Harold Laski

Harold Laski

A Political Biography

Michael Newman

MERLIN PRESS

© Michael Newman, 1993, 2009

First published in 1993 by The Macmillan Press Ltd
First published in paperback with a new preface in 2009
by The Merlin Press Ltd
6 Crane Street Chambers
Crane Street
Pontypool
NP4 6ND
Wales

www.merlinpress.co.uk

ISBN. 978-0-85036-696-9

British Library Cataloguing in Publication Data
is available from the British Library

Printed in Great Britain by
Lightning Source UK Ltd

To Kate, Hannah and Zack

Contents

Preface to paperback edition   A1

Acknowledgements   viii

Introduction   x

1   Divided Loyalties   1

2   Political Education   16

3   A Pluralist in North America   31

4   A Fabian Intellectual?   65

5   The General Strike and After   90

6   Empire, Race and Identity   110

7   Democracy in Crisis   133

8   Freedom in Danger   152

9   Dilemmas of an anti-Fascist   179

10   Laski's War   204

11   Political Trials   258

12   Zionism, Jewish Identity and Socialism   310

13   'I Build my Policy on Hope'   346

14   Constructive Contradictions   354

Notes   375

Bibliography   415

Index   428

Preface to Paperback Edition

Harold Laski (1893-1950) was one of the most famous socialist intellectuals of his era and there were already several books about him when I began my research in the late 1980s. Yet I felt that none of them did justice to his life and work, and that the time was right for a reappraisal of his contribution to the Left. I was not alone in this, for Isaac Kramnick and Barry Sheerman were simultaneously working on their book (*Harold Laski – A Life on the Left*, Hamish Hamilton, 1993), which was published just after mine. Although we had never made contact while chasing each other around the archives in pursuit of the 'real Laski', there was a fortuitous division of labour (or at least a difference of emphasis) between us. While Kramnick and Sheerman concentrated more on the personality of the man and the events in which he was involved, I was particularly interested in the relationship between his political thought and action. I hope that, in their different ways, both works played some role in reviving interest in this key socialist figure, and I am very grateful to Merlin Press, and particularly Tony Zurbrugg, for publishing my book in this new paperback edition.

It is significant that these reappraisals of Laski coincided with the collapse of the Soviet bloc, for his work had never fitted the constraining categories of the Cold War. For example, his centenary introduction to the Communist Manifesto in 1948, which simultaneously celebrated Marx as part of the enlightenment and democratic traditions while totally rejecting Leninism, was hardly designed to conciliate the Communist movement of the era. The latter also condemned his actions, for he played an important political role in blocking the mergers between Communist and Social Democratic parties in Western Europe sought by the Soviet leadership after the Second World War. But Laski's thinking and actions were perhaps rejected still more bitterly by the 'Western' camp. For he insisted on the crucial importance of Marx in any concept of socialism just as an attempt was being made to purge all traces of Marxist influence from liberal-democracy. And, once again, Laski's 'crime' was that he did not confine his thinking to the academy, but also sought to use his influence on the Left against the conventional claim that the Soviet Union was a military and political threat that needed to be countered by the projection of Western power across the world. After his death, neither Social Democrats nor Communists therefore included Laski in their pantheon of glorious figures and in the West in particular there was a rather conscious effort to play down his importance. My own research was based on the belief that Laski's socialism had significance for the post-Cold War world – a significance that had been anathema in both camps at the height of the East-West division. For he constantly endeavoured to combine elements that were conventionally regarded as incompatible, particularly by seeking a synthesis between liberalism and Marxism.

Much of Laski's work in this interface between different theoretical and political traditions has enduring relevance. In this brief Preface, I will discuss his thinking in relation to three themes that have particular significance for our own times: his attitude to liberal-democracy, his beliefs about the relationship between the nation-state and the international system, and his view of the United States. The discussion of each theme begins by considering some of the key issues and then explores them in relation to Laski's own insights.

Socialists have always found it difficult to define their attitudes towards liberal-democracy and its relationships with class and state power. One tendency within Marxism has been content simply to insist that the democratic elements have masked and legitimised the power of capital and its inextricable relationship with the state. From this perspective, it may seem unnecessary *either* to take the claims of democracy seriously *or* to consider the nature of the political system that might be established in a post-capitalist context. At the other extreme, as Ralph Miliband argued in his classic work *Parliamentary Socialism* (1961), Social Democrats have often become so attached to the constitutional trappings of liberal-democratic systems that they have totally lost sight of socialism. Indeed, more recently, they appear to have abandoned the concepts of class and class conflict almost entirely, failing to acknowledge the embedded relationships between capitalism and the state. Many discussions of democracy are therefore dialogues of the deaf between Marxist and Social Democratic 'fundamentalists' – with the former concentrating solely on relations of class power and the latter on constitutional form rather than socioeconomic content.

It is here that the work of Laski is so significant for, unlike most protagonists, he understood the importance of what each side was saying, since his own political evolution involved stages of deep commitment to differing theoretical positions without abandoning any of them. This meant that his attitudes to democracy were *multi-layered*, rather than mono-dimensional, and for more than three decades he strove to bring about a theoretical and practical reconciliation between differing positions. His earliest work was a form of radical pluralism in which he celebrated the maximum possible diversity of social and political allegiances, characterising the situation as one of 'contingent anarchy' because people would refuse to obey the state unless it was able to *demonstrate* that it was worthy of support. He was thus convinced that both individual fulfilment and worthwhile forms of democracy were possible only through active participation in a rich associational life, and there are some obvious similarities between this early Laski and the outlook in 'new social movements' in our own era. But subsequent experiences and critical reflection led him to qualify these early convictions and during the 1920s these themes appeared to be overlaid by other currents of socialist thought. In the first half of the decade he became increasingly attached to the Fabian notion that a strong state was necessary to bring about greater socioeconomic equality, while after 1926 – and still more, after 1931 – he embraced a Marxist view that the state reflected and defended the class power of capitalism. But Laski's thinking never constituted a linear progression from one theory to the next. Some of his earliest work included statements about the role of the state in protecting the power and privileges of those with property, while the themes of radical decentralisation and participation were repeated at the end of his life. For he never conformed to the intellectual and political straightjackets of any conventional socialist position. He recognised the validity of elements in liberal constitutionalism, radical pluralism, social democracy and Marxism and he constantly attempted to reconcile them. Even though he did not – and could not – fully succeed, his efforts have continuing relevance for our times.

It is, I think, clear that he would never have subscribed to the view that contemporary liberal-democratic systems provide an adequate form of democracy. Since he was one of the founders of the National Council of Civil Liberties (now *Liberty*) it is, for example, difficult to imagine him acquiescing in the increasingly repressive measures brought in by the Labour government in the period since 9/11. And he would not have been surprised by the current world financial and economic crisis or the fact that the banks have been bailed out at the expense of ordinary people. In fact, his shift towards Marxism owed much to his observation of the way in which a crisis in the international banking system was transmuted into intense political pressures on the Labour government. In September 1931 he thus told his friend, Felix Frankfurter, that 'the present spectacle is one of the definite sacrifice of the working class to men whose financial policy is very largely the source of our contemporary weakness'. Nor did he doubt that the dominant classes, who would always seek to preserve their privileges by limiting democracy to a narrowly defined political realm, would be engaged in ongoing conflict with the majority, who needed social transformation both to achieve social justice and as a prerequisite for effective political participation. In 1948 he was well aware that the Labour government had not made any attempt to penetrate the 'citadel' of capitalist power and until his death he remained convinced that:

> There is a point, never capable of exact definition, up to which the men of property are willing to buy off the opponents of capitalism by measures of social reform. But when that point is reached there is always the gravest danger that men of property, if they have to make their choice between their possessions and democratic institutions, will prefer their possessions, and destroy democratic institutions (Introduction to the 1948 edition of *Liberty in the Modern State*, pp.27-8).

It would, of course, be possible to move from this kind of observation to a purely negative Marxist critique and to argue that discussions of democracy diverted attention from the urgent need to overcome capitalist class power. But Laski did not take such a step, for he never doubted the overwhelming importance of democratic forms of government, which simultaneously celebrated diversity and upheld constitutionalism. This, I believe, is equally important now, for the history of the twentieth century demonstrates the inadequacy of the notion that the political form of a post-capitalist system can safely be left to take care of itself. There must surely be some relationship between the ideas that inspire a process of transformation, the policies and practices that might bring it about, and the system that is subsequently established. Nor is this simply a matter for a hypothetical future, for one of the most powerful propaganda triumphs of the Right has been its success in associating socialism with dictatorship. This makes it highly probable that any revival of the Left also depends upon it manifestly exhibiting genuine democratic credentials. Laski's simultaneous critique of the existing system and passionate advocacy of participation and pluralism therefore has enduring value.

The second key element in his thinking concerns the interrelationships between the domestic and the international realms. Clearly, one of the most obvious features of our own era is global interconnectedness – demonstrated dramatically by the current international financial and economic crisis. While the exact nature of these interrelationships remains contentious and it is clear that the term 'globalisation' has been used to justify neo-liberal policies, few would now claim that states can plausibly be treated as discrete and autonomous actors. There are, of course, also crucial questions about what the position *should* be: whether, in general, the aspiration is for more supranational and transnational forms of political and economic organisation or whether the nation-state offers some protection against international capitalist forces, so that the transcendence of the state could be considered only in a post-capitalist world order. Laski had enduring insights into these questions, which have recently been examined in depth by Peter Lamb in *Harold Laski: Problems of Democracy, the Sovereign State, and International Society* (Palgrave Macmillan, 2004).

He was deeply conscious of the relationships between the domestic and the international spheres from 1914 onwards, both because of his loathing of war and because of his belief that power needed to be divided and decentralised. He was also simultaneously aware of potentially contradictory pressures, for he was equally convinced of the importance of national self-determination and the need to tame state sovereignty through increasingly robust systems of international control. In his magnum opus, *A Grammar of Politics* (1925), he attempted to specify the ways in which legal, socioeconomic and political powers could – and must – be divided on a functional basis between states and forms of international government. Yet the evolution in his thought again meant that his enthusiasm for international federalism was tempered by scepticism about what was likely within an international system dominated by capitalist states. In *Nationalism and the Future of Civilisation* (1932), he thus stressed the link between sovereignty and capitalism arguing that both provided obstacles to necessary developments for the future of a world community – genuinely international law and economic equality. Having previously been cautiously optimistic about the League of Nations as an embryonic form of international government, he therefore became increasingly pessimistic about this, emphasising the extent to which international institutional forms reflected the socioeconomic system that underpinned them. While he continued to believe that new forms of international co-operation to supersede state sovereignty were *necessary*, he doubted their possibility unless they were established by states that had themselves transcended capitalism. Yet there were some tensions between his conviction about the importance of constructing new forms of international co-operation *irrespective of the socioeconomic system* and his scepticism about the possibility of doing so on a capitalist basis. Certainly, he believed that the necessary international changes were far more likely under socialism, but he was aware that these would not simply come about through a change in the economic system. And after the Second World War he condemned socialists for normally confining their internationalism to rhetoric while consolidating the exclusive claims of the nation-state in practice. He now believed that new forms of functional federalism were urgently needed and could not be postponed until capitalism had been superseded.

Once again, these insights have resonance for our own times. Laski died just before the Schuman proposal launched the first key initiative to bring about European integration. Since then socialists have engaged in ongoing disputes as to whether this has simply been a capitalist project or an important step towards supranationalism. It is not entirely clear what view Laski himself would have taken. I suspect that he would have cautiously welcomed it as a step in the right direction, while also fearing that a purely regional bloc might simply replicate the dangers of the nation-state at a higher level. And since he also recognised the extent to which the state both served the interests of domestic capital, and provided a focus for legitimation through nationalism, he would not have been surprised by the current difficulties in European integration: the reversion to forms of national protection, the inequalities between core and periphery, and the growth of xenophobia. Yet it seems unlikely that, with his long-term beliefs about the importance of transcending the nation-state, Laski would have favoured any reversion of power to the separate states. Similarly, I believe that he would simultaneously favour a strengthening of the United Nations and international economic regulation, while anticipating the likelihood that the most powerful states would be reluctant to cede any domestic control to an international body. Of course, all this is necessarily speculative, but there was a particular quality about Laski's approach that helps us to think constructively about such crucial questions in our own times. For he constantly combined a genuine socialist internationalism with a recognition of the fact that any initiatives would be limited and constrained by capitalism and state power. All this was closely related to the third theme – his attitude to the United States.

At the end of the Cold War it seemed possible to believe that a genuinely 'new world order' might be constructed. However, it became increasingly evident during the 1990s that this was, in fact, a new era of US hegemony and expansion, which was reinforced under the Presidency of George W. Bush. The failure in Iraq, the rise of China and other 'emerging economies', the international recession, and the replacement of Bush by Obama, may all mean that this period has now ended. Nevertheless, it is unlikely that there will be any dramatic collapse of US pre-eminence and it seems more realistic to assume that America will continue to exert a major influence over economic and political decisions across the globe. How does Laski help us to make sense of the meaning of US power?

His attitudes to the country were deeply ambivalent, but he was an acute observer of America and grasped its supreme importance in world terms far more quickly than most of his contemporaries. He had first made his reputation as a political thinker and activist in the United States during the First World War, and he constantly returned. In particular, almost as soon as Roosevelt announced the New Deal, he recognised its enormous significance, not only in domestic terms, but also *internationally*. This became most evident with the outbreak of the Second World War, for he was immediately convinced that the main hope for creating a genuinely new world depended not only upon defeating fascism, but upon the US supporting an international 'revolution by consent' that would transform the post-war. Of course, he was to be disappointed and his major post-war book, *The American Democracy* (1948), lamented the growth of reactionary conservatism and systematically demonstrated the way in which the power and values of business permeated every aspect of American life. He was still more vehement in denouncing the international impact of this transformation, for he now regarded the US as a counter-revolutionary force that sought to legitimise its policy by making bogus claims about the Soviet 'threat'.

At the end of his life he was, hardly surprisingly, pessimistic about the 'American dream'. In his last visit there in 1948 he had experienced in personal terms the anti-left witch-hunt that would culminate in McCarthyism, and he also witnessed the counter-revolutionary nature of US foreign policy in the early stages of the Cold War. Yet Laski was never 'anti-American', always recognising the positive features in US democracy. After a sabbatical there in 1938-39 he emphasised the variety of ways in which the British could learn from the Americans, suggesting that there was 'a quality of democracy in their social relations we have not yet begun even to understand'. (Quoted in Robert Frankel, *Observing America, The Commentary of British Visitors to the United States, 1890-1950*, University of Wisconsin Press, 2007, p.213). Similarly, he objected to Europeans, and particularly certain French commentators, who patronised the US and disparaged it glibly. He realised that it was necessary to interpret developments there in the context of American, rather than European, experience. This enabled him to understand the importance of Roosevelt's New Deal, while other European socialists (and particularly Communists) were still wondering whether it should be viewed as a step towards fascism. He justifiably saw Roosevelt as offering something quite new in the US experience with the potential to bring about important international changes.

I would suggest that Laski's attitude to the American New Deal contains some important lessons for the perspective that should be adopted in relation to Barak Obama's Presidency. He was well aware that Roosevelt was no socialist or even particularly radical. Soon after he became President Laski argued that he was answering the call of the American people to rein in the capitalist system so that it would be the 'servant' and not the 'master' of the public. Roosevelt was 'the logical expression of social forces and could hardly have acted otherwise if he wished to retain the characteristic contours of American life'. (Quoted in Frankel, p.186). Nevertheless, he had no doubt that the change in the US had immense significance for the world as a whole. Similarly, Obama has limited left-wing credentials and is clearly constrained by the system in which he has taken power, but there are two elements in Laski's view of Roosevelt that have particular relevance for the current world. First, he recognised the extent to which the international system would be shaped by the US, for he had no doubt that the major international power would play the key role in determining the nature of that system. Secondly, he also understood that the orientation of the domestic order would determine its international policies. If the US, as the leading power, was at least partially progressive, it would be possible to construct a more progressive international system. If reactionary forces controlled America, they would seek to ensure that these characteristics predominated in the global order. But this also meant that there were obvious links between this insight and the two other themes that I have considered. For new forms of international governance that partially supersede the nation-state cannot be created if the United States is intent on imposing its own system on the rest of the world. Nor is it possible to construct genuine systems of democracy within and between states if America accepts only one form and seeks to subvert others. In this sense, as Laski recognised, the nature of the regime that prevailed in the US was of crucial importance for all the other issues of the era.

No doubt, in his desperation about the situation in Europe, he initially exaggerated the progressive features of the New Deal. Later he both understood the way in which reactionary forces undermined many of the initial reforms and he was also bitterly upset by Roosevelt's own conservatism in foreign policy during the Second World War. Similarly, it is very possible that Obama will disappoint many of his supporters and that later historians will stress the continuities in American policies rather than the differences from the Bush administration indicated by some of the early initiatives. But this leads to one final point about Laski. However discouraging the political climate seemed to be, he always sought change and, as he said, just before he died, 'I build my policy on hope'. As a thinker, inspirational teacher, public intellectual and socialist activist, he engaged in the political world with constant passion and commitment. This too has continuing relevance for own era.

Acknowledgements

A great many people and institutions have helped me with this book. I am grateful to the University of North London for giving me an extensive period of leave, and to the Nuffield Foundation and the United States Information Service for grants to enable me to carry out research on Laski in the United States. I am also grateful to the owners or holders of papers quoted: the Bodleian Library, Oxford; the British Library of Political and Economic Science; the Brynmor Jones Library at the University of Hull; the Churchill Archives Centre, Churchill College, Cambridge; the family of John Winant; the Franklin D. Roosevelt Library; the Hartley Library, at the University of Southampton; Harvard Law School Library; the International Institute of Social History (Amsterdam); King's College Library, Cambridge; the Library of Congress; McGill University Archives; McMaster University Library; Manchester City Council Department of Libraries and Theatres (City of Manchester Leisure Services Committee); Manchester Grammar School; Manchester Jewish Museum; New College Library, Oxford; the National Museum of Labour History, Manchester; the Public Record Office; the Rockefeller Archive Centre; University College Library, Oxford; the University of Illinois Archives; the University of Sussex Library; and Yale University Library.

I am also gratcful to Columbia University, Cornell University, the Fawcett Library, the National Library of Scotland, the National Sound Archive, the University of Chicago, the State Historical Society of Wisconsin, and Syracuse University for allowing me access to archives or supplying me with copies by correspondence.

Archivists and librarians in numerous institutions provided invaluable assistance and I would like to record my thanks to them all. Bryan Dyson of the Brynmor Jones Library in the,University of Hull and Stephen Bird at the Labour Party (subsequently the National Museum of Labour History) provided help over long periods of time and I am particularly grateful to them.

I would also like to thank all those who helped by providing references and, in particular, Ian Bailey, Fred Leventhal, Kevin Morgan, Brian Thomas, Dennis Dean and Denis Judd. I am also very grateful to Frances Condick for her extremely thorough copy-editing and Margaret Cornell for compiling the index.

Many people gave me assessments of, or opinions on, Laski in discussions, and I am particularly grateful to the following: Bill Williams, for helping me to understand the family background in the Manchester Jewish community; Nancy Gilbert and Mrs T. Bristow for talking to me about the relationships between Harold and Frida Laski and their daughter, Diana; and Gordon East for information about Laski's role at LSE. Ian Mikardo provided some important insights into Laski and the Labour Party, while Sir Isaiah Berlin, Ralph Miliband and John Saville gave me stimulating and differing interpretations of his theoretical contribution. My interview with Michael Foot was more significant to me than he could have realised: he helped me to place Laski in the context of British socialism and, of still greater value, he reinforced my belief that the subject was an important one.

Andrew Mathewson, one of Harold Laski's grandsons, played a major role in my research. He lent me material in his possession, gave permission to quote from Laski's letters, and made many useful suggestions. I am very grateful to him, and his wife, Jackie, for their encouragement.

To Marc Karson, one of Laski's last PhD students, I owe a special debt. In several long discussions he provided me with an enormous amount of relevant information and interpretations; he explained key features of the American situation to me; and he read and commented on much of the first draft of the book. He has also been a living proof of the extent of Laski's political influence and personal magnetism. I cannot thank him enough for his contribution to the book.

Finally, I want to thank my family. My father read and commented critically on the whole draft, and my brother, Jeff, highlighted elements of Judaism and its possible influence on Laski for me. As always Ines has been a constant intellectual and emotional support. Her contribution was vast in all respects, and she helped me to understand Laski as a whole person. Our children were supremely tolerant of my obsession with the book and provided the antidote to excessive earnestness. Zack's initial delight when he mistakenly believed that I was about to write a book on Lassie has remained with me ever since and has helped to keep the whole project in perspective!

It is to Kate, Hannah and Zack that I dedicate the book.

Introduction

Harold Laski was arguably the most famous socialist intellectual of his era. He had already achieved a reputation as an outstanding political theorist before the age of thirty, but his scholarly interests were coupled with a burning political commitment, and his fame was based on action as well as thought. As a prolific writer, inspiring teacher, and intimate friend of leading political figures, his influence was felt in the USA, India, and mainland Europe, as well as in Britain. While *A Grammar of Politics* (1925) and several of his other works were translated into numerous languages and were regarded as highly significant theoretical works, Laski's fame extended far beyond the traditional academic elite. During the New Deal era he was at the centre of debate on every campus across the United States, was an intimate friend of many members of the administration, and knew Roosevelt personally. Similarly, he was friendly with Nehru and Gandhi, and after the achievement of independence a well-known Indian political leader stated that there was a vacant chair at every Cabinet meeting in India, 'reserved for the ghost of Professor Harold Laski'.[1] Above all, in Britain itself, he achieved the unparalleled position of being constantly elected to the Labour Party National Executive Committee – heading the poll throughout the Second World War – although he was never a member of Parliament. However, as Chair of the Labour Party in 1945, he also became notorious when Churchill made him the *bête-noir* during the General Election campaign. With this prominence in so many spheres, it seemed no exaggeration to claim, when he died, that future historians might talk of the period between 1920 and 1950 as the 'Age of Laski'.[2]

Yet his fall from grace after his death was very rapid. This was revealed extremely clearly in 1953 when two publications appeared: the biographical memoir by Kingsley Martin, and the two-volume collection of letters between Laski and the American Supreme Court Judge, Oliver Wendell Holmes Jr.[3] In both cases, the majority of reviewers appeared to relish the occasion as an opportunity to destroy the reputation of their dead protagonist. Two years later a further blow was struck with the publication of the *The Political Ideas of Harold J. Laski* by Herbert Deane, which concluded that 'Laski's political teachings were not of major philosophical significance or profundity'.[4]

It is, of course, legitimate to criticise the contribution of any theorist or practitioner of politics, and Laski had always been a controversial figure. However, there was something different about the nature of this posthumous attack: in my view, it was largely a product of the Cold War and was a quite deliberate attempt to confine Laski to the 'dustbin of history' because he did not subscribe to the orthodox Western version of the conflict. There were two main prongs in this attempt to discredit him: character assassination and a distortion of his political views. I will deal briefly with each.

As this book will show, Laski was a highly complex personality. He was ebullient, entertaining, inspirational, incredibly articulate, unbelievably knowledgeable, and generally regarded as one of the kindest and most generous of people. But he was also excessively anxious to be accepted by eminent people, he was gushing in his praise, and always needed to be at the centre of everything. He was, in fact, a 'larger than life' character, with greater virtues and weaknesses than most of us. However, those who wanted to undermine his reputation after his death focused on one further characteristic, claiming that he was dishonest.

Generations of staff and students at LSE had enjoyed Laski's 'tall stories' about encounters with the 'great and the good'. Throughout his life there were some who found this irritating but, after his death, this character trait was used to discredit him. It was argued that he was a notorious liar who lived in a world of fantasy. Overall, the suggestion was that Laski was a liar and that his politics could therefore be discounted. As Malcolm Muggeridge put it in a particularly vicious piece:

> Laski was physically small, a Jew from Manchester, fabulously quick-witted, and as fabulously untruthful. . . . What he resented was not established authority, as such, but rather his exclusion from it.[6]

There is no doubt that Laski embellished his stories. As a colleague, H. L. Beales, put it in 1945: 'Sometimes his desire to dramatise a good story leads him to an over-artistic arrangement of its incidentals.'[6] But Beales also noted that Laski was aware of this foible, and therefore played on it. Moreover, Laski obviously regarded Beales' point as fair comment, for he regarded the article as 'absurdly generous'.[7] However, a second crucial point is that most of the important 'stories' contained a substantial basis of truth. A few examples may be used to illustrate this.

In his letters to Holmes, Laski claimed that he played a role in the Anglo-Irish settlement of 1921 by giving advice to Churchill.[8] Since Laski had only been in Britain for a year at the time – after a six-year period in North America – and was a twenty-eight-year-old lecturer, this seemed inherently unlikely. One reviewer therefore wrote to ask Churchill (then Prime Minister) if it was true. He received the reply that Churchill 'does not remember ever having heard of him in connection with the Irish settlement of 1921.'[9] This was then used as grist to the mill in the anti-Laski campaign. However, Martin Gilbert's massive biography shows that Churchill did indeed discuss the Irish question with Laski in 1921.[10] Secondly, in January 1931 Beatrice Webb doubted Laski's claim that he was constantly in touch with American Zionist leaders over British policy towards Palestine.[11] Yet, as will be seen in Chapter 6, he was certainly in very close contact with them. In fact, several times in the research for this book, I began with an attitude of scepticism towards a particular claim made by Laski, only to find that the balance of probability was in his favour. Of greater importance, it was often possible to substantiate assertions made by Laski about his political involvement in various episodes, with references in other correspondence or archives. This is not to claim that everything that Laski said was true. In particular, I have not been able to verify the most disputed of all his tales – that he had a private meeting with Stalin in August 1946 – and I discuss this in Chapter 11. But I believe that Felix Frankfurter, his closest friend, should have the last word on the subject of Laski as a 'fantasist'.

In 1952, when Kingsley Martin was writing his biography of Laski, he was troubled by the whole question and wrote to Frankfurter suggesting that he might not realise the extent to which Laski had been a 'romancer'.[12] After having read the Holmes-Laski letters twice, Frankfurter replied:

> The upshot of my matured conviction is that it isn't much of a problem. . . . No doubt, here and there Harold did some embellishing, no doubt he infused with his own enthusiasm and style what other people said to him. . . .
>
> The striking thing that does emerge from Harold's letters is the accuracy of his quotations and of his references, the extent to which what on a quick glance appears to be implausible is verified.
>
> To be sure, some of the conversations that he quotes as having had with the great sound like whoppers. For instance, what Curzon

told him and what he told Curzon. But, then, I reflect on a conversation between Harold and Halifax the first time they met, and I believe the only time. It so happens that I was present . . . Had I not heard what I heard but merely had read an account by Harold of what I heard, I would have been extremely skeptical that Harold said what he could have quoted himself as saying, and even more skeptical that at the first crack Halifax should have said what he did. Or again, has Julian Huxley ever told you his fantastic adventure with Harold during the war by which they were enabled to get from Canada to the States? As Julian told me, if he hadn't been a witness, he would never have believed Harold if he had told him, what actually took place, as a yarn. In telling it to me, Julian indicated that he had little doubt that Harold, in narrating the adventure, remarkable as it was, would embellish it. And so what! . . . that's a characteristic – perhaps one should say, part of the art – of raconteurs.[13]

If Laski's 'stories' had far greater substance than his critics admitted, this is the least important element in his defence. Of far more importance is the fact – generally acknowledged by those who have been prepared to discuss it – that he was scrupulously honest in his serious work. His writings were meticulous and often extremely detailed, with careful attention to source material. Nor did he shirk the sometimes painful duty of speaking the truth to individuals. In August 1940, for example, Joe Kennedy, the American Ambassador in London, asked him to write an introduction to a book by his son, John F. Kennedy. Laski had reason to cultivate Kennedy senior at that time and liked his son, whom he had taught at LSE. Nevertheless, he refused to write the introduction, saying that the book should not have been published as many final year students could have written a work of the same standard:

I care a lot about your boys. I don't want them to be spoilt as rich men's sons are so easily spoilt. Thinking is a hard business, and you have to pay the price for admission to it. Do believe that these hard sayings from me represent much more real friendship than the easy praise of 'yes men'.[14]

Above all, Laski had the honesty to re-appraise his own political position in the light of changing circumstances and to do what he believed to be right even at the cost of personal sacrifices. Kenneth

O. Morgan is therefore right to reject the cruel travesty of Laski's character perpetrated by his opponents, and to argue instead that he should be regarded as a 'man of transcendent intellectual integrity'.[15]

The second element in the Cold War campaign against him concerned his thought. That Laski had always provoked sharp disagreements was not surprising, since he had become increasingly radical as time went on, and his theory contained some unresolved contradictions. But the attacks upon him at the height of the East-West confrontation were of a different order. The tone was set by Sidney Hook, the American philosopher, who argued that Laski had been carried away by his own eloquence, and had no real intellectual distinction. He claimed that the early theory had collapsed at the touch of logical analysis and had been replaced by a crude and mechanistic 'vulgar Marxism' and economic mysticism.[16] But the real onslaught came with Deane's book, which pronounced a categorical verdict on Laski as a thinker:

> It would be difficult to deny that his originality and intellectual vigor began to decline after 1930; in the last decade of his life his published works were repetitious and rhetorical to the point of bombast. His style became increasingly labored. The accents were those of a man who, although exhausted, was making a desperate effort to go on talking, in the belief that sheer repetition and volume of words would convince his audience of the truth and the importance of his message. His intellectual deterioration in this last phase is so striking that one is tempted to conclude that just as he had attained intellectual maturity at an unusually early age, so he became tired and old at the comparatively early age of fifty.[17]

This was highly effective as a critique because, at first sight, it appeared to be a detached analysis by a young academic with no political axe to grind. Yet, for all its apparently dispassionate stance, the book was a partisan job of political demolition. It repeated the character assassination, it misrepresented Laski's assumptions, and it showed no understanding of the historical context in which he had been writing. Above all, it was vitiated by an American Cold War perspective in which Laski was effectively denounced as an apologist for Stalinism. However, it was in harmony with the dominant assumptions of the era and was therefore greeted with enthusiasm by Laski's old antagonists. For example, Arthur Schlesinger Jr declared that Deane's book exposed Laski as someone who dwelt in a world of political fantasies. It presented 'an analysis of Laski as a political thinker from which it seems unlikely that his reputation can ever recover'.[18] This was clearly the aim and Deane's interpretation has been extremely influential.

The Cold War campaign against him did not wholly succeed in undermining Laski's reputation. His books have continued to be read and republished, and there were particular efforts to keep his memory alive in India.[19] Since the mid-1960s, there has also been a revival of interest in him.[20] In 1966 Martin Peretz published an excellent article which analysed the importance of Laski's ideas, and their relevance for the contemporary student revolt. Two years later B. Zylstra re-examined his early thought far more sympathetically than Deane. In the mid-1970s David Nicholls also analysed Laski's pluralist phase (as did Paul Hirst in 1989). In 1979 an Italian Marxist philosopher, Claudio Palazzolo, wrote a sympathetic study of all the major stages in Laski's theoretical development, and two years later W. H. Greenleaf also wrote an important article emphasising the essential consistency of the ideas. Attention has been paid to Laski's life as well as his thought, with the publication of a paperback edition of Kingsley Martin's biography in 1969, a second biography (bordering on hagiography) by Granville Eastwood in 1977, and an illuminating short piece on Laski's role in the British Labour movement by Kenneth O. Morgan. Yet considerable damage was done to Laski's reputation by the earlier attacks upon him and the later works have not been able to redress the balance.

This book therefore seeks to re-establish the position Laski deserves as a thinker and an historical actor. It is not uncritical, but it attempts to rescue him from some of the unfair attacks that he received – particularly the expert mauling by Deane. A final prefatory note is necessary on the method I have adopted.

Laski wrote an unbelievable amount. His range was vast, and some of the work was rather esoteric. At the same time, he was involved in a bewildering number of political movements, pressure groups, and committees. He died relatively young, but as one of his friends put it:

> has anyone ever packed so much into 56 years . . . He lived and worked at twice the pace of any man I know. So it was not only a packed but in reality a long life.[21]

It would take a very big book to deal with all this. Instead I have attempted to encapsulate and explain his political outlook and its

development over time. Sometimes this has involved looking at his
ideas, and sometimes the emphasis is more upon events, for Laski
himself oscillated between thought and action.

According to Bernard Crick, Laski's advice to students when
studying Rousseau was as follows:

> Do not falter at the formal contradictions of his arguments, which
> are legion, but endeavour to discover what is the animating in-
> wardness of the man.[22]

As Crick suggested, I have tried to apply the same principle to Laski
in an attempt to discover and explain his 'animating inwardness'.

1
Divided Loyalties

> Often enough, a man's political creed is born, not of an economic situation, but of an intense psychological dislike for the atmosphere of his family.[1]

There was an obvious autobiographical reference in Harold Laski's generalisation, and great insight into his character and thought can be derived from an understanding of his background, and his reaction to it.

Harold's father was Nathan Laski, who had been brought to England as a baby in 1863, by his parents, Naphtali and Esther, who had left Poland to escape the restrictions on Jews there. While their economic position was certainly not comfortable, they were not as poor as many immigrant Jews of the era, and Naphtali worked as a travelling jeweller.[2] During Nathan's childhood the family had moved to Manchester where he began work at the age of thirteen as a clerk and office boy in G. P. Guanis, a shipping firm. He was extremely energetic and determined, and quickly rose up through the firm. At the age of twenty-two he went to India for the first time on behalf of the company (he was to make forty-nine such visits, staying there on business practically every winter) and soon became a partner, and ultimately the senior partner. In 1889 he married Sarah Frankenstein. She was then twenty-years old and the daughter of Philip Frankenstein, whose family had immigrated to Britain during the 1840s, and now owned a factory which made waterproof garments. Nathan and Sarah had therefore already established themselves as 'middle-class' at the time of the main wave of Jewish immigration to Britain in the last years of the nineteenth century.

In 1891 their first child, Neville, was born, followed by Harold in 1893 and Mabel a year later. By now the family was fairly prosperous and, at the turn of the century, Nathan formed his own cotton export house, based on trade with India and, as the children grew up, his firm became increasingly successful. By now the Laskis were prominent members of North Manchester's Jewish middle class and in 1906 they moved to a large house in Smedley Lane, off Cheetham Hill Road.

At that time Cheetham Hill was full of small synagogues and Jewish shops and clubs, and Nathan and Sarah were deeply involved in the life of the area. They were observant United Synagogue Jews of the era. This meant that, although they had abandoned some of the traditional clothes and customs that distinguished the new refugees from Eastern Europe, they kept a kosher home, maintained the restrictions on work and travel on the sabbath, and celebrated the Jewish festivals. Moreover, they played a very active part in the religious life of the community with Nathan becoming President of Manchester's Great Synagogue at an exceptionally early age during the 1890s. Both Sarah and Nathan also played a leading role in numerous Jewish charities and the Jewish Board of Guardians. Their attitudes were, no doubt, paternalistic, but they were certainly generous with both their time and money.

While their primary base was the local Jewish community, Harold's parents were equally active in secular public service. Nathan was appointed a magistrate (a position he was to hold for thirty-five years), and he became increasingly prominent in Manchester organisations. As a devotee of Gladstone,[3] he also played an important role in the Liberal Party and Winston Churchill, the candidate in 1906 and 1908, sometimes stayed in the Laski house. Although Sarah did not play quite such a prominent role when the children were young, she also became well-known in the secular community, being first elected to the Board of Guardians in 1913 (which she subsequently chaired) and later also becoming a city councillor. If both Nathan and Sarah were Liberals, they were hardly radical, and during the 1930s the Conservative Party did not even oppose Sarah on the city council.

Harold's parents were genuinely public-spirited, but they were also ambitious and motivated by a clear vision. Nathan wanted to become recognised as a leader of the community (an aim which he had largely achieved by the turn of the century) because he had a strategy for overcoming the anti-semitism which Jews experienced in a number of spheres in Manchester.

On the city streets they were quite likely to encounter abusive remarks, particularly as new waves of East European immigrants, with clearly 'foreign' customs, settled in the city. And, at the other end of the social scale, Jews often faced discrimination if they wanted to join sports clubs or cultural societies. The Laskis' policy for conquering these problems involved a combination of integration and separation.

The first requirement was an emphasis on patriotism, and absorption of British cultural values. The Jewish community would be fully accepted only if it demonstrated its complete 'Britishness'. In the case of Nathan and Sarah themselves, this involved emulation of the British elite, not only in the obvious public sphere, but in smaller, apparently personal actions. Thus, for example, Nathan endowed Manchester Grammar School with the 'Laski cup'[4] for cricket and Sarah wrote a book on her trip to India in 1903. This was written as a travelogue by a member of British high society who spoke of 'our history', and recommended India to men who liked sport and club life and women who wanted to be relieved of household cares and duties. The proceeds were to go to the Manchester Ladies Visiting Association to help teach the poor the laws of health and hygiene.[5] Not everyone could aspire to such heights, but the Laskis hoped that new immigrants could be moulded into acceptance of British norms of behaviour as soon as possible, and Nathan clearly believed that it was his role to exert leadership in this direction. But while they believed that anti-semitism would be diminished if Jews demonstrated their patriotism, they were equally insistent that Jewish religious and cultural traditions must be maintained. Their objective was thus to bring about a situation in which Jews would be fully accepted as British citizens of Jewish faith.

One negative feature of this vision was a lack of tolerance for those who did not share it. Despite his personal generosity, Nathan was autocratic and unwilling to tolerate dissent. Pearl Binder, the author, thus recalled that when she became involved in Left-wing politics, and started to move away from the community, Nathan wrote to her and asked her to work for him, although she had never met him. She was outraged when he told her how she should dress, but thought that the Laskis:

> ... were a kind of surveillance of the general community; they felt it was their job to see the kids didn't go astray. ... I think Mr Laski felt responsible that no Jewish person ... went off the rails.[6]

Nathan and Sarah had views on the dress, behaviour, company and political views that were appropriate for Jews. In order to secure leadership of the community, Nathan sometimes made concessions: for example, he kept contacts with Zionism and Reform Judaism despite his lack of sympathy for such ideas. But, in general, Nathan expected both his family and the Jewish community to comply with his opinions. All this, he thought, was necessary if Jews were to gain full acceptance within Manchester and Britain.

Harold's parents were certainly successful in achieving this status themselves. Nathan must have felt that his life's goal was realised when, on receiving an honorary degree at Manchester University, he was described as a Jew who was proud of his Judaism and 'an Englishman of whom Englishmen are justly proud'.[7] And when he was killed in a car accident in 1941 his death was bemoaned by the then Prime Minister, Winston Churchill, as well as by the Jewish Establishment. Similarly, when Sarah died four years later, a memorial service was held in the local church as well as the synagogue.[8] They also handed the family tradition down to their elder son, Neville, who was to marry the daughter of the Sephardi Chief Rabbi in 1914 and, between 1933 and 1940, become an ultra-patriotic President of the Board of Deputies of British Jews and a High Court judge. And his sister, Mabel, never departed from the Manchester Jewish community. However, the impact of this background upon Harold was to be far more complex.

As a child, Harold was physically very slight and prone to recurrent bouts of ill-health. Perhaps partly because of this, he also had immense intellectual curiosity and probably developed one of his outstanding characteristics at a very early age: an ability to read at enormous speed and to absorb and retain the details of what he had read. Moreover, he had a voracious appetite for books of all kinds, both as a reader and as a collector, from childhood.

As a young boy, he was sent to a local private school, where approximately half the annual intake was Jewish.[9] There he quickly revealed another character trait – an extreme precociousness of intellect and personality. One of his contemporaries later recalled that he sometimes began lessons by reading the leading article from the *Manchester Guardian* and opening a discussion on it. On one occasion, when his teacher expressed a Conservative viewpoint, he is said to have replied: 'tell your parents to give up that rag, the *Daily Dispatch*, and take in the *Manchester Guardian*'.[10] This story may be apocryphal but it is plausible. Laski's tone was always authoritative and he related easily to people much older than himself, apparently assuming that he was on the same level as they were. This may have made him an obnoxious child, but it followed from the fact that, intellectually, he was far older than his years. Moreover, no doubt he had already revealed the other characteristics which always offset his arrogance: warmth, generosity, and humour. When he was a young adult, these characteristics would explain his ability to befriend a succession of eminent individuals much older than himself.

When he was eleven, he transferred to Manchester Grammar School – one of the outstanding academic schools in the country. While providing a competitive, elite education, this school also facilitated the merging of British and Jewish identities, for there were about 150 Jewish boys there, with daily Jewish prayers and no Saturday morning school. Moreover, the headmaster, J. L. Paton, was a genuine liberal humanitarian who was sensitive to the needs of his Jewish pupils and sometimes even attended Jewish prayers. In Laski's case, the home-school link was taken even further, for Paton was a family friend.

At Manchester Grammar Laski followed a predominantly classical and historical education. He also founded a Junior Debating Society, and was an active participant in debates throughout the school. His ability to articulate his thoughts with speed, clarity, humour, and an amazing recall of detail, was legendary in his later life, and was already evident during his childhood.

Simultaneously, he attended a Jewish religion school which taught him Hebrew and Jewish tradition and prepared him for his *barmitzvah*. There is little direct evidence of his early attitudes to Judaism, but when he was at university he wrote a scarcely veiled autobiography, *The Chosen People*, which implies that he had been strongly attracted to it.[11] No doubt the festivals and ritual struck a chord with the deeply emotional side of his character, while the emphasis on Jewish scholarship appealed to his intellectualism. It is thus highly likely that, at the time of his *barmitzvah*, he felt very much at home as a member of Manchester's Great Synagogue, accepting both the religious and the cultural aspects of his Jewish identity.

As a young teenager there was therefore every reason to suppose that Harold would achieve the goals that his parents had envisaged for him. The only apparent problem was his continuing ill-health – particularly a weak heart and chest. Indeed, he was so frequently absent from school that his exam results were often indifferent or poor. In the rigidly streamed Manchester Grammar School he started in 'good' forms but then dropped into a lower stream from the age of thirteen. When he was sixteen, acute appendicitis led to an absence of nearly a year. However, he continued to devour books in classics and history during his absences and at seventeen he was the only boy in the Lower Division to gain an award at Oxford (to read history at New College).[12] Paton certainly never had any doubts

about Harold, writing in a subsequent reference that he had been
one of the ablest pupils within the last ten years and that it was
presumed from the first that he would win a good scholarship to
Oxford.

> he picked himself out, already in the junior forms as one who
> could acquire knowledge for himself. He was never afraid of a big
> book, or a subject which most people would have said was be-
> yond him. He could always keep his end up in a discussion, and
> he showed marked promise of literary style.[13]

Illness had not therefore been a barrier to success (although it
would be a recurrent problem throughout his life, and as an adult
of five foot seven inches, he still weighed less than eight stone).[14]
However, by the time he was sixteen Harold was experiencing
inner conflicts which would lead to a major crisis in the Laski family
– a crisis which certainly affected Harold's life and subsequent
development.

The implication of *The Chosen People* was that the first problem
was his loss of faith in God. He himself was to attribute this to the
triumph of reason which undermined the possibility of believing in
a supernatural being for which there was no scientific evidence. It is,
of course, debatable whether faith is ever destroyed solely by intellectual processes or scientific evidence, and there were no doubt
other reasons, of which he may not yet have been conscious, for his
change of attitude. In any case, at first he may have thought that the
loss of religious belief would present him with no particular problems. Since he viewed it as an intellectual matter, he appears to have
expected others to respond to the change in the same way. However,
he was soon to find himself in a much broader conflict with his
parents. As he later wrote:

> I hated so much the standard of life I found. It seemed to mean
> that your children were to be kept ignorant of what you do not
> know, to be penniless unless you chose to endow them and de-
> pendent on you for . . . permission to breathe . . . To have ideals
> and to think for yourself, to refuse in any way to become a copy
> of the traditional type was to damn yourself.[15]

By the age of about sixteen he was beginning to find his parents'
home stifling and, while there is no evidence of the specific issues
involved, it can be presumed that they concerned features of Jewish

life. For if Harold had lost his religious faith, it is also highly likely that his enthusiasm for going to synagogue, and observing the dietary laws and the restrictions on activity on the Sabbath were also waning. He was never someone who would easily compromise or act hypocritically and he was probably unwilling to 'go through the motions' of a religious Jewish life once he had ceased to believe in its underlying rationale. However, the loss of faith raised questions well beyond the narrow limits of his parents' toleration. For if, in the final analysis, Jewish separateness stemmed from a religion in which Harold no longer believed, why maintain the separation? If his parents wanted Jews to be accepted as fully British, why not abandon the lifestyle which made them separate? It is not possible to pinpoint the precise moment at which he formulated such questions, but it may be assumed that he was already half conscious of them by late 1909. Otherwise he would not have taken the steps which would inevitably lead him into total conflict with his parents.

In December of that year Harold and his brother, Neville, were staying in Halesowen, near Birmingham, where Harold was convalescing after the operation on his appendix. There they met a young woman called Frida Kerry. She was currently teaching physical education at a nearby teacher-training college but, during her vacations, she worked as a masseuse at Halesowen, where she also lectured to interested patients. She was twenty-five years old, from an upper middle-class, gentile, landowning family in Suffolk.

Harold was immediately captivated by her. He took every possible opportunity to see and talk to her, and soon substituted her interests for his own. Until then his whole emphasis had been upon the humanities. Now he spent all his spare time mastering the theory of evolution and the current controversies in genetics.[16] He managed to persuade her to let him study with her during the summer and, after having won his Exhibition to Oxford, he dropped history and was accepted for science instead. He left school in December 1910 and, between then and the summer of 1911, he studied eugenics in London, with its prime exponent, Sri Karl Pearson. But eugenics and Frida were indissolubly connected in Harold's mind. He made his first coded declaration of love to her in August 1910 after they had worked together for the first time, and he expressed his feelings ever more openly until finally making them explicit in the spring of 1911.[17]

At first Frida could not take a schoolboy nine years her junior seriously when he told her he was in love with her; but her resistance was overcome by his adoration, and by her own admiration for his intellect. As she recalled at the end of her life:

> I might have been talking to a boy but what I heard was the voice of a man seeking the spark that would kindle the fires within him. I believe I was that spark.[18]

The initial basis of their relationship was discussion of every conceivable subject and, according to Frida, 'In any argument, he got the better of me and did it with a puckish humour I couldn't ignore'.[19]

By Easter 1911, she hesitatingly accepted his declaration of love. By June she was clear that she felt the same for him and they began a sexual relationship and planned to marry. In the summer, Frida's mother found out about the affair and told them that she would inform Harold's parents. Instead of ending the liaison, this hastened the marriage. On 1 August, when Harold was just over eighteen, the couple eloped in Scotland.

If love can never be explained fully, it is at least possible to go some way in accounting for Frida's attraction for Harold. In the first place, her age and greater experience were relevant, given Harold's customary ease with people older than himself. Secondly, and more important, she was the perfect complement to him in numerous ways. She was intelligent, where he was over-intellectual. His ebullience was coupled with introspection and even melancholy, while she was simply direct and optimistic. As he put it, she always gave him the 'right cheery word' whenever he felt hopeless.[20] She was practical where he was ethereal. She was physically fit, while he was unhealthy. She was certain of her beliefs where he was sometimes prone to doubts.

But they were also united in rebellion against the conventions of Edwardian England. Frida had had to struggle hard to emancipate herself from her parents, who believed that the only acceptable profession for their daughter was that of governess. She had thus been virtually disowned by her mother when she had insisted on going to a Swedish gymnastics college to train, and she had subsequently been forced to earn her living in Belgium for two years without any parental help. Such experiences had given her an iron will to do what was right in her own eyes, whatever the consequences. Since Harold was in the midst of conflict with his own parents when he met her, Frida's past struck an immediate chord with him. As he later put it:

then I met you and in all you wrote and spoke to me there was the note of a joyous and frank rebellion and a rejection of the modern standard of right and wrong . . . [21]

Frida's particular rebellion had not only been against the conventions of the older generation, but more particularly against the allotted role of women. Her wish to be a gymnastics teacher had broadened into a general demand for the emancipation of women and she was a militant suffragette. Whether Harold had seriously considered the role of women before meeting Frida is unclear. His own mother was unusually independent for this era and, at first, he had compared the two women.[22] But as soon as he met Frida, he became a sincere and enthusiastic supporter of women's rights. As far as he was concerned, a woman's freedom to choose her own life was part of the more general right of people to develop as they wished without being forced into a traditional mould by the older generation. Inevitably this belief would also cause tensions within an orthodox Jewish family, where there is a sharp differentiation between the assigned roles of the sexes. Indeed, by the time he wrote *The Chosen People* he had come to believe that Judaism was a barrier to full female emancipation.

In fact the relationship with Frida was an assault on the whole world outlook of Nathan and Sarah Laski. As soon as he decided to pursue her he was, consciously or unconsciously, declaring war on his parents' values. For orthodox Jews, marrying 'out' is a shameful act – even a sin. The perpetuation of the Jewish people through all the centuries of oppression had been regarded as a religious duty. Jews were to maintain the traditions of Judaism and hand them down to successive generations through their children. Intermarriage dispersed and 'diluted' the Jewish people and the taboo against intermarriage was therefore reinforced by religion and cultural tradition. Since observant Jewish families inculcate such beliefs in their children from an early age Harold obviously knew exactly what he was doing when he and Frida decided to marry. He took the decision to elope because he knew that there was absolutely no chance of their agreeing to him marrying a non-Jewish woman. Indeed, he no doubt fell in love with her because he had already rejected his parents' values.

He had not, however, rejected them as people. He still retained a deep affection for them and, in a sense, he was testing their love for him. Which was the stronger: their love for him or their acceptance of Jewish orthodoxy and the inter-marriage taboo? At times, he sounded confident, telling Frida: 'My people will be tremendously mad for a year or two, but they can't do without me and once they know you how could they help loving you'.[23] At other times, he was more apprehensive and anticipated a fight in which he would say: 'here is my wife, as you loved me love her – if you cannot accept her reject me also'.[24]

But in any case, he was absolutely determined to go ahead with the marriage. Moreover, while the coming conflict was obviously personal, he also saw it in universal terms. Both he and Frida firmly believed that individuals were entitled to do what was right according to their own consciences rather than being circumscribed by customs or religious doctrine. He knew that he would be accused of betraying his parents and that he would cause them anguish. But, as he was soon to write in *The Chosen People*:

> I prize so highly the freedom of my soul, the liberty to think and say and act with all the power and insight I have, that the unhappiness their sadness will bring is a price that I feel it is not dishonourable to pay.[25]

Conscience and personal freedom thus superseded all other considerations. Here was the seed of a political philosophy which Laski would develop in subsequent years.

The Chosen People suggests that this period was one of torment for him, as he oscillated between his happiness with Frida and his foreboding about the inevitable conflict with his parents and their subsequent unhappiness. But he did not have long to wait to discover the reaction of his parents. Warned by Frida's parents that the marriage had taken place, Neville and an uncle were sent to Scotland the next day to bring Frida and Harold back to Manchester. According to Frida's later account, when they arrived they found Nathan prostrate, overcome by shock and nervous exhaustion, following an attack of hysteria, while Sarah rushed out of the room weeping.[26] After a painful session, the family extracted the following promises: that Frida would not use the name of Laski; that the couple would not cohabit, and that they would not meet while Harold was at Oxford (where he was due to go in October) without their permission and without supervision. They were to spend that night in separate bedrooms and Frida was to go back to Glasgow the next morning. In return for meeting these conditions, Harold would be allowed to go to Oxford with a small allowance, but he would receive no more help unless Frida converted to Judaism.

They accepted the condition of immediate separation, and the secrecy of the marriage, because Frida insisted that Harold should go to Oxford to complete his education. At first they also intended to maintain sexual abstinence for the next three years, not because of the promise to Nathan and Sarah – which Harold regarded as 'worthless and less than binding' – but because he did not yet think himself sufficiently mature for fatherhood.[27] But they were both deeply frustrated and could not maintain this position. However, their meetings were very rare during Harold's three years at Oxford: they could not afford the travel expenses and Nathan and Sarah continued to exert maximum pressure to enforce their separation. This was, of course, very distressing for Harold and Frida, but it did not undermine their relationship or lessen their commitment to one another. The crisis with the Laski family was far more serious.

In *The Chosen People*, the character representing Nathan expressed his view on the meaning of the marriage:

> You are no longer my son. You have chosen to go counter and wilfully counter to the belief which you were aware was dearest of all to me. What crime have I committed that my son should thus throw overboard the faith I and my Fathers have held for countless generations. Is the stainlessness of our history nothing to you. Do you hold so cheaply that great rabbinic tradition of which my family has been so long and so rightly proud?[28]

For his wife's sake, he would 'allow time to heal the wound' if 'Frida' adopted Judaism and promised to observe it 'as your mother observes it, literally and with a heart full of love and esteem for the ritual', and if they pledged themselves to bring up their children 'to a wholehearted belief in the truth of Judaism'. Otherwise 'let there be an end to our kinship'.[29] Harold was absolutely determined that he and Frida would never accept such conditions. In August 1911 the eighteen-year-old Harold Laski had thus effectively renounced his family and background.

The crisis was traumatic. It called into question his whole sense of identity, family relationships and beliefs. Having been disowned by his parents, it became still more crucial for him to be accepted by others. His subsequent craving to be well regarded by those he respected was at least partially attributable to his early break with his family. However, he never had any doubts about his decision.

His marriage was the anchor in his life. It was a relationship of rare happiness for both partners, and Harold never stopped telling Frida of his love. Years later, when she was over sixty he still wrote, as he had written so many times:

> You are the most generous-hearted wife any man could hope for, and you make me feel very humble by the endless greatness of spirit you show. It was a marvellous day for me when you appeared that morning at breakfast at Halesowen. I can't bear to think of what I might have been if I had not found you. As it is, after all these years, I feel with all my heart that I begin to love you afresh every day. And to have you believe in me is the rock on which I can build my truth.[30]

And it is clear that Frida, who was so much the more psychologically stable of the two, played an incalculable role in all his subsequent achievements. This is not to say that she simply subordinated herself to his career in the conventional marriage style of the era. She continued to work as a physiotherapist for many years, and remained actively involved in a variety of organisations. In later years she was also a Labour Party Councillor and a magistrate. However, when she married she was consciously abandoning an element of freedom that she had previously valued. As she told a friend a few years later:

> It's no little change in an independent woman's life. . . . As keen as I was it took me a very long time to decide when it came to a question of marriage; you see I had the notion one could do without that – but I found I was wrong.[31]

Subsequently, although she was always active and maintained considerable independence, she seems to have believed that one of her primary tasks was to support him. Whether he was quite as solicitous to her needs is unclear, but at least he acknowledged his debt to her in fulsome terms on numerous occasions.

Harold Laski's ideas would change considerably during his adult life. Yet there was an essential core of values, and a spirit, which can be traced to his early background and the crisis which resulted from his marriage to Frida.

At a conscious level, the first impact of the break with his family was a complete rejection of 'Jewishness'. Of course, he had already rejected religious belief before the crisis. But the trauma was so deep that he felt the need to write a book on the subject (*The Chosen People*) which was really an attack on his whole background. Judaism, he now argued, had provided inspiration in the past, and eighteen centuries of ruthless Christian persecution had been 'unflinchingly borne and marvellously survived'. But the ghetto had meant years of 'ceaseless codification of a creed that became increasingly outworn'. Moreover the preservation of the religious tradition inevitably meant the continuation of the ghetto spirit, cutting Jews off from the indigenous community. Yet they simultaneously wanted to integrate into it and this led to a double life in which Jews tried to make their emulation of the conventions of their adopted land as complete as possible, while insisting on orthodoxy at home. Such practices were anachronistic and prevented the full integration of Jews into their adopted country. Liberal Judaism was no solution, because it was still based on untenable religious claims and could not even provide the ritual and spirit which had 'stamped the personality of Judaism'.[22]

Since religion was no longer sufficient to persuade the young that they should maintain physical separation from the indigenous population, there were now appeals to 'racial solidarity' and the inter-marriage taboo. But such separation cut Jews off from the mainstream of human intellectual progress, and the only tenable position in the modern world was full assimilation. Yet if this implied Laski's renunciation of his Jewish background, there were, even at the conscious level, some factors which made his rejection of his past less than total.

In *The Chosen People*, in fictional form, he describes his plight when he had wished to marry Frida:

> You come up so suddenly against the heredity of nearly six thousand years and you are made willy-nilly to realise your own powerlessness. All your pride in your race, all your belief in its future counts as nothing. You have betrayed it. You do not follow in the path of rigid faith and it casts you aside. Would that I could talk to my people . . . and make them see that even if I love someone of an alien faith yet the spirit with which my ancestry has imbued me goes on. It cannot die – it is the most essential part of me . . . [32]

There is little doubt that this expressed a genuine belief. He always regarded himself as Jewish and took some pride in the heritage of 'a common history and a great history'. And, even after the break with his family, he believed that there was a Jewish nation united by 'its spirit of intense determination to achieve [a] mighty end'.[33] This Jewish consciousness may have remained dormant for several years but it would be re-kindled by frequent experiences of anti-semitism and, above all, by Nazism. It may also partially explain his tendency, particularly in the United States, to form close personal friendships with other non-religious Jews, who had also broken away from the Jewish community.

But the unconscious imprint of his background was still more important. First, there was the drive to succeed, which Nathan and Sarah had instilled in him. Harold Laski, backed by Frida, knew that he had a formidable intellect and he never really doubted his ability to make an impact in the world. The break from his parents only reinforced his determination to 'make his mark'. Secondly, there were some intangible, but crucial features of his outlook, which owed much to his early years. In Judaism there is little distinction between 'scholarship' and 'religious duties': the point of study is to understand more fully what needs to be done. But this was analagous to Laski's subsequent refusal to draw a distinction between the academic and political worlds. Similarly, his unwillingness to kowtow to those in authority probably owes much to a religious background in which rabbis are teachers rather than leaders and the community is urged not to put confidence in princes.[34] However, the attempt to *renounce* his past influenced his life and thought as much as the background itself.

He insisted that Jewish identity was anachronistic and that religion was nothing more than superstition. Instead he sought the truth in terms of the Enlightenment values of 'rationality' and intellectual debate. Yet his rebellion was, of course, *emotional* as well as intellectual. And it was based on a deep belief that there was a gulf between the *actual* and the *possible*. He wanted to play his part in the creation of a world in which there would be 'beauty, truth, and love'.[35] And in *The Chosen People* he argued that both science and 'dreams' were necessary if the goal were ever to be attained.

Laski expressed such feelings more openly in his youthful letters to Frida and in *The Chosen People* than he would in his more sophisticated later works. And the means by which he believed the new world could be attained changed several times over the next four decades. Yet there was continuity in his belief that there was a divorce between existing reality and the more rational and just world that could be attained. His ambition was therefore never solely personal: it was always to act as a 'soldier in the liberation army of humanity'.[36]

In other words, there is a real sense in which Laski retained a religious drive, even though he was a professed rationalist. His Jewish background, and the personal sacrifice involved in severing himself from it, gave him a spirit and a vision which remained with him for the rest of his life. It provided him simultaneously with the courage to follow the dictates of his conscience and a craving for acceptance. It gave him great insight into the human condition and the conditions under which freedom might be possible, but it also made him apocalyptic and frenetic. His political creed was indeed the product of his background and 'an intense psychological dislike for the atmosphere of his family'.

2

Political Education

On the eve of the Second World War, Harold Laski was to recall: 'I have, I suppose, been a socialist in some degree ever since the last years of my schooldays.' The diverse factors leading him to this position were, he claimed, the influence of a great schoolmaster [Paton] who made us feel the sickness of an acquisitive society', the effects of his Jewish upringing and being treated differently from others for no obvious cause, the books of Sidney and Beatrice Webb, and a speech he heard in Manchester just before going to Oxford, by Keir Hardie, 'whose account of the effort of the Scottish miners to form a trade-union made me begin, at least dimly, to understand the price the workers have to pay for the social reform they achieve'.[1]

These were, no doubt, important influences, but Laski's conversion to socialism was a more gradual process than he implied. This chapter examines his intellectual and political development until the summer of 1914, when he and Frida left Britain for Canada.

By the age of sixteen, Laski had already demonstrated formidable abilities to absorb information and theories, and to articulate arguments authoritatively, with an exceptionally mature command of language. But he had not yet developed a distinct political or theoretical position. He had certainly assimilated liberal values from both his school and his home. Indeed, he would always remain deeply committed to the notions of free speech and discussion and relished the exchange of ideas. Yet by the time he met Frida he was beginning to break away from the politics of his parents and felt 'very keenly' the 'bankruptcy of modern liberalism'.[2] However, he also told Frida:

> I cant go as far as the socialists. It is hard to stand between two parties; bagging some ideals from one and some from another.[3]

This was a dilemma that was to remain with him for years.

In fact, Laski was still highly impressionable. He was aware of the crisis of Edwardian liberalism but had no clear view as to how the problems could or should be resolved. When he met Frida his affiliations (as well as his sense of identity) were in a state of flux. Captivated by her, he adopted her interest – eugenics.

Eugenics is now so closely associated with Nazism and racism that it is difficult to believe that liberals and socialists could ever have been attracted to it. Yet in the Edwardian era, it appealed to a whole swathe of progressive reformers, including the Fabians, J. A. Hobson, Keynes, Bertrand Russell, and H. G. Wells. Indeed, many of them maintained their support for it until well after the First World War.[4] While this does not *justify* support for eugenics, it suggests that Laski's endorsement of it was less surprising than it might appear at first sight.

The 'science' was effectively founded by Sir Francis Galton, who coined the term in 1883. Convinced that civilisation had been in decline since the end of the Greek era, his objective was to raise the physical and mental level of the 'race':

> This idea was based on two propositions: first, that desirable physical and mental qualities were unevenly distributed throughout the population and, second, that those who had the desirable qualities could be identified and encouraged to multiply faster than the others. This . . . could be accomplished partly by various forms of state intervention and partly by placing a high social value on the fertility of the better stocks in society.[5]

Eugenics research attempted to measure the allegedly inherited characteristics in mathematical terms, and a so-called Biometric Laboratory was established under Sir Karl Pearson, for this purpose. This undertook empirical studies to demonstrate that current fertility patterns were leading to an increase in weaker stocks and a decrease in stronger ones, and suggested policy changes to reverse this allegedly catastrophic trend.

The theory of heredity underlying eugenics was crude, with a tendency to assume that all observable physical characteristics were inheritable. It also claimed, with still less evidence, that types of behaviour and morality – such as criminality – were hereditary. The normal conclusion was that certain groups of 'undesirables' – such as the 'feeble-minded' – should not be allowed to breed at all, whilst the 'better stock' should be encouraged to have more children. What, then, was the attraction of eugenics to progressive liberals and Fabian Socialists?

In the first place, it possessed the status of 'science' at the turn of

the century. Darwinian evolutionary theory had transformed understanding of biology, and attempts to apply it to society excited
intellectuals across a wide political spectrum. Secondly, it could be
used to justify reform on the grounds that assistance which was
directed to 'healthy stock' in the working classes would help elevate
society as a whole. Indeed, in 1909 Sidney Webb addressed the
Eugenics Society to argue that the Minority Report on the Poor Law
was based on eugenic principles.[6] Thirdly, eugenics could be held to
lie to the left of traditional liberalism, since it could justify greater
state intervention to promote social goals. As one commentator
argues:

> one may . . . locate three related ideas as common to the mentality
> of eugenists and reformers: the evolution of human rationality,
> orientation towards the future, and their concomitant – planning.[7]

Despite the importance of contextualising the thought of the era,
rather than simply condemning it because of its later associations,
eugenics still seems morally repugnant. It also appears to be a middle-class doctrine. Its adherents often denied this, claiming that they
wanted to foster larger families amongst 'good stock' in all classes.
However, they normally correlated 'social value' with existing positions in society, effectively concluding that working-class fertility
should be reduced, whilst that of the middle and upper-classes
should be increased. Although the adherence of Frida and Harold
Laski to eugenics may therefore be viewed as comparatively common for the progressive middle classes in their era, there is no need
to sympathise with their stance. But what specific influences brought
them to eugenics?

Two factors had attracted Frida. The first was her intense interest
in physical fitness and physiotherapy. The second, according to her
own memoirs, was the conflict with her mother, leading her to
analyse the development of her own character and the relative weights
of hereditary and environmental influences in its formation. She first
came across eugenics while estranged from her parents in Belgium,
and became a convert. For her, it was a science which would study
the way in which 'fine human offspring' could be produced, and
would show the extent to which characteristics were inherited.[8] In
addition to the appeal of 'science' and the general factors which
attracted progressive liberals to eugenics, there was a further important element in it for Frida: it could co-exist with, and reinforce,

feminism. For if crucial inherited characteristics depended as much on female as male genes, how could there be any justification for regarding women as less important than men? Since women were the eugenic equals of men they should have equal rights to choose their marriage partners, careers, and political rulers.

Militant suffragist and evangelical eugenist: this was the Frida with whom the sixteen year-old Harold Laski fell in love. Consciously or unconsciously he saw eugenics as the way to her heart. However, it probably also attracted him because it offered the combination of scientific 'truth' (rationalism) and mission which might replace religion. In any case, he threw himself into it, eager to demonstrate to Frida the depths of his convictions and intellectual understanding.

Within a few months – while still at school studying for a history scholarship to Oxford – he published his first article on the subject.[9] In this, he used his formidable talent to explain eugenic principles in a literary style which would have been impossible for most scientifically-trained adherents. He showed occasional signs of the more progressive interpretation of eugenics. Whereas a right-wing eugenist might oppose the Education Act for penalising healthy parents by making them support their children for longer (thereby reducing their incentive to breed), Laski thus argued that the solution was the introduction of a minimum wage. But the main thrust of his argument was that:

> The decline of every great nation is probably to be traced to the fostering of the unfit at the expense of the fit, and their consequent over-propagation.[10]

At present, the differential rates of fertility pointed to a 'future swamping of the better by the worse' so that 'as a nation, we are faced by racial suicide'. Progress could not be secured 'unless we prevent the propagation of the unfit'.[11] The solution was to change public opinion in such a way that 'society will look upon the production of a weakling as a crime against itself'. All this led to the stirring conclusion that:

> Upon the framework, with which genetics provides us, we must build a strong political superstructure. We see the necessity of a radical reform in the basis of our life; we have realised that the science which enables us to elevate it lies ready to our hand.

Society will work out its own destiny without eugenics; but with its aid it can accomplish its salvation.[12]

Such words impressed Sir Francis Galton, who invited Laski to tea and was astonished to find that he was only just 17. Convinced that Laski was a prodigy 'with stamina and purpose', Galton projected him into the centre of the eugenics world.[13] Between leaving school in December 1910 and going to Oxford the next autumn, he was invited to study with Sir Karl Pearson at the Biometric Laboratory in London, and he continued his involvement in eugenics during his first year at university. Indeed, he was so committed to the doctrine that it was the subject of his first speech in a debate at New College, and he arranged for Pearson to speak on it to university undergraduates.[14] Nevertheless, he was probably beginning to have some doubts. He started attending Oxford University Fabian Society meetings during his first year and, as a member of its Political Science Group, agreed to give a paper in May 1912 on 'Some Problems of Eugenics'.[15] Whether he was referring to technical problems within a eugenics framework or was raising more fundamental issues is unclear. But although one more eugenics publication in which he participated came out in 1913,[16] the work for this had been done much earlier, and he appears to have lost interest in the subject by the end of his first year at university. This was no doubt partly because his political opinions were shifting to the Left, and partly because of problems he had been encountering in his academic work.

Although he had come second in the history examination into New College,[17] and planned to work for at least eight hours a day, his first year at Oxford was hardly plain sailing. In his second term he obtained permission to postpone his divinity exam – then compulsory – until December.[18] This was because he needed to read the New Testament for the first time in his life (perhaps because he refused to ask for an exemption on religious grounds). Far more seriously, he encountered major problems with science. His theoretical work was excellent, and at first his tutor told him that he was already at finals level in some aspects of biological theory.[19] But he was hopeless at practical experiments and classification, and clearly had no future as a scientist. At the end of his first year he failed his preliminary examinations and was told that he must pass them in December.[20]

This brought the problem to a head. Laski had switched to science because of Frida: the failure must have demonstrated his mistake to them both. He was now allowed to transfer back to history, although conditions were imposed. During the first term of his second year he was forced to study history and science (as well as divinity!) In December, it was reported to the meeting of the Warden and Tutors:

> that Mr Laski had failed for the third time in the Science Preliminary, and ordered that unless he passes all the Preliminary Examinations for his Final School by June, he will not be allowed to reside further until he has done so.[21]

This was perhaps less threatening than it appeared. Almost simultaneously the College awarded him a private exhibition on the strength of his work in history. But he had abandoned science completely and appears to have taken no further part in eugenics.

What then was the significance of Laski's eugenics phase? It is again necessary to emphasise the extent to which eugenics and Frida had been intertwined in his mind. Before their marriage he thus told her:

> I'm perfectly sure we're going to do great things together and if Pearson writes the Groundwork of eugenics we'll do its principles and we'll make it a tremendously fine book spinning it out of our souls.[22]

But if there was an indissoluble bond between Frida and eugenics in his mind, he was still 'responsible' for his own views. Three other points must therefore be made about this phase in his beliefs.

First, it demonstrated an elitist strand in his outlook. Eugenics assumes an ineradicably uneven distribution of inherited characteristics. In other words, there are elites in society (in intellectual and physical terms) whose prowess stems from biological characteristics which must be fostered. This is hardly a concept which would appeal strongly to an egalitarian. Secondly, his support for eugenics was coupled with a disdainful attitude to charity and paternalist social reform. This followed from eugenic principles for, according to the theory, such well-intentioned actions could have the damaging result of helping the weak at the expense of the strong. But Laski's attitude was probably rooted in more fundamental factors than his temporary support for eugenics. Since his parents' involvement in social welfare work was of exactly the kind which he now attacked, it is highly probable that his condemnation of charity was part of his rebellion against the values of Sarah and Nathan. It was to remain long after his eugenics phase had passed. Thirdly, his support for the doctrine was enthusiastic. He quoted with approval Galton's statement that 'we must hold the eugenic ideal of parenthood with the fervour of a new religion' and he saw it as the 'salvation' of society.[23] This was typical of the way he would commit himself totally to doctrines which he supported.

Fortunately, eugenics was a fleeting episode in his life which was soon replaced by two mutually reinforcing influences, which had a far greater impact on his political thinking in the long term: the intellectual climate of historical and political thought at Oxford, and the challenge to the Liberal government by direct action movements – particularly the suffragettes.

Laski's early intellectual promise had been in history and he was clearly most suited to the humanities and social sciences. As a schoolboy he had already shown extraordinary gifts of historical empathy and the ability to offer stimulating and penetrating interpretations in a highly authoritative manner. For example, at the age of seventeen he wrote an essay on Macaulay for the school magazine. In this he sought to explain why Macaulay was the most successful of modern British historians although:

> He has expounded no philosophy of life. He has left us no searching criticisms, no profound generalisations to which posterity will ever cling, and which the world will not willingly let die.

His answer was that 'his work abounds in the commonplace' and was in exact accord with the ideals and emotions 'acceptable to the ordinary man'.

> The ideal of a scientific history, stern and impartial, unswayed by emotion, untouched by feeling, is not one that would appeal to the untrained mind. But a history that combines in itself all the best qualities of a novel; a history, moreover, that has an unsurpassed dramatic interest; that abounds in brilliant descriptions of thrilling action, is bound to secure popular favour. . . . It is the constant occurrence of the truisms of life, its mutability, its beauty, its pathos, that win the ordinary man's heart. It is the same with Macaulay. . . . He was not a philosopher; he was not an analyst. He was a narrator; and from Homer to our own time it is the narrator who secures the public ear . . .

His work is essentially superficial, and, to use a paradox, profound in its superficiality . . .

He was pre-eminent in those qualities that make for the more obvious success. And when literary psychologists of the future attempt to dissect the movements of the nineteenth century, they will determine that, though men like Mill and Spencer did work of profounder significance, Macaulay was the mightiest influence.[24]

He was thus able to detect the qualities in Macaulay which were to make him A. J. P. Taylor's 'model' historian. Laski's style was perhaps pretentious for a schoolboy, but it never really changed, and he was already revealing his talent as an essayist, who could make an important point in a few words.

In fact, from an early age, his real love was for history, both for its own sake and as a means of understanding the evolution of ideas and institutions. His failure in science was therefore an intellectual liberation for him. (Indeed, given his pledges to Frida that they would devote their lives together to eugenics it would have been difficult for him to have made the decision to abandon science himself.) In any case, he now threw himself into the study of history, intent on covering the three-year syllabus in two. Unlike many politically active students, who have little patience with the more obscure medieval debates, he enjoyed all aspects of the curriculum both for their intrinsic intellectual interest and for their relevance in understanding the present. He thus won a university essay prize on 'The Colonial Administration of Lord Grey, 1846–52',[25] made a special study of the Domesday Book,[26] and, in his final year, analysed the workings of the Exchequer and system of national finance at the end of the fourteenth century.[27] But his real love was political thought and his work on this at Oxford would be crucial in his subsequent formulation of 'pluralist theory'.

The study of history was important in undermining the eugenics phase. This was partly because his abandonment of science removed any reinforcement between academic study and biological theory, and also because history led him to lose faith in mechanistic and deterministic theories of human behaviour. However, of still greater importance was the shift in his political sympathies and activities, particularly through his involvement in the suffrage movement.

When Laski went to Oxford, Frida became more actively involved in the Scottish branch of the suffrage movement. She also often visited the Pethick Lawrences' flat in London, which acted as the headquarters of the Women's Political and Social Union (WPSU), where she helped to compile and distribute the paper, 'Votes for Women'.[28] Laski sometimes saw her there and, through the Pethick Lawrences, they met many of the suffragist leaders. During his first year at Oxford Laski became an active suffrage campaigner in the overwhelmingly male university.

At the beginning of his second year, he was the second speaker for a motion favouring female suffrage in an Oxford Union debate. He emphasised that women were the intellectual equals of men and that the suffragists:

> would not regard even women in Parliament as an end in itself, far from it. They looked upon the granting of the vote merely as a symbol of a wider movement, a movement in which women were striving to win a larger and fuller comradeship in the study of great political questions which it was their duty to solve.[29]

The motion was lost (by 179 to 200), but the student journal, *Isis* congratulated him on a very good first appearance.[30] However, Laski's motive was not to gain applause in the training ground for future politicians: he was passionately committed on the issue. When he next spoke on the subject in a Union debate a year later, the government had introduced the so-called 'Cat-and-Mouse-Act' under which women hunger strikers were released for short periods to restore their health and then re-arrested. This time the motion was: 'This House disapproves of the policy and administration of His Majesty's Government with regard to militant suffragist outrages' and Laski's tone was far more strident than in the previous year:

> there was not a single Suffragist prisoner who had been committed by the judges of this country who had been guilty of a crime; the crime had been committed by His Majesty's Government. Women, who were fighting thus for a movement that was unequalled in the history of this country, were willing that they should suffer torture for the cause, in the way of forcible feeding, and under the Cat and Mouse Act. The Government was the culprit in this matter. There had been a suffrage movement in this country for 40 years, but until 1906, no one knew of its existence as a real political force. The point was that they had to waken up public opinion, and it was then that the country were prepared to give some attention to their demands. But what kind of attention

had the Government given to the suffragist movement? All they could see was an unwillingness to hear their case. The situation, which the Government had created, had made rebellion a virtue, and imprisonment an honour.[31]

His speech was not applauded and the motion was again defeated (by 137 to 162). But *Isis* noted that it was Laski's 'day out' as he was one of the leaders of the militant branch of the suffragist movement, 'and he revelled in his subject'.[32] A few weeks later it described him as one of only three speakers who treated the House to some genuine oratory, partly because he was a 'fanatic' – a term which was also used by *Oxford Magazine*.[33] Even his allies were sometimes surprised by his vehemence on the issue. For example, in November 1913 he was part of a suffragist deputation who saw Lloyd George when he visited Oxford. H. W. Nevinson, the radical journalist who led the deputation later recalled:

> Laski . . . set upon the unhappy Minister with a fury of a little gamecock, and a passion of the indignation far surpassing the careful restraint of us older men.[34]

The previous month the *Isis* reporter had also expressed the fear that Laski's 'vigorous and sincere eloquence will one day bring him within the prison gates'.[35] This may have been said in jest, but the danger of arrest was much nearer than the writer realised. For, in addition to his public activities on behalf of the campaign, Laski was also prepared to undertake illegal action. This ranged from comparatively trivial matters, such as tearing up his census form, to direct action.[36] It is unclear whether or not he was involved in the destruction of an Oxford boathouse – causing approximately £3000 damage – on 3 June 1913.[37] More serious still, he placed a bomb in a lavatory in a railway station in Oxted (Surrey). No-one was hurt, but he only narrowly escaped detection, when Frida borrowed a car, and drove him to Dover. From there he took a boat to France and stayed for a few days in Paris.[38]

It must be presumed that the bomb was intended to damage property rather than people. Nevertheless, this support for direct illegal action is highly significant, for Laski attached overwhelming importance to non-violence and was passionate in his belief that change should be brought about through 'reason', argument, and legal processes. However, when the Liberal government treated suffragists so viciously, he was prepared to depart from conventional politics. He had no doubts that the principle of equal rights for women transcended obedience to the liberal state. He also showed considerable bravery in campaigning for the principle in an exceedingly hostile environment. Even to speak in favour of female suffrage in the Oxford Union at the time required some courage, but he went much further than this. According to his later recollections, he was, for example, thrown down a flight of steps in Bristol by anti-suffragists, and the Warden of New College threatened that he would be 'sent down' if he organised any further disturbances at public meetings.[39]

Involvement in the suffrage campaign was also to carry Frida and Harold into the Labour movement, for they supported Sylvia Pankhurst when she broke with her sister Christabel and tried to unite the women's struggle with that of the workers. Thus in early 1914 Laski played an important role in the Oxford branch of the Men's Political Union for Women's Suffrage – in which G. D. H. Cole also became involved – inviting speakers such as George Lansbury to meetings.[40] Other influences were also driving Laski to the Left. The University Fabian Society had been radicalised by an upsurge of industrial unrest, including a local tram drivers' strike in May 1913. This shift brought Cole to the fore, and in February 1914 he took over as President and tried to push the society towards Guild Socialism and away from the more bureaucratic 'statist' influence of the Webbs.[41] This new mood affected Laski and in February 1914 he was the main speaker in an Oxford Union debate in favour of the motion 'Parliamentary Action is discredited as a solution for labour disputes'. He bitterly condemned the Liberal government and Parliament as a whole and supported strikes as the only method by which the working classes could 'alter their conditions when they became intolerable and too hard to bear'. He also proclaimed that 'one of the most remarkable facts in modern politics was the complete futility of the Labour Party in the House of Commons'. Labour, he argued, had gone to Parliament to alter industrial conditions but 'It had failed to do anything of that kind, and had become simply an adjunct, and not a very handsome adjunct to the Liberal Party'.[42]

During his final year at Oxford his political views were thus moving to the Left. Striving to combine insights and experience drawn from contemporary events with those derived from his academic work, he had come to believe that the existing system was in decay. But he was not clear about the fundamental source of the problems, or the way in which they might be resolved. He was certainly critical of the dominance of the executive, and believed that this was reinforced by the party system. This meant that he sometimes appeared to look back with nostalgia to a bygone age in which MPs were independent and governments really needed to convince Parliament of the wisdom of their policies.[43] But he was also attracted by the arguments of Guild Socialists, telling Frida in the summer term of his final year that they:

> are very right in arguing that the root-evil of today is the regarding of labour as a commodity that can be bought and sold. Immediately you do that you obviously give the power to the capitalist whether personal as a man or impersonal as a trust or state and I think because political power follows economic power . . . it doesn't make the vote you give the worker of any use so that the change I would advocate would be one in the point of view about labour that it is not a commodity the workman has to sell but absolutely his life. Then one sees what a change must come and how futile even collectivism is as a remedy just because . . . it is really only substituting one master for many and not touching the heart of the evil.[44]

As he also believed that 'the beginning of a group system is very obvious indeed', it is evident that he had begun to move towards pluralist theory while still an undergraduate. But his views were not defined with any precision.

Laski graduated from Oxford with a First Class degree in the summer of 1914. The performance of New College in history was outstanding that year, for it gained four of the thirteen First Class degrees awarded. He was therefore not necessarily the most highly regarded of his peers – perhaps partly because of his unorthodox views and approach.[45] Nevertheless, he was capable of an extraordinarily high level of analysis even within the rigid constraints of the Oxford examination system.

He had no doubt that he wanted to be an academic. However, there were no immediate opportunities when he graduated and he was now forced to find some other form of employment. Since Frida had not converted to Judaism, his parents now withdrew the financial support that had taken him through university. He and Frida could live together for the first time, but he needed some money to make this possible, particularly as Frida now left her job in Glasgow

to join him in London. Fortunately, their suffragist connections came
to the rescue. They were loaned a house by a wealthy suffragette,
and George Lansbury offered Laski temporary employment on the
recently established *Daily Herald*.[46]

Although he was there for only a few weeks and was just twenty-
one, Lansbury soon recognised Laski's unusual talent and allowed
him to write some editorials as well as book reviews. Here again his
viewpoint on domestic issues was somewhat fluid, with 'guild socialism' perhaps being the most dominant characteristic. He was
thus scathing in his attacks on the Liberal government for surrender-
ing to the Ulster Protestants on Home Rule, while repressing suffragists and workers, and concluded that 'the law is class-law'.[47] He
therefore urged greater militancy by both workers and suffragists as
the sole way to achieve their ends.[48] And he sought greater economic
equality, while opposing the domination of society by centrally controlled parties and Parliament.[49] However, he had not yet reached
firm conclusions about the way in which these problems should be
resolved, when domestic issues assumed secondary importance as
war approached.

With the mounting international tension in the summer of 1914,
Laski shared the general opposition of the *Daily Herald* to working-
class involvement in a 'capitalist war'. On 3 August – the eve of the
conflagration – he was at his most eloquent, urging brotherhood and
solidarity and the refusal of workers to immolate themselves on the
altar of despotic capitalism:

> The people of England have a great inheritance, won at the cost of
> blood. It is our duty to hand down that torch of freedom
> undimmed. Let our united efforts destroy this war. Let us ask no
> privilege for ourselves or for our nation in which others cannot
> share. Let us strive and work that the sword may be beaten into
> the ploughshare and the flag be furled.
>
> The Angel of Death is very near; we can almost hear the beat-
> ing of his wings. Amid this vast hush of gloom we must take
> thought for the morrow. If there is war, not we alone shall suffer,
> not ourselves alone shall we curse. It is our children who will
> inherit the tradition of our agony and our hate. It is surely greater
> to stand united against this thing.
>
> We are under no debt to France, we have no bond with Russia;
> the workers of Germany are our brothers, and not our foes. Every
> ambition we can cherish, every cause we advocate, makes for

peace. Little by little we are trying to make of this civilisation a fairer thing than our ancestors have known. Can we consent to turn Europe into one vast shambles, to heap grief on grief, to add to the workers' burden the agony of widow, the wail of orphan child, deprived of kin for an end that brings neither honour nor prosperity.

The workers are the trustees of the future – it is theirs to fashion as they will. Let them say clearly that they will have no war. Let them point to the splendour of a vision of peace. There are great things crying out to be done, real wrongs demanding redress. Into those channels let the national energy be directed.[50]

But once Britain entered the war, the *Daily Herald* accepted the inevitable: it denounced the mistakes of the past, while defending the condition of the workers, and urging peace without aggrandisement.[51] Laski shared this shift in position and on 14 August, with citations from Burke and Hegel (!), he insisted that the British had no quarrel with ordinary Germans:

Let our minds be fixed neither on English aggrandisement nor on German humiliation, but on peace.[52]

Accepting that, to an extent, militarism arose out of human instincts, he also argued that it was necessary to find 'A Moral Equivalent for War':

It lies in the creation of a civic sense. We must engender a hatred of the errors of our civilisation, a hatred so bitter and compelling that men will not endure wrong because they will regard it as sin.

For the soldier's pride, the task was to:

substitute for it a pride in the tools of labour, be they the miner's pick, the surgeon's knife, or the weaver's loom. We must learn to regard ourselves as an army waging ceaseless warfare against our enemy – Nature. As the soldier's business is to destroy life, so it be our's to preserve it. And not to preserve it merely. Let it be ours to make it shine forth in a new splendour and a new fulness.[53]

And once again he used his favourite phrase from Heine: 'We, the civic soldiers, we are fighters in a war that will liberate humanity'.[54]

By August 1914 Laski – like many in his generation – was experiencing such challenges to his beliefs that it becomes increasingly difficult to characterise his position. His radicalism, with its left-liberal and socialist influences, was reinforced by his characteristic sense of a moral crusade. But alongside this there were also vestiges of patriotism and it was this – perhaps coupled with a sense of guilt that others would be slaughtered while he lived in comparative tranquillity – that now led him to volunteer for military service. However, he was rejected on medical grounds because of his weak heart.[55]

Any dilemmas about his next course of action were resolved almost immediately. Another academic, who had been accepted for a Lectureship in History at McGill University in Montreal, wanted to fight in the war but would not be released from his post unless a substitute was found. The Warden of New College asked Laski to go and he and Frida decided to accept. The only hurdle was that McGill insisted on reimbursing the fare after Laski's arrival, rather than advancing the money. This meant that he was forced to ask his parents for the money – a request that Nathan accepted only on condition that it was repaid as soon as they arrived in Montreal. Nor would Nathan and Sarah even say 'goodbye', although they had no idea when they would see their son again. Instead, a leaving party was organised by Sylvia Pankhurst.[56]

In September 1914 Frida and Harold set sail for Canada. It was there that he would try to draw together the lessons from his involvement in the suffragist movement, his growing awareness of the problems of workers, and his dilemmas about the war. The result would be a theory of the state which was also derived from his study of history.

3

A Pluralist in North America (1914–20)

Laski arrived at McGill University with great enthusiasm, intent on becoming a successful teacher who would make a major contribution to his subject. He achieved this goal, but his two years in Montreal did not fulfil his hopes. The whole ethos of the university was completely at variance with his ideas and character. Despite the multilingual nature of the city, McGill was then the university of English-speaking Montreal, and seemed determined to maintain this stance. Moreover, the Principal was Sir William Peterson, an austere Scottish classicist, who looked back to the 'home-country' and regarded Montreal as 'the outskirts of the Empire, in Britain's chief colony'.[1] History was a minor part of a science-dominated university and Peterson was anxious to build stronger links with Montreal commerce – an aim with which Laski had no sympathy. However, Peterson was prepared to raise his salary and confirm his appointment for a second year only on condition that he gave some time during the summer vacation 'to the interests of the proposed school of Higher Commercial Studies'.[2] Finally, the two differed totally on the war. For Peterson, it provided a sense of purpose, for he now saw his main responsibility as ensuring that Canada played its full part in maintaining the Empire. Laski remained ambivalent about the war itself and completely opposed to any sign of imperialism. It seems that the Principal's position was far closer to the general view for, when Laski gave an address attacking Lloyd George's war policy, there were urgent demands for his dismissal.[3]

He was equally unhappy within the Department of History. He thought it ludicrous that a Canadian university did not study the United States, and believed that there was no plan behind the courses.[4] They had, he believed, been arranged 'according to the taste of a professor who wrote his lectures eight years ago (when he knew nothing) and is too lazy to write new ones'.[5] Laski's own approach was far too radical for his new colleagues. Thus in 1916 he set the following examination paper for final year students in Political Science:

DO FIVE QUESTIONS

1. What is the place of reason in political thought?
2. Discuss the demands of labour in the modern state.
3. 'All politics relate to the psychology of the average man'. Discuss this view.
4. How would you improve industrial organisation?
5. Discuss the control of industry by the State.
6. Give some account of (a) socialism; (b) syndicalism.
7. What is the probable future of the party system?
8. What is the place of education in the modern state?
9. Is revolution a valuable method of social advance?
10. What does the term 'good' mean in politics?

The comments from other members of his department were: 'It's an impossible paper. What books could the men get the answers from'?; 'If that's what political science is about I'll give up teaching it'; 'I've never thought about those questions myself'. 'There isn't a question about Aristotle in it'.[6] In fact, he was completely out of keeping with conventional McGill. He and Frida also no doubt shocked local university opinion by inviting students to their home, and teaching trade unionists as well as undergraduates.[7]

The other major problem was financial hardship. His salary was very low and when, in the autumn of 1915, Frida became pregnant, he insisted that they moved into a furnished flat which cost half his monthly income. In addition to this he was forced to pay doctor's and hospital fees. All this was exacerbated when their dog allegedly bit a neighbour and they needed to pay for legal advice. Peterson refused to raise Laski's salary despite an earlier assurance that he would do so, and he was forced to borrow – a situation which he hated.[8] He now began regular reviewing and writing so as to alleviate their financial straits, and his subsequent tendency to write far too much stemmed, in part, from his difficulties in these years. Finally in May 1916 their daughter Diana was born with a life-threatening intestinal obstruction, which required hospital treatment. However, after several frightening weeks, Diana survived.[9] Since Laski had, by then, accepted a post at Harvard, the family's situation finally appeared to be improving.

He had wanted to move from McGill almost as soon as he arrived and by July 1915, he had already decided that he wanted to teach 'his curious political ideas at Harvard'.[10] His opportunity to do so was facilitated by Felix Frankfurter.

Frankfurter, like Laski, was Jewish, irreligious, and, at that time, radical.[11] He had already worked as a government adviser on two occasions and, again like Laski, believed that academic and political work should be combined. He had been appointed as a Professor of Law at Harvard in 1914. In the spring of 1915, Norman Hapgood, the drama critic, had visited McGill and told Frankfurter that he had met Laski there who was 'the most extraordinary young fellow I've ever come across anywhere'.[12] In the summer Frankfurter decided to visit Laski while in Canada. In 1961 he recalled his first impressions:

> Everything that Hapgood said about his extraordinary qualities was verified within an hour. I was charmed by his mind. I was charmed by his manner. His quickness, his eagerness, his liveliness, his range of interests . . . made me realise I was in the presence of a very unusual person . . . [13]

Frankfurter was to become Laski's closest friend for the rest of his life. They were to differ considerably after Frankfurter became a Supreme Court judge in 1939 and became more conventional in his political views. But their mutual affection – even love – was to be unbreakable.

As soon as Frankfurter returned to Harvard he suggested to the Dean that Laski should be appointed. This was agreed at the end of January 1916, and he was to take up his post as an Instructor and Tutor in History the following autumn. He moved during the summer to find a flat and furnish it so that it would be ready for Frida and the baby when they arrived. According to her memoirs:

> I turned up . . . in September to find Harold . . . blissfully enmeshed in writing but lost like a small boy in a flat that stood 'starkers' except for one bedstead – no bedding – and a desk with reams of headed writing paper. I was speechless with anger but couldn't stay that way for long, Harold being as he was the most impractical of creatures, half-man, half-child and maddeningly dependent on me.[14]

They were to stay at Harvard for four years and, at least until 1919, this was a period of considerable fulfilment. In the first place, it was there that he discovered that: 'it was my vocation to be a teacher, that in whatever other fields I might wander, this was the activity, above all, to which I should devote my energies'.[15] Clearly, he was an outstanding success in this capacity at Harvard. One of his students later recalled that:

He bubbled over with enthusiasm and excitement over the subjects of his courses. . . . His lectures were one long outpouring of
fact and commentary which opened up a world of ideas to his
young and probably immature disciples.[16]

Part of his achievement as a teacher depended on natural abilities:
his extraordinary memory, individuality of interpretation, and quick-
ness of repartee. But his success was also built on very hard work
and a particular conception of a university, in which the relationship
between academic staff and students was the central element. On the
one hand the lecturer was to be demanding: students were not
'spoon-fed' with summaries of books but were forced to read original and difficult texts, to think for themselves, and to be prepared
to discuss and defend their ideas. On the other hand, Laski believed
that, whatever their abilities, ninety-nine out of every hundred students had 'a divine spark in them somewhere which sympathy and
enthusiasm is sure to light'.[17] Academic staff should build a large
part of their lives around their students, offering them interpretations, debate, and encouragement in the development of their ideas.
This task was not to be restricted to the confines of the working day
and in Cambridge Harold and Frida invited students to their home
for discussion and debate. This was unprecedented in the highly
traditional atmosphere of Boston society, particularly as women
students from Radcliffe were also invited. It was also frowned upon
by conservative academic opinion. As the official history of the
university expressed it in 1930:

> Laski had a provocative influence on many undergraduates. At
> his house could be heard some of the best conversation in Cam-
> bridge; his experiments in academic freedom furnished much of
> the conversation elsewhere.[18]

However, it was perhaps this total commitment to his role as a
teacher which led the Harvard student journal to describe him at the
time of his departure as 'an intellectual genius' whose influence had
been 'stimulating and inspiring'.[19]

He also found fulfilment in his years at Harvard because of the
intellectual stimulation derived from his colleagues. At first he not
only taught history and political thought, but also enrolled as a law
student himself. He gave the latter ambition up after one term because it emphasised business jurisprudence instead of politico-legal

theory,[20] but he continued to play a role in the Law School as well as in his own area, and to work with colleagues in a wide range of subjects. If he derived satisfaction from the discussions, he also infected other academics with his own enthusiasm. His approach was both international and inter-disciplinary: in 1917–18 he became the only person ever to act as book editor of the *Harvard Law Review* without having a Law degree. Roscoe Pound, the Dean of the Faculty, congratulated him for having 'done wonders' and making the reviews' section 'promise something worthwhile' for the first time.[21] In an obituary note, one of Laski's friends and colleagues recalled that he:

> had the great merit of freshness. He brought us a wealth of new facts and problems from contemporary England and from the development of France during the last hundred years . . . And there has never been any book reviewing in the [*Harvard Law Review*] . . . to compare with the product of those two years, both what he wrote himself and what he had the gift of persuading others to write . . . He opened the eyes of American lawyers to a new range of books, and he also showed we could learn from a new kind of reviewer.[22]

Being accepted as a person whose views were valuable brought Laski two other major causes of satisfaction: influence and new friendships.

From his base at Harvard, he became involved in a whole range of new associations. As an increasingly well-known academic, he was invited to lecture in many other institutions and was a founder member of the New School of Social Research in New York. But he also became deeply involved in journalism and political life. Of particular importance was his association with the recently established journal, the *New Republic*. At the time he was friendly with the journalist and writer Walter Lippmann and, partly through him, he met many of the leading American liberals and trade union leaders. In 1917–18 he even had a brief spell working with the American government, when Felix Frankfurter chaired the War Labor Policies Board of the American Department of Labor and used Laski as a special advisor on the European labour movement issues that might arise at the Paris Peace Conference.[23] While at Harvard, he therefore appeared to be well on his way to fulfilling his ambition of combining academic work with political influence.

Friendship was of supreme importance to Laski. Later he was to say that it had provided him with 'a sense of fellowship that has given to life a happiness beyond the power of sorrow to destroy'.[24] The need to love and be loved was crucial to him, and Frida was well aware that even she could not fulfil this role alone. As she told Walter Lippmann, 'I look for so much from your friendship with Harold. You know I can't think of anyone who needs friends as much as he does'.[25] Once again, it was in the United States that he formed his closest friendships. Apart from that with Frankfurter, the closest was also the most incongruous: that with the eminent Supreme Court Judge, Oliver Wendell Holmes. When Frankfurter introduced them in July 1916, Holmes was already seventy-five while Laski was only twenty-three; Laski was radical, ebullient and an optimist, while Holmes was politically conservative, sceptical and even pessimistic. Yet they saw each other regularly while Laski was at Harvard, and corresponded until Holmes' death in 1935 (although it was a one-way correspondence after 1932 because Holmes could no longer respond to Laski's letters). Initially, perhaps Laski was attracted to Holmes partly because he was so eminent, but this was not the basis for their enduring relationship and, when their correspondence was published, there was much speculation about this. The most interesting interpretation (by Edmund Wilson) was that Laski saw Holmes as a father substitute (given his difficulties with Nathan) while Holmes saw him as a substitute for the son he never had.[26] But Laski also revered Holmes because his attitude to law was simultaneously principled and flexible. As he had expressed it in his *Common Law* (1881):

> The life of law has not been logic: it has been experience. The felt necessities of the time, the prevalent moral and political theories, institutions of public policy, avowed or unconscious, even the prejudices which judges share with their fellow-men, have had a good deal more to do than the syllogism in determining the rules by which men should be governed.[27]

Laski's veneration of Holmes was based on a genuine respect for a man of principle. He was no doubt also fulfilled by the evident fact that Holmes adored him and found that Laski's enthusiasm and intelligence gave him a new lease of life.

With his joy in teaching and academic life, his political activities, and his new friendships, it is not surprising that Laski was later to describe his period in North America as 'the most fundamental experience of my life'.[28] It was also during these years that he established his reputation as a writer, and his contribution as a theorist must now be considered.

Many commentators have regarded Laski's pluralism as the peak of his intellectual achievement. It has thus been studied extensively by academics, and has been quoted as a source for federalism, decentralisation, and self-management. As recently as 1989, extracts of his pluralist writings (with those of Cole and Figgis) were published by an editor, who saw them as a valuable antidote to Thatcherite centralisation.[29] Yet there is a paradox here for, although Laski's early theories have been widely quoted, there has been little agreement as to their ideological orientation or their relationship with Laski's political pre-occupations.

While some analysts have seen his pluralism as 'academic' and detached from political concerns,[30] others have effectively viewed the theory as a mask for unavowed political aims.[31] Similarly, while such authors as Deane and Elliott have seen it as essentially syndicalist or socialist throughout the period, Kingsley Martin argued that Laski was more 'liberal' than 'socialist', and was only radicalised by a crisis at the end of his stay in North America. The only common element in these interpretations is a tendency to regard the theory as relatively static between 1914–20.

The following interpretation of Laski's pluralism differs from all these positions. It argues that 'academic' and 'political' concerns were always combined in his thinking, but that an important shift in his outlook, which strengthened the 'socialist' aspect, took place in the middle of 1917.

EARLY PLURALISM, 1914–17

Laski assimilated a wide range of political and legal thought while in North America, and was influenced by his observations of the workings of a federal system. He was also struck by the insights of William James, and became increasingly interested in contemporary French thought.[32] Yet the most important influences upon him remained British and, in particular, those that he had absorbed as an undergraduate.

Before the First World War the influence of the neo-Hegelian Idealism of Green, Bosanquet and Bradley on Oxford political thought was still very strong.[33] British Idealism was a reaction – within liberalism – against the laissez-faire approach of the industrial revolution era. This earlier phase of liberalism had insisted that there was a contradiction between individual freedom and state 'interference', so that freedom would be maximised if the state was restricted to its minimum necessary functions. This view had been contested both in theory and practice for much of the Victorian era, but by the late nineteenth century it was becoming increasingly clear to many liberal theorists that the minimal state was now anachronistic. In practice, state intervention in the economic and social spheres was now increasing, and liberal doctrines were being challenged from both the Right and the Left. In these circumstances theorists who did not equate laissez-faire with the essence of liberal doctrine were seeking a justification for the 'positive' state. Idealism was one such response.

T. H. Green, who taught at Oxford from 1860 until 1882, played the major role in adapting Hegelian Idealism to the British liberal tradition. His objective was not to make the state an 'absolute', but to transcend the earlier assumption that the interests of the state and those of the individual were potentially or actually in opposition to one another. Instead he argued that there was an organic unity – or harmony – between the individual, society and the state. An increase in the powers of the state did not in itself decrease the realm of freedom. On the contrary, it could enlarge freedom by removing obstacles to the full development of the individual. Green's theory thus elevated the society and state over the individual. The individual could not have rights against the state, for the state harmonised the social relations on which the individual depended for personal fulfilment. Yet this did not mean that Green emphasised the state's coercive powers over the individual. On the contrary, he saw the foundation of the state as resting on a 'will'. The state defines rights and legislation, but it does so through a common rational will by which a society is bound in the pursuit of common aims.

If Green's philosophy was still recognisably 'liberal', his followers, Bradley and Bosanquet, took the Hegelian aspects of the theory further. Green had seen the state as necessary for the elimination of the obstacles to individual fulfilment and, as such, it acted for moral purposes. But it was not the *source* of morality which was ultimately derived from Christianity. Moreover, the state was limited in the international realm by ethical constraints emanating from the need to consider the welfare of humanity as a whole. With Bradley, and still more with Bosanquet, the progressive message of Green's philosophy was diluted while the metaphysical notions were expanded. The emphasis was increasingly on the state as the embodiment and source of an ethical will, while individuals found freedom through submerging their interests in those of the community as a whole. Although Bosanquet cannot be accused of proposing an absolutist state, he no longer indicated any way in which it could be judged by independent ethical criteria. The sovereign state was now seen to incorporate the highest morality. The implication was therefore that the actions of the existing British government expressed an elevated morality and will.

While Idealism remained a powerful influence at Oxford during Laski's years there, it was also being challenged. Two historians – F. W. Maitland and J. Neville Figgis – played a key role in mounting a counter-attack in the name of 'pluralism'.[34]

Influenced by the work of the German jurist Otto von Gierke (which he translated), Maitland argued that in all societies certain enduring groups or associations arise. Such associations had a collective consciousness and will, over and above that of its individual members, and possessed a real personality. These groups, which included religious organisations and professional associations, were often at least as important to the individual as was the state. They were also often the source of both customs and laws in societies. Maitland had developed such ideas a decade before Laski went to Oxford (particularly in his introduction to *Political Theories of the Middle Ages*, 1900), and H. A. L. Fisher, who was one of Laski's tutors at New College (and also Maitland's brother-in-law) published Maitland's collected papers just before Laski started history.[35] He was therefore fully exposed to Maitland's work.

Figgis, a clergyman, believed that all important social groups – for example, trade unions, colleges, and families – had a status which should be protected. However, his main concern was to provide a justification for the independence of the church. In *Churches in the Modern State* (1913), he argued that the church was a corporate association with a distinct personality, and as a 'corporate person', its rights and privileges should be protected in the same way as those of the individual. For individual members, loyalty to the church was as important as loyalty to the state. Its purposes must therefore be recognised by the state, which was not entitled to control it. Laski read Figgis' book as soon as it was published and, despite his lack of sympathy for religion, he was immediately interested in the notion of a church as an association, with rights and privileges with which the state must not interfere.[36]

The works of both Maitland and Figgis influenced Laski enormously, as he frequently acknowledged. (Indeed he felt so indebted to Maitland that he and Frida gave Diana the second name of Maitland in recognition of this fact.) When, for example, he argued in his first book that, in the 1840s the Church of Scotland, as a complete and self-sufficient personality, was justified in defying the British state, he was clearly applying the general conclusions of Figgis to a specific episode.[37] Similarly, when he maintained that groups had personalities of their own, which must be recognised by the acquisition of legal powers and responsibilities, his perspective owed much to Maitland's work on medieval guilds.[38]

But *why* was he so influenced by pluralism? Laski himself implied that Ernest Barker, his tutor at New College, played a major role in his conversion, but this is unlikely. For although Barker recognised that 'all the emphasis recently laid on rights of associations suggests lines of thought which are valuable and likely to be fruitful',[39] he was reluctant to abandon the Idealist conception – particularly Green's progressive liberal version. He was thus highly sceptical about some of the claims made on behalf of groups and saw the state as a 'general and embracing scheme of life' and 'the common substance in which very different elements are so firmly knit together that they can rejoice in their membership'.[40] It is true that Barker read a paper in New College on 'The Discredited State' just before Laski took his finals, but this did not suggest that it was discredited in his own eyes.[41] If we are to explain Laski's attraction to pluralism, we need to look at his own life and interests.

Given Laski's political views in the pre-war period, it was inconceivable that he could have accepted the Idealist tradition at that time. The attribution of moral characteristics or a rational will to the Liberal State, as it lurched from crisis to crisis and resorted to repressive tactics against suffragists and strikers, would have been unthinkable for him. Nor would he have been willing to accept Barker's intermediate position between Idealism and pluralism, for this was extremely cautious on the problem of 'obedience'. He claimed that when the 'social conscience' had implicitly acknowledged that a group possessed a right which the state had not granted, it was *possible* that resistance was justified. But there could be no moral obligation to resist, for the state was a moral being:

If we challenge the State, we must challenge it in fear and trembling. The presumption is always against us. The whole system of acknowledged rights is almost certain to claim, and to deserve, a higher allegiance than the most ideal of ideal rights.[42]

With his deep involvement in the suffragist movement, Laski would obviously have rejected this doctrine, for he was quite adamant that the right to sexual equality deserved a higher allegiance than obedience to an increasingly brutal state. And as he moved further to the Left under the influence of Guild Socialist ideas, he would also have rejected the claim that support for the state should supersede a commitment to trade unionism. In these circumstances, it is easy to understand the attractiveness of Figgis's pluralism. For although Laski was irreligious, the doctrine legitimised his view that the morality and rights of the state did not necessarily supersede those of other associations. As he later told Bertrand Russell:

My interest in liberal Catholicism really dates from 1913 when I read Figgis' Churches in the Modern State at Oxford; and while I was writing my first book I came to see that, historically, the church and the State have changed places since the Reformation and that all the evils of unified ecclesiastical control are slowly becoming the technique of the modern State – if they have not already become so.[43]

But if this suggests that Laski's political and moral concerns were of fundamental importance in leading him to pluralism, were these preoccupations primarily 'liberal' or 'socialist'?

This question is difficult to answer both because of the general problems of defining ideologies and the boundaries between them and, more specifically, because Laski never fitted neatly into any category. Indeed his stress on individual conscience was so strong that elements of his thinking even resembled classical nineteenth-century liberalism. Yet he was obviously fundamentally opposed to the notion that freedom depended on the minimal state,[44] and he remained close to the concerns of the Labour movement.

As soon as he arrived in Canada he had tried to understand trade unionism there, and began teaching economics to trade union workers. In private correspondence with George Lansbury he outlined his ideas for a constructive programme for a workers' party,[45] and even in his first published book, which dealt primarily with church-state relations, he wrote:

I should be prepared to argue . . . that in the England before the war the ideal of the trade-unions was a wider ideal than that which the State had attained, one is tempted to say, desired to attain.[46]

Some critics have therefore argued that 'as often as not Mr Laski's use of pluralistic theories advances the church and other institutions and associations in the state as stalking-horses for the unions'.[47] In other words, it is suggested that, from the start, he was (covertly) propounding a socialist or syndicalist theory. Laski's correspondence with Russell offers some support for this interpretation, for he told him that after writing his first book:

It then struck me that the evil of this sovereignty could be shown fairly easily in the sphere of religion in its state connection where men might still hesitate to admit it in the economic sphere.[48]

However, the undeniable fact that he was more interested in trade unions than churches does not mean that he adopted pluralism solely, or even primarily, because of a commitment to working-class politics. For his major worry was that which he frequently stated: the potential threat to liberty emanating from excessive state power *in all respects*. His concern for trade unions was incorporated within this outlook, but did not yet dominate it. This becomes clear if another of his preoccupations is considered: the war.

Little attention has been paid to Laski's subsequent recollection that, when he went to McGill, his ambition was 'to write a book on sovereignty – an issue which seemed to me to lie at the root of the war'.[49] Yet this was a crucial factor in the formulation of his early theory.

We have already seen that in August 1914 his attitude to the war had been highly ambivalent, and in North America he remained torn between conflicting emotions. He thus told an American friend that the war was 'hellish'[50] and that he hoped that the USA managed to keep out of it: 'it will be something in the future to think that in an age of utter madness you managed to keep a sane head'.[51]

Yet he also remained conscience-stricken that he could not fight. In October 1915 he was extremely upset when his brother Neville was injured while fighting in the Dardanelles.[52] This incident was not serious, but when he heard of the deaths of friends he was not only sad but tortured by feelings of guilt. In November 1916, for example, he confessed to Holmes:

dark places . . . come to me too often – come because most of me is in Europe aching to be fighting there and feeling a poor, stupid nonentity because I can only watch and hope when the youth of my generation are giving up their lives with so supreme an idealism.[53]

Again on 4 June 1917 he described himself as 'festering' on 'in a curious effort to get outside the war and to believe that it is honest to go on thinking when others are dying to make it possible for me to think'.[54]

The only way he could justify his position to himself was with the belief that his theoretical work would have some real importance. In May 1917 he thus told Felix Frankfurter that his ultimate aim was to 'do a real service by showing how this war has really precipitated a crisis in the theory of liberty': 'It seems to me an opportunity to do some real work for the things we care for, where physique and things like it don't matter'.[55]

His anguish is understandable. Almost one-third of his former classmates at Manchester Grammar were killed in the war,[56] and the preface of his second book reveals his feelings about his contemporaries at Oxford:

I began my other book with a sense that it might give pleasure to my friend A. R. Herron. He was killed before I could finish it. This book would have gone to my friend Frank Haldinstein, scholar of Christ Church and captain in the Royal Engineers. But his name, too, has been added to the list on which the Oxford of my generation will, with undying pride, write those of Arthur Heath, of Nowell Sievers, and of A. D. Gillespie – all of them of New College. When I look back on certain magic nights at Oxford and re-read these pages in the light of their memory, I realise how halting they are compared to the things they would have said. But I take it that for them the one justification of this conflict would have been the thought that we who are left are trying in some sort to understand the problems of the state they died to make free. To have known them was an education in liberty.[57]

One aspect of the linkage between Laski's pluralism and his attitude to the war was revealed in an unpublished critique of a book by a German academic (Professor Boas). The book, he argued, was very bad when it dealt with Germany and the origins of the war:

The whole of these pages is a plea that we must judge the morality of nations by a standard different from that by which we judge the morality of men. . . . Von Bethmann Hollweg had *no* choice on August 2nd – he had a clear duty and that was to uphold the sacred character of the public law of Europe. He violated that law and the only thing Boas or anyone else can do is to plead not for a verdict but for a mitigation of sentence.[58]

The relevance of this argument (in relation to pluralism) was the assertion that states should be bound by morality and international law. For if they were answerable to law, they could not be the source of it. This again was to deny state supremacy.

In an appendix to his first book, he traced the implications of his doctrine more precisely. Germany, he argued, had unity of sovereignty and sought a conformity of outlook. The result was that no-one in Germany doubted that it had been right to sink the *Lusitania*. But this was:

> simply evidence that in Germany today necessity has exacted the sacrifice of right to authority. Faith there is more urgent than thought. We prefer a country where the sovereignty is distributed, where the richness of the corporate lives is insurance against such sterility of outlook. . . .
>
> There can be no servility in a State that divides its effective governance. The necessity of balancing interests, the need for combining opinions, results in a wealth of political thought such as no State where the real authority is single can attain. The price of liberty is exactly divergence of opinion on fundamental questions. The well-ordered and neatly arranged products of recent German thought on politics testify to the existence of its opposite.[59]

Pluralism argued that power should be divided internally, and that states should be answerable to a higher morality or law. Laski's belief that such goals were more likely to be achieved in Britain than in Germany provided a rationale for his support for the Allies. Laski thus turned to pluralism for a variety of reasons, which cannot easily be incorporated within any conventional ideological 'label'. What was distinctive about his theory?

One notable feature was simply the assertive and clear manner in which it was expressed. But, more fundamentally, his approach differed from that of other pluralists because of the breadth of his attack on the sovereign state. Even when he was using historical examples of church-state conflicts, he incorporated legal and political thought to advance the case that state supremacy could not be justified in theory, practice, or morality. Moreover, Laski's doctrine was more fundamental than that of his predecessors in undermining theories of sovereignty while upholding the sanctity of the individual conscience. As we will see, this exposed the theories to criticism. But it also forced critics to reconsider first principles, for Laski was asking – in the most stimulating and provocative way – whether individuals and groups owed any allegiance to the state.

His negative aim was to discredit the state. His main response to Idealist theory was simply to expose the gulf between theory and practice. The state was said to embody ideal purposes, but its actions were carried out by agents (governments) which, in practice had no such elevated characteristics. What then was the point of attributing ideal and abstract goals to the state when these bore no relationship with its actual policies? It was far better, he asserted, to judge the state by its *consequences*. However, Idealism was only the most overt justification for state supremacy, and he was equally anxious to undermine any other rationale for the sovereign or 'monist' state. For example, the attribution of a 'general will' (*a la* Rousseau) to the state was equally invalid. For there was no such 'will' – only diverse wills. Since there was no empirical basis for ascribing generality to the state's will, any such ascription was either meaningless or dangerous. Indeed, he wanted to refute any doctrine which elevated the state above all other groups and individuals in society. This was difficult when (following John Austin, the nineteenth-century theorist of positive law), the rationale was expressed in apparently neutral terms: that is, that the state was the sole fount of legal sovereignty. However, he tried to rebut this by showing that, *in practice*, in various eras, the state had been unable to enforce its will and had been forced to submit to recalcitrant groups. Once again, he was therefore basing his argument on a form of 'consequentialism'. What was the point of claiming that the state was sovereign if, in fact, it was often unable to secure compliance with its commands, even when these were reinforced by laws? But the argument was also again moral and based on his primary assumption: that is, that there was no *a priori* reason for supposing that commands or laws were 'good' or that they *should* be obeyed because they emanated from the state.

The positive side of Laski's doctrine lay in his attitudes to the individual and groups. His most fundamental assumption was that the state must recognise individuality and the sanctity of a person's conscience. But this stress on individual conscience – no doubt based in part on his own rebellion against his parents and the pre-war Liberal government – was coupled with an equal emphasis on groups.

Associations such as clubs, churches and trade unions gave vitality to social life and provided the channels through which individual personality was expressed. Associations were thus the life-breath of the community. But recognition of this fact also had implications for the theory of the state. For if people were – and should be – members of associations, it followed that they had a 'plurality' of allegiances. There was no reason to assume that allegiance to the state would supersede a person's loyalty to a church or trade union. In some circumstances it was indeed patently obvious that loyalty to the primary association would be the stronger, and the state would fail if it tried to insist on its pre-eminence. He anticipated a criticism:

> It may seem that this view gives a handle to anarchy. Well I cannot help that. It does not, I believe, give any greater handle to anarchy than it already possesses.[60]

However, he accepted the need for a state. His point was that it could not secure allegiance by claims of its inherent superiority over all other organisations. It could do so only by winning support through being based on 'right conduct',[61] and having 'sufficient wisdom to obtain general assent'[62]. For the state was simply one association among many and, in one of his more provocative formulations, he claimed that it did not differ fundamentally from a baseball club.[63]

Laski's doctrine has been extensively criticised from various perspectives. Some have argued that he confused legal sovereignty and political absolutism,[64] and it is true that there is no necessary connection between them. But Laski believed that there was an historical or political linkage. That is, if state supremacy is constantly justified, there will be no basis for dissent, particularly when additional legitimation for sovereignty was provided by Idealist theory.[65] It was on these grounds that he criticised contemporary German doctrine and practice. Some critics have also been shocked by his proximity to anarchism, and it has even been argued that this kind of questioning of law and order destabilised the state and eventually led to Fascism.[66] But Laski was far more worried about the tendency towards an increasing concentration of state power, particularly during the war. He did not believe that active disobedience would be common, but simply wanted to demonstrate that the state must *win* allegiance and that if it failed to do so, there should be no presumption that the protest was unjustified.

Yet even for sympathetic critics, there are several problems in Laski's theory. It is clearly true that individuals will sometimes follow the dictates of their conscience rather than comply with the state and it is, in my view, crucial that such a stance is acknowledged as valuable. But the consequences of submission to 'conscience' are less straightforward than Laski implied. He obviously felt that the state should have submitted to the demands of suffragists (and that their consciences in refusing to comply with state demands should have been respected). But we also know that he was completely opposed to Asquith's submission in the face of the threats of Ulster Protestants. Are we then to argue that the Protestant rebellion was not dictated by 'conscience'? If so, is 'conscience' present only when we sympathise with the cause in question? Laski may have claimed that he was simply demonstrating that the state was not sovereign because people resisted when they felt sufficiently strongly about a principle. But it is unlikely that he felt that all consciences were equally important or that they should always be respected by the state. If so it is clear that additional principles needed to be invoked to justify support for either the state or the dissenters. But, at this stage, Laski did not provide any guidance on this.

This leads to a second allied problem. Laski was arguing that the state must win allegiance and obedience. In principle, this is an attractive doctrine, but it is, in many respects, as 'idealist' as the theory he was seeking to discredit. For he was not arguing simply that some states rest on greater popular support than others, but was implying that, in a pluralist state, people would comply with laws enthusiastically and without the need for coercion:

> The members of the state agree to obey the decrees of government simply because those decrees are infused with good will and because, without such agreed submission, the state, like any other group, becomes impotent and impossible.[67]

It is not surprising that Laski was seeking such a state, for harmony of this kind was his life's quest. But he did not explain *how* the non-sovereign state would provide such benefits that allegiance would be secured without the use of sanctions.

A third problem was his failure to examine the internal life of the associations to which he was ascribing such importance. In fact, of course, he knew from his own experience that religious organisations could be highly intolerant of deviant behaviour amongst their members. Yet he said nothing about the way in which associations might treat their adherents, presumably on the somewhat simplistic assumption that membership was voluntary. Nor did he deal sufficiently with the external actions of groups. One critic thus asked pointedly whether the Ku Klux Klan should simply be treated as an association.[68] Clearly Laski would not have thought so and would, no doubt, have argued that group actions must be bound by morality and law in just the same way as he believed that states should be. But he was placing so much emphasis on groups and individuals that he did not explain the genesis of these wider ethical and legal notions. He was content to rest his case on the notion that a rich associational life was the key to diversity and political freedom.

Two further criticisms may be advanced which have particular relevance when considering the ideology of the doctrine. First, Laski did not deal with issues of inequality either between individuals, groups, or social classes. Secondly, he gave no real indication of the kinds of policies that are required if the state is to secure allegiance, particularly from the working class. But if these questions were not addressed in the theory, it is difficult to see how it can be regarded as a socialist doctrine.

Until mid-1917 it therefore seems that, both in emotional and theoretical terms, Laski should be regarded as a left-wing liberal. He hoped that the working classes would secure greater opportunities and material advances through trade unions and their impact upon the state. But he also remained distinctly elitist in many of his attitudes. The pursuit of liberty, diversity, and justice were his primary political values, and he believed that these could be secured by associational activity on the one hand and a 'non-sovereign' state on the other.

PLURALISM AND CLASS CONFLICT, 1917–19

The shift in Laski's outlook was not sudden. At Oxford he had already expressed the view that there was a fundamental conflict between capital and labour, and he repeated this opinion to Holmes in September 1916.[69] However, he had not yet highlighted it within his analysis. This changed with the overthrow of Tsarist autocracy in Russia, and the general increase in industrial and political unrest in the latter stages of the war. Laski's interest in working-class movements was reactivated, and he decided to make it the central feature of his work. He therefore abandoned his intention of writing a further volume of church history and concentrated instead on the Labour movement.[70]

In April 1917 he told Holmes:

Once accept the postulate that political power is the handmaiden of economic power – which seems to me a historical truism – and I think it follows that the state which manipulates that power is also a capitalist institution. The fight between labor and capital . . . seems to me part of a historic process which one day will take us out of the capitalist system just as in the sixteenth to the eighteenth centuries we got away from the feudal system.[71]

But if the conflict between capital and labour was the decisive feature of contemporary society, and if the state was tied to capitalist interests, how could the situation be changed? And, more particularly, how could any conception of change be reconciled with pluralist theory? For pluralism could be negated by either a reformist or revolutionary conception.

Fabian and other reformist socialists argued that the position of the working class needed to be alleviated by material and social improvements carried out by the state. But how could this be achieved without a strengthening of the state? And if it were strengthened, would this not reinforce its supremacy and threaten associational activity? On the other hand Marxists generally argued that, since the dichotomy between capital and labour was the fundamental feature of society, there could be no solution unless capitalism were overthrown. Pluralist goals, it might be claimed, would perhaps be achievable after the capitalist state was 'smashed', but it would be utopian to believe that they could be attained in any other way.

Laski's position was therefore problematic, but he accepted neither of these alternative views. Instead he insisted that pluralism could help resolve the issues of class inequality and conflict. He did not abandon his perspective: he 'stretched' it to incorporate his growing preoccupation with the Labour movement.

The most important statements of his new position came in two texts which he wrote during the winter of 1917–18. The first (originally delivered as three lectures to Smith College in early 1918) was published under the misleadingly dry title, 'The Problem of Administrative Areas'.[72] The second was an introductory chapter of over 120 pages, in *Authority in the Modern State*. There were differences between the two works: the first dealt primarily with Britain and made some concrete proposals, while *Authority* was more philosophical and international, drawing particularly on French material. *Authority* also made it clear that Laski regarded his arguments as generally applicable to advanced capitalist democracies. However, there were substantial similarities between the two works, and the following summary draws on both of them in order to encapsulate the main features of his thought at this stage. His most fundamental assumptions were again that the goal was: 'a balance of associations which is the safeguard of liberty', and that there needed to be diversity and a decentralised structure if creative impulses were to be given full play.[73] Similarly, he continued to stress the importance of conscience and the need for individuals to decide the direction of their allegiances. However, he now argued that these pluralist goals were threatened not only by the sovereign state, but also by features of capitalism. In particular, he now identified two additional, and closely related, barriers to the attainment of pluralist goals. The first was the fact that workers did not participate actively in the majority of associations and institutions. To some extent this was because it was impossible to exercise full citizenship when illiterate, poverty-stricken and exhausted by physical labour. But it was also because political democracy had failed to change the basic conditions of the workers who could not therefore accept the state 'as in any fundamental sense the representative of the community'.[74] This was related to the second, and still more intractable problem: class conflict.

Laski now believed that the interests of capital and labour were so divergent that there was no possibility of any permanent harmony between them. Furthermore, the state was 'profoundly affected by the views and purposes of those who hold the keys of economic power'[75] and could not 'aim at fundamental disturbance of the economic status quo'.[76] What then did he propose as the solution?

One aspect was acceptance of the need for the state to take on a more interventionist role in securing the partial equalisation of economic and educational provision and in the reduction of the inequalities between different areas. This would help alleviate some of the obstacles to working-class participation. But the other main element in his strategy for change was to promote such activity immediately. Territorial decentralisation could be an important element in this (although he warned that Britain was an economic unit), but he now placed still greater faith in 'functional federalism'.

The idea was to organise the interests of producers 'by working out a delimitation of industry and confiding the care of its problems to those most concerned with them'.[77] The governing body of each industry would soon discover its interconnections with other sectors and would need to find a basis for establishing their mutual interests. Since all forms of industry were interdependent, the various units would ultimately form a federation. This federal council of producers would deal with such issues as output, wages, hours and training and:

> the more this ideal is approached the more will it tend to create an economic sovereignty either outside the legal sovereignty of Parliament, or using the latter merely as an organ of registration.[78]

For Laski a crucial element of such experiments in industrial democracy was that it would elicit the 'idealism it is so necessary to introduce into political processes'.[79] Industry could not be governed well 'until the thoughts and aspirations of its workers find a full place in its institutions', but:

> A workshop that elects its own foreman, a clerical staff that chooses its own chief, heads of departments who choose their own manager, have a far more real interest in the firm for which they work than if the bond between them and their employers is the merely nominal bond of wages.[80]

Industrial councils would also bring about systematic meetings between employers and workers, which would help promote the interests of labour. Discussion of industrial questions would broaden out into wider social and economic issues, thereby affecting political programmes at both national and local levels. Experiments in industrial democracy would also mean training in self-government. The ideal would be the creation of a whole hierarchy of structures on the industrial side – from works to district, from district to national industry, and from national industry to the whole system of production. This would mean, in effect, a state-equivalent on the functional side, representing producers.[81]

While Laski's proposal embraced much of the syndicalist case, he also saw dangers in it. There needed to be safeguards against the narrow selfishness of groups of producers, and trade unions should not be idealised.[82] Industrial councils must not therefore pass beyond their powers, and some forms of parliamentary, legal, and governmental control would still be necessary. The solution was therefore two parallel, decentralised structures with the central body of producers balanced against a national legislature, elected on a territorial basis. The state would still exist to represent the overall needs of the community, the courts would secure an extensive role of arbitration, and a bill of rights might be necessary to embody an overall concept of justice.[83]

Laski's argument was thus that industrial participation could simultaneously both provide an outlet for the creative energies of workers and help to transform the system. A pluralist society could therefore be attained – at least in part – in the post-war world. The settlement would not be permanent because of the enduring conflict between labour and capital, but it could bring about an adjustment which would reconcile the opposing interests temporarily.

It is not difficult to criticise the theory, from a number of different perspectives. On a practical level, the problems of representation and co-ordination within the industrial councils were hardly addressed, and Laski failed to deal with the complexity of the relationships between the spheres of production and consumption. Nor did he really examine the role of the state in relation to the producers' council on the one hand and the legislature on the other, or the ways in which changes in policy would be effected. Theoretical problems are equally apparent. If he believed that there was a fundamental conflict of interest between capital and labour, and the state was the servant of the prevailing economic system, a Marxist would argue that the theory did not address the issue of the ultimate overthrow of capitalism. On the other hand, since he was actually proposing a gradual and peaceful change, a reformist socialist would ask why a left-wing party was given no role in influencing public and parliamentary opinion. However, such criticisms are based on *conventional* perspectives. Laski was seeking to define his own theory and, if we are to understand his position, it is more instructive to consider its relationship with other doctrines than to concentrate on the weaknesses.

How, in the first place, did he maintain pluralism while embracing the notion of a more positive, interventionist state? One aspect of Laski's answer was to concentrate upon the *goals* of such intervention. Laski was thus arguing that the provision of minimum material and educational standards was a prerequisite for participation – a crucial pluralist goal – rather than an end in itself. But there was another, more paradoxical, strand in his argument, for he was also claiming that the additional functions would *divide* the powers of the state, rather than strengthen it. At present, he argued, there was a concentration of state power because it was wielded on behalf of a particular class. But recognition of rights would both benefit the working class by providing reasonable social, economic, and educational services, and diversify power. While there was centralisation in the interests of a particular class, the people were powerless.[84] A dilution of the concentration would empower more people, thereby permitting a greater degree of pluralism. This emphasis on class power immediately raises a second question: what was the relationship between Laski's position and Marxist theory?

His formulation of the conflict between capital and labour, and the role of the state appeared to resemble that of Marxism. His criticisms of reformism were also very similar. He thus argued that electoral victory for the Labour Party would not lead to a gradual evolution in favour of the working classes because the House of Commons simply sought the harmonisation of the interests of consumers with 'the demands of the prevalent economic system'.[85] Yet Laski was seeking peaceful change rather than revolution, and Marx was not a significant influence on his thinking. He attributed the insight 'that political power is the handmaid of economic power' to Harrington, the seventeenth-century English theorist,[86] and Laski's definition of the state-class relationship and his notion of the ultimate goal differed from those of Marx.

A Marxist analysis of the state takes its relationship with the mode of production as fundamental and unbreakable. Because the interlocking between class power and the state is seen as so total – even in versions that stress the 'relative autonomy' of the state – two further conclusions follow: first, that revolution in some form is held to be necessary and secondly, that post-revolutionary society will need to establish a new form of state. However, Laski did not accept any of this. He now came close to embracing the Idealist conception that the state could be discussed in terms of its *purpose*: the 'development' of the fullest capacity for good possessed by its members'.[87] The problem was that those who held the keys of economic power profoundly affected the government:

> That does not necessarily mean that government was consciously
> perverted to the ends of any class within the state . . . But when
> power is actually exerted by any section of the community, it is
> only natural that it should look upon its characteristic views as
> the equivalent of social good.[88]

While some Marxists might agree that governments do not necessarily *consciously* follow policies which benefit a particular class,
there was nevertheless a crucial difference in Laski's position. For he
was arguing that the goal was the achievement of a situation in
which the state *would* fulfil its purposes. Admittedly, he did not
believe that any ultimate reconciliation between capital and labour
was possible. But he obviously felt that a new equilibrium could be
obtained in which the state would seem worthy of allegiance by the
working class. This could occur if the purpose of the state, as revealed by its actions, was morally superior to those of other organisations.[89] Moreover, a central aspect of his thinking was that 'the
logic of reason' was the means of progress.[90] This meant that reason
could be detached from class-interest and used to convince decision-
makers of the need for change. It was on this assumption that he
argued that the notion of a 'minimum equality', as well as liberty
and federalism, was implied in the goals of the state.[91] Nor was he
arguing that the capitalist state needed to be destroyed: he was
attempting to transform its nature by broadening its conception of
the social good, and by adding greater outlets for the representation
of working-class interests.

The difference between Laski's position and that of 'orthodox'
Marxism in terms of the ultimate goal also distinguished him from
other forms of statist socialism. For he opposed the notion of centralised state management of the economy:

> to surrender to government officials not merely political but also
> industrial administration is to create a bureaucracy more power
> ful than the world has ever seen. It is to apotheosise the potent
> vices of a government department. It is to make certain a kind of
> paternalism which, perhaps above all other systems, would pre
> vent the advent of the kind of individual freedom we desire.[92]

He accepted that nationalisation might solve the basic problem of
property ownership and lead to an increase in wages, but this was
'in no real sense the root of the matter'.[93]

The real demand of labour is for the democratization of industrial processes, by which is meant that the truths of popular political government are applicable to industrial government as well.[94]

Certainly, he believed that the satisfaction of material needs was a prerequisite for active industrial democracy, and that capitalism was an obstacle to the advance in working-class living standards. He also called for the state to take greater control over industry and to transform it from of a system of 'chaotic autocracy'.[95] But he saw the real problems as spiritual: the thwarting of energies which could be fulfilled only through participation in decision-making. The replacement of capitalism by nationalised industry would be counter-productive in this respect:

> the trade unions would be compelled to fight against an established order for the opportunity of industrial self-expression; and the fight against a state is notoriously more difficult than the fight against private capital. . . . And, indeed, government, even less than private enterprise, is . . . prepared to tolerate democratisation of control.[96]

Laski never even considered the possibility of decentralised public ownership. He therefore believed that pluralist goals could be advanced more fully by the growth of industrial democracy within the existing system, than by the replacement of capitalism by state socialism.

Such ideas appear to place Laski close to Guild Socialist and syndicalist conceptions and he was certainly influenced both by G. D. H. Cole, and by French syndicalist thought. Yet, as already noted, he feared that producer groups and trade-unions could be self-interested. He would therefore not accept 'the attitude of the anarchist who denies . . . the need for authority at all, or the attitude of the syndicalist who emphasises only the producer's interest'.[97] In his vision, industrial democracy was not designed to supplant the parliamentary system, but to supplement it. The interests of workers and producers needed representation but so did those of geographical areas. State policy needed to be influenced by diverse pressures rather than those exerted by the capitalist class alone. But the population as a whole had varied interests which could differ from those of producers and workers, and these also needed to be articulated and defended.

How then should we appraise Laski's theoretical contribution in the latter stages of the war? Certainly, if viewed from any conventional perspective, it appears contradictory. Certainly, it failed to deal adequately with some of the problems to which it alluded. But these defects are scarcely surprising if the task that he was undertaking is considered. For he was trying to propound a pluralist conception which would draw on other traditions and yet transcend the limitations of liberalism, reformism, guild socialism and Marxism. He failed, but his insights were far more stimulating that many theories which are successful within narrower frameworks. One other important factor should be noted: he was now prepared to describe himself as a socialist. In May 1919 he thus told Holmes:

> almost any system must be better than one which gives some men economic power over others. I am not a socialist in a Marxian sense; but I am against the inheritance of great fortunes, against the refusal to allow labor a share in the control of business (an increasing share), the unwillingness to establish proper human conditions in the factory. I believe there is a real class-war and that progress towards a fuller development of human capacity comes out of the growing strength of the workers. What mainly impresses me under present industrial organisation is the wastage of capacity which for me is the worst sin. And we try to remedy by the second sin which is social reform – a name for multiplying the number of clerks and teachers and dethroning spontaneity for paternalism.[98]

His conception of socialism was by no means fixed, and it was to continue to co-exist with substantial elements of liberalism. But Laski would regard himself as a socialist for the rest of his life.

CRISIS AND DEPARTURE

By 1919 Laski had become an established theorist with a growing reputation, particularly in radical circles. For example, the reviewer of *Authority in the State* in the American journal *The Nation* was ecstatic:

> To say that Mr Laski's new book is important would be a gross understatement. It is a book which no student of politics, law, or

sociology can afford to leave unread and unmastered. . . . It leads through the vast labyrinth of events, legal decisions, and theoretic discussion – the whole ferment in which the transformation of the State is being worked out – and brings us to a point where we can see the foundations of a new political order.[99]

However, his work was obviously also controversial because it was imbued with political purposes. Bertrand Russell, who was in sympathy with Laski's views, believed that the 'book is as admirable as it is unusual'. But he also noted:

His manner is academic and learned, his appeal very sober and scholarly; but beneath this disguise we discover the opinions of a Guild Socialist, almost (where France is concerned) of a Syndicalist. He has the art of making these opinions seem (as indeed they are) the most reasonable and sensible imaginable, and such as would naturally result from any unbiased study of the facts. For this he deserves our gratitude.[100]

However, conservative forces were unlikely to share Russell's attitude, and Laski's shift towards socialism had coincided with a sharp move to the Right in the USA.

In the era of the Bolshevik Revolution, an American 'red scare' was unleashed, which threatened anyone with radical views. Socialist leaders, including Eugene Debs – who had obtained nearly a million votes in the 1912 Presidential Election – were sent to jail on the basis of statements they had made, and there was a general climate of intimidation against the Left. At the same time employers undertook a major assault on trade unionism to restore uncontrolled capitalism. However, there was also growing labour militancy, with a General Strike in Seattle, and the so-called 'Great Steel Strike' both occurring in 1919. Employers' groups denounced all forms of working-class unrest as 'Bolshevik', and often used violence and vigilante forces to break the strikes. The anti-Left hysteria intensified in April 1919 when the Attorney General, A. Mitchell Palmer, received a letter-bomb through the mail. He then established a new section in the Department of Justice, headed by J. Edgar Hoover, which launched notorious attacks on the 'Reds'.

In this climate of repression and intolerance, liberal conceptions of free speech were inevitably undermined. In May 1918 the Espionage Act was reinforced and the federal government began a series of prosecutions. The most notorious was that against Abrams and others who had distributed leaflets calling on munitions workers to stop producing war materials that could be used against revolutionary forces in the Soviet Union. They were sentenced to twenty years' imprisonment with a fine of 1,000 dollars, and the judgment was subsequently upheld by the Supreme Court (with Holmes and Brandeis dissenting). In this situation, academic freedom was also threatened. Laski would therefore have been vulnerable even as an 'ivory tower' academic. Since he was never prepared to adopt such a stance, by 1919 his position was far more exposed.

Naturally, he was aware of the new pressures and, for some time, he had been worried about the relationship between the business community and the universities. In January 1919, he wrote:

> In every American university, from the best to the worst, the hand of the trustees lies heavy upon the academic body. Unquestionably, it is possible to be a radical without hindrance in Indic philology; but it may be doubted whether there is a single institution in America where a distinguished socialist . . . could be regarded as its main ornament. In every subject that nearly touches the business world heterodoxy is at a discount; and this makes itself felt in every aspect from the choice of a President to the social life of the Professor.[101]

He was therefore quite conscious of the dangers of speaking out against the dominant view. By now he was well-known in radical circles as an increasingly outspoken critic of conventional America and a forceful advocate of increasing the power of the labour movement. Boston society had formed the impression that he was a 'dangerous man' and, as a comparatively junior lecturer and a foreigner, he was obviously in a vulnerable position.[102] An undercurrent of anti-semitism was a further factor in the situation. The roots of the crisis were therefore present long before it finally erupted in the autumn of 1919. The occasion was to be the Boston police strike.[103]

Pay and conditions in the Boston police force were deplorable, and on 2 August the men decided to apply to affiliate to the American Federation of Labour (AFL) – a request which was granted on 9 August. Two days later Police Commissioner Curtis tried to forbid this step, but he was defied and on 18 August the new Police Union elected its officers, who were immediately informed by Curtis that they would be charged with insubordination. The mayor then stepped in and, in an attempt to find a compromise, established a special committee to examine the issues. However, Curtis was less interested in this than in preparing for a showdown by enrolling volunteer police in case a strike broke out. This call immediately involved Harvard for, on 27 August a Professor of Physics (Edwin Hall) wrote to the *Boston Herald* urging students to return early to act as volunteers. More than 400 members of Harvard were soon assembled and the President of the University, A. Lawrence Lowell, urged returning students to prepare themselves for such service by maintaining law and order. The mayor's committee reported on 4 September, but Commissioner Curtis took no notice of its conciliatory proposals (which were accepted by the police although they involved disaffiliating from the AFL), and on 8 September he confirmed the dismissal of the officers of the new police union. That night the police voted for a strike by 1134 to two.

The forces of order were well prepared. In addition to the volunteers, powerful private and public institutions had hired their own guards and were ready to withstand the strike. Tragic events also played into their hands. There had been considerable unrest in Boston in the months before the police action and, once the strike started, there was an outbreak of looting and mob violence, and eight people were killed. This made it comparatively easy for conservatives to justify the use of overwhelming force. On the first day of the strike the State Guard was sent in and 3,500 men were soon patrolling the Boston streets with machine guns and light artillery. Within a week Calvin Coolidge, the Governor of Massachusetts (and future President) took personal control of the situation. He was totally opposed to any concessions, gave full backing to Police Commissioner Curtis, and eliminated all possibility of the mayor finding a compromise solution. The Guard thus remained in the city almost until Christmas, none of the strikers were ever allowed to return to work and by December a completely new police force had been recruited.

From the beginning of the crisis conservatives had also unleashed a propaganda war. There was, they claimed, an attempt to establish 'red dictatorship', and the Boston press resorted to extreme nationalism and anti-semitism in the attempt to mobilise support against the strikers. Harvard University may have been less hysterical in its language, but the majority of academics and students viewed the conflict in the same way as the rest of middle-class Boston.

Laski must have seen the dangers of speaking out in this situation and, at first, tried to exert influence without drawing attention to himself. He was appalled by the University President's original invitation to the students to act as strike breakers and on 10 September he wrote to Walter Lippmann to ask the *New Republic* to take a position:

> I wish you would say something about the general advisability of keeping university students neutral in a labour conflict. Quite apart from the fact that they don't understand the rights and wrongs of the matter, nothing is better calculated to impress the labour movement with the belief that universities are capitalist institutions.[104]

Two weeks later he defined his position further, again in private correspondence:

> I was not in favour of the police joining the AF of L. . . . But I don't think . . . a 'recognized' private union is adequate. It doesn't take enough account of the police-force as a source of livelihood and dwells too much upon the legal aspect of the police-function. I'd like to see emphasised the fact that, AF of L or not, policemen will go on strike when their grievances seem to them to justify it.[105]

In fact the *New Republic* remained cautious, simply stating in an unsigned article of 1 October that it did not support the strike, but thought the police grievances had been badly dealt with. Laski now went further in public. He told the student newspaper that the strikers' demands had been justified, and accused Curtis of creating the crisis. This immediately caused a stir, with a professor from the Department of Government in the university (Professor Carver) dismissing 'the stand taken recently by another member of the instruction staff' as that of a 'boudoir Bolshivist' [*sic*][106]. Professor Hall, who had originally called for police volunteers within the university, now wrote to the *Boston Herald*, claiming:

> Last spring I listened very attentively to his [Laski's] exposition and defence, yes, glorification, of bolshevism, delivered in a certain church parlor. He told us there plainly and convincingly that we must accept the practice of this doctrine or fight, and his whole manner showed that he did not expect us to take the second alternative. That is where Mr Laski and those who agree with him have made their great, their mortifying, mistake. The rest of us are

not playing the game as the bolshevists planned our part for us, and they seem to be hurt in their feelings by our conduct. At the end of Mr Laski's talk last spring I joined in the vote of thanks tendered him by the audience. The fact is that I felt toward him a certain measure of gratitude, the same that I should feel for a rattlesnake that had given me timely warning.[107]

But this was only the beginning of the crisis. On 15 October Laski addressed a meeting of the wives of the striking police. He ended on a resounding note:

> We are told that the police are deserters. The deserter is Commissioner Curtis, who was guilty at every point of misunderstanding of his duties and failure to perform his functions. . . . The Commissioner has learned that labor is more unified than ever as a result of this issue. Labor will never surrender.[108]

This statement brought the wrath of Boston society down upon him. The *Boston Transcript* asked whether Mr Laski was 'an instructor in American government or Soviet government' and suggested that the parents of Harvard students should urge the university to dismiss him.[109] The student newspaper defended academic freedom (while distancing itself from Laski's views), but calls for his dismissal were taken up within the university and by alumni. A Wall Street millionaire informed President Lowell that the Laski affair would lead to a reduction of donations to Harvard.

Although Lowell disapproved of Laski's speech he refused to dismiss him, and the matter was referred to a meeting of the Board of Overseers on 27 October, which referred it to a sub-committee. At the time Laski sounded optimistic, telling Holmes:

> I have had a fight here, but am, I think, out of danger. Lowell was magnificent and I felt that I had a president in him I would fight for. My protest in the police strike was against the stupidity of dealing in absolutes. It is useless to say you are *fur oder gegen* the union. The problem is what conditions led to its formation? Could they have been remedied? Was an attempt made to remedy them? My insistence was that Curtis and Coolidge bungled the whole situation and the Republicans, naturally, did not like it. But the atmosphere is clear again and I don't think there will be any difficulties over academic freedom in the future.[110]

Later, however, he qualified his account, claiming that Lowell told him not to expect promotion from the university.[111] He was also warned to restrict his speaking to classroom lectures and his social evenings with students were restricted.[112] And although he subsequently made light of the interview with the overseers, at the time he told Bertrand Russell that they had asked him:

> (a) whether I believe in a revolution with blood (b) whether I believe in the Soviet form of government (c) whether I do not believe that the American form of government is superior to any other (d) whether I believe in the right of revolution.[113]

Meanwhile, some papers were demanding that Yale University Press should withdraw his books from circulation on the grounds that they preached anarchy.[114]

Why had he spoken out when the dangers were so obvious? Partly, perhaps, because of a kind of naivete which often led him to believe that his persuasive powers were so great that he might ward off an almost inevitable attack. But of far greater importance was the fact that he stood up for the strikers because he believed that it was his duty to do so. In view of the 'anti-red' hysteria, this took considerable courage. Yet the aftermath was far worse than he could have anticipated.

On 16 January 1920 – after the strike had been crushed – a student paper, the *Harvard Lampoon*, devoted a whole issue to a vicious attack on Laski. For sixteen pages writers used all forms of anti-semitic prose and visual images to 'crucify' him for being a Jew and a 'Bolshevik'.[115] To label him a Communist was, of course, a total distortion of his views, but was perhaps predictable. The vicious anti-Jewish caricatures were more deeply wounding.

He had already sensed anti-semitism at Harvard before this episode. In August 1919 he had asked Bertrand Russell to intercede on behalf of a Jewish philosopher (Sheffer) who, he believed, was being victimised by most of his department because of a 'combination of anti-semitism and that curious university worship of social prestige which plays so large a part over here'.[116] But since Laski had consciously broken away from his background, denounced the 'ghetto mentality', and effectively argued that assimilation was the solution to anti-semitism, he would have been reluctant to accept that anti-Jewish prejudice was prevalent in the university. The *Lampoon*'s use of his Jewish identity as part of its attack must therefore have been extremely painful for him.

What were the long-term effects of the episode upon him? Kingsley Martin argued that the police strike, and its consequences, were of decisive importance in the evolution of Laski's views:

> Trade union wages and academic freedom were apparently separate, unconnected questions, but either of them might suddenly expose the hidden class struggle. . . . In short, Harold had discovered at first hand the weakness of the liberal philosophy in which he had been brought up, and had taken a long step towards a predominantly Marxist view.[117]

I disagree. Both the shift towards socialism and the recognition of the relationship between academic freedom and class power had pre-dated the police strike. But he would now move towards Fabianism rather than Marxism. In fact, paradoxically, because his personal crisis was so painful, the lessons that he derived from the police strike were rather limited, at least in the short-term. His American experience had become bitter, so it was against the USA, rather than capitalism in general, that he tended to vent his anger. Indeed he would never again believe that the American university system was conducive to learning or compatible with genuine academic freedom. But the Boston strike led to no immediate leftward shift. Instead, his own experiences, coupled with the general political climate of the United States at the end of the war, made him desperately keen to return to Britain.

Even before the *Lampoon* episode he had been in touch with Graham Wallas, the Professor of Political Science at the London School of Economics, in the hope that a position could be found for him.[118] He now told Holmes that he longed for 'clearer skies', and confessed to Russell that he was 'heartily sick of America'.[119] He was thus delighted when, in March 1920, through the mediation of Wallas, he was offered a post at LSE to take effect the following autumn.

He had no doubts about accepting the move. His only difficulty was to tell Holmes:

> You will know what I mean when I say that my love for you and Felix is the one thing that holds me back. It is one of the two or three most precious things I have ever known and to diminish the personal contact that has lit up these last four years so much is not easy. Yet I think it has gone deep enough to make space, I do not say unimportant, but irrelevant. Wherever I am and whatever I do you would be one of the greatest joys I could have.[120]

The reply was uncharacteristically emotional:

> Your decision sounds right to me. . . . But oh, my dear lad, I shall miss you sadly. There is no other man I should miss so much. Your intellectual companionship, your suggestiveness, your encouragement and affection have enriched life to me very greatly and it will be hard not to look forward to seeing you in bodily presence. . . . If we should not meet again you will know that you have added much to the happiness of one fellow-being. Give my love to your wife.[121]

On 19 June, after a series of farewell dinners and the presentation of several volumes of antiquarian books by staff and students at Harvard, the Laskis set sail for Britain. His time in North America had ended with a bitter experience, but the USA was now very much a part of him. Not only would he return frequently, but his consciousness of American society and politics would influence his thought at critical stages in years to come. For the moment, however, he and Frida were keen to rebuild their lives in London.

4

A Fabian Intellectual?
(1920–5)

The first five years after Laski's return to Britain were highly satisfying for him. This was partly because it was a period of personal happiness and outstanding achievement, but also because he genuinely believed that his academic work, public service, and political role were important and mutually reinforcing. By 1925 it seemed that he had become a Fabian intellectual, who was critical of the British system, but confident about the way it could be changed and the contribution that he could make. In fact, this harmony between thought and action was a temporary phase, which would gradually be undermined in subsequent years. Nevertheless, it was a crucially important stage in his life when he wrote his most influential book, *A Grammar of Politics* (hereafter *Grammar*). And this work reflected the integration that he had achieved between the different aspects of his activities.

This chapter is divided into three sections. The first outlines important features about his life at this time, the second explains the general evolution in his political outlook, and the third examines the argument in *Grammar*.

REINTEGRATION

Within a few months of his return, he was reconciled with his parents. This had previously appeared unlikely since the situation in 1920 was exactly as it had been left six years earlier when he and Frida had gone to Canada. In other words, Nathan and Sarah were unwilling to make peace unless Frida converted to Judaism. Nevertheless, Laski visited them in Manchester almost immediately he returned to Britain. He reported to Holmes.

I went because I thought I ought to show them that there was a real eagerness on my part for the resumption of our relationship.

I don't think it did any good. They've become very wealthy and my income and prospects are not on the plane which interests them very greatly; and since I'm finding it impossible to rent a house and cannot buy one under £3,000; and since they must give us the £3,000 since I don't possess it, I am afraid we'll have to live in S. James Park until they feel that Diana and Frida can be palatable even though they were not born Jews. Do you mind if I consign all religions to external damnation?[1]

However, after they moved into a rented flat in Onslow Gardens with the help of Frida's family, Nathan and Sarah began to unbend a little. According to J. S. Paton (the Head of Manchester Grammar), who was friendly with both sides in the dispute, Harold's parents still had 'feelings' but were proud of him and could see that it would be hypocritical to convert unless there was a sincere intention to adhere to Judaism.[2] And by September, Laski was able to tell Holmes that his father 'came out a trump':

for though he won't come to see us, and persists in regarding my marriage as a crime, and Diana as an illegitimate child . . . he offered to pay for the furniture, with the result that the house is supremely comfortable.[3]

Finally, at the end of October a full reconciliation took place, with Frida playing the major role. She felt sincere gratitude to Nathan and Sarah for helping them financially, and thought that the only way to repay them was by becoming Jewish. She therefore found a sympathetic rabbi herself and began the long process of conversion.[4] Harold had been 'dead against it',[5] but he was obviously delighted by the effect of Frida's decision, telling Holmes:

My best news I keep to the last. After negotiations that were as agonising as they were absurd my family and I have made up the ancient quarrel. Largely it's due to Frida's common sense and courage – and to their amazed perception that I don't give a damn for their money and had therefore better be left to my own vicious views and a penniless career. The result is that my father has gone to India happier than he has been for years, full of almost extravagant delight in Frida and me, and with copies of my books in his trunk that he may talk to me of them when he comes back. . . . I'm very glad over it all, for it brings Frida into her own.[6]

The relationship would never again become really intimate, but every year Harold (and sometimes Frida and Diana) spent at least a week in Manchester, and Nathan and Sarah supplemented his income with generous presents. Both sides were clearly gratified that the feud was over and that Diana was accepted into the family. Harold was now even prepared to conciliate his father by accompanying him to a synagogue when he visited Manchester.[7] However, the relationship remained awkward. In reality, Harold's renunciation of his parents' values remained as complete as ever and he never felt at ease in the Manchester home. Similarly, Frida's conversion was in form rather than spirit: she never felt Jewish and, despite her pledges, Diana was not brought up in an observant environment.[8] Indeed Laski was so adamant that she should be educated with secular values that he once claimed that when he believed that he was about to die in a car crash his first thought was: 'was there any danger of Diana receiving a religious education from her grandparents'?[9] But if there was no real meeting of minds between the generations, Harold was now on cordial terms with his parents. The one aspect of family life that never really improved was his relationship with his brother, Neville.

Harold had probably never forgiven Neville for fetching him from Scotland and siding with his parents at the time of his secret marriage to Frida, particularly as he knew that Neville also resented their overbearing attitudes. For his part, Neville could probably never reconcile himself to the fact that, however much he moulded himself on Nathan, the brilliant and humorous Harold remained the favoured son. Every subsequent stage in their lives reinforced their antipathy. While Harold had married a non-Jewish feminist, Neville told his wife, Sissie, the daughter of the Sephardic Chief Rabbi: 'Thank God, dearest, we both unite in a love of orthodoxy, children and home'.[10] While Frida favoured a simple lifestyle, Sissie was highly snobbish and materialistic, and even looked down on Sarah for having a couple of 'scruffy little maids' instead of having a personal servant, as befitted the 'lady of the house'.[11] According to Frida, Neville also suspected that she had converted in order to 'curry favour' with the family.[12] While Harold was a socialist and internationalist, Neville was Conservative and would become an ultra-patriotic President of the Board of Deputies of British Jews. The two brothers maintained contact all their lives, and Harold sometimes tried to like Neville, but it was obviously an uphill battle. Nevertheless, the difficult relationship was an irritant, rather than a major problem in his life.

If the ending of the family trauma, and his home life with Frida and Diana provided the basis for happiness, Laski was also extremely enthusiastic about LSE. At this stage he liked William Beveridge, the Director, found many of his colleagues very stimulating, and was particularly close to R. H. Tawney. He loved his teaching, still finding perpetual delight 'in youthful enthusiasm'.[13] He was less enamoured with university committees,[14] but played an active part in administration. He also had plenty of experience of other universities, including Cambridge, where he held a part-time appointment at Magdalene College for two years from 1922. By now he was well-known throughout Britain and also received invitations to lecture in other European countries. However, LSE remained the focus of his attention and in 1923, when Graham Wallas retired, he was promoted to become a Reader and acting Head of Department. Two years later he was appointed as Director of Research.

This rapid elevation was based on his outstanding record as a theorist. He had already published a series of works, which culminated in 1925 with *Grammar*. This was widely acclaimed as a major work at the forefront of political thought. Even one of his fiercest critics accepted that Laski's theories had been his 'greatest stimulant' and that in *Grammar*:

> one can not help finding a book written in the great tradition. It belongs to the effort made by a few figures in each generation to reinterpret political phenomena in a way that is true to the prevailing philosophy of the times and prophetic of the direction which political reforms will take. No one, without being completely and dogmatically lost to reason, could fail to acknowledge the stimulus which Mr Laski has given contemporary theory.[15]

Grammar was therefore the basis for the final stage in his promotion. Early in 1926 he became the Professor of Politics at London University (held at LSE). His application had been supported, in the most glowing possible terms, by several referees from Britain, the United States and Austria. As A. D. Lindsay, the Master of Balliol College, Oxford, put it:

> I am sure there is no one of Mr Laski's standing who is doing work in political science comparable to his, and I do not think there can be anyone whose claims to a Professorship in the subject can be anything like as great as Mr Laski's.[16]

Laski had aspired to academic recognition: to be promoted, at the age of thirty-two, to the Second Chair in Politics in Britain was naturally highly gratifying.

An almost equal cause for satisfaction was the forming of new friendships with eminent figures in all walks of life. On his return to Britain he had projected himself into intellectual and political 'high society'. Indeed, within a few years, he knew all the leading figures in the Labour Party, Fabian Society, and trade union circles. He was also on close terms with many Liberals and progressives, and was even friendly with some Conservatives. He also met many of the leading writers and artists of the era and, of course, academics in all subjects. He and Frida also entertained an endless stream of intellectuals from the continent and the USA and, following a visit to Paris in 1922, he became particularly well acquainted with French writers and political figures. His letters to Holmes thus read like a travelogue through the radical intelligentsia of the era. Amongst those whom he certainly knew relatively well in this period were Lord Haldane, the former Liberal Minister, who became Lord Chancellor in the 1924 Labour government; Mr Justice Sankey (later Lord) who would hold the same position in the 1929 government; the Webbs; H. G. Wells; H. N. Brailsford, the radical journalist; and Bertrand Russell. Acquaintanceship with such people was of particular importance to Laski, partly because of his need to be accepted, and partly because of his love of discussion.[17] However, it was also related to another characteristic: his wish to exert influence.

It is significant that, when explaining his decision to return to Britain to Holmes, Laski said that one consideration was that 'It brings (I dare to hope) some very real political influence within my grasp'.[18] In fact, his ambition was more complex than this stark statement implies for, at this stage, he believed that the *elaboration of doctrine* was ultimately more important than involvement in practical politics. However, he certainly also sought influence in the narrower sense of hoping to persuade political leaders to implement the decisions that he favoured, and he had every justification for believing that he was playing a growing role in this respect in the first half of the 1920s.

As soon as he returned to Britain he joined the weekly editorial discussions of the liberal-left journal, *The Nation*, and remained closely associated with it until Massingham, the editor, was dismissed in 1922 (largely for aligning it too closely with the Labour Party). This immediately established Laski as an important commentator on current political events and constitutional issues, and he quickly became involved in discussions about a possible Liberal-Labour alliance against the Lloyd George coalition. In 1922 he also joined the Executive of the Fabian Society and used his expertise and writing skill to advance both the theoretical and practical case for Labour. His expertise in the machinery of government, disseminated through Fabian tracts, influenced both the Parliamentary Labour Party and the leadership.[19] When the Labour government was elected, MacDonald therefore offered him the opportunity to carry out unofficial work on its behalf and he appears to have acted as a kind of 'trouble-shooter', writing memoranda, interviewing candidates for positions, and carrying out missions for Haldane.[20] At the very least, he was given an inside view on government policies through discussions with ministers – particularly Haldane and Sankey – and sometimes with MacDonald himself. It is even possible that his pamphlet *The Position of the Parties and the Right of Dissolution* (1924) may have influenced MacDonald's decision to hold an election in 1924.[21]

Certainly, he exaggerated his influence. There is little doubt that he played a role in Liberal-Labour negotiations to bring about an anti-Lloyd George grouping in 1921–2 but he was not so central as he implied in his correspondence.[22] Similarly, he was less important than he suggested in mediation attempts between the government and the miners in April–May 1921, in providing a compromise formula for Irish independence at the end of that year, and in acting as a conciliator between the Labour government and the dockers in February 1924.[23] Yet these exaggerations should not obscure the fact that Laski was certainly consulted by political leaders in all parties. For example, he saw Churchill, who had stayed in the Laski home in pre-war Manchester, on several occasions and they obviously discussed the Irish situation. He also met Baldwin when he was already Prime Minister and was genuinely impressed by his apparent determination, energy, simplicity and depth of character.[24] He remained equally positive about the Conservative leader in subsequent meetings and they no doubt discussed current issues.[25] It is unlikely that Laski had any real influence over him but, as a prominent Fabian intellectual with access to the Labour leadership, his views received attention even in Conservative circles. And some Labour ministers clearly took his advice seriously.[26]

By the mid-1920s Laski therefore seemed to have achieved everything to which he had aspired in terms of personal ambition. Indeed it seemed that he had been reintegrated into the society that he had challenged before the war. Certainly he remained on the Left but, as a Fabian intellectual and university professor, he now seemed far closer to the mainstream of political life than he had been previously. However, despite the 'name-dropping' and bonhomie, Laski remained very serious about his politics. He was able to act as he did because he genuinely believed that he was contributing to a process of political change that was both necessary and possible. In order to appreciate his strategy in this period it is necessary to understand his general political assumptions.

AWAY FROM PLURALISM

Laski's outlook shifted once again after 1919. There were three crucial changes of emphasis which started to become apparent even before his return to Britain. The first was discernible in his political associations and allegiances.

While still in the United States he began corresponding with the former Liberal Cabinet Minister and theorist, Lord Haldane. Their mutual regard was immediately evident. Haldane believed that Laski's 'Problem of Administrative Areas' was 'wonderful'.[27] Indeed he was so impressed with it that he played a major role (with Wallas) in securing Laski's position at LSE.[28] But the influence was reciprocal. Haldane saw education of the workers as a crucial element in social change and Laski was an immediate convert to the cause.[29] Soon after he returned to Britain, he became Secretary of Haldane's Institute of Adult Education and a very active member of the movement.

But Haldane also had views which were more directly political, telling Laski in April 1920:

> I am trying to find a new outlook which will secure Liberalism and Labour equally without prejudicing their special programmes.[30]

Laski was attracted to this idea and when he returned to Britain he saw Haldane regularly. Through him he met Sankey – another former Liberal now *en route* to the Labour Party – and, as already noted, he became involved in *The Nation*. He and Frida were now Labour Party members, but between 1920 and 1922 one of his main concerns was to effect an alliance between the two anti-Conservative parties.

He therefore called for 'good men to unite' against Lloyd George 'lest their apathy be one day adjudged the chief instrument of his sinister determination'.[31] Nor was this simply a tactical ploy for, at first at least, he obviously found it easier to 'relate' to Liberals than to trade unionists and working-class Labour MPs. He thus told one American correspondent that he saw Haldane and the Liberal elder statesman, John Morley, as 'worlds beyond anything else in England'[32] and another that he found his comfort 'largely from people outside the Labour movement altogether'.[33]

Yet he also actively supported trade union causes, particularly that of the miners whose publicity committee he joined in 1921,[34] and he campaigned actively for the Labour Party. And once the Conservatives ousted Lloyd George and regained their independence, he worked for a Labour government and saw the decline of the Liberal Party as inevitable. However, he remained less enthusiastic about the Labour Party than his public stance implied. While the first MacDonald government was in office, he thus described his feelings about it to Holmes:

> Some people are in it because they really have a considered social philosophy; others because they have a vague pity for the working class; others again on religious grounds. It is a queer mixture, and I have sat through many a meeting which made me feel with Halifax that 'ignorance maketh a man enter into a party, and shame preventeth him from leaving it'.[35]

In many ways he still hankered after a form of 'new liberalism' invigorated by socialist principles. But:

> liberalism today in England is so completely void of influence or meaning that to dwell even casually in its halls is like spending your time in the archaeological section of the British Museum.[36]

If the period from 1920 to early 1926 is considered as a whole, it is therefore evident that these new political associations constituted an important shift in emphasis. Previously, he had paid comparatively little attention to political parties: now he became deeply involved in party political activity. Previously, he had emphasised the role of trade unions and industrial activity; now he seemed to prefer working with the radical intelligentsia. These changes were connected with a second important evolution in his position: his attitude to direct action by the working classes.

In 1920 the power of trade unionism in Britain was far greater than it had been six years earlier when the Laskis had left for Canada. Moreover, there was a major wave of industrial militancy and a constant climate of tension. This reached its peak in April 1921 when the miners, who rejected drastic wage-cuts, were 'locked out' and the government declared a state of emergency and moved troops and machine guns to the coalfields. The so-called Triple Alliance of railwaymen, transport workers, and miners had pledged a national strike response but, on the notorious 'Black Friday' (15 April 1921), this collapsed and the miners were left to fight alone. After this the strike wave receded (until the General Strike of 1926) and the government appeared to gain ascendancy. However, such events – in an international context of revolution and counter-revolution – revealed Laski's underlying ambivalence about 'direct action'. On his return home, he thus supported the 'Hands off Russia' movement when dockers refused to load a ship destined to help the Poles fight against the Soviet Union, but made it clear that he believed that such actions should be limited to events of this kind.[37] Similarly, he favoured the miners' strike in 1921, but saw the solution as mediation rather than outright victory by the trade union movement.[38] And, more generally, his whole emphasis was now upon progress through parliamentary rather than direct action. How should this shift in emphasis be explained?

One factor may have been that, at this stage, Laski remained an intellectual and social elitist. This would be substantially reduced over time as he became increasingly involved in working-class politics. Indeed by the time of the Second World War, he had a genuine, unbounded enthusiasm for 'ordinary people'. But, despite having written passionately and sincerely of the workers' wish for decentralisation and control over their own lives, this had not been based on prolonged, personal involvement with workers. When he returned to Britain in 1920 his underlying snobbish attitudes thus came to the surface. He was shocked to see one Labour MP finish the half-drunk beer of another,[39] and he was sceptical about the intellectual abilities of the working-class leadership of the trade union movement. Like John Stuart Mill in the previous century, he feared the consequences of the achievement of power by the working class before education levels had been raised, and this was part of his initial rationale for supporting Haldane's work in adult education.[40] However, elitism was less important in changing his attitude towards direct action than another factor: his abhorrence of violence and revolution.

In 1919 Laski had been prepared to believe that the Bolshevik strategy in Russia had been mainly justified.[41] But this had not been based on very substantial information. In August 1920, however, he saw Bertrand Russell, who had just returned from Russia 'impressively hostile'.[42] He accepted Russell's account and felt that 'much of the confusion in Russia [was] due to the attempt to run an impossible system'.[43] He now felt that the cost of revolution was too high and that it was doubtful whether it achieved the purpose for which it was initiated.

This change in attitude was not surprising for Laski had always hated violence and intolerance. When he had previously praised the movement for industrial democracy, he had not faced the issue of *conflict* in any concrete sense. However, the post-war climate raised such questions in an acute form throughout Europe. He now became vehemently opposed to revolution and the forces that favoured it. He saw Marxism as a 'gospel of impossible despair' based upon hate, and he coupled Lenin with Mussolini on the grounds that both had abandoned the path of reason.[44] Yet this did not mean that he became more 'conservative': the answer to revolution, he constantly affirmed, was to bring about fundamental change peacefully so that the working classes would not turn to violence.

The third sign of the shift in Laski's outlook was closely related to the first two: a far more favourable attitude to state action, and to Fabian conceptions of socialism, than had previously been the case. The evolution in this respect, which had begun in his later phase of pluralism, now became increasingly pronounced and, even before he left the United States he started to accentuate his criticisms of G. D. H. Cole and Guild Socialism. When a new edition of the Webbs' classic history of trade unionism appeared, he thus told Holmes that it was:

> colossal – accurate, shrewd, penetrating, profound. What I . . . like best is seeing the expert in armor on the novelties – there are half a dozen pages in which guild socialism is dissected about as neatly as an intellect can perform an operation.[45]

In particular, this involved a substantial evolution in his attitude to nationalisation.

At the end of the war the miners had insisted on nationalisation as the major element in solving the problems of wages and conditions, and a Royal Commission under Justice Sankey had been established.

In the event, this failed to reach agreement (although seven out of thirteen of the Commissioners favoured public ownership) and Lloyd George used the lack of unanimity to reject the proposal. But the significant point for Laski was that both the miners themselves and people such as Haldane, Sankey and the Webbs, favoured nationalisation. This suggested that it was time to review some of his own opinions. He still argued that the miners' main motives were spiritual rather than materialistic.[46] But he now also praised Haldane and Webb in comparison with Guild Socialists and, on his return to Britain, he immediately collaborated with Tawney to publish Haldane's evidence to the Coal Commission. In their introduction they stressed both the demands of the workers and the need for efficient public servants to run the industry.[47]

This was an early sign of a shift towards a more 'Fabian' conception of socialism and a move away from pluralism, which was confirmed in *The State in the New Social Order* (1922). This did not mean that his earlier ideas simply disappeared: indeed they continued until the end of his life. But between 1920–5 he certainly adopted a more 'statist' approach in which nationalisation was viewed as a crucial component of a socialist strategy.

Overall, therefore, the three shifts in emphasis amounted to this. Laski no longer believed that decentralised, industrial democracy was an adequate strategy or goal given the reality of state power, and its role in the economy. Having witnessed industrial confrontation, and read of revolution and counter-revolution, he instead sought to advance the cause of the working class by capturing state power through a political party working through Parliament. There is one final aspect of his assumptions in this period which needs to be considered before *Grammar* is examined: his conception of the way in which change could be effected.

Despite some moments of anxiety about the instability of the situation in 1920–1, Laski's general belief was that, at least in Britain, there was a possibility of gradual change through peaceful, constitutional means.[48] This did not mean that he was complacent. He saw education, propaganda, pressure politics, elections, party government, and constitutional reform as necessary elements in a reformist strategy, and he attempted to play a part in all of them. He had no doubt that a fundamental reconstruction of society was vital and urgent, but after 1921 he assumed that there was some time in which this could be effected. He was therefore philosophical about the defeat of the Labour Party in the 1924 election in the belief that the electorate would ultimately accept the appeal of socialism through a steady process of political education.[49] In the meantime, he was convinced that Baldwin was 'sane and sympathetic' and clearly felt that the Conservative victory posed no threat to the prospects of gradual change.[50]

His 'Fabian' outlook on political change was thus in harmony with his talents and ambitions. He could educate both students and the working classes; he could undertake propaganda through journalism and public speaking; he could advise the Labour Party on constitutional issues; and he could 'permeate' through his innumerable acquaintances in all political parties. Above all, he could attempt to formulate a 'doctrine'. This requires further explanation.

Throughout this period Laski received invitations to stand for Parliament as a Labour candidate. Had he done so, he would certainly have risen very quickly within the party hierarchy and would probably have achieved a ministerial position before the end of the decade. At times he was probably tempted, for he told Frankfurter in October 1921 that he had 'conditionally' promised to stand in a by-election following the next General Election.[51] However – reinforced by Frida – he always declined the prospect of a political career. This was partly because of his love of academic life, but also because of his belief in the importance of ideas.

In June 1923 he told Holmes of 'a wonderful dinner' with the Liberal elder statesman Morley, who was trying to persuade him to stand for Parliament.

> This, said he, is an age not of doctrine but of occasions; you can seize them only in the House of Commons. The constituency you need can be addressed only from a platform and that must needs be the place where the great decisions are made. I answer that occasions are only moments charged with doctrine; and it is more important to furnish the doctrine than to seize the pith of other men's thought. . . . The statesman on the modern stage is inevitably a pigmy; the writer who knows his business, even more the teacher, watches hundreds who never heard of him rediscover the truths he has uttered.[52]

Because Laski also always wanted to be at the centre of things, he sometimes needed Frida to reinforce this belief. But in this period, at least, he maintained the view that in the long run the theorist was more influential than the politician.[53] And this was related to his life-long assumption that it was possible to demonstrate the need for change through argument and the use of reason.

In other words, he believed that he was capable of contributing to the establishment of a democratic socialist doctrine which could be adopted by politicians. And he was particularly enthusiastic about his theoretical work at this stage because the belief in the importance of 'doctrine' was in harmony with his general view that fundamental political change could be effected by progressive politicians, armed with the appropriate theoretical and practical tools.

After his return to Britain he thought constantly about the in-adequacies of his former theoretical position and the ways in which these could be remedied. Once he had abandoned the notion of industrial decentralisation as the key element in his outlook, he sometimes appeared pessimistic about the whole concept of demo-cracy in large states.[54] He feared that:

> the transformation of the scale of life has really made most polit-ical problems insoluble. . . . It is horrible to go into a London tube at six at night and to remember that good government means translating the inarticulate wills of those rows on rows of tired faces into something like reality.[55]

But he was determined to try to find a way forward. While the Labour government was in office, he thus worked steadily on *Grammar* and told Holmes that to disentangle the relationships be-tween liberty and equality was 'worth all the cabinet offices a man was ever able to enjoy'.[56]

This book therefore represented his highest aspiration: a serious academic work which could simultaneously convert its readers to democratic socialism. What, then, was the theory which Laski had worked so hard to develop?

A GRAMMAR OF POLITICS

A Grammar was the 'magnum opus' that Laski had set out to write in 1917. Its scope was vast, for he not only sought to explain and justify a political philosophy, but also to deal with its implications for political, economic and legal institutions, outlining the necessary reforms in each sphere.[57] The evolution that had been taking place in his thought since 1919 was evident in the work. He now envisaged a far stronger role for the state and was prepared to describe the economic system he envisaged as 'frankly collectivist'.[58] In comparison with the position that he had held in 1918, the power of associations and industrial councils that he advocated was also severely circumscribed. Nevertheless, there were some important continuities with pluralism and it would be quite wrong to assume that Laski had simply abandoned his earlier conceptions in favour of a Fabian version of bureaucratic control. For he still adhered to a vision of participation and creativity at grass-roots level, and remained opposed to the centralised state.

Throughout the book he stressed that his goal was the creation of a situation in which people could realise themselves through their own activity, and he emphasised the sanctity of conscience as vehemently as ever. Power, he maintained, was poisonous to those who exercised it 'unless their authority is checked always by urgent criticism, and, if need be, in the end by resistance'.[59] The solution was decentralisation on the one hand and citizen involvement on the other.[60] Authority must be 'federal' and:

> The will of the State must be compounded of the separate and varying consciousnesses that are affected by its willing.[61]

Each person had a plurality of interests, goals and allegiances, and the state could not in any sense be 'imperial' or a unity to which the individual's will should be subordinated. If the state was to secure allegiance it had to validate this, not by eliminating other loyalties (to trade unions or churches), but by demonstrating that any change 'is not an imposition upon those fellowships but a growth from their experience'.[62] This entailed a need for permanent and continuous organisations which were consulted before decisions were reached so that they would grow from the largest range of people and associations that could be encompassed.[63] Within the general framework established at governmental level, there should be as much devolution to the local and industrial levels as was possible.[64] Co-ordination was essential, but he insisted that his conception necessitated:

> that the co-ordination shall grow from within, and not be imposed from without. It argues that the experience of no group of men is ever wide enough or true enough to make it possible for them to be entrusted, in any other way, with final powers. It agrees that a coercive authority is necessary, but is distrustful of a

coercive authority. It is distrustful because the psychological penumbra which surrounds coercion deadens those who exert it to the needs and wants of others.[65]

To suggest that his model remained one in which there was constant criticism and participation is not to claim that he was necessarily successful in resolving the contradictions in his position. Nor is it to deny that a very real shift had taken place. But it is important to emphasise the continuation of his pluralist convictions and his commitment to the goal of an active citizenry. Nevertheless, while the *aim* may have been constant, the evolution in his thinking meant that these aspects of his thought appeared secondary in comparison to the more 'statist' version of reformist socialism that he now embraced.

Laski was attempting to elaborate a theory which would simultaneously demonstrate that the state had obligations to its citizens and that individuals had duties to society as a whole. A doctrine of 'rights' played a key role in both aspects of this enterprise.

Despite his continued antipathy to notions of state sovereignty, he used an idealist notion of the state's purposes in order to condemn its failure to realise them in reality, and to define the direction of reform. The goal of the state was to provide conditions in which all citizens could realise their 'best selves'. Its adequacy in achieving this goal could be judged by the extent to which it protected people's rights.

> Rights . . . are those conditions of social life without which no man can seek, in general, to be himself at his best. For since the State exists to make possible that achievement, it is only by maintaining rights that its end may be secured. Rights, therefore, are prior to the State in the sense that, recognised or no, they are that from which its validity derives.[66]

However, if the recognition of rights imposed requirements on the state, their possession also entailed duties. Individuals had rights which meant that they could make demands on the state to provide the necessary conditions for the development of their 'best selves'. But they then had a duty so to develop. Moreover, he now saw the private realm as insufficient. Individuals lived in a society on which they were dependent for life, material conditions, and various forms of protection. This meant that they had an obligation to society: the realisation of 'best self' contained a social element. Poets, artists, and writers should be guaranteed the kinds of conditions which would enable them to produce their work. But the result was social as well as individual, for the deliberate and conscious striving of each person in each generation increased the social heritage from which all benefitted. What were these rights which simultaneously imposed obligations on the state and on individuals?

Citizens had a right to work and society must provide such opportunities, for the full realisation of human personality was impossible without access to the means of existence. Work also involved the production of a share of goods and services for society: it therefore contained the social service element in self-realisation. If society was unable to provide work it must provide benefits until employment could be found.[107] Furthermore, the right to work also included the right to an adequate wage to provide the kind of living standard without which creative citizenship would be impossible. It should also be necessary only to work for a 'reasonable' number of hours for, in order to be a citizen, a person needed time for thought. Therefore 'the right to reasonable hours of labour is the right to discover the land of the mind'.[68] In *Grammar* he saw an eight-hour day as the maximum, but envisaged further diminution as mechanisation continued. Similarly, everybody had a right to education for there was 'a minimum level below which no citizen can fall if he is to use the necessary intellectual instruments of our civilisation'; and the citizen must 'be made to feel that this is a world in which he can by the use of his mind and will shape at once outline and substance'.[69]

In addition to these 'social' rights, Laski also elaborated a series of more overtly political ones. Every citizen had a right to political power in the sense of having direct access to the sources of authority. This involved an unrestricted franchise, and the assurance that all classes and groups would be represented in positions of authority (for otherwise those without representatives would be excluded from the benefits).[70] The right to freedom of speech and all that made it effective was absolute in both peace and war, and was coupled with the rights to free association. Finally, all citizens should possess the rights of full judicial safeguards, coupled with an independent judiciary, separated from the administration.

Many of these rights were, of course, part of the normal liberal catalogue. However, through them Laski immediately introduced a critique of current society. For example, he argued that the current industrial system infringed rights in terms of pay, the length of the working day, and the almost total power of owners to hire and fire, which he regarded as a mitigated form of slavery. Workers should share in the making of decisions, which affected them as producers, and they had a right to representation in industrial government so that their personalities should be expressed. Moreover, there was a notable absentee from the normal liberal list: property. For he specifically claimed that the right did not exist 'beyond that extent which enables the decent satisfaction of impulse'.[71] Ownership of more property than this was not needed to ensure the development of a person's 'best self', but to secure power over others or as a means of defending other possessions.

Laski believed that his doctrine of rights had implications upon liberty, equality and property. Liberty was 'the eager maintenance of that atmosphere in which men have the opportunity to be their best selves'.[72] It was not incompatible with compulsion to obey common rules because such rules were necessary for social living. It was, however, essential that the prohibitions should be 'built upon the wills of those whom they affect'. Restraints were felt as evil when they frustrated the life of spiritual enrichment, for each person desires 'room for our personal initiative in the things that add to our moral stature'.[73] This involved liberties in the private, political and economic realms. But Laski insisted – as against de Tocqueville and Acton – that the concept of liberty was totally intertwined with that of equality. Liberty meant the absence of special privilege for, unless individuals had the same access to power as others, they were denied an opportunity. This led to an acceptance of an allotted station in society, thereby curtailing the spontaneity which was the essence of freedom. Nor was there liberty where the rights of some depended upon the pleasure of others. If a person's livelihood could be destroyed by the whim of an employer, he or she could not be free. Similarly, a group of citizens would not possess liberty if the state was biased towards another social entity. All this implied the need for equality, for no group should have such economic advantages as to be able to deny the rights of citizenship of others, or to exert unequal pressures upon the institutions of society.[74] Laski was thus presenting a radical critique of existing society where inequalities of wealth made freedom impossible for the majority. In his view government, the judiciary, and the education system were all dominated by those who controlled economic power. It was therefore necessary to find a source of power outside property so that the ordinary citizen could achieve freedom.

If people had rights in order to enable them to be their best selves, this entailed a share of the national dividend so that their primary material wants could be satisfied. But no one had the right to live parasitically off the effort of others. There was therefore a justification for property derived from fulfilling a social function, but not for the possession of property without service. Laski's elucidation of these ideas on equality and property ownership reveal him as occupying a midway position on the socialist spectrum.

He did not believe that it was possible to bring about complete equality of opportunity because he neither anticipated nor desired the disappearance of the family, although he saw it was an inevitable source of inequality. Nor did he believe that complete equality of income was possible in the foreseeable future. However, he stressed two fundamental principles. First, that everybody must have a sufficient material adequacy to meet their primary needs. On these grounds he advocated the introduction of a minimum wage. Secondly, he argued that inequality could be justified only on the basis of reason.

For example, a government minister should not be oppressed by material anxieties, and those who worked particularly hard or who had additional skills and responsibilities should secure an extra reward for the contribution they were making. He accepted that the communist vision of total equality was more attractive than this idea in the sense that it would equalise people's 'pull' in society far more than anything else. But it had the disadvantage that, while all needed to make an effort if society were to achieve the productive possibilities which would enable all to live amply, equality of payment would give equal reward for unequal effort. He therefore claimed:

> The property of a doctor, a sailor, an inventor, a judge, all represent a definite return for definite service. Such property is legitimately the embodiment of rights because it is accompanied by the performance of duties. It comes from the fact that its possessor has fulfilled a station in society. He has endeavoured to pay his way. He has sought to return to society the cost of his maintenance before the years of maturity. He has not been parasitic upon the body politic. He has sought to be a citizen in the sense of pooling his effort in the enrichment of the social whole. He represents a definite addition to the productivity of those who live by what is produced.[75]

If all were 'removed from that haunting dread of insecurity and inadequacy which now poisons the lives of most',[76] he believed that it might be possible to base a theory of wage differentials on consent about approximate estimates of social value. However, he also argued that if rewards were to be related to service to the community, this justified the removal of a large section of industry from 'functionless owners'. Instead it should be controlled and owned in different forms – through nationalisation, consumers' co-operation, or co-operative production. The right to inherited property should also be severely limited as no-one was to secure rewards without providing a service through his or her own efforts. Finally, major controls over industry that remained in private hands would be necessary so that workers achieved the rights of citizenship. The state would need to control rates of pay, hours of work, and conditions for dismissal.

Laski argued that nationalisation was the only solution in monopolistic industries whose operation was 'essential to the welfare of the community'.[77] Elsewhere different forms of ownership were possible and for luxury goods, such as cosmetics, the main role of the state would be to establish standards and to protect workers. Private enterprise would thus operate within a much narrower range of activity and under stringent controls. Some people might still make fortunes, but these would be subject to heavy income tax and still heavier death duties. Moreover, each industry would be subjected to very extensive state controls under the direction of a Ministry of Production. Prices would be controlled in the interests of the consumer, and each important industrial sector would operate under a council which would consist (in addition to the owners) of workers, users of the products and government. Such councils would have the power to lay down binding conditions about each firm within an industry. Profits would be limited to a 'reasonable rate'. Wage levels would be specified, and the conditions of factory life would be subject to rigorous control. The realm in which the entrepreneur would remain autonomous would be closely defined. The compensation, he argued, would be that business would become the servant of moral principle, and industry would be transformed into a profession. The relations with the workforce would be based on co-operation rather than fear, leading to a greater likelihood of inventiveness and energy. Industrialists would also be able to plan because the Council to which the firm belonged would be able to provide information about the industry as a whole.[78]

The protection of industrial workers would also involve non-material matters. They would have rights in management in the same way as lawyers and doctors, and would be consulted over the making of policy. Managers would retain responsibility, but works committees would be given wide functions through which the will of the individual worker would have 'full opportunity of expression'.[79] Workers would also be involved in all kinds of advisory and research bodies giving the results of their experience. For example the Seaman's Union would give advice on the design of ships, the Miners' Union on safety, and barristers' clerks on the ways in which the legal profession could be improved. While employees would still need to submit to the will of others, all would be free, for in the new situation the worker

> is made the servant, not of other men, but of the logic inherent in social organisation. He, in fact, helps to make that logic, and his service is thus a function which he masters as he fulfils it.[80]

Such proposals obviously threatened the interests of the current owners of capital and Laski realised that they might try to resist or to sabotage the policies of a reforming government. He even saw the possibility of fascism arising from such a conflict.[81] Yet he did not believe that this kind of bitter conflict was inevitable. It could be averted by prudent statesmanship and a willingness to compromise. For example, he urged the payment of compensation to the former owners of nationalised industries, even if this was illogical since they would then receive rewards without providing any service.[82] It was, he believed, worth making such a gesture so as to win goodwill and prevent a recourse to sabotage.

In comparison with these socio-economic changes, his ideas on political and legal reform were mild. His most radical political proposals were for the abolition of the Second Chamber – already foreshadowed in his Fabian pamphlet on the subject – and for the introduction of payment for local councillors, so as to enable greater working-class representation. Otherwise his institutional recommendations were mainly non-statutory. He urged a greater use of parliamentary committees, more dynamism and co-ordination of policy in the civil service, and a far more extensive role for advisory committees, which would involve the consultation of affected interests prior to the enactment of legislation. Similarly, his judicial proposals were limited, focusing on the need for a broader legal education to combat conservatism (his model here was still the Harvard Law School), reorganisation of the structure of the profession, and the need for free legal advice for the poor.

The moderation of these legal and political reforms was based on his general assumption that the inequality of wealth was the fundamental cause of the other weaknesses in the system.[83] Institutional reform was therefore of secondary importance. And although his model continued to stress the goal of active participation, he now believed that this could be secured without major changes in the political structure. He now accepted the need for party government to impel a sense of direction into society, and opposed proportional representation because it might lead to weak coalitions which would undermine political leadership. He was now also quite certain that the state must have overall responsibility for society. He therefore rejected his own earlier proposals for a division of responsibility between producers' councils and Parliament. Fundamental socio-economic reform, coupled with limited institutional change, could bring about the desired synthesis between participation and political leadership. If the state both recognised rights and implemented the appropriate policies, it would be possible to institute a regime of liberty and equality in which active citizens could use the opportunities to realise their best selves.

Grammar was a highly ambitious book, which attempted to integrate theory and practical proposals over a vast range. In this sense it was in the classical tradition of political thought and seemed to pre-date twentieth-century works with their increasing specialisation. Of course this was deliberate, for Laski was convinced of the need to maintain the broadest possible approach if modern political developments were to be understood and controlled. This breadth was responsible for both the strengths and weaknesses of the work.

Its strength lay in Laski's ability both to elaborate a theory and then to draw out its practical consequences in substantial detail. Moreover, the theory itself was multi-dimensional. Take, for example, the notion of 'Rights' from which he sought to derive so much. Laski was well aware of the objections to the doctrine of 'natural rights'. He knew that it was highly problematic to suggest that people had inalienable and unchanging rights irrespective of time and place. However, he was certainly not prepared to accept that only those rights which had already been incorporated in a code of law had any status. Historically, the oppressed had demanded rights to which they felt entitled, but the content of the demands changed with social development. At any given time it was possible to see that particular benefits could be realised only if they were acknowledged as rights. Thus rights:

> are not historical in the sense that they have at some time won their recognition. They are not natural, in the sense that a permanent and unchanging catalogue of them can be compiled. They are historical in the sense that, at some given period and place, they are demanded by the character of its civilisation; and they are natural in the sense that, under those same limitations, the facts demand their recognition.[84]

This was not a conventional philosophical approach, but one which was imbued with an understanding of historical development and political reality. And, more generally, Laski's concepts often incorporated insights from history, philosophy, legal thought, and institutional analysis, as he sought to show that pluralistic socialism was rooted in historical evolution and conceptions of justice, and could be effected in practice.

Yet the range of the subject matter also led to weaknesses in his analysis. In particular, it is evident that his knowledge of economics was limited. Indeed he sometimes relied *solely* on moral arguments to rebut possible objections to this ideas. For example, he claimed that it was no ethical answer to his position to suggest that current productivity was inadequate to provide sufficiency for all. Instead it was necessary to reorganise the instruments of production so that human demands could be satisfied. He even admitted that, in its early days, the new society might be materially poorer than the current one:

> But it will be a society of deeper spiritual values, from which the worst tyranny, that of man over man, will have been banished.[85]

In one sense, of course, this was an honest acknowledgment of the difficulties. However, a more substantial analysis of the economy would certainly have strengthened his argument.

The very range of the work also raised other difficulties. It may be asked, for example, whether it was really necessary to enter into details of the promotion opportunities of civil servants, or the intricacies of legal education, in a book which was attempting to elaborate an overall *theory* of politics. Might it not have been worthwhile to have discussed the underlying assumptions, and the advantages over contending theoretical perspectives, more fully? Yet such objections are based on a misunderstanding of Laski's aims.

It was, he believed, essential to explain the intricacies of practical reforms because he was attempting to show *how* the essence of theoretical ideas could be embodied in concrete proposals. In other words, the objectives were to demonstrate both the necessity and practicality of fundamental change. This also explains his unwillingness to go further in justifying his theoretical position against contending perspectives. For he was trying to demonstrate that his conclusions followed from a theory *that had already been accepted*. In other words, he was attempting to show that his proposals must be endorsed by all who agreed that the state should be 'an organisation for enabling the mass of men to realise social good on the largest possible scale'.[86] This involved refutation of theories that explicitly rejected this perspective: for example, idealists who believed that the state already realised this purpose or Guild Socialists, who argued that it never could do so. But his doctrine was based on the assumption that this conception of the state's *raison d'être* was already accepted – at least implicitly – by the broad spectrum of liberal opinion. His task was therefore to persuade his readers that the only way to achieve the goals in which they already believed was by accepting the need for the state actively to intervene on behalf of the working classes. He was thus trying to show that liberal objectives could now be achieved only by the creation of a more equal society – socialism. The aim was therefore to convince his readers that they already accepted the doctrine and that, once they understood it properly, they would also appreciate the necessity for fundamental change. They would, in fact, realise that liberalism entailed socialism. The book was therefore an integral part of Laski's general conviction at this time that there could be 'the slow permeation of economic relationships by the democratic principle.'[87] *Grammar* was intended to help this process of 'permeation' by providing a doctrine.

Despite the power of his advocacy, his work could not transcend ideological differences or secure acceptance as inherent within liberalism. In fact, he had presented a *moral* justification for democratic socialism, which was based on assumptions which were obviously controversial. Thus the notions of people having a duty to realise 'their best selves' and attain 'moral stature' could easily be dismissed as meaningless or purely subjective by those who were unsympathetic to his argument. Similarly, his insistence that the right to privacy must be complemented by a social duty is more controversial than he implied. That is, his arguments may be *attractive* and persuasive. But this is not the same as regarding them as *compelling* on logical or empirical grounds. Naturally, those who were close to Laski's political perspective were far more likely to accept his doctrine than were non-socialists. Indeed, he encountered this experience immediately with two people, for whom he had enormous respect. Sidney Webb regarded it as a triumph:

> I always regarded [it] as one of the (usually unfulfilled) duties of 'scientific' authors to make each book inclusive and supercessory of all that has gone before! You must have come near doing that. It is a great gain to get it done on *our* assumptions instead of our opponents' assumptions.[88]

However, Holmes – with evident embarrassment – gave a very different judgment:

> I am worried by this letter – because I have read your book and it does not command my sympathy and I hate to have any words but praise for you. . . . I never read so penetrating a socialist book – but . . . I don't believe your premises and . . . the elaborate construction of an imaginary society seems to me premature and like the constitution makers of the 18th century. . . . I take no stock in abstract rights, I equally fail to respect the passion for equality . . . [89]

These divergent views encapsulate Laski's (inevitable) failure to present a doctrine which might appeal to all. This leads to a second point.

He argued that his doctrine was the expression of 'reason'. But he was clearly aware that he might fail to convince his political opponents of this. He therefore backed his case with a further, more pragmatic, argument. The continuation of the status quo was, he claimed, impossible because the working class would no longer tolerate the existence of capitalism. Unless change came about through the use of reason, the workers would ultimately turn to revolution. Even if, as he expected, they failed, this would be disastrous because:

> its defeat will destroy the prosperity of capitalism, on the one hand, and imply such an iron dictatorship of the capitalist, on the

other, as to usher in a period of guerilla warfare almost certain to ruin the prospects of civilisation.[90]

He thus conceived his argument as:

an attempt to make possible the triumph of reason in a vital department of human affairs. Frankly, it demands from the economic rulers of society a sacrifice greater than they have ever been called upon to make. Frankly, also, it admits that their refusal of such sacrifice involves unthinkable disaster. We have reached a moment when institutional change is bound to be rapid, in either a backward, or a forward, direction. The one . . . implies the end of coherent civilisation; the other offers, at the least, the prospect of an ordered society built upon justice.[91]

This may be regarded as a prophetic warning, but sceptics no doubt shared Holmes's view:

I do not accept any prophecy with confidence. The unforeseen is generally what happens.[92]

Laski was obviously unable to convince everybody that socialism was just and rational, or that the alternative would be catastrophic. But for the moment he remained cautiously optimistic about the future of British politics. As he was also so happy in his personal life and academic career he had every reason to feel content. Yet almost as soon as *A Grammar of Politics* was published he could see the storm clouds gathering and, over the next few years, his mood would gradually change to one of deep pessimism.

5

The General Strike and After (1926–9)

In *A Grammar of Politics* Laski had elaborated both the doctrine and practice for a reformist socialist government. In June 1929 a second minority Labour government was elected to office. In the intervening years, his political thought had not undergone a major shift or transformation. Yet he was constantly reviewing his assumptions in the light of both concrete experiences and considerations of theory, and this led to some subtle – but significant – changes in attitude. None of these affected his political stance in an overt way, but the underlying evolution that was beginning to take place helps to explain the *apparent* change of course that occurred during the 1930s.

The catalyst for Laski's partial reappraisal of his position during the second half of the 1920s was the British General Strike of 1926. This chapter therefore begins by examining his role in the strike, and the immediate impact of the experience upon his outlook. It then considers the related evolution in his attitudes towards peaceful change, Marxism, and the Labour Party.

THE GENERAL STRIKE

The General Strike of May 1926 was an event of pivotal importance in the history of the British Labour movement. On the one hand, the strike itself was the greatest challenge to the state ever mounted by the trade unions; on the other hand the fact that the TUC called it off after eight days without securing any of the original demands represented a total defeat. Moreover, the result weakened the trade union movement: membership declined and its powers were restricted by the Trade Disputes Act of 1927. The union leadership soon placed its faith in the Parliamentary Labour Party to secure an electoral victory, and in collaboration with industrialists over the economy in the so-called Mond-Turner talks, which began in 1928.[1]

The origins of the strike lay in the desperate plight of the miners, which had led to an upsurge in militancy between 1919 and 1921. There had then been a partial abatement of tension until April 1925 when Churchill, as Chancellor of the Exchequer, had announced the restoration of the Gold Standard with sterling at its pre-war parity. This immediately increased general industrial costs and intensified the problems faced by the economy as a whole. But the situation for the coal industry was further exacerbated by the resumption of German competition following the Dawes Plan. By June 1925 the industry was running at a loss of £1 million pounds a month, and 300,000 miners were out of work. At the end of June the mine-owners announced that the existing agreements would end on 31 July, after which they were proposing immediate wage reductions of between 10 and 25 per cent, the abolition of the national minimum, and a return to local wage bargaining. These proposals envisaged the maintenance of a standard rate of profit however low wages fell, thereby explicitly overturning the principle of linking wages and profits, which the miners had finally won in 1921.

The Miners' Federation immediately turned to the General Council of the TUC, which endorsed their refusal to negotiate on the basis of reduced wages or increased hours. In a similar situation in April 1921, the miners had been let down by their partners in the so-called Triple Alliance (railwaymen, transport workers), but this time greater solidarity appeared likely, particularly as it was clear that defeat for the miners would probably lead to a widespread reduction in wages. On 29 and 30 July Baldwin appeared to rule out any subsidy to the industry, but he soon realised that the TUC was not bluffing and that there was a real prospect of a general strike. Having failed to secure any concessions from the owners, he backed out of an immediate confrontation by guaranteeing to subsidise wages at their current level for nine months while a new inquiry (under Lord Samuel) was established to investigate 'the methods of improving the productive efficiency of the industry for the purpose of increasing its competitive power in world markets'.[2] Whatever Baldwin's own motives may have been, other members of the Cabinet had approved the continuation of the subsidy so as to buy time in order to defeat the unions. Their preparations included a readiness to use extreme Right 'volunteers' to maintain supplies in the event of a general strike.

Laski was always aware of the suffering in coal villages. He had lectured in mining areas, had joined the miners' publicity committee in 1921, and had even been pressed to stand for Parliament to represent a mining community.[3] He therefore had no doubts about the justice of their case in 1925. But he also wanted to interpret Baldwin's intentions as favourably as possible. He liked and respected the members of Samuel's Coal Commission, whom he helped unofficially, and he hoped that they would propose a solution acceptable to the miners, the TUC and the government.[4] This was always a forlorn hope, for it was never likely that the miners would accept a worsening of conditions or that the government would continue to subsidise the industry. In any case, it became clear that the Cabinet was not wedded to conciliation when the police, under the direction of the reactionary Home Secretary, Joynson-Hicks, arrested twelve leading Communists and charged them with seditious libel and incitement to mutiny in October 1925. At the end of November they were found guilty and five of them, including Albert Inkpin, the party General Secretary, and Harry Pollitt, secretary of the National Minority Movement (and future Party General Secretary) were sentenced to twelve months' imprisonment. The others received six-month sentences when they refused to promise to renounce all further association with 'an illegal party carrying on illegal work'.[5]

In his *Grammar*, published a few months earlier, Laski had already taken a clear position on such issues:

> from the standpoint of the State the citizen must be left unfettered to express either individually, or in concert with others, any opinions he happens to hold. He may preach the complete inadequacy of the social order. He may demand its overthrow by armed revolution. He may insist that the political system is the apotheosis of perfection. He may argue that all opinions which differ from his own ought to be subject to the severest suppression. He may himself as an individual urge these views or join with others in their announcement. Whatever the form taken by their expression he is entitled to speak without hindrance of any kind. He is entitled, further, to use all the ordinary means of publication to make his views known. . . . To be able to do any or all of these things, with the full protection of the State in so doing, is a right that lies at the basis of freedom.[6]

In the concrete situation of the Communist trials of 1925, he was equally adamant. He believed that the original police action was probably illegal,[7] and was certain that the government's case was poor, and that the convictions could come about only if the jury was 'passionately prejudiced'.[8] Once the accused were found guilty, he joined the massive protests against free speech, speaking at the public meeting at Queen's Hall.[9] But the main impact of these events was to make him far more pessimistic about Baldwin and British politics than he had been previously.[10]

As the crisis moved towards its climax, he seemed resolute in support of the miners. At the beginning of March 1926 he was convinced that the Labour movement was solidly behind the miners and he tried to convince the wavering PLP leadership to stand firm.[11] However, the publication of the Samuel Commission's report on 10 March did not provide much basis for hope that the conflict would be averted. It was unacceptable to the miners because it ruled out a further subsidy and called for wage reductions (justifying them as a temporary expedient until prosperity revived); and the mine owners were equally hostile to the call for the reorganisation of the industry. Laski saw it:

> as an impressive economic analysis which is void of any construc-
> tive plan for the immediate crisis and is amazingly timid in the
> long-term views it is prepared to take.[12]

The government effectively backed the owners in regarding wage cuts as the crucial issue and, in any case, argued that it was up to the two sides to reach agreement. This was, of course, inconceivable and, over the next few weeks, the movement to the final break-down appeared inexorable as the owners prepared for a lock-out and the miners for the strike. The TUC was still pledged to back them, though it was clear that some members of the General Council were seeking a way out through talks with the government. It is probable that, by now, the majority of the Cabinet was against any further compromises. In any case, the unofficial action of the *Daily Mail* printers in refusing to print an anti-strike editorial was given as a pretext to break off negotiations and, on 3 May, the General Strike began.

Laski had been in the USA for a month from the end of March and only returned to Britain just before the start of the strike. But on 1 May he wrote an open letter to the American journal *The Nation* saying that 'one hopes without hope' that a way out would be found. He still thought that Baldwin had 'humanity, shrewdness, insight', but feared the influence of 'pinchbeck Mussolinis' like Churchill and Joynson-Hicks. If Labour were defeated and the occasion was used for a general attack on its standards 'the way will lie open directly to a revolutionary temper'. If that occurred Baldwin and his colleagues would find that a subsidy was a small thing compared to the ultimate cost that they would have to pay.[13] The next day he told Holmes:

I have a deep sense that before the general strike begins . . . Baldwin will somehow have found means of accommodation, for, as I wrote to him last night, the breakdown seems to me rather the misunderstanding of tired men than any ultimate difference. I hope so; for a general strike, if at all prolonged, would loose forces of a kind that make for changes too vast to come rightly or wisely without deliberate plan.[14]

Once the final confrontation became imminent, Laski thus grew increasingly worried about its consequences. However, he had no doubt that the government was to blame for the strike. Indeed he believed that Churchill and Joynson-Hicks were intent on the confrontation and had forced Baldwin to use the refusal of the compositors at the *Daily Mail* to print the editorial as the pretext for calling off the final negotiations.[15] His view of the strike as a regrettable necessity was fairly similar to the majority of the TUC General Council and, as soon as the strike began, he volunteered to help them. For eight days Frida therefore drove Laski and Arthur Pugh, who chaired the TUC, to its headquarters where Laski helped produce the daily strike bulletin. In one draft he wrote:

Every observer of the situation, both British and Foreign, is impressed by the good order everywhere maintained. It constitutes a record for a dispute of this kind. It shows how thoroughly the workers accept the insistence of the General Council that this is a purely industrial dispute. The General Council congratulates trade unionists on their magnificent response to appeal for discipline.[16]

This is highly significant for it indicates Laski's fundamental preoccupations once the strike began: anxiety that peace and order should be preserved, and an insistence that its aims were industrial rather than political. He also hoped that it would be settled as quickly as possible and, given his extensive contacts, he could not resist the attempt to play a mediating role.

The central figure in the negotiations to end the strike was again Samuel, the President of the Coal Commission. On 7 May he met the

TUC negotiating committee and the next day he saw both the owners and the government, suggesting that a settlement should be based on agreement on reorganisation, a TUC assurance to accept the main proposals of the Samuel report of March, a continuance of the subsidy until the end of the May, the end of the lockout, and restoration of the previous wage levels. The official reaction of the government was to refuse any suggestion that Samuel was authorised to speak on its behalf or to commit itself to any proposals that he might make. An hour later Tom Jones, the Deputy Secretary of the Cabinet met Laski and reported his words as follows:

[Laski]: "I spend all day at Eccleston Square. I take Pugh home every night. I think I know their minds there. Of the twenty-six known to me not more than three are out and out revolutionists". [Jones] "What about Bevin?" "Bevin has a niggling mind and I don't think he is straight. Thomas on the other hand has won the confidence of Herbert Smith by the way he has fought for the miners. Herbert Smith would consent to 15 per cent off the wages of the hewers and 10 per cent on an average off the rest".

Laski then produced a written scheme for a settlement, signed by himself, but one with the general lines of which he felt sure Pugh was in accord. I went through it carefully, discussing it clause by clause, and putting what I deemed would be the Government's objections. His scheme was a conditional withdrawal of the strike with arbitration on unsettled points in the Report and the decision of the arbitrator to be enforced on the parties by the Government, if not accepted. I struck out the offending parts, and told him I would show the document if he liked as thus amended to the P.M., leaving his name out. (This I did within an hour.) My general advice to Laski was to get Samuel to knock the heads of the owners and miners together and bring any agreed proposals to the PM.[17]

Jones then told Baldwin 'the substance of the Laski interview'.[18]

If Jones's account is accurate there are three notable points about this interview. First, there seems to have been little basis for Laski's claim that J. H. Thomas, the Labour MP on the Right-wing of the TUC General Council, had 'won the confidence of Herbert Smith', the President of the Miners' Federation. Indeed there was a stormy meeting later in the day, when Smith and A. J. Cook, the Miners'

Secretary, assailed the General Council for negotiating behind their backs.[19] Secondly, his assertion that Smith would consent to wage reductions of this kind appears highly improbable. Thirdly, it is difficult to know what to make of Laski's statement that Pugh was in accord with the general lines of the proposal. Had Pugh authorised him (unofficially) to put such an offer to the government? If so, the TUC Chair was already intent on settling over the heads of the miners. Or was Laski himself trying to force the pace without even consulting the TUC? There is no evidence either way.

The next three days consisted of increasingly desperate attempts by the TUC General Council to secure acceptance of Samuel's pro- posals as a general basis for a settlement. This involved some further concessions towards the miners' position in the final draft, which Laski probably wrote.[20] However, it was still unacceptable to the miners' executive because it implied (unspecified) wage cuts for a large number of mineworkers. By now the leading figures in the TUC General Council were totally frustrated by this 'stubbornness' and, on 12 May, they met Baldwin and called off the strike. The government made no commitments in return and made no signi- ficant concessions. This has justifiably led to the charge of a TUC 'betrayal' of the miners. However, Laski was convinced that the government had reneged on a pledge to accept the Samuel Memor- andum. What was the basis for this?

The official record provides no justification for his view for, on 8 May, Samuel had received a letter on behalf of the Cabinet clarify- ing its position:

> it is imperative to make it plain that any discussion which you think proper to initiate is not clothed in even a vestige of official character.[21]

And Samuel was quite open with the TUC about this.[22] Yet Laski genuinely believed that the government would accept the Samuel Memorandum. Indeed, the day after the strike was called off, he obviously thought that it had done so, for he sent a letter to the Cabinet secretariat which implied that it was only the miners (and not the government) who had failed to agree to it.[23] And on 19 May, when outlining the events for *The Nation*, he explained that on 12 May, when the General Council had gone to Downing Street, they had asked for negotiations on the mining issue to be renewed:

Formally, it was the 'unconditional surrender' the Government was compelled to ask after the position it had assumed. Actually, everyone knows that it was the result of a 'gentlemen's agreement' in which, without formal documents, the basis upon which negotiations were to be resumed on both sides was well understood.[24]

However, on 23 May he told Holmes that, by threatening to resign, Churchill had compelled Baldwin to introduce changes that the miners could not reasonably be asked to accept. The next day he wrote bitterly to Frankfurter:

> It was called off on a gentleman's understanding which the Cabinet broke. The Secretariat was perfectly definite to me that if a man of Samuel's standing intervened he could pledge his honour to the T.U.C. that the Govt would honour his terms if the strike was called off first. The terms were hammered out, Samuel seeing Steel-Maitland (Minister of Labour) throughout and informing the T.U.C. of his attitude. And I think on this we were entitled to assume that in all except form we were negotiating with the Govt.[25]

Yet this was naive. For even though government sources no doubt encouraged the negotiators to believe that Baldwin would accept new proposals despite the official stance of 'unconditional surrender', Laski had no reason to believe this. In reality he, like the majority of the General Council, was so keen to reach a settlement, and so anxious to believe that Baldwin was 'reasonable', that he was willing to clutch at straws. However, he was on firmer ground in arguing that, in *tactical* terms, the miners might have been wiser to have accepted the Samuel Memorandum. This would have made it far more difficult for the TUC to have betrayed them and would have put the government on the defensive. Indeed it is possible that, as Laski argued, Baldwin might even have been forced to resign in this situation:

> It is true that: (1) the document was unofficial, (2) that Sir Herbert Samuel told the General Council it was unofficial; (3) that the government would have been gravely embarrassed had the miners accepted it. But it must also be remembered that: (1) the

Minister of Labor knew of each stage of Sir Herbert Samuel's efforts; (2) that the Prime Minister knew of its inception and general outline; (3) that unofficial negotiators other than Sir Herbert Samuel were informed by unimpeachable authority – I speak whereof I know – that such intervention would be acceptable to the government; (4) that the embarrassment caused to Mr Baldwin by an acceptance of the Memorandum would have lain in the two facts (a) that its terms were an overwhelming defeat of the owners and (b) that public opinion was so definitely pro-miner and anti-owner *at that stage* that the government would have been compelled to implement them. The miners, I believe, were right in the sense that the Council had no document signed by the Prime Minister; they were quite wrong in the sense that all the moral certainties were on the Council's side. It is probable that Mr Baldwin would have had to face three resignations had the miners accepted the Samuel terms and had attempts at their enforcement followed; but I have good authority for saying that acceptance without enforcement would have led to one resignation which would have brought the Baldwin government to an end.[26]

However, the miners' leaders were, understandably, uninterested in such tactical considerations and were not prepared to accept a proposal that would add to the suffering and poverty already experienced so widely in coal-mining communities.

The truth is that in 1926, when it came to a real confrontation between the workers and the government, Laski was not a militant. If the TUC betrayed the miners, Laski must be regarded as one of the 'guilty men'. But why did he act in this way?

He had no doubts about the justification for the original strike by the miners. He was well aware of their hardships, and had genuine admiration for their powers of endurance, describing them as 'unbeatable people'.[27] Nor did he accept any of the propaganda about a General Strike being 'unconstitutional' or revolutionary – assertions which he effectively countered in various articles in Britain and the USA.[28] He also believed that rank-and-file trade unionists were 'wonderful'.[29] His behaviour was not based on any criticism of the strike call, or of its operation during the nine days. It arose from his fears of what would happen should it continue.

When, in March 1926, he had called for Labour Party and trade union solidarity with the miners, he had clearly believed that such pressure would force the government to make concessions. By May it seemed clear that this would not happen. He was thus expressing his innermost thoughts when he told Holmes, on the eve of the strike, that 'we tremble on the verge of terrible events here and I do not know what will happen.'[30] And immediately the strike was over he claimed that, although the solidarity of trade unions had been demonstrated in a triumphant fashion:

> it is . . . pretty clear that a general strike for industrial purposes will not be called again in my lifetime. For . . . it cannot continue on its massive scale without becoming revolutionary. The Government will, through the use of troops and blacklegs, seek to provoke it to violence.[31]

He maintained this view over the next year arguing that, faced with a determined government, a General Strike could not succeed unless it developed into a revolution. And even if it did so develop he believed that it would be defeated 'except in such circumstances as a protest against war, or against a dictatorship'.[32] This fear of violence was obviously also his major preoccupation during the strike itself. He could see the troop movements and feared that Churchill was going to take action. As he told Holmes:

> Churchill was contemptible and on two or three occasions we had high words. He saw himself as a pinchbeck Mussolini, and if he had not been restrained, he would have done infinite mischief. I know no tragedy so great as that where men of goodwill are kept from each other's minds, and that is the tragedy Winston precipitated.[33]

He thus feared that if the TUC had continued by calling out more strikers, it 'would have meant violence and from that anything'.[34]

Whether or not this was a correct assessment of the situation, it was consistent with Laski's general political position. For he was still opposed to revolution and violence, and desperately hoped that this situation, like all others, could be resolved by compromise and reason. It was this that led him to maintain his faith in Baldwin during the strike and to believe that negotiations would succeed. Even after the defeat he hoped that the government would see the need for magnanimity and on 13 May he therefore appealed to the Prime Minister (through Jones) not to allow victimisation:

I venture to write this because you will know how earnestly I, in common with a group of your friends, have worked to make the Trade Union Council move towards pacific measures. Earlier in this crisis we discussed the danger of a Carthaginian peace. The Prime Minister has begun so courageously to avert that danger that I hope we may expect him to continue upon the path that secures the prevalence of the good-will out of which real peace may come.[35]

He was to be disappointed. Baldwin made no real move towards the miners, who were forced to return to work at the end of the year. The next year he also passed the vindictive Trade Disputes Act, against which Laski helped the TUC to campaign.[36] His hopes were therefore illusory. Subsequently, he no doubt felt guilty about this and continued actively to campaign on behalf of the miners.[37] Yet it would not be fair to accuse him of betraying his principles, for his most fundamental goal was still to bring about change through peaceful means.

PEACEFUL CHANGE AND THE CHALLENGE OF MARXISM

The General Strike did not lead to any dramatic shift in Laski's political outlook. He wanted to maintain his optimistic view about the possibility of change through peace, reason and compromise. His faith in Baldwin was soon restored and by May 1927 he had even forgiven Churchill.[38] However, there is a difference between *adhering* to an assumption and the attitude with which it is held. And the General Strike certainly led Laski to question his political premises and precipitated bouts of pessimism about their validity. For example, in July 1927 he predicted the likelihood of a Labour-Liberal Cabinet (following the next election) which would encounter House of Lords' opposition to its moderate programme. This would, he thought, lead to a growth of communism, fascism and revolutionary sentiment. Having also argued that fundamental economic reorganisation was necessary, he continued:

It is, historically, at least dubious whether parliamentary institutions are capable of making that transformation successfully. Their success has been in the direction of consolidating after a revolution – of bringing political liberty rather than abandoning eco-

nomic privilege. Their success, moreover, demands an atmosphere of concession in public life which is increasingly rare in
England. In the nineteenth century, concession was easy because
the margins within which concession was possible were so wide.
That is not the case today. The concessions which are elementary
cut at the root of the power held by the property-owning classes.
I know of no instance where such a class has acquiesced in its
own supercession.[39]

Since he maintained in the same article that 'the Tories, like the
Communists, would fight for their position', he confessed that he
found these 'comfortless and even gloomy speculations'. Yet the fact
that he periodically felt that such a prognosis was justified indicates
the underlying pessimism that was beginning to challenge his more
hopeful vision. Furthermore, it contained all the ingredients of the
viewpoint that he would express more categorically in the thirties:
that the demands of the working classes for greater equality were
irreversible and could be met only by ever-increasing concessions;
that these could now be granted only by eroding the privileges of
property-owners; and that it was unlikely that the latter would
concede without a fight. Hence constitutionalism was now threatened by the socio-economic pressures of the post-war situation.

   This perspective appears close to Marxist theory, which he examined more seriously in the light of the General Strike. However,
before considering his attitude to Marxism after 1926, it is necessary
to summarise his outlook on it earlier in the decade.

   As was shown in Chapter Three, in 1918–19 Laski's view of class
conflict and the relationship between the state and the 'ruling class'
had *resembled* Marxism, but had actually differed substantially. Subsequently, he devoted little attention to the subject until 1921 when
he began work on a Fabian pamphlet, entitled *Karl Marx*. This was a
highly critical work in which he argued that revolution could come
about only with a complete breakdown of the state, and control by
the revolutionaries of the army and navy, which was unlikely except
with defeat in war.[40] More fundamentally, he criticised Marx for
failing to consider the psychological impact of violence on society
and the way in which this could preclude the communist goal rather
than proving an avenue to it 'for the condition of communism is the
restraint of exactly those appetites which violence releases'.[41] He also
argued that Marx had no real concept of rights, or democracy and,
perhaps most perceptively, he claimed that Marxism contained no

analysis of the way in which a post-revolutionary dictatorship of the proletariat could effect a transition to democracy.

> The special vice of every historic system of government has been its inevitable tendency to identify its own private good with the public welfare. To suggest that communists might do the same is no more than to postulate their humanity.[42]

And if in fact they did surrender power, this would, he maintained, vitiate the truth of the materialistic interpretation of history since their motives for so doing would not be economic.[43]

Despite these pertinent observations, the pamphlet was marred by a complete failure to distinguish between Marx and his Bolshevik successors, by inadequate attention to economic doctrine, and by some dismissive and sweeping generalisations. These weaknesses stemmed from a factor which is of great significance: Laski's deeply emotional reaction to Marxist theory.

This had been evident as soon as he started his research for the pamphlet. He thus told Holmes that Marx was 'all phrases of part truth with a series of semi-mathematical formulae that are entirely worthless'.[44]

> I can't extract from him a single fundamental novelty; there's no history (except bad history), no psychology, no perception that an economics entirely divorced from ethics is likely to rebound upon itself.[45]

A month later he proclaimed:

> Really I loathe the fellow even while I recognise his powers. And I don't doubt that he really did want a tip-top revolution with all the blood possible . . . [46]

He toned down his invective in the published work, acknowledging the pre-eminent importance of Marx in the development of socialism, but he maintained that his theory was built on hatred rather than the love which had inspired earlier socialists. It was therefore a 'gospel of impossible despair'.[47]

The fundamental reason for Laski's emotional reaction was clearly that he was simultaneously attracted and repelled by Marxism. He recognised the proximity of his own views to those of Marx, but the latter threatened his outlook and even his *raison d'être*. If valid, Marxism appeared to preclude the possibility of change through consent, compromise and constitutionalism based on a conception of 'reason' which transcended class differences. It also undermined the prospect of intellectuals *persuading* politicians of the truth of socialist doctrine. But he also acknowledged the force of the challenge and the crucial importance of demonstrating progress through peaceful means so that the Marxist message could be rebutted by concrete evidence. He maintained this position for some years,[48] and it was only in the second half of the twenties that it showed any sign of shifting.

By coincidence he was working on a book on communism at the time of the General Strike. That experience would, he told Holmes, 'enable me to write a much better book . . . than I could have done before'.[49] Clearly the intensity of the conflict was leading him to reappraise and examine the Marxist alternative more seriously. Three months later he told Frankfurter that the book:

> has been perfectly fascinating to write, and one of the main things I have learned from it is an enormous admiration for Lenin – the biggest figure in European history since Napoleon.[50]

This was perhaps a back-handed compliment to Lenin, and much of the book reiterated the criticisms of Marxism which were contained in the 1921 pamphlet. But while the line of argument had not changed significantly – and Laski still assumed the continuity between Marx and contemporary communism – the critique was fuller and more serious. Moreover, it is clear that Laski was now wrestling more constructively with the threat that communism presented to his own position. He now acknowledged that it offered an alternative and very powerful view and, even if rejected:

> it compels the adjustment of one's own philosophy to a richer and wider perspective. It emphasises neglected aspects of history and, by the authority of its emphasis, translates them into demands.[51]

In particular, he saw the materialist interpretation of history as generally valid in explaining the relationship between the economic base and the institutional and ideological superstructure. However, he still insisted that materialism should not be pushed too far as it could not wholly explain the actions of an individual, and he also criticised communists for treating historical tendencies as if they were firm laws.[52] The essence of his argument was that communism made a powerful appeal to the working class, which would be countered only by 'the alteration of the present social order by concessions larger in scope and profundity than any ruling class has so far been willing to make by voluntary act'.[53] This is significant for it suggests that his increasingly gloomy prognosis was not only based upon personal bouts of pessimism, but was rooted in a theoretical framework, which he was developing in full awareness of Marxism.

The next year he attempted to summarise the relationship between his own position and Marxism in a short article. At first sight, this seems to indicate a conversion, for Laski now declared that 'The Marxian philosophy of history is, as a doctrine, at once simple and true'.[54] As for the 'economic foundation upon which the theory rests':

> It is simple folly to deny the large degree of truth this analysis contains. That political power is the handmaid of economic power has been insisted upon by every thinker who has at all carefully scrutinized the nature of social organisation. That a mere ballot-box democracy is, as a consequence utterly unreal in the presence of large inequalities of property will be evident to any one who considers the history of any modern State like England or France or Germany.[55]

Similarly, he claimed that the influence of property upon ideas, law, journalism, education and the social outlook of the churches 'is in all large outlines quite final as a determinant', and that Marx had shown 'with unsurpassed clarity' that there was no common interest between owners and workers and that the balance of power was overwhelmingly tilted in the interest of the employers.[56] Furthermore, he now argued both that Marxian doctrine was generally valid with reference to the current situation of class inequality, and that 'It seems, moreover, to be true that capitalism cannot maintain its early successes. It results in combinations and crises'. Furthermore:

> it provokes to revolt those over whose destiny it presides; the law of its being is conflict, and this, in the end, is fatal to prosperity.[57]

Yet Laski had not become a Marxist. He still believed that the theory of surplus value was erroneous, that Marx's interpretation of history gave too little room to the significance of non-economic factors, that it was a doctrine of violence, and that revolution was unlikely to succeed and, if successful, that it could result in a dictatorship that served the interests only of the dictators.[58] In what sense, then, did he accept that the Marxian philosophy contained 'seminal truths'?

Marxism, he now maintained, had a truth as a social philosophy even if aspects of the theory were false or reductionist. It was 'true' in the sense that it provided insights into the historical process and the nature of capitalist society. But its power came above all from its appeal:

It is the inevitable creed of men who suffer from economic oppression. It draws its nourishment from every refusal to act with justice and generosity. It is fed by the conflicts which, at every margin of civilization, haunt our lives with the instinct of coming disaster.[59]

And, given the power of its message, the 'Marxian faith is held by its adherents with an intensity as passionate as ever moved the protagonists of a religious creed.'[60] This meant that the only way to counter the 'truth' and power of this inspirational social philosophy was to prove 'that the hill can be breasted by a different and easier path'.[61] In other words, he was arguing that the 'truth' was *contingent* rather than necessary. It could still be refuted by a demonstration that peaceful change was possible. However, he now stated:

Nor is it *yet* fair to predicate that social justice is unattainable peacefully through the normal channels of representative government.[62] [My emphasis]

And that:

The effort at constitutional transition . . . loses nothing by being attempted; and much may be lost by its willful [sic] and deliberate abandonment.[63]

The very language indicates Laski's fear that failure was probable. Moreover, he now attributed the basis for his growing pessimism about peaceful change to Marx.[64]

THE LABOUR PARTY

These shifts in perspective were also coupled with a greater scepticism about the Labour Party, and particularly its leadership. Until late in 1927 Laski's relations with MacDonald were very cordial, although he was sometimes critical of him in his private correspondence. For example on 23 September 1927, he and Frida invited the Labour leader to dinner and the next day he told Holmes:

> He is a fascinating creature. To watch him is like observing a really temperamental prime donna. He is brilliant, jealous, eager for applause, quick, incoherent – the last person who ought ever to lead a party. He dismayed me a little by his vivid certainty that God is on his side; hardly less by his perception of politics as a struggle in a theatre between contestants for the limelight.[65]

However, in November 1927 Laski expressed some of his true feelings in an article in the *New Republic* in which he discussed the annual party conference:

> not a single proposal was accepted by the Conference which could even remotely be called socialistic; one eminent delegate, indeed, definitely asked for the exclusion of such proposals, on the ground that they antagonized Tory trade-unionists. . . . The present *mot d'ordre* is respectability. . . .
> Anyone who reads the famous program of 1918 and compares it with the proceedings of the present Conference will be driven to wonder if it is with the same party that he is concerned.[66]

There were, he argued, three major reasons for the change. First, there was irritation with Russia and communism and a rejection of anything which could be believed to emanate from a source suspected of communist leanings. Secondly, the aftermath of the General Strike had lowered the vitality and optimism of the party. Third:

> the leaders have a view of the present political situation which calls imperatively for moderation. Mr MacDonald himself has something like a horror of ideas; he is interested in the play of the parliamentary arena. He does not welcome anything which might jeopardize his power to dominate it. Mr Snowden has largely

ceased to be a socialist, and, in any case, he is a convinced adherent of Liberal-Labor cooperation; he wants nothing which might endanger its possibility. Mr Thomas never was a socialist; he is a brilliantly clever Trade Unionist Imperialist, a thorough political democrat, but without any profound interest in schemes or theories of economic reconstruction. What interests him is the moment; he can always take care of the morrow by an expedient invented twenty minutes before it is necessary. Mr Henderson, than whom no party ever had an abler or more devoted organizer, is naturally concerned with its mechanical rather than its intellectual problems.[67]

Labour, he concluded, might win office with this 'realist' approach:

But there are other things to remember. The driving-power of Labor in the country is its idealism. It has offered, especially to the young, the prospect of translating great hopes into fruition. . . . If it is merely to become the alternative to the Conservative party, with a philosophy that is as related to socialism as a jerry-built house to Westminister Abbey, it will not continue to attract those who still venture to dream of a new world built by high courage and arduous effort. . . . If the Labor party is to fulfill its historic mission, it will have to seek a new temper and a more audacious policy. Its present mood makes Mr Lloyd-George look like a reckless Bolshevist.[68]

This *cri de coeur* was hardly calculated to woo the leadership, and MacDonald immediately responded.

What you write. . . . greatly puzzles me . . . Not only are your facts very wrong and your selection of them most imperfect, but your logic is all at fault. I think it is a pity that foreign papers should be used for these criticisms. They should be kept for home consumption where the people who were present could see them.[69]

And after Laski defended himself, MacDonald wrote again, deprecating the publication of an article on the party in a foreign paper, which put the worst possible construction on its actions.[70] After this exchange, relations between the two deteriorated, and Laski became increasingly critical of the leadership in general for its cautious approach, and despaired of MacDonald in particular.[71]

Yet although Laski was sceptical of the abilities of the Labour leadership by the late 1920s, he had certainly not aligned himself wholeheartedly with the Left of the party. In August 1928, for example, he described as 'simply silly' the campaign of A. J. Cook, the miners' leader, and James Maxton of ILP, who were appealing to 'the workers of Britain' to build a militant rank-and-file movement against 'class collaboration'.[72] Indeed he fully supported the so-called Mond-Turner talks between the TUC and industrialists that Cook and Maxton were denouncing, arguing in March 1929 that:

> English trade unionism is marked by a new spirit. It has realised that a mere policy of negation will carry it nowhere. It is anxious for efficiency and reorganisation as a condition of prosperity for its own members. It has grasped the fact that rationalisation must inevitably come, and sees that the best safeguard for itself is a reconstruction carried out with its own consent and under its own supervision.[73]

And he argued that the answer to Britain's problems lay in a 'policy of moderate but continuous progressivism' which involved a recognition that social democracy was required.[74]

Both he and MacDonald were capable of opportunism as the General Election approached. The Labour leader called in Laski to counter communist propaganda in his constituency, and Laski agreed to do so, telling Frida:

> I felt that if we *do* form a government I want to sit on Commissions and things and I better have MacDonald in my debt.[75]

When the second minority Labour government was elected to office in June 1929 he therefore held two – potentially conflicting – attitudes simultaneously. On the one hand, he had campaigned eagerly and looked forward, with some excitement, to the prospect of involvement in a reforming government. On the other hand, he had grave doubts about the capacity of the leadership and the likelihood that it would tackle the problems in a radical or adventurous way. But these contradictory feelings about the prospects for a Labour government were in line with the overall evolution in his views since the General Strike. For, as this chapter has also shown, his perspective on closely related issues contained similar tensions. He was thus still deeply committed to the vision of peaceful change through constitutional means, but was far less optimistic about it than he had been when he wrote *A Grammar of Politics*. And he continued to reject Marxism, while finding it an increasingly compelling explanation of capitalist democracy.

Much of the shift in Laski's political position which was to take place during the 1930s was therefore foreshadowed in the second half of the 1920s. However, it would take further crucial experiences before the signs of change that have been discussed in this chapter assumed a more dominant position in his outlook. The second Labour government, and its fate, were to play a major role in this respect.

6

Empire, Race and Identity (1929–31)

In terms of Laski's overall political development, the most salient aspect of the record of the second Labour government was its failure in domestic economic policy and the collapse and 'betrayal' of 1931. However, for partly fortuitous reasons he was to be more involved in areas in which he had previously taken far less interest: imperial conflicts, particularly in East Africa, India and Palestine. In different ways each of these raised important issues, and forced him to confront his own attitudes towards questions of race and identity. The conflicts involved raised dilemmas for him which were also to have a marked effect on his political evolution, even though these were sometimes only apparent in the long term. This chapter therefore considers Laski's involvement in these three aspects of imperial strategy.

EAST AFRICA

Before 1929 his view of the Empire had been fairly typical of the Labour Party mainstream. He had been critical of imperialism in a general way and had wanted a stronger role for the League of Nations to ensure that indigenous peoples were treated 'justly'.[1] But he had not taken a particularly radical stance or treated the issues as very urgent. Moreover, his approach often sounded paternalistic and patronising. In *Grammar* he talked of 'the treatment of backward peoples' and suggested that the League should insist that the Mandatory Power should employ as administrators only those who had 'an adequate training in ethnology and anthropology' and an 'ability to understand native customs'.[2] Nor was he even categorical in denouncing forced labour, at least where public works were concerned.[3] In relation to Africa he showed no sign of envisaging independence in the forseeable future. Moreover, his private correspondence sometimes implied racist attitudes. In September 1923, for

110

example, he told Holmes that a young man from the southern states of the USA asked him 'if there any negroes at the School':

> I answered, I fear curtly, that their right to come was settled at Appomattox Court House just on sixty years ago. I did not add my doubts whether, in the main, they greatly benefit.[4]

Two months later, he told Holmes that he had addressed the Pan-African Congress in London:

> It was a most queer feeling to address four hundred black people. Luckily I was talking about a purely technical subject, and except your very able . . . Dubois, I don't think many understood me so I was spared more than a formal discussion.[5]

Overall, therefore, Laski's position was fairly typical of liberal-Left opinion in the era. He opposed the white supremacists in the southern states of the USA and southern Africa. But he maintained some implicitly racist assumptions, which also affected his attitude to imperialism. Under the Labour government, he became involved in such issues directly because of his friendship and association with Lord Sankey.

Laski had met Sankey soon after returning from the USA and had been on friendly terms with him for nine years. When the Labour government came to power in June 1929, Laski urged MacDonald to appoint Sankey as Lord Chancellor.[6] As soon as Sankey assumed this position he turned to Laski, for whom he had great respect, as an unofficial adviser.[7] In his capacity as Lord Chancellor, Sankey was involved in issues of constitutional change in the Empire and these were raised almost immediately by developments in East Africa.

During the 1920s the white settlers, particularly in Kenya, had become increasingly worried that Indians might achieve equality. Although their position appeared to have been safeguarded by the pro-white colonial policy of the Conservative government, a Commission which reported in 1929 talked of the 'paramountcy' of the protection of native interests and proposed a common white and Indian electoral roll.[8] The new Labour government was thus faced with an eruption of white settler protest. Given its generally liberal-paternalistic attitudes in Africa, the Labour Party was, for the most part, unreservedly on the side of the Indian community and opposed the wish of the dominant whites to create their own state. This was also Laski's perspective and in *Grammar* he had talked of the need to protect the 'native races' against white settlers, for the latter were 'there for profit, and it is obvious . . . that the trader cannot be trusted to do justice to the native'.[9] However, as Secretary of State for the Colonies, Sidney Webb (now elevated to Lord Passfield), was responsible for government policy, and his attitude was less clearcut. Beatrice Webb expressed his dilemma as follows:

> The sympathies of the British Labour Party, far from the scene of the racial conflict, have been and are overwhelmingly on the side of the exploited coloured wage-earner. . . . But it is not easy to turn back and withdraw the self-government of the Kenyan white settlers. The apparent alternative is to supersede or curb that power by other machinery of government dependent on Whitehall without rousing too overwhelming a reaction, or without involving too long a delay. 'You won't have a Labour government in power for long,' says Sidney. 'Get the most you can now, even if it is not all that you want, before the South African Dominion joins up with a reactionary British government'.[10]

In other words, he intended to compromise with the white settlers and, by October, he already knew that he would 'be denounced by idealists' and that no one would be satisfied.[11] Backbench Labour opinion was soon aware of the possibility that Passfield would 'appease' the whites and by the winter there was a strong possibility of a parliamentary revolt. Moreover, the Viceroy and Secretary of State for India were also alarmed by the impact that Passfield's policy would have in the sub-continent, and this led to a split in the Cabinet.[12] This resulted in the establishment of a small Cabinet sub-committee under Sankey to consider policy: in particular, the conflicting claims of the whites to maintain their supremacy, and of the Indians for a common European and Indian roll.[13]

Laski now worked behind the scenes with Sankey to counteract Webb's apparent inclination to appease the settlers. In December, he told Holmes that MacDonald had asked him to produce a critical analysis of Webb's proposed constitution for East Africa.[14] A few weeks later, according to his own account, he wrote a draft constitution for Kenya and found 'that Webb . . . was bitterly hostile, that Sankey was all for my draft, and that there was a grand fight in the Cabinet'.[15] In February he informed Frankfurter that it had taken Sankey four weeks to compel 'the quite impossible draft constitution' that Webb had written to be referred to a Cabinet committee, and that the alternative proposed by himself and Sankey 'is being fought by Webb with all his power'.[16] Finally, he reported in April that, when Sankey submitted a further memorandum that he had drafted with Laski, 'Webb . . . was the only person at the Cabinet who dissented . . . and Sankey was triumphant'. He also expressed his own satisfaction 'since the lives and fortunes of about three million African natives were involved.'[17]

He exaggerated in various respects. In the first place, there were many other influences on policy. Within the Cabinet committee, Sankey appears to have played a supportive role to Wedgwood Benn, the Secretary of State for India, rather than being the leader that Laski implied. Outside the government, there were other opponents of the white settlers, including the Labour Party's Advisory Committee on Imperial Questions, which submitted a highly critical memorandum on government policy on 15 April 1930.[18] Secondly, the final policy was far less radical than he implied, for Passfield warned that the settlers might become violent if the common roll was adopted, and the matter was referred back to the Cabinet committee. As a result, equality of status was postponed for the long-term future and the constitution was not changed. As an alternative, the party published a Memorandum on Native Policy in East Africa, which reaffirmed an earlier commitment:

> that the interests of the African natives must be paramount, and that if, and when those interests and the interests of the immigrant races should conflict, the former should prevail.'[19]

This may have sounded principled, but it failed to deal with the fundamental issues which were maintaining the subordination of the Africans, even though activists such as Jomo Kenyatta and the ILP campaigner Norman Leys had brought them to the attention of the government. As Gupta argues, bureaucratic paternalism had been reaffirmed against both the settlers and the champions of equal rights but, in the absence of equal rights or a more advanced form of intervention:

> paternalism could in practice turn out to be a form of indefinite political and administrative dominance by officials of a foreign country.[20]

The fact that Laski appeared satisfied with the prevention of an overtly pro-settler policy – rather than advocating a more radical stance – suggests that his attitudes on imperial policy in Africa had not yet changed significantly. In other words, he presumably still believed that benevolent rule on behalf of subject peoples was justified. On the other hand, the experience had certainly demonstrated the power of the Colonial Office in impeding the reformist intentions of a Labour government. Ultimately, this was a factor which led him to adopt a more radical stance against imperialism. Similarly, he eventually came to favour a more militant policy against white supremacists. At the end of the Second World War, for example, he was personally opposed to the inclusion of the South African Labour Party in the Socialist International unless and until it adopted multi-racial policies.[21] But the Kenyan episode did not have an immediate and tangible effect on his attitudes. His involvement in India was to be more substantial and to have a discernible impact upon him.

INDIA

The situation in India was immensely complex, with deep conflicts of religion, caste, and region, and a further division in that approximately one-third of the territory and a quarter of the population were nominally ruled by princes, rather than being under the direct control of the Viceroy.[22] Yet the most salient features of the situation were symbolised by two events in 1919. On the one hand, the British Empire presented its liberal face by passing the Government of India Act, which stated:

> the policy of His Majesty's Government, with which the Government of India are in complete accord, is that of the increasing association of Indians in every branch of the administration and the gradual development of self-governing institutions with a view to the progressive realisation of responsible government in India as an integral part of the British Empire.[23]

This was, of course, extremely vague in that it involved no precise definition of the extent of self government involved. Nevertheless, it led to a substantial increase in Indian participation and implied a constant movement towards self-determination.

On the other hand, Britain also presented the most repressive form of imperialism when General Dyer ordered his troops in

Amritsar, in the Punjab, to fire on a crowd of peaceful protesters, killing 400 and wounding more than a thousand. A subsequent enquiry exonerated Dyer.

British liberals tried to convince Indian political opinion that the first policy represented the true intentions of the Viceroy. They thus offered the prospect of gradual constitutional reform with the promise that at some stage, in the remote future, Indians would be allowed self-government. However, the message of the Amritsar massacre (reinforced by daily experiences) was far more potent for many Indians. In particular, it increased support for Gandhi who had now embarked on his campaign of civil disobedience (*satyagraha*).

The extent to which the British showed their 'hard' or 'soft' sides varied during the 1920s, as did the strength of the nationalist movement. But in 1927 a new focus for Gandhi's non-cooperation movement was provoked by a British decision to appoint the Simon Commission (to examine the working of the constitutional reforms of 1919) without including any Indians amongst its members. Before this Commission reported, the Labour government had been elected to power.

Laski had grown up with some consciousness of India through his father's trading interests here. Although he had never been to the sub-continent himself, he had encountered Indian nationalist opinion at Oxford and by 1915 he already said, of British rule in India: 'I hate it and I personally favour our withdrawal from there'.[24] Although he did not systematically study the problem subsequently, he expressed his conviction consistently. In 1924, for example, he was called as a juror in a libel case brought by Sir Michael O'Dwyer (the Governor of the Punjab in 1919) against an author who had criticised his role in the Amritsar massacre. The trial, which was extraordinary, because of Laski's frequent legal interventions as a juror, shocked him by exposing the 'depths of colour prejudice'.[25] At the end, when he was the sole dissenter against the verdict, which favoured O'Dwyer, he again concluded 'The truth is . . . that we ought not to stay in India. Literally and simply, we are not morally fit for the job'.[26] However, he also felt that there was 'nothing near the necessary degree of moral unity in India to enable us to withdraw'.[27] At times he believed that it would be better for Britain to get out despite his 'grave doubts' about the Indian capacity for self-government: 'If they fail, let it be their failure'.[28] In general, however, he certainly favoured a negotiated transfer of power. Shortly before the 1929 election he thus described the position as follows:

> The Indian problem is delicate and difficult. . . . Withdraw we cannot with honor to ourselves; to stay on any terms less than Dominion Home Rule is to risk a score of Amritsars after the Simon Commission has reported. To give Home Rule is to risk a government of caste, an internal Hindu-Moslem conflict, evil in its consequence to the poor. To refuse Home Rule is to outrage the pride of all but a handful of educated Indians. . . . One thing only is certain, that any policy less than generous will fail; and that failure in India will as surely poison English domestic politics now as in the eighteenth century. At the moment we tread a forked path either side of which seems not unlikely to lead us to armed conflict.[29]

He was now to observe the handling of the British dilemmas from close quarters.

In general, the Labour Party had not been particularly advanced in its attitudes to India during the 1920s, again favouring gradualism and the continuation of a 'trustee' role.[30] Certainly, the party was comparatively liberal in British terms, and some of its members had criticised the exclusion of Indians from the Simon Commission. However, MacDonald had overruled them, and Attlee and Hartshorn, the two Labour delegates, had co-operated closely with Simon. Nevertheless, by 1929 the Viceroy, Lord Irwin, was beginning to fear that the Commission would alienate moderate nationalists and he tried to circumvent it. In the summer he returned to Britain to consult with the new Labour government. As a result, it decided to call a Round Table Conference, with Indian representation and participation by the other British political parties, to discuss the next stages of the move towards self-government. It was also agreed that Lord Irwin should make a positive statement accepting the attainment of Dominion status as the eventual outcome of India's constitutional progress (which he did on 31 October 1929). The Labour government therefore seemed set on a liberal course, but did not favour any dramatic change and still looked to the Viceroy to take the lead.

The Simon report was finally published in June 1930 and recommended a reconstruction of central government, with the Viceroy and his council in charge of defence, and a federal assembly whose members would be indirectly elected by provincial assemblies. It did not mention the goal of Dominion status. Laski now became involved, for MacDonald asked him to write a memorandum on the report.[31] In his view, the report had 'everything in it except an understanding of the psychology of the situation':

It is no use treating a great nationalist movement as though it consisted of men who have only to be told of the complexity of their situation to agree at once that Great Britain must go on governing them.[32]

His fear was 'that India will become the Ireland of the next generation – a prospect to me of unmitigated horror'.[33] Wedgwood Benn, the Secretary of State for India, had exactly the same fear, and Laski was in sympathy with government strategy which was, in effect, to set aside the Simon Report and proceed with the Round Table Conference. Sankey was involved in the preparations for the Conference and its operation and again called on Laski to help him. This involved such activities as the preparation of memoranda, meeting Indian delegates, and discussions with Sankey about progress.

In fact the Conference, which opened on 17 November, had an air of unreality about it. On the one hand, Gandhi had successfully renewed the campaign of civil disobedience and was not present at the conference. On the other hand, Conservatives and many Liberals were opposed to any rapid or significant advance to Dominion status by India and were ready to block any such move if necessary.[34] The Labour government was not prepared to take any decisive lead and sought a compromise between all the British and Indian representatives involved. In the event, the question of Dominion status did not become a major issue because of divisions amongst the Indian delegates, and the princes pressed instead for an all-India federation, in the belief that their power base could be protected in this way. Although this was not a practical proposition, it enabled the Conference to end in relative harmony in January 1931 with a decision to reconvene in September.

Laski was cautiously optimistic, although he and Sankey had wanted to specify the standard for labour legislation at the federal level, rather than devolving it to the provinces, where it could be evaded by the princes.[35] Laski also feared that Indian religious differences were so deep that a settlement would be extremely difficult. But he felt that progress was being made.[36] Such hopes appeared justified for, on the basis of the conference, the Viceroy was able to negotiate a pact with Gandhi in March 1931. The non-cooperation campaign was called off in return for government concessions, including amnesties, and Gandhi was invited to attend the reconvened Round Table meeting.

Laski was now on sabbatical leave in the United States, but he was delighted by the news, telling Frida:

I was wildly excited today by the Irwin-Gandhi agreement – as big a justification of the lab govt . . . as the Irish treaty was of L-G [Lloyd-George].[37]

On his return to Britain in July he again worked with Sankey to prepare the ground for the Conference. Late in August a major complication occurred, for Sankey remained with MacDonald in the new National Government, to which Laski was bitterly and totally opposed. However, despite this break, both wished to continue the collaboration. Laski still liked Sankey and believed in his goodwill, and he hoped that the new government would continue Labour's Indian policy. He thus stayed on for the conference which Sankey was to chair. It was to be an important educative experience for him.

The economic crisis and change of government made a major difference to British attitudes to the Indian negotiations. When the Indian delegates arrived, the major political figures were preoccupied by the General Election and left it to Sankey to negotiate with Gandhi, whom Laski now encountered for the first time. He reported to Holmes:

It was fascinating to see Gandhi at work and try and penetrate his secret. It comes, I think, from what the Quakers call the inner light – a power of internal self-confidence which, having established its principles, is completely impervious to reason. At bottom it is an incredible egoism . . . sweetened by an indescribable sweetness of temper. He is also an amazing casuist, with a Jesuitical love of dubious formulae which would be amusing if it might not so easily become tragic. But the drama of this wizened little man with the whole power of the empire against him is a terrific spectacle. The basis of it all is, I think, the power of an ascetic over Eastern minds who resent the feeling of inferiority they have had for 150 years. And to watch his people hang on his words, he who has neither eloquence nor the gift of verbal artistry, is fascinating. Whether we can come to terms with him, heaven alone knows; much depends on Sankey's negotiating ability. But at least I understand now why Christianity in the first century appealed to the poor and the oppressed. Through Gandhi the Indian *ryot* feels himself exalted, he embodies for them their own impulse to self-affirmation.[38]

In fact, the outcome would not depend on Sankey and Gandhi alone because there were many other forces on each side. Sankey himself soon felt that Samuel Hoare, the new Secretary of State for India, was unsympathetic to the Round Table Conference and would not be unduly disturbed if it broke up.[39] And Gandhi was not the only influence on the Indian side, which was divided in religious terms, and between the Congress Party and the Princes. Laski was soon aware of this new atmosphere and felt that a settlement was unlikely 'with Tory impossibilism on one side and Indian extremism on the other.'[40]

He was proved correct, but it is not necessary to recount the details either of the failure of the Conference or of Laski's abortive attempts to prevent its breakdown.[41] However, certain points are of importance in relation to Laski himself. The first was his continued belief that if Gandhi, he and Sankey 'were left alone for a week we could have solved the whole damned business . . . in a way that would have commended itself to most reasonable men'.[42] This was, of course, quite unrealistic but demonstrated his continuing belief in the importance of securing a negotiated settlement. However, this was counteracted by a second point – his fear that 'reason' was not the dominant force in the situation:

> The real tragedy of work like this is the sacrifice, on both sides, of reason to prestige. At the back of the Secretary's mind [Hoare] is the complex that the white man ought not to be asked to give way to the black; and at the back of Gandhi's mind is the haunting fear that the white man in India will always take a yard for each inch of compromise. If ever one saw reason as the slave of the passions it is in this realm. And I am terrified of failure which means an India in flames in the next few years and out of that tragedies too vast even to think of. What makes it so terrible is that . . . it will offer a holocaust to pride without a moment's consideration of the cost. In a world like ours the only real thing to be is a mathematician or a physicist to whose work the human animal is irrelevant.[43]

Thirdly, he recognised Gandhi as a wholly new phenomenon, quite outside his experience, who would not negotiate within the existing rules of British imperialism.[44] And this led to the final important point, which occurred after the breakdown of the conference. For when Gandhi returned to India at the end of December, civil disobedience was renewed, and a week later he, and thousands of his supporters, were arrested and imprisoned. Laski's reaction was immediate:

Really it is almost useless any longer to try and do anything except protest. Reaction is in the saddle, and we must do other things than politics until more sanity comes from the experience of disaster.[45]

He did not, in fact, abandon the hope that eventually a transfer of power would be negotiated. But there was a definite evolution in his attitudes between 1929 and 1932. Previously, he had generally felt that it would be irresponsible to consider withdrawal until it was absolutely clear that there was an Indian administration which could assume control. Now he argued that, whatever the difficulties, self-government was an absolute necessity. This was vital, both for the sake of British politics, and because the Indians now saw everything from the perspective of nationalism:

Yet the problem of Indian nationalism is . . . of quite secondary importance from any ultimate angle. The big Indian problem is poverty. The reorganisation of the agrarian system, the develop-ment of Indian industry, a comprehensive effort to deal with the problem of public health and education, these, with such social problems as child marriage and the depressed classes, ought to be the real material of public discussion. No Indian politician can be persuaded to face them seriously until responsible government is in being. Until then, he will pursue the ostrich policy of attribut-ing all evils to foreign domination. There will be a continuation of that listless inertia in the face of momentous social difficulties which is the curse of India. Rhetoric will occupy the place of thinking; denunciation will comfort those who ought to be busy with constructive effort. Enthusiasm will be concentrated on the shadow, instead of the substance, of the large problems. The lines of division in Indian opinion will be utterly unreal because they will not be set by the material with which it is urgent to cope. India is the outstanding proof of the fact that only in self-government can the means of social regeneration be found. De-prived of that, the Indian lacks that sense of responsibility which is the condition of social progress.[46]

He never subsequently diverged from this position and soon became one of the most prominent campaigners for Indian independence in the British Labour Party. In 1932, when one of his former students, Krishna Menon, formed the India League with a commitment to complete independence for India, Laski became one of the office-bearers in the organisation.[47] He never had any illusions about the situation which was likely to occur following the transfer of power and he continued to believe that nationalism offered no solution to the fundamental problems. But he now saw independence as the essential prerequisite for any solution and, by 1935, believed that Britain's Indian policy 'demonstrates in a decisive way . . . that capitalist imperialism neither can nor will solve the problems of a subject people'.[48] His close observation of policy between 1930–2 had thus led him to take a far more decisive stance than he had done previously. It was because he was then prepared to participate actively in the campaign for independence – often criticising Labour Party caution – that he became so popular and influential in India.

PALESTINE

If the Indian crisis led to a progression in Laski's viewpoint, the problems of Palestine raised some questions about his own identity which he would have preferred to repress.

The contradictions of British policy in the region were embedded in the Balfour Declaration of 2 November 1917 – a highly ambiguous document. It was in the form of a letter from the Foreign Secretary to a representative of the Zionist Federation:

> I have much pleasure in conveying to you, on behalf of His Majesty's Government, the following declaration of sympathy with Jewish Zionist aspirations which has been submitted to, and approved by, the Cabinet:
>
>> 'His Majesty's Government view with favour the establishment in Palestine of a national home for the Jewish people, and will use their best endeavours to facilitate the achievement of this object, it being clearly understood that nothing shall be done which may prejudice the civil and religious rights of the existing non-Jewish communities in Palestine, or the rights and political status enjoyed by Jews in any other country'.
>
> I should be grateful if you would bring this declaration to the knowledge of the Zionist Federation.[49]

This contradicted earlier British pledges to Arab leaders, but some of them accepted it at the time. However, the real problem was that the subsequent conflict was rooted in a fundamental difference of interest. On the one hand Jews had been persecuted for centuries, particularly within Christian Europe and, in the age of nationalism, Zionism had developed to give concrete form to the age-old cry of 'Next year in Jerusalem'. On the other hand, at the end of World War One there were approximately 65,000 Jews in Palestine and some 700,000 Palestinian Arabs. The Zionist aim was always to secure a Jewish majority there by encouraging emigration. But how could this be done without prejudicing 'the civil and religious rights of the existing non-Jewish communities in Palestine'? Moreover, the Balfour Declaration was silent on the issue of economic rights, but Zionists aimed to buy land for Jewish settlers. Certainly they found absentee Arab landlords willing to sell, but the inevitable result was the creation of a landless Palestinian sub-class. Perhaps even this explosive situation might have been contained (temporarily?) had the settlement taken place in a pre-nationalist era, but the reverse was the case. Arab nationalism was now burgeoning and anti-Zionism was soon to be its focal point.

In some respects the Palestine conflict obviously resembled other colonial situations, in which an indigenous people was displaced by an economically dominant European settler population. But there were two added complications. In the first place, the settlers were themselves the victims of persecution. Indeed as anti-semitism grew more intense in Europe, Zionism became more attractive for Jews in the diaspora, and this was demonstrated within a few years of the Balfour Declaration by an influx of Jews from newly independent Poland. Secondly, many of the Zionists were also socialists and the kibbutz movement was widely regarded as an advanced form of communal organisation.

The seeds of conflict were always present in Palestine after 1917, but a period of comparative tranquillity was shattered in August 1929 by two events. The first was the holding of the sixteenth Zionist Congress. This created the Jewish Agency, with the implication that, henceforth, even non-Zionist Jewish organisations would actively promote emigration to Palestine; and it gave publicity to the Revisionist Zionists who condemned the leadership of Chaim Weizmann for being too conciliatory to the Arabs and too gradualist about colonisation. All this alarmed Arab nationalists and may have been a factor in fuelling the second event, which occurred after supporters of Revisionist Zionism staged a demonstration in Jerusalem. For Arab rioters in many parts of Palestine now attacked Jewish settlements, killing 133 and wounding 339. 116 Arabs were also killed and 232 wounded, but all the Jewish casualties were due to Arab action, while all those on the Arab side were caused by British police action, except for six killed in a Jewish counter-attack.[50] It was this situation to which the Labour government was forced to respond. Indeed, within a year the situation had been transformed from one in which optimists had some basis for their belief that Arab-Jewish harmony was developing, to one of acute crisis.

Palestine had not, thus far, been a major area of interest for the Labour Party, but those who had taken a stance had been generally favourable to Zionism as a force which would bring modernisation and socialism to the area, and MacDonald himself had expressed this view.[51] However, there are some signs that party opinion was becoming less sympathetic towards the Zionists by 1929,[29] and there were obviously other influences on the party leadership once it was in government. Palestine was an important strategic base for the Empire and many policy-makers valued stability there above all other considerations. Moreover, the Colonial Office was anxious that support for Zionism might alienate Moslem opinion in India, and the current High Commissioner in Palestine was deeply prejudiced against Jews.[30] Yet any appearance of reneging on the Balfour Declaration would cause a furore both with Zionists and a wide range of political opinion in Britain and the USA. The new government therefore played for time and, in September 1929, dispatched a Royal Commission to Palestine (the Shaw Commission) to inquire into the immediate causes of the riots and atrocities.

As the Secretary of State, Passfield's personal views were to be important in the definition of policy. He had previously appeared favourable to Zionism as a force for economic modernisation, and certainly sympathised with the Jews at the time of the riots. However, he was also impressed by the views of the Colonial Office and the High Commissioner about the negative effects on the Empire of a pro-Zionist policy, and he no doubt soon shared the outlook of his wife:

Is there any principle relating to the rights of peoples to the territory in which they happen to live? I admire Jews and dislike Arabs. But the Zionist movement seems to me a gross violation of the right of the native to remain where he was born and his father and grandfather were born – if there is such a right. To talk about the return of the Jew to the land of his inheritance after an absence of two thousand years seems to me sheer nonsense, and hypocritical nonsense. . . . This process of artificially creating new communities of immigrants brought from any part of the world, is rather hard on indigenous natives. The white settlers in Kenya would seem to have as much right, on this assumption, to be where they are, as the Russian Jews in Jerusalem . . . Obviously order must be maintained in Judea; and the responsibility for the looting and murdering must be fixed and proper action taken to prevent recurrence. But the case for the Arab has not yet been heard; whilst the case for the Jew has been vehemently and powerfully pressed on the government. The Zionist movement and the Mandate for a National Home for the Jews in Palestine seems to have originated in some such unequal pressure exercised by the wealthy and ubiquitous Jew on the one hand and the poor and absent Arab on the other.[55]

There were thus signs that Passfield would be sympathetic to a reinterpretation of the Balfour Declaration, and in March 1930 the Shaw Commission (which went beyond its terms of reference) gave him ammunition for this change of course. Its main recommendations were designed to reassure the Arabs that Jewish immigration and eviction of tenants would be controlled, and that the Jewish Agency had no share in the government of Palestine.[56] However, a Labour Party representative on the Shaw commission (Henry Snell) issued a minority statement which was more sympathetic to Zionist claims, particularly in its acceptance of their argument that the anti-Jewish atrocities had been orchestrated by the Arab leadership.[57] Many in the Labour Party sympathised with this viewpoint and, instead of simply accepting the Shaw report, MacDonald insisted on sending a new Commission to Palestine to investigate the land question. At first he had wanted to send General Smuts of South Africa but, after further thought, decided that he was too pro-Zionist, and agreed with Passfield to send Sir John Hope-Simpson, who was a British official with the League of Nations.

MacDonald's intervention, without reference to the Cabinet, demonstrated the fact that Passfield was not the sole source of Palestine policy. Laski had already been involved in promoting the alternative, pro-Zionist line and was now to play an increasingly important role in its development.

Laski had been brought up with an awareness of Zionism and had heard Weizmann speaking in Manchester in his youth. But he had been deeply sceptical about the movement by the age of sixteen and had rejected it with other aspects of Jewish identity two years later.[58] By the mid-1920s he had not changed his mind about Zionism, telling Holmes, quite simply: 'I abominate it'.[59] However, his closest friend, Felix Frankfurter, took a quite different position. He had held a 'watching brief' for American Zionists at the Paris Peace Conference – where he had secured a statement of support from Prince Feisal of Arabia[60] – and, with Louis Brandeis, whom Laski also knew, he had actively campaigned for the movement ever since. Even before Labour was elected to government, Frankfurter persuaded Laski to act as an intermediary with Ramsay MacDonald.[61]

Why did Laski agree to help Frankfurter and Brandeis when he was not a Zionist himself? First, he was keen to play a role in improving Anglo-American relations generally, and may not even have been immediately aware that Zionism would become the focal point in Frankfurter's representations to him.[62] Secondly, as already noted, support for Jewish settlements was, at the time, the more common position in the Labour Party. When Laski agreed to make representations on the Zionist side, he therefore believed that he was adopting a socialist position. The atrocities against Jewish settlements and the signs that Passfield was likely to oppose the Zionist viewpoint no doubt reinforced his willingness to help Frankfurter.

His first important action in his new role was to ensure that MacDonald saw Brandeis when he went to the USA on an official visit in October 1929.[63] This probably alerted the Prime Minister to Zionist suspicions of Passfield, and the likely reaction to a 'pro-Arab' report by Shaw. Such influences, in conjunction with majority parliamentary opinion, obviously convinced him that Palestine policy could not be left to Passfield alone and accounted for the dispatch of the Hope Simpson enquiry. But Zionists remained worried about the probable outcome of this second Commission, and on 27 May 1930 Frankfurter asked Laski to suggest to Arthur Henderson, the Foreign Secretary, that the British Ambassador in Washington should see Brandeis.[64] Laski seems to have done this and he also talked to MacDonald about the whole situation, after discussions with Weizmann.[65] But Brandeis now felt that Frankfurter should come to Britain to lobby directly. Laski dissuaded him in a cogently argued letter.

The government, he told him, would take no decision until after

Hope Simpson had reported, so that any discussion would take place in a vacuum and could not lead to action. Secondly, Frankfurter would have much less value if he used his arguments now because MacDonald would not want to hear them again later. Thirdly, there was the danger that Zionists – particularly Americans – could do grave harm by calling on too many people to exercise pressure, particularly as a temperamental person like MacDonald could be irritated by what looked like 'nagging'. The nub of his argument was that:

> I am convinced that we must influence only at a distance e.g. the press meetings, memoranda, until we have the report. Then, but only then, the maximum possible direct pressure if the report is unfavourable. That is the time to play the American card. But not before then. You must not omit the factor of national sensitiveness. Your case is known, you really could not add to it. I will pledge my whole judgment that this is the right course to take.[66]

His eloquence seems to have been effective and the visit did not take place. However, in the autumn the Hope Simpson Commission reported and was followed immediately by the publication of a White Paper by Passfield. From a Zionist perspective, the most salient issue in each case was the argument that Jewish immigration should be limited in the interests of Arab employment. This was coupled, in Passfield's White Paper, with the explicit statement that:

> Attempts have been made to argue in support of Zionist claims that the principal feature of the Mandate is the passage regarding the Jewish National Home and that the passage designed to safeguard the rights of the non-Jewish community are merely secondary considerations qualifying to some extent what is claimed to be the primary object for which the Mandate has been framed. This is a conception which His Majesty's Government have always regarded as totally erroneous.[67]

Laski anticipated the furore that would occur and had tried to persuade MacDonald to postpone publication and to allow Zionist comment on the draft. The Prime Minister rejected the advice on the grounds that the draft had been accepted by the Cabinet. He continued:

They were trying to hold the scales even between Jew and Arab and they thought they had succeeded. Nor could they submit a policy to alien strangers for comment before publication.[68]

Laski told him that:

he ought to realise the general consequences of what he proposed to do. I explained vigorously the effect on Jewish opinion, dwelling especially on the effect of his policy on Anglo-American relations. He replied only that I enormously exaggerated the position and that he was convinced the Jews would realise the bona-fides of the Government.[69]

After publication, when the storm broke, with protests from Zionists, much of the Jewish community, and British parliamentary opinion in all parties, the situation changed. According to Laski's account:

Henderson sent for me. He said that they were distressed at the reception of the policy and hoped I could help them to assuage feeling. I said I could do nothing. He then asked me to see the P.M. who asked me if I could do anything to assure my 'American friends' that the Cabinet would do all in its power to act justly. I said I could do nothing. I had warned him this would occur; he had treated my views with contempt. Now he saw I had underestimated the depth of feeling. Nothing could be done now unless he sacked Webb or withdrew the Declaration.[70]

He also told MacDonald that he saw no prospect of a modus vivendi while the Declaration stood. Subsequently, he met Weizmann constantly and kept closely in touch with him and tried to stir up Labour MPs. But he feared that the policy would stand while the Labour Party was in power 'unless foreign opinion is forcible, especially in America' and urged that it was fundamental for American Zionists 'to take nothing short of a withdrawal of the Declaration'.[71]

It was soon clear that the pressure was having its effect. On 1 November Laski phoned Passfield to tell him that the following day there was to be a great Jewish demonstration in New York and that, in response to enquiries from his friends there, he proposed to send a cable saying that British policy had been misunderstood.[72]

Passfield thanked him for his efforts 'towards dispelling the extraordinary Jewish misconceptions of our statement of Policy' which, he believed were, deliberate. He also enclosed a copy of a telegram which he authorised Laski to send 'as from yourself to your American friends' and informed him that the Prime Minister had offered to see Weizmann the following week. He also told him that the government might then 'decide to issue a statement, which would be in the sense of what I have given you'.[73] However, Passfield subsequently told MacDonald that he refused to sanction Laski's wording but, in view of his strong appeal, had authorised him to send, in his own name, the following message:

> I have definite assurance from British Govt that Jewish protests against Govt statement of policy are founded on complete misconception. Govt explicitly declare their intention of executing Mandate exactly in accordance with all its terms. They make no change whatever in the interpretation of Mandate adhered to by all successive Ministries since 1922. They neither enact nor intend any stoppage or prohibition of Jewish immigration, and they expressly provide for continuation of colonisation operations without a break. They set no limit to whatever expansion of National Home in accordance with terms of Mandate may prove practicable. It is indeed to make available additional land that Govt undertakes large scheme of land dvlpt and irrigation.[74]

Passfield described this as a terse statement of government policy 'which is so deliberately misinterpreted' (and he accused Weizmann of trying to stir up the passions of world Jewry to increase the flow of subscriptions).[75] In fact, he had obviously already accepted the likelihood of a 'climb-down' by the government, but presumably wanted MacDonald to believe that he had not been pressurised by Laski or Zionists. In any case, the retreat was now well under way, as MacDonald had already sought to assure pro-Zionist opinion that the government remained committed to the establishment of a Jewish national home.[76] On 6 November 1930 he met Weizmann and told him he planned to establish a Cabinet committee to re-examine the problematic clauses in the White Paper and that representatives of the Jewish Agency would be invited to attend, and he urged him to tell American Zionists about this conversation.[77]

The new committee was chaired by Henderson rather than Passfield. Since the Foreign Secretary had been in Geneva when the White Paper had been approved by the Cabinet, he had never felt committed to it and was therefore predisposed to make the requisite changes. Laski worked closely with Henderson and liaised with Zionist circles in an attempt to ensure that any new wording would be acceptable.[78] Indeed he later told Frankfurter that he worked on the issue for three hours per day for six weeks.[79] At the end of January Henderson informed the Cabinet that his subcommittee and the Jewish Agency had agreed on a statement explaining government policy which could be sent in the form of a letter from MacDonald to Weizmann.[80] This course was adopted and on 13 February MacDonald read the letter out in the House of Commons. This expressed pious hopes that 'no solution can be satisfactory or permanent which is not based upon justice, both to the Jewish and non-Jewish communities of Palestine'.[81] But the real impact of the statement was to tip the balance back towards the Zionist reading of the Balfour Declaration. Over the next four years the size of the Jewish community increased from 180,000 to 400,000. Since this would not have been permitted under the White Paper, the change in government policy was of great significance for the Zionist movement – and, of course, for the Palestinian Arabs.

Laski's role in reversing government policy was obviously only of minor importance. Nevertheless, the significance of his intervention was recognised by the Zionist movement. After his death Berl Locker of the Jewish Agency thus wrote to Frida:

When . . . after the . . . White Paper . . . the crisis in British Jewish relations started it was Laski who by private intervention especially with Arthur Henderson . . . was instrumental in bringing the Government to the establishment of a special Cabinet committee under Henderson's chairmanship which ultimately resulted in an agreement between the Government and the Jewish Agency in the form of the well known MacDonald letter to Dr Weizmann.

Dr Nahun Goldmann who was at that time present in London and took part as a member of the Zionist delegation tells me that in one or two meetings of the Cabinet Committee with the Jewish delegation, H. J. Laski was even present in a personal capacity.[82]

Since he had participated in a successful campaign, it might be expected that he would be pleased by the outcome. In fact, however, his emotions were far more complex, almost certainly because the episode raised awkward issues about his own identity.

As soon as it became clear that Passfield would be overruled, he showed increasing signs of irritation with the Zionists. On 30 November he thus told Holmes:

> I can't run daily to the Foreign Secretary because Brandeis has doubts about a semi-colon – at some point in a negotiation one has to assume that the cabinet really means what it says.[83]

A month later 'a further dose of Palestine' convinced him that 'Moses made a great mistake', and on 10 January 1931, when the new statement had been completed, he expressed the hope that 'Felix and Brandeis will be grateful for a job which has taken infinite pains and ought really to satisfy every decent aspiration to which they are entitled'.[84] A little later he told Frankfurter himself: 'I hope that I shall have peace from Palestine for the next ten years'.[85] Similarly, while on sabbatical in the USA he told Frida that a talk with Brandeis had been interesting 'especially as we steered clear of Zionism'.[86] All this reflected his desire not to allow his Jewish origins to influence his outlook. Similarly, he told Holmes that his difficulty with Jews is their tough resistance to assimilation, their pride in being different. . . '.[87] For assimilation remained his real wish, both for himself and for Jews as a whole. Yet when he recounted an emotional interview with MacDonald shortly after the publication of Passfield's White Paper, he gave a very different impression:

> He said he could not understand my bitterness since I was not a Zionist. I said my views on Zionism had not changed but that as a Jew I resented a policy which surrendered Jewish interests, in spite of a pledged word, to the authors of an unjustifiable massacre. No doubt when the Arabs killed the next lot of Jews, Webb would be allowed to expel all Jews from Palestine.[88]

In other words, when it came to a crisis, Laski still identified himself as a Jew even though he did not wish this fact to have any relevance to his opinions or actions. Similarly, he was sensitive to any hints of anti-semitism.[89] Palestine therefore presented him with a major problem for, although he did not really want to align himself fully with Zionism, he clearly did so during the period of his intervention. He believed that anti-semitism amongst British officials in Palestine was impeding Jewish settlement and he probably also suspected Passfield's motives, perhaps with justification.[90] He therefore temporarily overcame his reluctance to work with Zionists, although he hoped that 'a large measure of Arabo-Jewish cooperation' would be achieved.[91] Having helped to defeat Passfield, he wanted to detach himself from a partisan stance as quickly as possible.

This episode is highly significant for, although Laski *hoped* to forget about Palestine and Jewish identity, history would not allow him to do so. As he had actively supported Zionism during a crisis in 1930, the stand that he would take after the Nazi holocaust was already predictable.

In their different ways, the three imperial problems with which Laski had been involved during the Second Labour Government had all raised important issues for him, even if he did not necessarily resolve them immediately.

In 1929, despite his socialism, he was, at a fundamental level, a rationalist liberal, imbued in European values and preconceptions. When, for example, Bertrand Russell had visited China in the early 1920s, Laski could not really understand his enthusiasm, and maintained his preference for the culture and thought of ancient Greece.[92] Similarly, he always wanted to believe that religion and nationalism were anachronistic forces and that ultimately, secular and liberal values would triumph. As was noted at the beginning of the chapter, a racist element was also discernible in his attitudes. Similarly, while he was certainly critical of imperialism – and always thought that Britain should eventually withdraw from India – he had not treated the issue with any sense of urgency. How did his experiences in the subsequent two years affect these assumptions?

There was not a total transformation. Until his death Laski remained deeply committed to secular, rational values, and European, liberal conceptions. In 1932 for example, he maintained, in relation to India, that Moslem separatism 'is likely to fade quite rapidly as industrialism develops issues before which religious differences are bound to appear insignificant'.[93]

Yet there were certainly important developments in his attitudes. Through his involvement in the Round Table negotiations, he became convinced that Indian independence was an urgent necessity. Although he did not subsequently play an active role in African affairs, his stance on India soon broadened into a far wider condemnation of imperialism as a whole. Similarly, his participation in the India League probably affected his attitude to race as a whole, for I am not aware of any repetition of the implicitly racist statements that he had made to Holmes in the 1920s. However, the Palestine issue had also temporarily rekindled an awareness of his Jewish identity. He did not welcome this reminder and hoped that he would subsequently be able to resume his activities as a fully assimilated rationalist. Ultimately, however, Palestine and Jewish consciousness would have an even greater impact upon him than India.

Laski's experience of the three imperial conflicts was therefore important, and the lessons were absorbed into his general framework of analysis. However, MacDonald's 'betrayal' in the domestic sphere was still more crucial: it is this which must now be examined.

7

Democracy in Crisis
(1929–32)

It is clear that the collapse of the second Labour government in August 1931 made a major impact on Laski's political thought. However, it has been argued that there was a *total* break in his attitudes and assumptions at this point. Thus, according to Deane, until 1931, Laski's commitment is 'to the methods of rational discussion and peaceful change, and his basic outlook is that of an eighteenth-century rationalist'.[1] Thereafter:

> he joins the retreat from intelligence by calling for faith and fervor rather than reason and persuasion. He becomes the prophet, if not the advocate, of revolution and dictatorship as the inevitable road to the new socialist society.[2]

It is certainly true that, during the early 1930s, there was a new shift in Laski's political stance. He became identified with the party's Left-wing, and he adopted a perspective which owed much to Marxism. Nevertheless, the argument which will be developed here differs from that of Deane in every respect. Whereas he implies that there was a sudden change, I will suggest that it was very gradual; where he regards the shift as total, I see great continuities; where he asserts that Laski abandoned reason, I think that he sought to maintain it in an irrational era; and where he believes the evolution was unwarranted, I view it as easily explicable in terms of the historical situation and Laski's own experiences. As will be seen, my position does not involve an endorsement of all of Laski's judgments or theories: only a refusal to subscribe to the kind of Cold War orthodoxy which led Deane to condemn him so totally.

In Chapter Five it was argued that Laski was beginning to doubt the viability of his own strategic conception of piecemeal change long

133

before the General Election of 1929. Although he was then excited by the prospect of power, there was little in the new situation to allay his anxieties.

The government was similar in personnel to the previous MacDonald administration and, once again, was dependent upon Liberal support to maintain a majority.[3] Apart from a creditable record in European policy, its domestic measures were disappointing – even if the crucial area of the economy is discounted. There was a programme of urban slum clearance and land utilisation in rural areas, but the attempt to raise the school leaving age was blocked by the House of Lords in March 1931, and repeal of the hated Trade Disputes Act of 1927 was dropped because of Liberal opposition. There was therefore little to raise the spirits of someone – like Laski – who was hoping to see a Labour government demonstrate the possibility of establishing socialism through constitutional means. There were soon signs that he was anxious about the main thrust of government policy and its implications for his general political perspective.

In July 1930 he expressed some of his conclusions in a remarkable seven-page, pioneering article in radical political sociology.[4] The Labour Party, he argued, might be the largest in the House of Commons, and trade union officials were the largest element within it. Nevertheless, every member of the aristocracy who belonged to the party was a member of the government and, broadly speaking, no class of members in the party had been more rapidly rewarded for their affiliation. Middle-class Labour MPs were, on average ten years younger than working-class MPs, so that, as the Liberal party diminished in size and the Labour party became the natural residence of the radical-minded aristocracy, unless there were great social and economic changes, the likelihood was that, in a generation, there would be a working-class party 'officered' by aristocrats and intellectuals. After providing a profile of the class composition of other social institutions, he summarised the political aspect as follows:

> In a Labor Government the working class will have about half the government posts. None of its members will be in the House of Lords; none will be appointed to posts of importance abroad. They will have no part in a Conservative Government or even in its ranks within the House. Effectively they play no part in the civil service, none in the foreign service, none in the judiciary. They have a small part in the local magistracy, but the predomin-

ance of their opponents is so overwhelming that even equality is decades away. . . . Even under a Labor Government no royal commission or departmental inquiry of any kind has been appointed upon which people with Labor views have been in a majority. Under Conservative Governments, they have been given two or three places; but in so vital a commission as that on coal in 1925, there was no person of Labor views.[5]

Turning to the economic situation, he argued that, while the quality of trade unionism had improved and its status had been recognised, it had not attained any of its declared post-war objectives. Industrial direction was still centred on the banks – particularly the Bank of England – and they were ruled by the same class as before the First World War. This was also generally true in the railways, insurance, and the great industrial companies. The balance of essential control therefore remained unchanged and the impact of the Labour government was very limited. The underlying principle even in such schemes as slum clearance was of 'controlled individualism' rather than socialism, and 'it is well known that Mr Snowden's budget is a wholly admirable application of the complete canon of Gladstonian finance'.[6] He thus anticipated 'better factory acts, fewer hours of labour, more attention generally to the humanisation of industrial and social conditions' but no movement 'toward a social, as distinct from a political, democracy'. This was because there was no alteration in the ultimate disposition of economic power, which was held by the business class which inter-married into the old aristocracy:

> From this general angle the broad result of political democracy in England would seem to be less a change in the essential contours of its life than an admission that the number of those who are to share in its benefits is to be somewhat larger than in the past. Twentieth-century England will pay a little more heavily to maintain the characteristic structure of Victorian England.[7]

He highlighted three major points from this analysis. First, that the English governing class wielded such immense power that a vast sacrifice would be demanded if the Labour Party's ideals were ever to be realised. Secondly, that there was little scope for concessions in the current era, but that the fundamental agreement on which the parliamentary system was based could break down if there was a real attack on the rights of private property. Thirdly, that there had been a de-radicalisation of the Labour Party so that it was now a party of social reform whose basic principles did not diverge fundamentally from those of the pre-war Liberal government. His overall conclusion was therefore that:

> so far at least the accession of the Labor party to power cannot be regarded as a decisive challenge to the framework of traditional England; 1924 and 1929 are, like 1832, one more instance of the superb absorptive capacity of the English aristocracy. They still guide the middle class. They still dominate the mentality of the judiciary and the civil service. Membership of their class is still the supreme ambition of the business man. They may . . . be pardoned if they feel that in surrendering the shadow of political power they still retain its effective substance.[8]

While this article encapsulated his analysis brilliantly, it did not make it absolutely clear whether or not he was urging the Labour government to take a more radical stance. After all, the implication was that, if it did so, a breakdown of parliamentary government was more likely. However, other articles, written at about the same time, show that he believed it *vital* for reforms to be pursued more vigorously. For there was far greater knowledge of, and impatience with, social inequalities than ever before. Therefore:

> To conserve the gains of political evolution in the last century we have to satisfy a population more critical, and more explicit about its criticism, than ever before, that the foundations of our society inherently secure its happiness, its comfort, and its self respect. The peaceful transformation of society depends upon our ability to produce that conviction.[9]

And unless the Labour Party, in particular, and the elite in general, recognised the urgency of reform, the working classes would turn to communism. In order to convince an 'establishment' audience of this point he gave a provocative talk at the Royal Institute of International Affairs at Chatham House in December 1930. In this he deliberately tried to show how compelling the communist viewpoint was to the working classes if they looked at the contemporary reality of representative democracy:

if we watch the operation of a community which never surrenders the well-being of the whole unless it must; which only grants concessions when in the last analysis it is forced to grant concessions; if we remember that this community is, broadly speaking, characterised by that Machiavellian comment, 'Men will rather forgive the death of their relatives than the confiscation of their relatives' property'; then can we expect that the class asked to surrender its power will do so willingly and by the ordinary processes of democratic government? Is not democratic government, broadly speaking, no more than a sham?. . . .

If we can only expect a solution, granted our past experience, in terms of violence, is it not our business as a proletariat to prepare for the inevitable day?. . .

Is anything more futile than to live as the social democratic parties live, as very notably the English Labour party lives, in the pathetic belief that it will be able to enact Utopia by the use of the parliamentary machine, when if anything in the world is clear, it is that the moment the Labour party in office seriously confronts the citadel of capital, the advance guard of that capitalistic citadel will come out and destroy the effective authority of the Labour Government?[10]

Although some of his audience – and some later critics[11] – may have been confused by his method, it is absolutely clear that he was not advocating communism, but *the establishment of a viable alternative, which would undermine its appeal* . As he concluded:

It . . . becomes our obligation to the heritage which is ours to show that the consequences of a capitalist civilisation, as translated into the daily fabric of ordinary men's lives, is as compelling and attractive as that which stands as its antithesis.[12]

By the end of 1930 it is therefore clear that Laski recognised the immense difficulties in peaceful transformation, but believed that the task was nevertheless vital. He also felt that the Labour government was far too cautious, and feared that its failure would lead to a strengthening of communism. All this foreshadows the position that he would adopt after 1931. Moreoever, he already held a further belief that provides an element of continuity with his later position: an insistence on the need for constitutional reform.

The focus on potential constitutional barriers to a Labour government was not, of course, new. In the twenties he had advocated the abolition of the House of Lords as an ultimate goal, and had sought to lessen the potential power of the monarch over a Prime Minister in a minority government.[13] More generally, he had been concerned as to whether existing parliamentary institutions could cope with the increasing pressures exerted upon them by more complex economies requiring growing state intervention.[14] However, a crucial evolution in his thinking took place during the life of the second Labour administration. Whereas he had previously seen a resurgence of parliamentary vitality as an important aim, after 1929 his emphasis shifted towards a belief in the need for strong government.

In part, this change emanated from the general experience of the Labour Party in office. For it soon became evident that its legislative programme was blocked by the use of all possible parliamentary delaying procedures, which the Opposition parties were able to exploit to their full advantage against a minority government. It was probably this which led Laski to write in 1930 that:

> there is a growing sense that modern political institutions are utterly inadequate to the task they must perform. Slowness and obstruction are inherent in them; and it is ground common to all parties that they are overwhelmed by the sheer weight of business they have to bear. . . . it is clear that the rate of decisive change is, under parliamentarism, bound to be slow.[15]

These general reflections were sharpened by Laski's sustained consideration of some of the issues as a member of the Committee on Ministers' Powers established by the Labour government in October 1929 under Lord Donoughmore. Sankey had invited him to serve on this Committee, which was designed to refute a sensationalist Right-wing attack on contemporary government by Lord Chief Justice Hewart in his *The New Despotism* (1928).

The essence of Hewart's argument was that the supremacy of the courts and Parliament was being undermined by the growth of discretionary power exercised by civil servants and ministers. The underlying assumption was that freedom depended upon limited government. The terms of reference of the committee were to consider government powers by way of delegated legislation and judicial or quasi-judicial decision, and to report on the safeguards which were desirable or necessary to secure the constitutional principles of the sovereignty of Parliament and the supremacy of law. Since high-powered personnel were needed to deal with the arguments of a Lord Chief Justice, the committee contained eminent lawyers and civil servants, three Conservative ex-ministers and three Labour MPs, with Sir William Holdsworth, a Right-wing legal historian, and Laski as the academics. It held fifty-four meetings, at twenty-two of which oral evidence was submitted, and it published two volumes of evidence.[16]

Laski regarded it as 'a great committee, and a great subject',[17] took the work extremely seriously, and was forced to postpone a planned lecture trip to Yale in the spring of 1930 so that he could concentrate upon it.[18] He also played a key role in drafting the final report.[19] Although it was completed *after* the fall of the Labour government (in January 1932), Laski no doubt reached his conclusions at a much earlier stage and the report is therefore important in relation to his evolving views on the constitution.

In the first place, the committee was absolutely clear that delegated legislation was necessary and irreversible for a modern government for, unless Parliament delegated law-making power, it 'would be unable to pass the kind and quantity of legislation which modern public opinion requires'.[20] Moreover, Laski and Ellen Wilkinson, the Left-wing Labour MP, went beyond the rest of the committee in their approval of delegated legislation. He concurred with a note which she added, which argued that, rather than a necessary evil, delegated legislation ought to be widely extended in 'the conditions of the modern state, which not only has to undertake immense new social services, but which before long may be responsible for the greater part of the industrial and commercial activities of the country'.[21] Many of the existing parliamentary procedures were not dealing really effectively with the principles and general plan of proposed legislation, but were merely obstructive, and 'Nothing is so dangerous in a democracy as a safeguard which appears to be adequate but is really a facade'.[22]

Secondly, Laski added a dissenting note (supported by Ellen Wilkinson) which tried to limit judicial power over the interpretation of statutes. The object of this was to increase the likelihood that the spirit behind government legislation would prevail over conservative judges.

This apparently esoteric point expressed a long-term conviction that politicians rather than judges should make the law. Laski had often applied Holmes's axiom – that judges approached the law with

'an inarticulate major premise' – particularly to judicial interpretations of the law relating to trade unions and social policy.[23] He
therefore now disputed the majority view that the difficulty lay in
the faulty drafting of statutes which could be overcome by a strengthening of the Parliamentary Counsel's Office:

> When the Divisional Court held that attendance by school chil-
> dren at performances of Shakespeare's plays could not be re-
> garded as an object of 'educational' expenditure; or when it is
> held by the House of Lords that a power in Local Authorities to
> pay 'such salaries and wages as they . . . may think fit' means, in
> fact, such salaries and wages as the House of Lords may consider
> 'reasonable'; it seems to me clear that there is a discretion beyond
> the mere compulsion of words in the judicial interpretation of
> statutes. And this discretion, as I think, enables the judge to sub-
> stitute his private notions of legistative intention for those which
> the authors of the statute sought to fulfil.[24]

His proposal, which was rejected by the majority of the committee,
was that Parliament should add an explanatory memorandum to
statutes which would guide (but not bind) judges in discovering the
intention behind particular pieces of legislation.

In fact the final report made little impact, but it is significant that,
on both the major issues with which it was concerned, Laski endorsed the general view that the establishment of effective executive
power was a primary goal in the modern age. It did not mean that
he, or the committee, believed in an uncontrolled state. Indeed it
argued that continental critics were justified in pointing out the
limited protection for the citizen against the Executive, including the
fact the Crown could not be sued for tort. This had been one of
Laski's 'hobby horses' since his early pluralist phase, and he may
have been responsible for the committee including a recommendation that this 'lacuna in the rule of law' should now be filled.[25]
However, his support for the general emphasis on the need for
executive power stemmed from his current view that government
needed to be able to act quickly if the demands for social and economic change were to be implemented by constitutional, rather than
revolutionary, means. Yet he was becoming increasingly pessimistic
about the prospects long before August 1931.

He spent the spring and early summer on sabbatical leave at the
Yale Law School. This was not a great success, mainly because he

missed Frida and Diana desperately and vowed never to spend such a long time away from them again.[26] But he also felt alienated from American politics and society and continued to feel involved with the British Labour government. However, as he observed it from afar he became ever more dismayed at its economic policy and its failure even to repeal the Trade Disputes Act. By March he was contemptuous of MacDonald, whom he regarded as cowardly, shifty and secretive, and he was anxious for the defeat of the government.[27] In June he told Frida that it would 'be a tremendous relief to be in opposition' and that 'two more years of this would really be frightful'.[28]

Two years' experience of a minority Labour government had thus reinforced the more pessimistic mood that had been growing within him during the latter half of the twenties. And this was exacerbated by the deepening economic crisis and its political repercussions throughout Europe and the United States. Even if the Labour Party had simply been defeated, it is therefore probable that his faith in the gradualist perspective would have been further undermined by this second experience of government. Yet this is not entirely clear, for he also felt 'that going into opposition is the only way to prevent the disintegration of the party's morale', and he looked forward to MacDonald's replacement by Arthur Henderson, for whom he retained far more respect.[29] It is thus possible that, had the party political system continued in a conventional manner, he might have repressed his doubts by simply seeking to radicalise Labour for the next occasion in government. In any case, the debacle of August 1931 acted as a catalyst in the evolution of his political perspective.

There had been an incipient crisis in British politics ever since the Wall Street crash of October 1929 had marked the onset of the world depression. As the British economy had never really recovered after the First World War, the underlying weaknesses had been quickly exposed. The Labour government, which had promised a solution to unemployment, soon found itself powerless to prevent a sharp rise in the numbers out of work and, during 1930, it accepted Treasury financial orthodoxy in preference to any radical alternatives. By August 1931 unemployment, which had totalled 1,164,000 when Labour had taken office, had reached 2,800,000 and was still rising, and exports had plummetted by 40 per cent over the same two year period, while imports had remained constant. These problems in the real economy were accompanied by an international financial crisis which centred on London in the summer of 1931. The expert (but

orthodox) committee, established under Sir George May, reported at
the end of July recommending drastic cuts in expenditure, and it
became clear that the government would implement fiercely defla-
tionary policies. However, there was now an atmosphere of panic
in financial circles which the comparatively slow reaction of the
Cabinet did little to allay. All the ministers adhered to the orthodox
line that cuts were necessary, but there was disagreement about
their extent and nature. In particular, there was deep controversy
over the demand that wages and unemployment benefits should
be affected, and a meeting on 20 August revealed the extent of
TUC resistance to any such suggestion. This, and the attitude of the
Parliamentary Labour Party, reinforced opposition within the Cabinet and matters came to a head on 22 August.

Even with the projected economies, foreign loans were regarded
as essential, and American bankers had made it clear that these
would be forthcoming only if the government were supported by
the opposition parties. MacDonald and Snowden now made two
crucial announcements: that the parliamentary opposition would
sustain the government only if additional economies were made,
and (later the same day) that the American banks were insisting on
a cut in unemployment benefit. On 23 August the Cabinet accepted
the package of cuts by eleven votes to nine, but the majority was too
small to secure the loan. At this stage the whole Cabinet was expected to resign. However, MacDonald now accepted the blandish-
ments of the King and opposition leaders and, on 24 August, became
Prime Minister in a National government. Since only three members
of the Labour Cabinet (Sankey, Thomas and Snowden) joined him,
this was a Conservative-dominated administration, and it immediately made the cuts and secured the loan.

Laski was on holiday in France when the crisis broke, having
spent only one month in Britain since leaving for his American
sabbatical in February. However, he immediately returned and joined
Arthur Henderson in the attempt to rally the party in its new,
marginalised position. He now argued that there had been a deliberate plot by financial interests (including the Bank of England) to
bring down the Labour government and reduce wages.[30] Two of his
other instant reactions are still more significant.

First, he resolved that he would 'stay with the Left of Labour and,
if necessary . . . go to the extreme left'.[31] This demonstrates the
catalytic effect of the events of August 1931. Until now, his *analysis*
had increasingly placed him on the left of the party, but he had been

reluctant to assume any such position in organisational terms. It was MacDonald's action which now led him to associate with the left in factional, as well as ideological, terms. Secondly, he immediately put the crisis in a theoretical context which arose out of his longer term pre-occupations:

> For us, the issue is clear. Is policy to be made by the elected government, or by financial interests outside? If the latter, clearly Socialism cannot be attained constitutionally and the Bolsheviks are right. . . .
>
> The present spectacle is one of the definite sacrifice of the working class to men whose financial policy is very largely the source of our temporary weakness. This is the biggest gift Communism has had in our lifetime, for it throws the whole foundation of parliamentary government into jeopardy.[32]

Soon afterwards he returned to a similar point in relation to the forthcoming General Election. The Labour manifesto called for the nationalisation of the Bank of England, power, transport, and iron and steel, and pledged a restoration of the cuts. Although it still accepted the need for a balanced budget, it was denounced as catastrophic by its opponents – most notoriously by Snowden who now claimed that Labour's policy was 'Bolshevism run mad'. Laski, who played a major part in the election campaign, noted that the National government was asserting that a Labour victory would involve a flight from the pound. But, he argued, this meant that, even if Labour achieved a majority, it would have to accept 'as a presupposition of power, the theory of social action which suits the demands of finance-capitalism'.[33] Following MacDonald's acceptance of such demands in August, the implication was that 'Socialistic measures . . . are not obtainable by constitutional means'.[34]

The August crisis and its aftermath had focused Laski's attention – more pointedly than ever before – on the whole issue of peaceful change and constitutionalism. Yet his views have often been misinterpreted.[35] He was *not* saying that the communist position had been vindicated. On the contrary, he was arguing that, by accepting the bankers' conditions, MacDonald had implicitly endorsed the view that 'a socialist state cannot be built without a violent break with capitalism'.[36] But this had done 'the most considerable disservice to constitutionalism' in Britain in modern times.[37] In other words, Laski was implying that MacDonald need not have acted in this way, and that the bankers' ultimatum could have been rejected. But was the constitutional system sufficiently resilient to make it possible for a Labour government to operate against the wishes of those who controlled the levers of financial and economic power? Once the Labour Party had been routed in the October 1931 election – losing nearly two million votes, and returning only fifty-two MPs – Laski turned his attention to this question.

There is no doubt as to what Laski *wanted* to believe: he fervently hoped that peaceful, constitutional change remained possible. It was, he felt, quite evident that 'government by persuasion is invariably a more creative adventure than government by violence'.[38] Indeed, in the autumn of 1932 he inveighed against the prospect of revolution in quasi-religious terms:

> revolution, like war, is infinite tragedy, since, in its very nature, it means pain and suffering and the tragic confusion of means with ends. The innocent not less than the guilty are its victims. It is the enemy of Reason and Freedom – the twin goddesses whose triumph gives what of beauty there is in the ultimate texture of men's lives. Where there is social conflict, there also Hate and Fear rule the destinies of us all; and even if there is high purpose in the price they exact, it is a purpose stained by bloody sacrifice.[39]

But it was one thing to urge that peaceful change was incomparably preferable to revolution, and quite another to explain how it could come about. Obviously, hopes for the future were dependent upon the ways in which the past and the present were interpreted, and Laski now agonised over the meaning of the current situation.

The most tempting explanation for the failure of the Labour government was simply to blame MacDonald himself. For if all the responsibility for the inadequacies could be transferred onto a single individual, the party itself, and its general conception of change, could be absolved. Laski certainly *did* condemn the former party leader in the strongest possible terms, believing that he had been guilty of a great betrayal. However, he was aware that this was, at best, a partial explanation for a far more fundamental problem. His immediate reaction was to examine the British constitutional system itself, both to diagnose what had gone wrong in August and to prevent a recurrence of similar 'betrayals'. He first considered these issues at length in a booklet entitled *The Crisis and the Constitution: 1931 and After*, which was written in the winter of 1931–32.

He began with some comparatively limited considerations, arguing that some of the Prime Minister's powers should be transferred to the Cabinet as a whole; that executive dominance over parliament needed to be recognised; and that a smaller, more streamlined Cabinet should be established. Such recommendations were in line with his earlier evolution in accepting the necessity for stronger Executive power, (although the wish to strengthen the Cabinet *vis-à-vis* the Prime Minister clearly stemmed from MacDonald's action in August 1931). However, he also introduced new elements. In particular, he envisaged the necessity for the next Labour government to introduce emergency powers to control financial speculation. This would necessitate the House of Lords' consent and, quite probably, the King's agreement to create sufficient peers to pass the legislation in the event of difficulties with the Lords.[40] Moreover, even within the pamphlet itself, Laski's ideas about the extent of the changes that would be required seemed to escalate and he declared that the Labour Party:

> will need the kind of religious enthusiasm for its ends which Russian Communism displays; the ability to convince its opponents that nothing can turn it from its goal.[41]

Similarly, the trade unions needed to conceive themselves as a protective rampart for a Labour government:

> a contingently revolutionary force which could be called into play by any such betrayal or strategy as the last crisis brought into instant being.[42]

The problem was that he was aware that the constitution was only one aspect of the difficulties facing a Labour government. It might be true, in the British context, that constitutional ambiguities had provided anti-socialist forces with scope to act in 1931, and this might be diminished by institutional reform. For example, since the prerogative powers of the King had been unclear, it could benefit a future Labour administration to clarify them in the way that Laski suggested. But this would have less importance if, as he also believed, anti-socialist forces would be determined to prevent the implementation of radical measures, *whatever the exact nature of the constitutional provisions*. In this situation the prerogative powers of the King were less crucial than the fact that he could become a focus for Right-wing, 'patriotic' sabotage against a Labour government. Such considerations did not mean that constitutional clarification became unimportant. Indeed Laski became more specific about the contingency plans which would be necessary to ensure the King's agreement to Labour's constitutional proposals after an interview with the King's private secretary in November 1932. For this convinced him that:

> while in normal times, the King's influence is a pressure and not a force, once things are critical, it becomes immediately the active pivot round which things turn.[43]

But it meant that he saw the constitutional system as an element *within* the arena of social and political conflict rather than as a neutral framework which needed to be rectified in the light of weaknesses exposed by the recent crisis. Moreover, while considering such issues he became increasingly pessimistic about the wider context, and this led him to question the viability of constitutionalism itself. He thus told Frankfurter that he feared that progress in Britain would come only by 'catastrophic change' because 'the dice are too loaded' to establish a socialist society 'within the framework of existing conditions'.[44]

His despondency was not confined to Britain. He had also been depressed by his four-month stay in the USA in 1931. He had found American society excessively materialist, with a deep cynicism about politics.[45] Naturally, he condemned President Hoover for his inactivity in the face of 'terrible unemployment'.[46] But he was still more depressed by the fact that his radical friends 'seem just to give up hope of being able to do anything at all', and he feared that the Americans were moving 'towards a vast tragedy – bigness without depth'.[47] And he saw the situation in the capitalist world as a whole as moving 'with an almost awe-inspiring determination to catastrophe'.[48] The result was both deep despair about the survival of democracy anywhere, and an acceptance of extreme measures to save the principle of constitutionalism within Britain. It was in these circumstances that he wrote *Democracy in Crisis* in the summer and autumn of 1932.

This was, he believed, 'the most creative book' he had ever written.[49] In fact it was a tormented work in which his veneration for liberal democracy was counterbalanced by his pessimism about its future. The growth of individual liberty and parliamentary democracy in nineteenth-century Britain had been 'a remarkable tradition', with many admirable virtues.[50] However, it had been based on particular economic circumstances, which had now disappeared, leaving no apparent basis for a new compromise. The situation was paralleled elsewhere, leading to breakdown in Italy, Von Papen's emergency regime in Germany, crisis in France, disillusionment in the USA, and no sign of democracy in the majority of the world. The 'inner citadel' of the capitalist system had never been assailed by democratic governments and it was imperative to find the necessary conditions for a new equilibrium. But there was no guarantee that constitutional conventions would be accepted if there was *fundamental* disagreement over the whole system.[51]

It was on this assumption that he proceeded to make his most controversial statement on the situation which could arise in Britain in the event of a Labour victory. For he now envisaged a climate of potential civil war in which the government would need 'to take vast powers', 'suspend the classic formulae of opposition' and secure Conservative promises that 'its work of transformation' would not be repealed.[52] Such speculation indicated his state of mind, for the book was dominated by a prolonged inner debate between two Laskis: one who desperately wanted to save constitutional democracy and the other who saw this as increasingly improbable. If, as he assumed, the working-class demand for greater equality was irreversible, the alternatives were only 'between conflict with the workers or the surrender of privilege by the narrow class to which it is confined'.[53] But this meant that the only way to maintain peaceful progress was to ensure that a Labour government had sufficient power to effect immediate changes: hence the need for emergency powers.

The crisis of democracy was thus also a personal trauma, and Laski was quite unable to resolve his dilemma as to whether constitutionalism would survive. At times he held out the hope that in Britain at least the traditional deep desire for compromise might yet lead to peaceful progress. But even before January 1933 and the establishment of the Nazi regime in Germany, a deep-seated pessimism had superseded his vision of peaceful change, and he implied that the economic crisis was more likely to lead to revolution or Right-wing dictatorship.

At the beginning of this chapter, four propositions about Laski's position were counterposed to those suggested by Deane: first, that the change in his thought was very gradual; secondly, that there were great continuities; thirdly, that he continued to base his outlook on 'reason'; and fourthly that the evolution that occurred was explicable in historical terms. Each of these points may now be considered.

There had certainly been a shift in Laski's basic attitude of mind. In 1927 he had sometimes seemed despondent about the prospects for constitutional change, but he had normally remained relatively optimistic. Five years later these positions had been reversed. As he stated in the Preface to *Democracy in Crisis* :

> I am aware that my argument is a pessimistic one . . . I should have been happier if my conclusions had been in another direction . . . .[54]

The type of power that he now envisaged as necessary for the establishment of socialism had also changed. Before 1929 he had anticipated great difficulties for a reforming administration, but it was only after the experience of the MacDonald 'betrayal' that he declared that the Labour Party:

> will need the kind of religious enthusiasm for its ends which Russian Communism displays; the ability to convince its opponents that nothing can turn it from its goal.[55]

Yet, as has been shown, the change was very gradual. In 1930 he had already argued that socialism would probably not be introduced by the government because of the power of the ruling classes, the constitutional barriers, and the inadequacy of the Labour Party's ideological commitment. His advocacy of stronger executive power and a far more urgent approach to reform at this time foreshadowed the position that he adopted *after* 1931.

The gradual nature of the change is obviously closely connected with the second point: the continuities in his outlook. In April 1927 he told Frankfurter:

> I judge that the next five or ten years will be very critical. Granted an expansion of trade they might bring appeasement; if not, the narrow margin within which our economic system now works

means, to me at least, a definite drift towards social confusion and bitterness.[56]

He had thus already defined economic expansion as the critical factor in the situation. His belief, after 1931, that a really profound social and political crisis was probable as a result of the depression was therefore in line with the views that he had held in the aftermath of the General Strike. Another, perhaps more surprising, continuity is that by the end of 1932, his attitude to Marxism had hardly changed. He continued to extol its virtues as an overall social philosophy rather than as a 'science' which was valid in its particulars, and he still believed that its truth was only contingent. In other words its prophecies would be fulfilled *unless there was peaceful change or capitalist recovery in Europe and the United States* .[57] The change – once again – lay in his *attitude* rather than his *theory* . For he now thought it far more likely than he had done previously that Communist dictatorships would be established as a result of a refusal to reform.[58] Continuity in his *theory* was matched by continuity in his *practice* .

It is true that Laski now became more associated with the Left. After the fall of the Labour government he became involved with the various attempts to revitalise socialist forces within the party, and played a role in establishing the Socialist League in the autumn of 1932.[59] This group, in which Sir Stafford Cripps was the dominant figure, became the main organisational focus of the party's Left-wing after the disaffiliation of the ILP earlier in the year. It was to clash with the leadership almost immediately, partly because it also advocated the adoption of new emergency powers to introduce extensive socialist legislation.[60] Laski's view of executive power was therefore in harmony with that of the Socialist League. Yet he still maintained his contacts with people whose political stance was well to the right of his own position. He continued to work with the Labour Party mainstream, and did not even cut off all links with the National government. For example, he agreed to serve on a new committee on legal education which he persuaded Sankey to establish in 1932.[61]

These continuities are also related to the third point: Laski's continuing belief in 'reason'. Of course, there are problems associated with the concept of 'reason': supporters of a whole range of perspectives seek to appropriate the term to justify their own ideas. Nevertheless, Laski remained convinced that reason was the basis of his position. He believed that his analysis was grounded in the evidence and that his pessimistic prognosis was based on 'the obligation to follow the compulsion of the facts'.[62] But he also still hoped that 'reason' would triumph: that there might be peaceful, constitutional change and the establishment of 'a great civilization' based on reason and tolerance.[63] And he continued to believe – albeit with diminishing optimism – that he would be able to persuade people of goodwill that radical change was necessary.

This leads to the final question: were Laski's conclusions explicable in terms of the available evidence and his own experiences? Or had he, as Deane argues, joined 'the retreat from intelligence'?

Laski was hardly alone in moving to the Left in 1931–2. Other major British socialist intellectuals, such as G. D. H. Cole and R. H. Tawney also became more radical, while the Webbs began their love-affair with the Soviet Union, and John Strachey became a pro-communist propagandist, after a brief spell in Mosley's New Party. It is hardly surprising that in Britain, in the era of hunger marches, means' tests, wage cuts, mass unemployment, and the formation of the British Union of Fascists, many adopted a far more radical stance than previously. Indeed, for many, the horrific consequences of the economic depression throughout the world, seemed to demonstrate that capitalism was in terminal decline and that the only remaining alternatives might be fascism or communism. Since Laski was more aware than most of the *international* dimensions of the crisis, his evolution was surely easily explicable, particularly as he had already started shifting his position *before* the 1931 crisis. Nor did he accept that catastrophe was inevitable or that the only alternative to fascism was communism. He continued to hope that peaceful change was possible.

Laski's views were, I believe, warranted by the 'facts' and the general political perspective to which he adhered. This does not mean that he was 'right' in every aspect of his argument. For example, he may have overestimated the role of the monarch in the 1931 crisis.[64] A more fundamental weakness lay in his economic analysis. In particular, he failed to examine Keynes's economic ideas in any depth before concluding that socialism was the only solution to the crisis or that expansionist policies would never again be introduced within capitalism.[65] On the other hand, he realised that the resolution of the crisis was not simply a 'technical' matter, because divergent class interests were involved and pro-capitalist forces sought a solution in terms of lower wages which would be resisted by workers. For Laski the economic depression and its political repercussions were thus acute manifestations of the underlying problems of capitalism, which could not be eradicated by the adoption of particular policies. Certainly, he was comparatively weak in his economic analysis, but he was justified in believing that 'Keynesian' solutions would not be adopted at the time that he was writing.

If Laski was neither volatile nor irrational in adopting a pessimistic outlook by late 1932, this does not mean that his position was unproblematic. In fact, the worsening economic and political situation had exposed the underlying tensions in both his theory and practice. He was, with great regret, coming to believe that the communist analysis would probably be shown to be valid. But he had based his political life on the hope that justice would prevail through peaceful compromise. This inherent contradiction between his emotions and his intellect would lead to immense difficulties as his theory became more 'schizophrenic' and his activity grew ever more frenetic. Moreover, the pressures were to intensify as the world situation deteriorated after 1932.

8

Freedom in Danger
(1933–4)

From 1933 Laski was ever more prolific as a popular journalist, and became increasingly active in numerous Left-wing organisations, as well as the Labour Party. He also urged unity of action with the Communist Party. He remained as much of an 'intellectual' as ever, quoting with approval Goethe's aphorism: 'action is easy, it is thought that is so difficult'.[1] But he argued that intellectuals needed to have the courage to shun wealth and respectability and to speak the truth as they saw it. It was, he claimed, far easier to avoid doing so and to be accepted as someone with 'sound' views.[2] Later he proclaimed:

> I am . . . certain that the responsibility of the intellectual who sees the drift of his time towards the abyss is to mitigate its dangers by seeking, through the profundity of his alliance with the masses, to make their dreams and hopes seem practicable and legitimate.[3]

Once Hitler had assumed power in Germany, Laski thought that he could see the abyss and that his duty was to help persuade people to confront 'the central issues of the crisis . . . in rational terms'.[4] From then onwards he stretched himself beyond any normal limits to continue his academic work while becoming ever more deeply involved in political life.

His thinking in these years was complex as, once again, it contained both changes and continuities. It has been attacked for its inconsistency, and it is certainly true that his positions were sometimes difficult to reconcile with one another. But this was not because he was muddled or lacked depth or theoretical sophistication. It is necessary to ask *why* he could hold views which were, apparently, contradictory. This chapter will therefore seek to explain the nature and causes of his political development. It will be argued that both collective and individual experiences were important in the formulation of his outlook and theories, and that the contradictions 'made sense' in the context of the era.

THE IMPACT OF NAZISM

Laski had visited Germany in the summer of 1930 and described his impressions to Holmes:

> their organisation is remarkable. Whether it's the little steamer, or the ferry, or the village threshing machine, the people seem to fit into one another's needs remarkably. There are, of course, faults. There is a certain drab sameness about the talk you get. You don't find the individuality you always tumble upon in an English or American village. The people, like good Germans, are a little too respectful, and a little too neat and orderly. But they are full of common-sense. There is little or no bitterness about the war. The Republic is clearly firmly established . . .[5]

Two years later his complacency had vanished and he talked of 'the dark outlook in Germany'.[6] He was therefore not surprised by the accession of Hitler. Nevertheless, the event was of critical importance in his life, for Nazism was the antithesis of everything in which he believed. Indeed it was a denial of his whole being as a liberal rationalist, and as a Jew who had believed that assimilation was the answer to anti-semitism. At times he was in near despair, and was so obsessed by Hitlerism that his daughter, Diana, feared that he might collapse under the strain.[7] However, he also reacted positively, in absolute determination to play a role in countering it.

In the first place, he responded by trying to help some of the victims of the new regime by using his influence within the university world to find as many posts as possible for German academic refugees. He was not alone in this: Beveridge and others at LSE agreed to establish a fund, and eminent professors, such as Karl Mannheim and Herman Kantorowicz, were recruited to the School. However, Laski threw himself into this work with a sustained commitment, facilitating recruitment both to British and American universities.[8] Of course, he was always humanitarian, and ready to help individuals in difficulty. But he clearly felt particular empathy with these victims of Nazism as a Jewish socialist academic himself.

In general, he tried not to allow the Jewish question to dominate his attitude to Hitlerism. However, he obviously felt it deeply. He urged the British government to allow more Jews into Britain and was deeply critical of the 'low-key' stance of his brother Neville, now President of the Board of Deputies of British Jews. He thus wrote to Frankfurter:

The Jewish problem oppresses me night and day, especially as the policy my brother stands for seems . . . weak and indecisive. We shall get on only by a positive emphasis of our own; not by standing at the back door of foreign offices.[9]

Sometimes he was able to respond to the tragedy with his normal humour. A few months later, he thus reported:

I saw Neville yesterday . . . He suggested . . . that the best way in which H. M. government could mark its disapproval of Hitler was by conferring a knighthood on him as the 'lay head of the Jewish community in England'. I suggested that a baronetcy was more suitable, from which he did not dissent.[10]

Similarly, he recounted the plight of a German student at LSE in a light-hearted manner:

I was amused by a Nazi student from Berlin who asked me whether I was a Jew, and, on learning that I was, explained that he could not work under me. I sent him along to a colleague who told him that, for his subject . . . I was the only person from whom he could get help in England. So he complained despairingly that all the people who might help him in Germany had been dismissed and when he came to England for help he was assigned to someone with whom he dared not work! I was sorry for the lad, but his dilemma was really comic.[11]

In reality, he was deeply disturbed by the Nazi persecution, and became more involved in the 'Jewish question' and Zionism as a result.[12]

His second major response to Nazism was to support the Socialist League's United Front policy. In March 1933 the Communist Party, supported by the ILP, called for a United Front against fascism and, at its first annual conference in June 1933, the Socialist League passed a resolution calling for a united action by the whole working class.[13] The emphasis differed slightly in that the League saw the Labour Party as the focal point in rallying opinion in favour of socialism and against fascism, but the implication was of unity with the ILP and Communist Party. This, with the Socialist League's continuing commitment to the passing of emergency powers in the event of a Labour victory, was sufficient to incur the hostility of the Labour leadership, which was adamantly opposed to any common action with parties of the Left – particularly the Communist Party. Its attitude was symbolised by the policy statement 'Democracy versus Dictatorship' presented to the 1933 Labour Party Conference.[14]

This argued, in effect, that the way to save democracy in Britain was to refuse any form of association with anti-democratic forces – a category which included both communists and fascists. Any common action with communists would, it was claimed, simply increase the likelihood that conservative forces would turn to fascism. The leadership argued that democracy was strongly embedded in the British tradition and that the danger of fascism was remote. Association with communists would therefore *increase* the threat rather than diminish it, as the proponents of a United Front argued.

Laski was convinced of the fragility of democracy rather than its strength, and believed that the threat was not from the Left but from the ruling classes, who might withdraw their support for democracy as capitalism contracted. He was therefore a fierce opponent of leadership policy. In July 1933 he took part in a meeting at LSE which attempted to persuade Walter Citrine, the TUC General Secretary, of the validity of the Socialist League's position.[15] This failed and the next year the leadership, in the person of Herbert Morrison, implemented a policy of bans and proscriptions on association with communist-led organisations. In Laski's view the leadership was repeating all the mistakes of the German Social Democrats at the time of the rise of Hitler: instead of adopting a militant policy to protect democracy and working-class institutions it was, he thought, simply relying on constitutional forms in the belief that Britain was 'different'.

In 1933–4 he therefore became a strong advocate of some kind of 'United Front' against fascism. This did not mean that he supported the Communist Party (CP). On the contrary, he condemned the role of communism in the rise of Hitler, believing that the doctrine of 'Social-Fascism' had been disastrous.[16] And even when the CP softened its attacks on the Labour Party, he remained critical.[17] However, he certainly moved closer to the CP's analysis as he became convinced of the need for unity against fascism.

In *The State in Theory and Practice* (hereafter *State*) completed in October 1934, he attempted to analyse the phenomenon at length. By then a clerico-fascist regime had destroyed Socialist Vienna, and the Third Republic in France had also been threatened by extreme Right-wing forces. He now saw fascism as a general phenomenon and maintained that its rise and development confirmed the validity of the analysis which emphasised the contradiction between democracy and capitalism in a phase of contraction:

> If the phase of contraction is prolonged, it becomes necessary either to abrogate the democratic process or to change the economic assumptions upon which the society rests.[18]

The state, he claimed, is always biased in the interests of the owners of the means of production, who would not surrender their advantages unless compelled to do so. If threatened, they would attempt to suppress democratic institutions because:

> The maintenance of political democracy is not, as the experience of Italy, Germany and Austria makes manifest, an inherent purpose of the state as such. It is a form of government able to maintain itself only so long as it does not contradict the implicit needs of the class-relations a capitalist system requires.[19]

This analysis raises two immediate questions: was Laski suggesting that fascism was inherent or inevitable within capitalism – the line of the Comintern at least until the crushing of the German communists under Hitler? And was he taking the wholly reductionist view that fascism was simply an economic phenomenon arising out of a capitalist crisis?

He avoided taking a categorical position on the first point, but certainly emphasised the likelihood of the growth of fascism within all capitalist countries, given the world-wide economic depression. He stressed the growth of fascism in France, the way in which employers in the USA obstructed the New Deal and used violence to suppress trade unionism, and British Conservatives' interest in strengthening the House of Lords and monarchical powers against the threat of socialism. He never claimed that the National government was 'fascist', but did argue that there was 'the growth of a fascist temper in Great Britain'.[20] This was, he believed, symbolised by such measures as the 'Incitement to Disaffection Act'; the Trenchard police reforms, which strengthened the officer class through direct appointment; and the contrasting treatment of communists and fascists by the police and courts. He acknowledged that countries with longer experience of democratic institutions had thus far withstood the attacks from the extreme Right, but he emphasised the general malaise, and the fact that there was no example of peaceful transformation of the property system. This, he believed, meant that there was an ever-present *threat* of fascism.

His response to the second question was as follows. He acknowledged that non-economic factors had contributed to the growth of fascist doctrines, but argued that, without economic difficulties, the movements would never have been projected to power.[22] Once established, the fascist state interfered with 'freedom of enterprise', but 'the character of that interference, both in Italy and Germany, has been the interference of capitalists in the interests of capitalist recovery'.[23]

In the final analysis, fascism was thus the result of capitalist crisis. It was not a new ideology for, under close examination, it:

> proves to be nothing more than an ill-assorted rag-bag in which all kinds of remnants from the most diverse philosophies seek as best they may, to find a place . . .
>
> Stripped of all its rhetorical trappings, Italian fascism appears quite simply as an insistence upon compulsory obedience to a state whose purpose is to protect existing class-relations.[24]

He therefore avoided reductionism in the sense that he acknowledged the existence of factors other than economic ones. But he appeared to view them as so subordinate as to require little discussion.

There are two notable points about this analysis. The first is the minimal attention he paid to the specific features of Nazism and, in particular, to its racism. At one point he termed Hitler's takeover as a 'revolution' with the purpose of regenerating 'the German state by removing from influence . . . men and women of Jewish blood or Marxist ideas', and he acknowledged that anti-semitism was not a wholly economic phenomenon.[25] But such references were comparatively rare and hardly developed in any of his writings before the Second World War. Normally, he simply concentrated on the general relationship between capitalism and fascism without much attention to the specifics of Nazi barbarism. Yet we know that he was actually deeply affected by Nazi anti-semitism. Secondly, his analysis of fascism was fairly commonplace and uninspired. This is not to dispute his fundamental claim about the relationship between capitalism and European fascism in the inter-war period, but to argue that this kind of explanation still needs to take account of specific features in the countries in which fascism developed. Laski avoided some of the excesses of the Comintern's position, but failed to deal sufficiently with historical, political, and cultural factors. In fact, these two criticisms coalesce into one: had he dealt with the specificities of Nazism, he would have been forced to consider the explanation of its rise and development in greater depth. This might have enriched his analysis of both fascism and capitalist democracy. Why, then, did he not do so?

The first factor may have been emotional. Because Nazism threatened him in such a personal way, he may actually have found it easier to deal with on a general level. After all, concentration on Hitler's regime could have led him towards a more exclusive concentration upon aspects of Jewish identity. He wanted to help Jewish refugees from Nazism, but would not allow this issue to dominate his perspective. Secondly, and paradoxically, the validity of his insights in the pre-Nazi era may now have led him to over-simplify. That is, his justifiable pessimism about the future of liberal-democracy at the end of 1932 had the disadvantage that Hitler's accession to power could simply be incorporated into the existing framework of analysis. Laski had already developed his theory about the tensions between capitalism and democracy by 1932: the rise of Nazism *simply confirmed the viewpoint that he had already reached.* Similarly, the subsequent suppression of socialist Vienna in 1934 offered further confirmation. Since he had predicted pro-capitalist, anti-working class dictatorships, there appeared to be no reason to question his theoretical framework when actually confronted by fascist regimes. However, as we have seen, the weakness of this position was that his analysis was insufficient. He certainly prophesied that fascism could lead to a new 'dark age', but he saw this in terms of the destruction which would be wrought by an era of counter-revolution, revolution and war. He never predicted the possibility of the Holocaust because he was satisfied with his own explanation of Nazism as 'capitalist dictatorship'.[26]

This leads to a third factor, which must be borne in mind. The critic has the advantage of historical knowledge. We know that fascism did not come about in Britain or the United States and we therefore have the opportunity to analyse, in a leisurely manner, the reasons for the continuation of the liberal-democratic state. In so doing, it is easy to emphasise relevant differences in the circumstances of the fascist and non-fascist countries. Laski obviously did not have this advantage and was writing in circumstances when the growing threat of fascism across Europe seemed very real. The problem appeared to be the *general* threat rather than individual variations.

Finally, while Laski was trying to understand and analyse events, he was also attempting to make an impact upon them by *warning* of the dangers that lay ahead. *State* was simultaneously an academic work and a political tract which was calling for a United Front against fascism. He was urging unity because he sincerely believed that it was vital. But this purpose was not always easy to reconcile with a full theoretical analysis of the phenomenon.

One other feature of Laski's outlook in this period was indirectly related to Nazism and the United Front policy: his fuller acceptance of Marxism.

This was apparent in a number of texts written from the summer of 1933 onwards. In *State* the main thrust of the argument and much of the terminology was 'Marxist'. For example, he now talked of the relations between the economic base and the social superstructure, described the government as 'the executive committee of the class which dominates, economically', and acknowledged Engels' view of historical materialism as the basis of his analysis.[27] He did not explicitly claim that the book was 'Marxist', but, in an article celebrating the fiftieth anniversary of the Fabians, written at the same time, he clarified his position, arguing that the future of Fabianism was largely dependent upon relearning the significance of Marxism and 'its acclimatization to the British scene'.[28] After this he constantly stressed the need for the British Labour movement to adopt Marxism and eventually described himself as a 'Marxist'.

His conviction of the need to forge closer relations with the Communist Party coincided with his move towards 'Marxism', and his analysis of fascism reproduced some of the weaknesses of current Comintern theory. Yet it would be wrong to assume either that the 'Marxism was a kind of fashionable veneer applied to the timber he had long worked',[29] or that he was repeating a diluted version of Communist theory.

I argued above that some of the weaknesses in his analysis of Nazism stemmed from the fact that he had already predicted an era of 'capitalist-dictatorship' before 1933 and saw Hitlerism as confirmation of this prognosis. An exactly similar process occurred with his shift towards 'Marxism'. By the end of 1932 he had come to believe that Marxism would be shown to be valid unless capitalist democracy proved itself capable of adaptation 'at the eleventh hour'.

But the advent of Nazism, and the general spread of fascism, seemed to extinguish any remaining basis for optimism about European liberal democracy. Laski therefore now saw no rational alternative but to accept Marxism as an 'actual' rather than a 'contingent' truth. Yet he appeared to do so with ambivalence and inner doubts. There was thus a kind of reciprocal reinforcement in his political evolution. The advent of Nazism appeared to confirm his pessimism about capitalist-democracy and hastened his move towards Marxism. It also confirmed his belief that a more militant socialist policy was necessary in co-operation with the Communist Party. And such co-operation simultaneously reinforced his tendency to interpret the world through a framework of analysis that was heavily influenced by Marxism.

Nazism was therefore of crucial importance in his political evolution. It also affected his attitudes on a further question which now appeared increasingly urgent: the question of peace and war. In order to appreciate the development in his views on this issue it is necessary to examine his changing analysis of the problem over a rather longer period.

THE NATION STATE, PEACE AND WAR

As was shown in Chapter Three, Laski had experienced considerable stress between 1914 and 1918, having originally opposed the war and subsequently feeling guilty that he was unable to fight. Like so many others of his generation this had left him determined that there must never be another European war. Again, like the majority of the British Left, he had been deeply critical of the Versailles peace treaty and had normally regarded French policy as the main obstacle to conciliation during the 1920s. But he had also taken a *theoretical* stance on the issues.

Throughout the 1920s Laski had continued to view the sovereign state itself as the source of war. In *Grammar* he included a long final section, which argued that it was imperative to remove from state control all the major aspects of economic and military policy which could give rise to international conflict.[30] At the same time he saw a need for a very substantial increase in the power and functions of international institutions, and he was a committed supporter of the League of Nations. Furthermore, he took issue with legal theorists who argued that international law was not *really* 'law' because it lacked the means of enforcement. Against this, he claimed constantly and confidently, that the answer was to provide it with the relevant powers.[31] Failure to do so emanated from the ideology and power of state sovereignty, rather than from any inherent difficulty in the notion of international law. However, by 1930, with the breakdown of the facade of European stability which had existed between 1924 and 1929, he was becoming increasingly anxious about the possibility of a new war. And during the early 1930s, his general move to the Left was reflected in a gradual shift in his attitudes towards the nation-state and war.

The first stage in this process was evident in a lecture delivered to the Geneva Institution of International Relations in August 1931 – just before the fall of the Labour government. He outlined his normal views about the need to supersede the nation-state, but also stated – without any real development – that there was a relationship between capitalism and war because the expansionist drive of capitalist states was fuelled by domestic inequality.[32] These incipient tensions between his view of the nation-state on the one hand and his increasing tendency to perceive capitalism as the major source of international tension were shown more fully in a very thoughtful lecture on 'Nationalism and the Future of Civilisation' which he delivered in London in April 1932.

He began, in a manner reminiscent of John Stuart Mill, with an acknowledgement of the positive aspects of nationalism:

> In so far as we can give to each nation the power to express itself as a state it seems to me clear that we liberate a spiritual energy which . . . adds to the happiness of mankind.[33]

But he immediately differentiated between admitting 'the title of statehood to a nation' and accepting the implications of statehood as they had been understood in the last hundred years. For the interdependence of nations made it impossible to allow one nation-state finally to decide any questions in which other nation-states had a serious concern. The League of Nations must be granted, little by little, increasing authority so that the intolerable egoism of the nation state could be controlled: 'Either we must curb its excesses – which means the end of the sovereign-state – or they will destroy civilization.'[34] This again expressed his long-term position, but he now argued that capitalism led to imperialism by the very logic of its being. Capitalist states tried to avoid economic justice at home, leading to an era of economic rivalry and potential or actual conflict. However, although he now identified capitalism as one of the major obstacles to world peace, he did not believe that socialism would resolve the problems. Indeed, he claimed that it could make nationalism still more intense. The creation of a world community therefore still remained the only solution. At this point, Laski was therefore able to see the pursuit of domestic socialism and the strengthening of the League as overlapping, but separable, aims. However, this was not the end of his evolution and later in the same year he placed still more stress on the relationship between capitalism, nationalism, imperialism and war.[35]

The first signs came in a contribution for a book edited by Leonard Woolf. The entry, which Laski wrote during the summer of 1933, was so different from the pro-League emphasis of the other authors that Woolf inserted a special note on it in the introduction, pointing out that it was controversial and indeed that its conclusions would not be accepted by several of the other contributors. For although Laski still acknowledged the achievements of the League and agreed that there was no *a priori* reason why a socialist state should not embark on war, his whole emphasis was now upon capitalist-imperialism as the fundamental problem, and a far stronger Leninist influence was detectable in his explanation of the underlying processes.[36] Similarly, he now argued that the League's failure to prevent Japanese expansion into Manchuria showed that it would not be effective against the economic imperialism of major powers.[37] In theory, he argued, it might be possible to conceive of a capitalism which was both international in scope and willing to accept limitations to diminish the probability of war. In practice, however, this was shown to be unrealisable because capitalism was historically tied to the nation state and was incapable of making the necessary adjustments.[38]

> Our task, therefore . . . is to seek the transformation of capitalist society as the essential pre-requisite of an international community. . . . Such a transformation alone makes possible the abandonment of sovereignty in the form which strikes at the root of peace.[39]

It was true that socialism was not an absolute guarantee of peace, but 'economic democracy' would mean that war would no longer 'be a necessary function of the social order'. It was only once this position was reached that 'we shall be entitled to optimism about the future of mankind'.[40]

The evolution in Laski's thinking on the nation-state and war thus paralleled the shift that took place in his views on capitalist-democracy. Just as the rise of Nazism appeared to validate and reinforce his ideas about the likelihood of capitalist dictatorship, it strengthened his belief in the relationship between capitalism and war. Japanese expansion and the failure of Britain to act against it had already led him to doubt his previous faith in the League and the supercession of the sovereign state. Hitler's accession, and the increase in international tension, seemed to dispel any remaining 'illusions'. By October 1934 he therefore appeared to believe that the reconstruction of the class relations of modern capitalist society would *in itself* bring about a harmonious international order:

A society of socialist states is in a position, to which no other order of life can pretend, to consider its economic problems upon a basis of genuine mutuality and goodwill. For such a society, and no other society, can plan its life in a deliberate and coherent way. It is not oppressed by those problems of prestige which are inherent in the nature of the capitalist state because they are inherent in the class-relations of capitalism. Its interest in peace is the more direct since it is not perverted from allegiance to it by the peculiar psychology of patriotism which a capitalist society is driven to invent for its own preservation.[41]

This apparent loss of faith in the League of Nations led Philip Noel-Baker, one of its major proponents in the Labour Party, to complain that Laski:

who admits that the League is the only hope . . . spends his time sneering at it, belittling its achievements, using his immense influence and prestige to throw doubt, and indeed despair, into the minds of those who should be furnishing that driving power of public opinion without which the League cannot triumph.[42]

However, Laski's attitude to the League paralleled his view of the liberal-democratic state. In both cases, he *wanted* to believe that they embodied justice and were effective, but felt that contemporary reality negated his hopes. Nevertheless, his argument may be criticised for showing the same 'reductionist' tendency as his account of fascism. Capitalism may be a primary causal factor in war, but is there any evidence that it is the *sole* cause, as Laski was now implying? Once again, he had evolved towards this position over a comparatively long period. The evidence of imperialism, of economic conflicts between capitalist powers, of 'appeasement' of imperialist expansion when other Great Powers had no interests at stake, and of the general hostility to the Soviet Union, had all modified his previous belief that the fundamental problem was state sovereignty itself. He then found a form of Marxism the best way to interpret the processes that his earlier theory had not explained.

Yet his aversion to war and his increasing acceptance of a Marxist analysis of imperialism led him to a position with crucially important political implications. Since the capitalist state was essentially imperialist in its external activity, it could not be trusted to defend any interests other than those of capitalism. There was therefore no basis for agreement between socialists and their 'own' government in foreign policy. This would ultimately lead Laski to face a major dilemma in relation to the Nazi threat. At this stage, however, he believed that overcoming the danger of war was the vital concern, and that this involved a general socialist stance against both fascism and war. Since this was also the position of the CP it again made him a proponent of a United Front strategy.

By the autumn of 1934, Laski was therefore arguing that the major problems of the era stemmed from the continued existence of capitalism. How did this affect his attitude to the Soviet Union?

THE SOVIET UNION

Even in the 1920s, when he had equated Mussolini and Lenin as irrational architects of violence, Laski had been comparatively restrained in his criticisms of the Soviet Union. In 1924, for example, he had quarrelled with the American anarchist Emma Goldmann who had wanted him to join her in a total condemnation of the Soviet system.[43] His opposition to revolution and dictatorship *as general principles* did not mean that he was prepared to take a wholly negative stance on the Soviet system, and this position was typical of the Labour Party as a whole at this time. However, as he became more pessimistic about 'capitalist democracy', he grew more inclined to see virtues in the Soviet Union. In late 1932 he thus wrote:

Where Europe and America were sunk in pessimism, the whole temper of Russia was optimistic. The authority of its government was unchallenged; its power to win amazing response to its demands was unquestionable. Granted all its errors, no honest observer could doubt its capacity both to plan greatly and . . . to realise its plans.[44]

He acknowledged that the Soviet Union was a dictatorship, that there was little tolerance, and that a heavy price had been paid for progress. But these were comparatively mild criticisms since he was writing just after the devastation and death caused by forced collectivisation.

In the early summer of 1934 he and Frida visited the Soviet Union for the first time, for a month, at the invitation of Moscow University. While there he wrote two articles which reveal his attitudes at the time. He emphasised many negative features in the Soviet system. Those with ability would find opportunities provided that they were not hostile 'to the purposes of the dictatorship' which was 'real and omnipresent' and 'ruthless and relentless in suppressing all opinion . . . which it conceives to be hostile to its fundamental objectives'. He personally had seen nothing of the treatment of political prisoners or the kulaks, but:

Definite instances given to me, and certain general accounts, suggested that this is a very ugly aspect of the picture in which Soviet Russia has little to learn from either Hitlerite Germany or the Balkan dictatorships.[45]

The Communist Party was:

relentless, dogmatic, intolerant, too incapable of skepticism, permeated with an emotional attachement to its principles which makes it dangerously over-confident in its prognostications . . .

Its discipline was too rigid, it was too full of suspicion of its opponents' motives, it counted its ends as so vital that it was often indifferent to the means (and cost) by which the ends were to be attained, and it was far too dominated by the leadership and the 'line' which was being propounded.

He also felt that Russians were, in general, uninterested in foreign countries and that their analysis was often vitiated by dogma. This led him to conclude 'that the communist approach makes even men of first-rate ability lose most of their perspective in judging the situation abroad'.[46]

Nor did he intend to be complimentary when he claimed that 'Russian communism is as genuine a religion as any in the experience of man', and compared it with the Roman Catholic church and Cromwell's Ironsides. Finally, on the negative side, he argued that it was 'a regime of deliberate and organized repression which sweeps ruthlessly out of its path all who are unable to conform to its purposes' and that 'For the spirit which doubts, it means profound discomfort; for the spirit which denies, it means imprisonment and possibly death'.[47]

However, the criticisms were counter-balanced by positive comments. Many services were better in the Soviet Union than in the West, there was real factory democracy, more workers played an effective part in administration than elsewhere and their views influenced party policy. The administration of justice was 'generally simple, efficient, and straightforward'. The standard of living might be low in comparison with Britain or the USA, but conditions were definitely better than at any time since 1917 and the material and spiritual welfare of the masses was 'the primary and permeating objective of Soviet planning'. Therefore:

> Russia is a land of hope. The masses have no doubt that the sacrifices of today will be justified by the achievements of tomorrow. The mental climate is one of intense exhilaration, of a buoyant and optimistic faith I have never before encountered. The belief in the 'manifest destiny' of Russia, the conviction that it is succeeding in its experiment, is obviously both widespread and profound. That this makes the adventure worthwhile at least for all who have come to maturity since the revolution is, so far as my necessarily limited observation goes, quite unquestionable.[48]

Furthermore:

> the intolerance and repression characteristic of proletarian dictatorship are the symptoms of communist insecurity; they will disappear as conviction of security emerges in Russia. But for those who . . . are able to adapt themselves to the foundations of the new system there are opportunities, and therefore freedoms, comparable in volume to those of the early days of the industrial revolution. The class affected is, of course, both different and wider, and it does not depend upon its ability to procure the use of capital for its private well-being. For this reason, I believe the

claim of the bolsheviks that their form of state is a higher form than that of capitalist democracy to be well founded . . . [49]

Laski was trying to present an honest account of what he saw and he refrained from the eulogies made by the British Communist Party and its 'fellow-travellers'. It is also worth noting that he was writing before the assassination of Kirov and the new wave of repression that was unleashed at the end of the year. Nevertheless, it seems clear that he saw what he wanted to see. Perhaps this was because, as Beatrice Webb noted, the visit 'seems to have been mainly spent in being entertained and talking until two o'clock at night with different groups of the Moscow intellectuals'.[50] He was quite explicit about the repressive nature of the regime and declared that 'if I lived in Russia I should court difficulty from my sense of the need to found a Council of Civil Liberties'.[51] But the overall impression was certainly one of optimism about the general direction of Soviet development.

This more positive attitude towards the Soviet Union was in line with his United Front stance and was the obverse of his increasing pessimism about the future of liberal democracy. On his return from Moscow he was confronted with a personal crisis, which inevitably reinforced his fear that traditional liberties were now being eroded in Britain. This concerned academic freedom. But in order to understand its full implications it is necessary to consider his whole conception of his role at LSE.

LSE AND ACADEMIC FREEDOM

Laski had been deeply committed to LSE ever since returning to Britain in 1920. He regarded academic life as his primary vocation and saw no contradiction between this and his increasing involvement in politics. Indeed, as he had made clear in his inaugural professorial lecture in 1926, he believed that active participation in public affairs was an essential prerequisite for effective political analysis. Nor was he worried that his reputation for Left-wing views was in any way detrimental to this position as an academic. For he believed that impartiality was impossible and that 'the teacher's function . . . is less to avoid his bias than consciously to assert its presence and to warn his hearers against it'.[52] His position at LSE became an anchor in his life, perhaps secondary only to his relationship with Frida. It was the major focus of his work and the base for all his other activities. And at the School he remained a popular figure, particularly with younger staff and students, and was widely regarded as an inspiring teacher. However, by the early 1930s he also had many enemies, including the Director, William Beveridge.

This had not always been so. For several years after Laski's appointment their relationship had been harmonious. Indeed, Beveridge had defended Laski on at least two important occasions in the 1920s. The first was in 1923 when he rebutted protests from a group of the School's business governors about Laski's promotion to a readership. His political views, Beveridge maintained, were irrelevant and the promotion had been made on the basis of Laski's eminence as a teacher.[53] Similarly, he resisted the pressure of Sidney Webb (of all people!) who sought to prevent Laski from becoming Professor and head of department in 1926, on the grounds that he spent too much time on extra-mural activities.[54] By the late twenties, however, relations were already becoming strained. Political differences were the major factor, but these were related to wider disputes involving the university as a whole, and the nature of social science.

As Director, Beveridge wanted to increase both the status and size of the School and, from 1925, had been encouraged by the Rockefeller Trustees to look to the Foundation for research funds. This resulted in a grant of nearly £200,000 to create new Professorships and endow research in the social sciences. By the late 1920s Laski realised that this strategy had major implications which were, in his view, highly disturbing. In the first place, it threatened to reproduce the situation that he had condemned so bitterly in the United States, where external 'benefactors' exerted influence over academic life. In particular, he feared the development of a situation in which the expression of radical opinion could be curtailed in order to conciliate the sources of private finance. He therefore began attacking the power of foundations in articles which Beveridge was bound to view as a criticism of his whole approach.[55] Secondly, Laski was out of sympathy with the whole concept of research involved in the Rockefeller application. He remained a highly traditional, 'liberal' academic, who believed that scholarship involved individual thought and writing on major themes. He therefore deplored the idea of collective work on issues which private foundations believed to be 'useful' and he also attacked this idea.[56] But this raised a third element in the dispute: the concept of social science itself. Beveridge believed in a highly empirical method which would, he thought, form a bridge with natural science, and he expressed a particular interest in social biology.[57] Laski was deeply sceptical about 'scientific' approaches to politics and indulged in the kind of abstract speculation that Beveridge criticised. As Laski grew more interested in Marxist political theory, the gulf between them widened and was reinforced by other powerful forces within the School. In 1929 Lionel Robbins became Professor and Head of the Department of Economics which soon became a bastion of neo-classical doctrine. The economists were soon at loggerheads with Laski, and Beveridge was now ideologically close to them.[58] A major conflict between the two was therefore almost inevitable, particularly as the Director's mode of management was also highly autocratic. The turning point came in 1930, when Beveridge believed that Laski had made 'a rather savage speech' which turned a student dinner into a protest meeting against the School.[59] Their relationship now became increasingly frosty.

By the early 1930s, Laski was one of the major publicists of the Left in Britain through his numerous political and journalistic activities. This, combined with the rather lower profile of Tawney, had given the School an (unjustified) reputation as a centre of Left-wing activity and, as Laski had prophesied, Beveridge now found that this could adversely affect his success in attracting outside funding. This was the context for the Professorial Council's decision in 1932, that, although the School's constitution guaranteed to its teachers, 'absolute freedom in both speaking and writing':

> they should nevertheless regard it as a personal duty to preserve in such writings or speeches a proper regard for the reputation of the School as an academic centre of scientific teaching and research.[60]

However, in the same year Laski extended his popular journalistic output by contributing a regular series of political profiles in the *Daily Herald* . The 'explosion' came in 1934 when Beveridge was convinced – probably wrongly – that Laski was encouraging student protest and was interfering in a particular case where Left-wing activists were due to appear before a disciplinary panel.[61] The Director therefore wrote to him, stating that his utterances might be harming the School. In a subsequent interview, Beveridge also drew attention to Laski's *Daily Herald* articles, arguing that these might be incompatible with his position as a full-time Professor, and stressing that a lower rate of pay was reserved for those with substantial external earnings.[62] He also insisted that 'the School and your subject are worth your undivided allegiance'.[63] Laski agreed that all this should be considered by the School's Emergency Committee, but was devastated by the attack. He consulted Sidney Webb (an ironic choice!), who cautioned him not to exaggerate his differences with Beveridge who had not, so far, been 'out of order'.[64] Laski then submitted a long letter to the Chair of the Governors demonstrating the enormous extent of his academic activity in teaching and research both in the School and internationally.

However, he offered to discontinue his *Herald* articles if the Governors disagreed with his view that they enhanced the reputation of LSE as a place in which unorthodox views might be freely expressed. Before the Emergency Committee had met to consider the matter, a storm broke over Laski's Moscow lectures.

This began in the *Daily Telegraph* on 6 July. The Moscow correspondent provided his own summary of Laski's lecture under the heading 'The Hope of Revolution in Britain', and the leading article reinforced the attack. Both acknowledged that Laski had stated that there was little prospect of revolution in the immediate future, but the leading article implied that he was disappointed about this. It concluded:

> Mr Laski was wise to discourage extravagant hopes at Moscow. . . . But it is none the less an outrage on British public opinion that a Professor of London University should parade his pestilential programme for producing strife or civil war in England for the delectation of a Communist Academy in Moscow.[65]

Laski replied on 10 July. His lectures, he claimed, had been delivered under the auspices of the Institute of Soviet Law, not the Communist Academy. They had been an academic discussion of the development and future of parliamentary government, evaluating its present crisis and possible future and, in the third lecture, he had explicitly argued that the communist method was inapplicable to the current British situation. All his quotations had been taken out of context with the exception of a phrase that he had used about the 'gentleman of England' adapting the constitutional conventions in indefensible ways to preserve their privileges. Finally, he insisted that his lectures had been a version of his *Democracy in Crisis*, which had been followed on each occasion by a fierce communist attack for their defence of social democracy. The *Telegraph's* comment was therefore based on a misunderstanding of their real substance.[66]

The restrained tone of Laski's letter suggests that he knew that this was only the beginning of the furore. The next day the matter was raised in Parliament by some Conservative MPs who suggested that he ought not to have been issued with a passport, or that the government should reduce its funding of LSE. Attlee and Cripps jumped to Laski's defence but Duff-Cooper, for the government, simply stated that the University of London made its grant allocations on the advice of the University Grants Committee (UGC) and that it did 'not seem necessary to take any action'.[67] This could be taken as a veiled suggestion that London University should *itself* decide to reduce its funding, and was followed the next day by a letter to the 'quality' daily papers from the Vice Chancellor and Principal Officer of London University. This extraordinary intervention stated:

it would clearly be improper at this stage, before the facts have been precisely ascertained, for the University to express an opinion on Professor Laski's action, which will doubtless form the subject of an enquiry by the appropriate body.

We feel it our duty, however, to make plain immediately that, if Professor Laski's statements have been correctly reported, the University can accept no responsibility for personal expressions of opinion by any of its professors, and such expressions of opinion should not be taken as representing in any way the views of any responsible person connected with the University.[68]

This raised the temperature and five of Laski's colleagues immediately wrote to the *Times* defending the principle of academic freedom. The *New Statesman* struck a similar note and the *Manchester Guardian* warned the chiefs of London University that Laski would 'find himself supported by a large body of opinion drawn from all parties' if there was an attempt to muzzle professors.[69] But the next day the MP for London University went still further in a letter to the *Daily Telegraph*. Laski, he asserted, ought to be disciplined by the LSE governors, but they probably would not do so since the School had long been regarded as a 'hotbed of Communist teaching'. As the government could not take action unless a revolutionary teacher actually broke the law, he encouraged the Court of the University to do so by reducing its allocation to LSE.[70]

Beveridge was not responsible for the escalation of the attacks, but the pressure on LSE no doubt reinforced his view that Laski's activities endangered the future of the School. It is also safe to

assume that the Vice-Chancellor of the University was well aware
that the Emergency Committee at LSE was already scheduled to
discuss the 'Red Professor's' position. It was therefore almost inevitable that some action would be taken against him to demonstrate the
School's 'reliability'. However, it was also evident that the appearance of victimisation could transform the affair into a *cause célèbre*
with far-reaching repercussions. On 19 July the Committee therefore
decided that Laski's work for the *Daily Herald* was a breach of its
rules on professorial salaries, and that 'the development of public
opinion concerning Professor Laski's recent more popular utterances' was 'against the best interests of the School'.[71] As a result,
Laski agreed to end his regular articles and to limit his extra-
curricular political activities.[72]

On one level, Laski was justified in his claim to a friend that he
had 'won' the dispute and that his defiant attitude would make it
harder for the university authorities to take action against the next
'offender'.[73] For he had already agreed to stop writing the articles for
the *Herald* and the committee held that it was the 'development of
public opinion' rather than the 'utterances' themselves which threatened the interests of the School. And although Laski did not limit his
subsequent political activities, Beveridge felt unable to take further
action against him, and the Director's own position grew increasingly weak until his resignation in 1937. However, this was a pyrrhic
victory for Laski.

In the first place, it alienated him from LSE to which he felt that he
had devoted himself for fourteen years.[74] Until Carr-Saunders took
over as Director almost three years later he was therefore unhappy
at the School. Given its central importance in his life this must have
been a shattering experience for him. Secondly, despite his claims of
'victory', the episode obviously made him feel more cautious and
constrained. He believed that the first round of the conflict had
ended in his favour, but that this was certainly not the end of the
affair.[75] Thirdly, and of the greatest importance, it led him to fear for
the future of academic freedom.

For Laski, the meaning of the conflict had been quite clear: there
had been an attempt to limit or curtail the expression of Left-wing
views, while liberal or Right-wing opinions could be voiced with
complete impunity. Naturally, he believed that Beveridge had been
a 'swine',[76] but he was, in some ways, still more disturbed by the
attitude of many of his colleagues, particularly the economists. Overall, he doubted 'if we had more than a bare majority in favour of

academic freedom', while the governors' 'only real concern was endowments'.[77] He acknowledged the support of most of the lawyers and was obviously gratified by the attitude of academics outside LSE, such as Keynes, who had written a very powerful letter in his defence in the *New Statesman*.[78] But, in general, he was very disappointed by the way in which so many academics 'fell down completely' on the issue.[79] He was therefore upset in a personal sense, but also thought that there was far more at stake than his position as an individual.

Only a month before his conflict with Beveridge had erupted he had published an impassioned article on 'Freedom in Danger'. In this he had argued that the growing insecurity of the governing class meant that authorities were threatening 'to trample upon the claims of freedom' all over the world.[80] It was, he argued, possible to act in a positive way by helping German academic refugees:

> If we made up our minds that none of these teachers should lose by the tyranny to which they have been subjected, we should strike a dramatic blow for freedom which would resound all over the world. If we took action now publicly to proclaim that any teacher who was dismissed on the ground of race or color or opinion would be given the chance of continuing elsewhere in his vocation we should rapidly end the insolence of dictatorship in this sphere.[81]

It was surely inevitable that he would see some parallels between his own position and that of the German academics. This did not mean that he viewed his situation as comparable with their dire position. But his experience must have reinforced his general fears about the erosion of freedom in liberal-democracy. Nor was he alone in this. Keynes's forceful letter in the *New Statesman* put the case in the international context and argued that such episodes, coupled with developments such as the Government's Sedition Bill, emphasised 'the extraordinary importance of preserving <u>as a matter of principle</u> every jot and tittle of the civil and political liberties which former generations painfully secured.'[82] Mary Stocks, in a letter to the *Manchester Guardian*, was even more pointed in drawing an analogy between the action of the Vice Chancellor and Principal of London University and their counterparts in Germany who had participated in the Nazi purge of academics.[83]

Laski was gratified by the support.[84] But there was a final point of comparison, which none of his defenders mentioned, but that Laski himself could hardly have missed: anti-semitism. This surely was the implication of the *Daily Telegraph's* comment:

> The ordinary, decent Englishman would blush to talk thus in a foreign capital, but Mr Laski is a *cosmopolitan* Socialist.[85] [my emphasis]

And one of the MPs who raised the matter in Parliament was still more explicit:

> Is it not a fact that Professor Laski is *an avowed Communist as well as of alien origin* ?[86] [my emphasis]

In such circumstances the threat to his position as an academic must have reinforced his pessimism about the future of liberal democracy and, almost certainly, depressed him deeply. One piece of circumstantial evidence for this lies in the fact that, for the only time in their whole correspondence, he failed to write to Holmes for nine months. Since the old man had told him in November 1931 that Laski's letters were 'one of the greatest pleasures of my waning life', and since Laski normally conscientiously continued to write without receiving any replies, it is safe to assume that he felt very unhappy in this period.[87] The crisis at LSE was almost certainly a major contributory factor, which reinforced his general pessimism about liberal-democracy in the fascist era.

Yet if the advent of Nazism, the fear of war, and his personal experiences all led him towards Marxism, there was one countervailing force: the revitalisation of American democracy.

ROOSEVELT AND THE NEW DEAL

In 1932, when unemployment had mounted to thirteen million, Laski had been gloomy about the prospects for democracy in the United States. Nor was his attitude immediately transformed by Roosevelt's election victory in November of that year. Like many others, he had not discerned any bold or clear strategy in the new President's campaign. He thus told Holmes:

> I have a sense of relief at Hoover's defeat; but though I greatly like Frank Roosevelt, I am not able to feel enthusiasm at his victory. I

thought he fought a second-rate campaign, evasive and timid; and I am no admirer of most of the people on whose advice he is going to depend. . . . I shall watch with enormous interest; but I suspect that this in fact a pill to cure an earthquake.[88]

His public reaction was equally cautious. Roosevelt, he told Labour Party members, had many likeable qualities, but 'no-one would . . . describe him as a bold and enterprising man, nor one gifted with any special vision'.[89] True, he was 'teachable' and anxious to make a big reputation for statesmanship, but he was not as determined as Woodrow Wilson and he was surrounded by rich men, with a typical business outlook. His domestic programme would therefore 'not contain very much that an average Tory Government in this country might not pass without discomfort', and his victory gave little ground for any new optimism in world affairs.[90]

Yet even before the election he had acknowledged that Roosevelt had at least 'recognised the existence of the common man'[91], and a few months after his assumption of power, he sounded more optimistic about his aims.[92] His admiration grew as he watched the President's determination to implement radical reform during the first 'hundred days'. In August 1933 he told Frankfurter:

> We follow your 'revolution' with absorbed interest. From here it looks like touch and go. I can't pretend to more than the sympathy of half understanding. It looks to me as though F. R. still underestimates the opposition which will organise against him at the first opportunity. But without the feel of your opinion I can only guess in a darkness. At least he has energy and courage. . . .[93]

Laski's knowledge of the United States, and his friendship with Frankfurter and other supporters of the new President, immediately gave him a quite different attitude to the New Deal from the majority of the British Left. Whereas the Communist Party saw the New Deal as a form of fascism – a view which was shared by many members of the Socialist League – Laski always saw it as a positive move. The strengthening of the Executive, which Roosevelt had asked for in his inaugural speech, did not worry him because it was exactly what he advocated for the Labour Party. By the beginning of 1934 he was thus coupling Roosevelt's United States and Stalin's Russia as 'the only two countries in the world where something is being done about which men are entitled to hope'.[94] He now also sought to convince both the British and American Left that the New Deal must be supported. Roosevelt, he argued:

> is the first statesman in a great capitalist society who has sought deliberately and systematically to use the power of the State to subordinate the primary assumptions of that society to certain vital purposes. He is the first statesman deliberately to experiment on a wholesale scale with the limitation of the profit-making motive. He is the first statesman, again in a wholesale way, to attack not the secondary, but the primary, manifestations of the doctrine of laissez-faire. He is the first statesman who, of his own volition, and without coercion, either direct or indirect, has placed in the hands of organised labour a weapon which, if it be used successfully, is bound to result in a vital readjustment of the relative bargaining-power of Capital and Labour. He is the first statesman also who, the taxing-power apart, has sought to use the political authority of the State to compel over the whole area of economic effort, a significant readjustment of the national income.[95]

This enthusiasm did not mean that he was necessarily optimistic about Roosevelt's ultimate success, or that he exaggerated the degree of radicalism of the programme. Conservative and financial forces would, he argued, do their utmost to sabotage the New Deal which was in any case quite inadequate from a socialist perspective. But it was experimental, imaginative, and convinced the ordinary person that it really offered a 'new deal'. Moreover, it was the last chance, for if Roosevelt failed seriously:

> the next epoch in America will be an iron age of industrial feudalism. Out of his failure will emerge all the forces which have made the Italy of Mussolini and the Germany of Hitler the ugly things that they are.[96]

In fact, Laski remained fairly pessimistic about Roosevelt's likelihood of success throughout 1934. This judgment was quite realistic, since the early recovery which had reduced unemployment by 2,000,000 and had raised national income by 25 per cent, had given way to a static phase. Moreover, Roosevelt was now faced with challenges from Right-wing demagogues, an upsurge in labour discontent, and business fears of increased regulations. Laski thus told Holmes in December that Felix:

> appears to retain deep faith in the New Deal – more, I imagine, than I can permit myself. But he can't outdo me in admiration for Roosevelt as a person even though I don't believe he can succeed. . . . Even at this distance one has a sense of something big being tried; and the superiority of effort to our policy of do-nothingism is immeasureable.[97]

Laski's admiration is easy to understand if his fundamental attachment to liberal values is recalled. For, despite his pessimism about the future of capitalist-democracy, and his increasingly Marxist-inspired analysis, he still *wanted*, more than anything else, to believe in the possibility of peaceful, constitutional transformation. He was therefore not only thinking of the USA when he considered the meaning of the New Deal. As he said of Roosevelt a little later:

> if he is able to make his policy work, there will be a revival of progressivism all over the world. He can dispel the disillusion which is the psychological rampart of fascism, and is the main reason why the average elector, with insecurity about him everywhere, shows so profound a fear of drastic reconstruction. If Mr Roosevelt fails. . . . I do not think anyone can preserve social peace in Europe in the next generation . . . We have seen the Russian way to . . . liberation; it is bloody, it is brutal, but it is unquestionably effective. Mr Roosevelt seems to me the one statesman whose people are, differently from ourselves, still experimental enough to be willing to take the risks an alternative route implies. If he has the big vision to embark upon this adventure, he may change the face of the world by the forces he will unleash.[98]

Laski's support for the New Deal thus emanated from his view that it represented the real 'third way' to which he was committed. If it succeeded, fascism could be avoided without the violence and repression that he associated with communism. It was this 'message' – rather than the details of the programme – which was so resonant for Laski and led him to feel such a strong emotional indentification with Roosevelt's project.

LASKI'S AMBIVALENCE

Once the many strands of Laski's thought and experiences are examined, it is easy to understand the apparent contradictions in his position. He was pessimistic about the future of capitalist democracy, saw an increasing danger of war, and tended to rely on a form of Marxism as his basic framework of analysis. All this led him towards a more positive evaluation of the Soviet Union and support for a United Front against fascism and war. But part of his mind simultaneously recoiled from communism because of his enduring liberal values of freedom, constitutionalism and tolerance, and he remained opposed to violent revolution. A few years later, when he explained why he was a 'Marxist', he thus declared 'What I have seen at first hand, no less than what I have read, *has left me no alternative* '.[99] [my emphasis] The implication was that he would have preferred an alternative, and in 1934 his inner debate between liberalism and Marxism was manifested in the pages of *State* .[100] For this reason he desperately wanted the New Deal to succeed. Yet he did not think it would do so because capitalist forces would ultimately refuse to accept their own erosion. He thus rejected communism because of its denial of liberalism, and remained pessimistic about the New Deal because he interpreted it in Marxist terms and believed that controlled capitalism was, in the long run, 'a contradiction in terms'.[101]

He was obviously searching for a viable synthesis through 'revolution by consent'.[102] But he had not yet managed to define the way to this goal and thus vacillated uncomfortably between liberal democracy and Marxism. This was to cause him a series of dilemmas as he tried to define his policy positions as the war approached.

9

Dilemmas of an Anti-Fascist (1935–9)

The second half of the decade began with an event which caused Laski great sadness, although it was hardly unexpected: the death of Holmes. He had not seen the old man since April 1933 and was about to visit him again when he heard the news. The Judge had long ceased to influence Laski and had not been able to write to him for over two years. Yet Laski's respect and affection for him never waned. Perhaps this was partly because his obvious importance to the old man, who was so highly regarded, also helped maintain his own self-esteem. In 1931, for example, he had attended his ninetieth birthday celebration when both the President and Chief Justice had broadcast special messages. Laski had reported to Frida:

> While they spoke the tears rolled down the old man's cheeks and he said to me 'to have you here for this day is the completion of my happiness'. He said just a few words at the end so strongly and so bravely that it was difficult not to cry. Then I left him with the pledge to come back . . . Dearest he was really majestic.[1]

He knew that Holmes was devoted to him and for Laski, who craved affection, this was extremely important. He was not therefore exaggerating when he told Frankfurter that, with Holmes's death, he felt that he had lost a limb: 'I loved him and . . . he is a big part of the things in life that make me care for its continuance'.[2] It is also possible that his letters to Holmes had a therapeutic function for Laski himself: his attempt to maintain the old man's spirits by concentrating on the brighter side of life may have helped to maintain some optimism himself. If so, this was an outlet which he desperately needed during the 1940s.

In other respects, Laski's personal life settled down once more as the crisis at LSE receded. Frida was now flourishing as a Labour Councillor in Fulham, where she became a member of the Public Health, Maternity, Child Welfare and Library Committees (sub-

179

sequently becoming Chair of the latter two and Vice-Chair of the Housing Committee).[3] For years she had subordinated her career to his, and had concentrated more on the home. Although he also became an Alderman on the Council, where he remained until 1945, she played a more prominent role. She took a lead in public health provision, concentrating particularly on the establishment of birth control clinics and the reorganisation of the maternity service. He seems to have been proud of her achievements and to have welcomed her sense of fulfilment, even telling Frankfurter: 'She really makes me feel damned humble. I do the talking, and she does the doing.'[4]

Diana was now a young woman. She was lively, and enjoyed reading, but was not particularly academic.[5] Laski had made a terrible mistake in encouraging her to attend LSE. It would, he had said, 'be thrilling . . . to have her at the School . . . and talk over her lectures in the evening'.[6] This would no doubt have been a bad idea for Diana at any time, but as she was actually there when her father was in the midst of his crisis, it must have been disastrous. She failed the exams at the end of the year and left the School.[7] Fortunately, she was subsequently accepted at Lady Margaret Hall College, Oxford, where she read History. She was happy there and met her future husband, Robin Mathewson. After graduating in 1938, they spent a year in Cambridge, Massachusetts (he at Harvard, she at Radcliffe College) where they married.

Since the family was extremely close, Frida and Harold naturally missed Diana once she left home in 1935 to go to Oxford. But at the same time they bought a country cottage in Little Bardfield, Essex. This was to be a haven for both of them, and he subsequently did most of his writing there, safely shielded from the hoards of visitors in their London house. Another cause for contentment came in 1937 with Beveridge's replacement by Carr-Saunders as Director of LSE. Laski saw him as a 'trump' and his faith in the School was restored: indeed he described it as an 'idyll'.[8]

Yet if Laski remained happy at home and was again fulfilled in his academic life, any implication of tranquillity would be wholly misleading. He often worked fifteen or sixteen hours a day and, like most of his generation, he was preoccupied with the international crises and the sense of an inexorable movement towards war. But, like many others, this also forced him to consider the position that he had reached by the end of 1934. In particular, was the United Front against fascism and war the main priority? Or were there circumstances when it was necessary to support a capitalist state against a greater evil? Laski was confronted by some difficult dilemmas which ultimately forced him to make choices which departed from the stance that he had held in 1934. This chapter examines the way in which his assumptions were tested by the pressure of events. It begins by considering his attitude to the USA, before examining the complexities that he faced in Europe.

LASKI AND ROOSEVELT

In March 1935 Laski left for a four-week visit to the USA. His first impressions were unfavourable. He felt that there was a lack of confidence, a sense of drift, and that the rich were completely un-reconciled to the New Deal. He also detected an immense amount of latent fascism and anti-semitism, and feared the influence of extreme Right populists on the lower middle classes. He therefore found Frankfurter's defence of Roosevelt 'attractive but unconvincing'.[9] He was obviously looking for some evidence of the positive impact of the New Deal and, at first, was clearly disappointed. However, this was to change when he met Roosevelt in person.

Before coming to the USA, Laski had told Frankfurter that he would, if possible, like an hour with the President.[10] Frankfurter had told Roosevelt that he would find Laski delightful, stimulating and informative on the European, and particularly the English, situation. The President replied that he wanted 'very much to see Laski'.[11] The meeting was arranged for 24 April and was obviously a success. Laski, who had first met Roosevelt during his years at Harvard, was now deeply impressed by his determination and warmed to him personally. The 'chemistry' between the two clearly worked, for Laski was to see the President again in April 1936, April and October 1938 and May 1939, and to write to him (and receive friendly replies) far more frequently. When he left the United States shortly after their first meeting, Laski's doubts about the New Deal had been allayed and he was ready to help it through favourable publicity in both the USA and Britain. In return, he hoped to be able to influence the President.

Between 1935 and the outbreak of the War Laski promoted the New Deal in his academic, journalistic, and political roles. When the Supreme Court tried to thwart Roosevelt's reforms, he likened its opposition to fascism and suggested tactics which might be the most effective in preparing American opinion for constitutional changes.[12] When the Republicans sought to undermine the basis for state intervention by invoking laissez-faire, he tried to persuade them that they needed to formulate a rational conservative opposition, which actually implied acceptance of the main features of Roosevelt's strategy.[13] But Laski's most important attempt to help the President through favourable publicity came in his book, *The American Presidency*.

This began with a letter in which Laski asked Roosevelt if he might dedicate a book to him on the subject of the Presidency – based on six lectures he was to give at the University of Indiana.[14] Roosevelt replied that he would be 'honoured and happy' with such a dedication, and Laski finished the book just before the war. He then informed Roosevelt:

> I have written a book on the Presidency which, maintaining all the proper spirit of what the professors call 'objectivity' will, I hope, make your enemies furiously angry. Few things are more pleasant than to write a book in the guise of a scientific treatise.[15]

He was right to poke fun at the book's 'scientific' pretensions for it was, in effect, a defence of Roosevelt's Presidency. Its essential argument was that the constitution of the United States had been based on weak government in an era of laissez-faire, but that the society was now in the same kind of capitalist crisis experienced in Europe. In this situation, strong government was necessary. The only way to deal with the crisis was through purposeful leadership, and the sole focus for this lay in the Presidency. It was therefore necessary to strengthen this institution through granting a third term, allowing it greater scope in foreign policy, and ensuring that it maintained sufficient autonomy vis-a-vis the Cabinet, both houses of Congress, and the Supreme Court. Roosevelt would not have agreed with all Laski's arguments, but the overall impact of the work was just what Laski had intended – a defence of the current Presidency. Indeed Eleanor Roosevelt reviewed it during the war, claiming that Laski had identified the key problems, and that the book would be useful for future Presidents.[16]

Purists might criticise him for producing an 'apologia' in the form of a scholarly work, but he was undoubtedly sincere in his evaluation. Numerous private letters to Frankfurter and others demonstrate his real admiration for Roosevelt and the New Deal –

particularly after the Supreme Court attempted to limit its scope.[17] Moreover, despite his general attempt to 'promote' the New Deal, he also sometimes publicly criticised Roosevelt. In a major academic article, written in 1938, he thus pointed to the President's lack of any considered or systematic philosophy, and his failure to understand that the problems lay in the system itself rather than in evil men or excesses. He also condemned the manner in which he had tried to defeat the Court by side-stepping it. Nor did he disguise the fact that he regarded him as essentially 'conservative'. However, he also elucidated the reasons for offering him support:

Since 1933, we have mostly been accustomed to a democracy seemingly in slow process of grim erosion; it has been uncertain of itself, unable, accordingly, to seize its opportunities, bewildered about its values, and slow to meet its emergencies. The America of Roosevelt has offered a heartening contrast. No one, I think, could reasonably say that it has fully met, much less overcome, any of its central problems. No one either could reasonably deny that its approach to them has been affirmative and not negative in character. In five breathless years, it has lived the intensity of a generation. Men have had the sense that something was being done. They have been given the exhilaration of hope. They have been shown that a people can, if it is adequately led, move swiftly to action without losing the democratic right to be master of its own destiny. The American remains a citizen capable of deliberately willing change; he has not, as in Fascist countries, become the inert recipient of orders that he must obey without scrutiny under sanction of the concentration-camp. If our age emerges successfully from this period of blood and iron, I believe that the Roosevelt experiment . . . with all its blunders and follies, will be regarded by the historian as having made a supreme contribution to the service of freedom. For it will have shown, in that event, that the principle of responsible and democratic self-government has still enough vitality left to persuade men to die and, even more, to live for the fulfilment of its objectives.[18]

Given the stakes he believed to be involved, and the sincerity of his support for Roosevelt, it is perhaps not surprising that Laski was prepared to provide an academic gloss to works of propaganda. And, of course, he now believed that strong government was a general necessity if democracy were to survive.

If Laski tried to promote support for Roosevelt, how did he try to influence him in return? He constantly urged him to adopt a bold approach in confronting conservative forces in the United States. As he wrote in May 1939:

> Please keep your courage and your belief in the big things. You cannot appease your enemies. I want your administration to end with the grand gesture that makes the historian say 'He ended even more splendidly than he began.'[19]

But he also hoped to persuade him to exert pressure against British foreign and defence policies.[20] In other words, he not only *contrasted* the progressive role of the New Deal with the reactionary policies of the National government, but consciously sought to use Roosevelt as a force against his own rulers.

It is unclear whether he actually exerted any influence over Roosevelt. The President's replies to his letters were normally friendly, but relatively non-committal, and it is inherently improbable that a British Left-wing intellectual would have played any significant role in Presidential decision-making. On the other hand, Roosevelt may well have thought Laski's power base in Britain was stronger than it was in reality – a belief that Laski no doubt encouraged. And he was the intimate friend of Frankfurter, who certainly had some influence over Roosevelt – particularly once the Supreme Court issue became so important.[21] He also knew many of the other 'New Dealers', who had advised Roosevelt.[22] Roosevelt quoted Laski's views with approval in government circles and some of his advisers believed that he took Laski's views seriously.[23] For example, he was approached at least twice to write to the President to suggest Frankfurter's nomination to the Supreme Court on the grounds that a supportive letter could be influential.[24] Laski resisted such requests on the grounds that intervention by a foreigner might do more harm than good. This was a wise decision, since Frankfurter's opponents cited his friendship with Laski in the attempt to prevent ratification of his appointment to the Supreme Court in January 1939.[25] In general, Roosevelt probably saw Laski as someone whose views were worthy of consideration and who was a useful conduit for attracting foreign and domestic support for his own administration.

Laski may have overestimated his influence in Washington, but he was generally satisfied with his role there. His positive attitude to Roosevelt remained highly significant in restoring his faith in liberal democracy. And acceptance by the President and 'New Dealers' was obviously very important to him psychologically. It was during the latter part of the 1930s that the United States really became his 'second home'. He returned increasingly often, culminating in a sabbatical year at the University of Washington in Seattle in 1938–9. Important though it was to him, however, it remained a 'sideshow' – the one relatively unproblematic aspect of his thought and action. He certainly believed that, both by example and concrete policies, Roosevelt's fight in America kept alive 'the dream of what still may be in Europe'.[26] But his real preoccupations and dilemmas were nearer home. It is these that must now be considered.

THE UNITED FRONT

The position of Laski and other proponents of co-operation with Communist Parties was facilitated by the seventh and last Comintern Congress in the summer of 1935. Following Dimitrov's definition of the new line, the CP now adopted the policy of a Popular Front for the defence of liberal democracy more wholeheartedly and softened its attacks on social democracy. Since Laski and the CP took a broadly similar stance in identifying capitalism as the main force behind fascism and war, there appeared to be few problems in co-operation. Nor did it seem necessary to differentiate between domestic and foreign policy as the National Government was identified as the main immediate problem in both spheres.

1935 was an important year in the history of 'appeasement'. In April the so-called 'Stresa front' of Britain, Italy and France was formed in the wake of Hitler's open violation of the military restrictions of the Treaty of Versailles. However, the apparent unity was immediately shattered by two events: the British government's separate naval agreement with Germany, and Mussolini's invasion of Abyssinia. The year then ended with the British government solemnly protesting its faith in 'collective security' on the eve of a General Election, while planning a deal which effectively acquiesced in Mussolini's victory as soon as it was re-elected (the so-called 'Hoare-Laval' pact). Laski's view of these events gives an insight into his general interpretative framework at the time. He was bitterly critical of the appeasement of both Hitler and Mussolini. The Anglo-German Naval Agreement was, he argued:

symptomatic of a profound pro-Hitler movement among the elect here; and its basis, in my belief, is a desire at all costs to come to terms with Hitler in the West on the assumption that if he chooses Eastern ambitions that is not our concern.[27]

Similarly, he was appalled by the government's handling of the Abyssinian crisis, although he had predicted the 'sell-out' before the election:

At present it is very 1914 – Abyssinia = Belgium, the League = sacred treaties and so on. They have still to learn that this govt and France do not really mean sanctions in any effective sense. . . . I predict that at the end the League will . . . virtually give Abyssinia to Mussolini and reserve the film-rights for the Emperor.[28]

He believed that Mussolini could be stopped by effective sanctions, but that Britain and France had never been serious.[29]

However, he was equally adamantly opposed to rearmament. He took this stance for two reasons: first, because the National Government was an imperialist force, which would only fight for capitalist interests, and secondly because an arms race would eventually lead to war.[30] He was so certain of this that he wrote to Roosevelt in November 1935 to ask him to pressurise the British government into reducing naval armaments, presumably in the hope that Hitler would also be forced to accept a new agreement.[31]

All this was in line with the general view that a United Front campaign against the National Government could simultaneously preserve the peace and defeat fascism. Early in 1936 he took two important steps in this direction.

The first was to respond favourably to the CP's request to affiliate to the Labour Party. The proposal was made immediately after the 1935 General Election, and was supported by the Socialist League. Laski had long admired communist zeal, but had previously been highly critical of the Party's centralised control and frequent changes of line.

Yet he was so anxious for unity that he now argued that it was morally obligatory for the Labour Party to enter discussions with the CP to see whether an adequate common basis of action could be found. He maintained that the communists had been guilty of grave and indefensible errors in the past and that there were considerable remaining differences between the two parties, but claimed that discussion might contribute to the adoption of a coherent philosophy by the Labour Party.[32]

The second important step was his acceptance of an invitation by Victor Gollancz to join John Strachey and himself in establishing the Left Book Club. Gollancz had been a contemporary of Laski's at New College before the First World War where they had campaigned together on the suffrage issue. By now a successful publisher, he was desperately preoccupied by the threats of fascism and war and envisaged the Club as a popular front campaigning organisation.[33] Strachey was probably the most brilliant populariser of Left-wing ideas in the era and, at this stage, was effectively a communist.[34]

The Left Book Club, which was launched in May 1936, was to become the most important Popular Front organisation in Britain, ultimately achieving a membership of 57,000, with 1500 study groups. Its local meetings and major rallies were often far more successful than those of the Labour Party, and its monthly newsletter and books played an important role in influencing the movement of opinion on the Left. But despite its appearance of independence, and Gollancz's frequent protestations that he and Laski were both members of the Labour Party, the Left Book Club was largely controlled by the CP. Strachey was prepared to defer to the CP leadership, and Gollancz consciously strengthened the relationship between the Club and the Party. As will be shown below, Laski was probably unaware of the extent of the CP's role, and sometimes struck a note of independence. Nevertheless, his association with the Club indicated the strength of his support for the United Front and reinforced his commitment to its positions on defence and foreign policy.

Two months after the launching of the Left Book Club his sense of urgency about the need for Left-wing unity was heightened by a further critical event: the outbreak of the Spanish Civil War. For Laski, as for the Left as a whole, this was to symbolise the struggle of the decade. He saw the government's policy of 'non-intervention' as a cynical ploy which would aid Franco, and he was appalled by the decision of the 1936 Labour Party Conference to support the strategy.[35] This decision was of pivotal importance in leading him, with others, including Cripps and Aneurin Bevan, to take another decisive step in the development of the Popular Front campaign. Immediately after the Conference, plans were discussed for launching a new Left-wing weekly (*Tribune*), and a 'unity manifesto' on behalf of the Socialist League, the ILP and the CP.

The manifesto was issued to the press in the names of the two parties and the Socialist League on 18 January. It declared that the unity campaign was 'for action, for attack, for the ending of retreat, for the building of the strength, unity and power of the working-class movement'. It stood for 'unity of all sections of the working-class movement . . . in the struggle against fascism, reaction and war, and against the National government . . . in the struggle for immediate demands, and the return of a Labour Government as the next stage in the advance to working-class power'. The manifesto also proclaimed that the movement should not wait for General Elections, but should win organised support for thirteen immediate social and economic demands.[36] It also proclaimed:

> the fight for peace demands unbending hostility to a National Government that can in no circumstances be trusted to use armaments in the interests of the working class, of the peoples, or of peace.[37]

As soon as the manifesto was published, various well-known figures on the Left, including Laski, Brailsford, Cole, Bevan and Strachey, added their names to it.

The campaign itself opened with a vast meeting in Manchester on 24 January and a series of rallies were organised throughout the country on a scale which surpassed anything that had been witnessed for years. The National Executive of the Labour Party responded on 27 January with a demand that its members should withhold support from all 'organisations which are clearly formed to pursue "United Front" or "Popular Front" activities', and disaffiliated the Socialist League. It was therefore quite clear that continuation with United Front activity carried the risk of expulsion.

Laski had anticipated this threat, having told Frankfurter on 20th January:

> I shall be sorry to be thrown out. But I certainly can no more allow the party to control my political affiliations (when the right wing goes its own way) than I can allow the university to control my ideas. So that is that.[38]

He now denounced the NEC's action in *Tribune*, ending with a call on fellow members of the Labour Party to 'see to it that our faith in Socialism is not made a ground for our expulsion'.[39] The article contained forceful arguments, but was also disingenuous in insisting that he had had not been 'a party to the negotiations which preceded' the Unity Manifesto and had simply added his signature after learning 'of its contents from the daily press in the same way as millions of other citizens'.[40] It may be true that he had not been involved in the actual negotiations, but he probably had a good idea of the likely outcome.

He also participated, with G. D. H. Cole, in the CP's *Labour Monthly* conference in February 1937. His speech was defiant. He was, he proclaimed, prepared to stand on the same platform with any 'member of a working-class party who is ready to fight against the twin threats of war and fascism'.[41] He asked the conference to accept the principle that the philosophy of the British Labour movement must be built upon full acceptance of Marxist philosophy, and declared the need for opposition to the rearmament programme of the National government. The defence of democracy and socialism with a Popular Front government, in alliance with the Soviet Union would, he argued, be justified:

But is there anyone here who believes that this is the purpose for which the Baldwin Government rearms? Is there anyone here who believes that this purpose is compatible with the logic of class-interests upon which it is built? Is it not likely, rather, that this Government will take us into a shambles worse than 1914? Cannot we learn the lesson of the last war which Lenin so clearly drew?

He coupled this with some criticisms of the CP's past role and current psychology, but insisted that overall, 'in the policy to-day of Pollitt, of Dutt, of Dimitrov, there is a large common ground it is our business jointly to occupy'.[42]

On the surface, he appeared to maintain this position for the rest of the year. When, in March, the NEC formally proscribed membership of the Socialist League, he told Frida that he and his associates 'must grin and bear it' if they were thrown out of the Party.[43] And in July he condemned the Parliamentary Labour Party's decision to abstain on the defence estimates, rather than to oppose them as it had in previous years.[44] He thus continued to sound like an intransigent opponent of the leadership and now took one more significant step on behalf of the United Front campaign.

At its spring conference, the Socialist League had decided to disband itself rather than risk mass expulsions from the Labour Party. However, the campaign for unity continued and Laski, with the three Left-labour MPs, Cripps, D. N. Pritt, and Ellen Wilkinson, now stood for the NEC on the basis of the policies of the Unity Manifesto. As Laski anticipated, the annual conference in October rejected their proposals. Nevertheless, the unity candidates were elected – perhaps because delegates hoped that they would bring some of their dynamism to the Party. Laski was now in the rare position of being a non-MP elected to the NEC – where he would remain for twelve years.

DOUBTS AND TENSIONS

Once elected to the NEC, he immediately devoted himself to a Spanish campaign, and spoke to packed meetings in various parts of the country. But although this was an issue on which the Left of the Party had always played the major role, it was no longer so divisive as previously, for the 1937 Conference had finally rejected the policy of non-intervention. It was therefore a subject on which the Party as a whole could mobilise support against the government. This did not mean that Laski was avoiding controversy, for he was soon involved in a campaign to back a boycott of Japanese ships, following the invasion of China in July 1937, and faced considerable opposition, particularly from the trade union leadership.[45] But his major responsibilities on the Executive were confined to areas of policy which were not associated with the Left: he was appointed to a defence sub-committee,[46] and he helped to initiate, and serve on, an inquiry into the organisation and personnel at Labour Party headquarters.[47] As usual he invested enormous energy in these tasks, but the work had little to do with the United Front.[48] In fact, by early 1938, his position was shifting once again and, although this would not become clear for a few more months, there had been signs of tensions much earlier.

The first factor which indicated a potential difference between Laski and the United Front was discernible as a nuance rather than a definite policy divergence. It concerned the crucial realm of foreign and defence policy and had begun as long ago as 1935. In November of that year, when appalled by the government's appeasement of both Nazi Germany and fascist Italy he had confessed to Frankfurter:

I even find myself eager for Winston to be in the Government; he would be the one person solidly set against an Anglo-German understanding. Without him I fear that gravely.[49]

This is not decisive evidence that Laski's private thoughts differed substantially from his public statements, for it was *possible* to yearn for a more resilient anti-Nazi stance without this meaning that he would have abandoned his opposition to an 'imperialist war' had Churchill been a Cabinet minister. The same could be said of his heartfelt remark in May 1936 that the government seemed helpless before Hitler – 'their one object to keep us out on almost any terms'.[50] But at the beginning of 1937, he set out his private thoughts at greater length:

We live in the nightmare world of preparation for a war that seems inescapable; for Hitler is in a vice from which the gamble of war is, in the long run, his only escape. That is why the timidity of the Baldwin government is unpardonable. To give him piecemeal victories is to refresh his prestige; and the more it is refreshed, the more he demands. I want the anti-Fascist powers to unite and say 'No further'. The alternative is his attack on Spain today; tomorrow it may be Prague; and the day after will be Armageddon. But if we said 'No' now, he would, like every bully, retreat, and for him a loss of face is the beginning of downfall. If he does decide to fight, then for my part I would go forward. Civilisation and Fascism are literally incompatibles. He betrays the elementary decencies of life. And the British government halts only because it fears Communism if he falls . . . But all this is merely to whet the appetite of dictators who can live only by foreign conquest. We are in one of those decisive epochs where evasion of choice is worse than no choice. England, France and Soviet Russia are unitedly strong enough to put a term to the career of these pinchpack autocrats. If our governing class will not do so for fear of their own privileges, a dark age might well descend over Europe in which the very condition of civilization may easily be lost . . .[51]

There was nothing strictly incompatible with the United Front strategy in these words. Yet the tone was quite different. For the implication was surely that Laski would have welcomed a strong lead from the National government and would have been prepared to accept war if this was the consequence of resistance to Hitler's demands. It is true that he presumed that a decisive lead would have entailed alliance with the Soviet Union, and many other supporters of the United Front accepted the possibility of war on these terms. However, there is more than a hint here that Laski's most fervent hope was for genuine resistance to fascism and that this emotion was beginning to supersede his belief that the *prevention* of war was the principal objective. By 1937 he was thus more ambivalent about the legitimacy of war than he implied and, in these circumstances, his attitude to defence was also likely to shift. Once on the Executive, and involved in concrete consideration of military issues, his position changed fairly quickly and by February 1938 he had probably tacitly accepted the need for rearmament.

This shifting stance on defence and foreign policy coincided with long-term tensions in his relationship with the Communist Party, which came to a head at about the same time.

One element concerned his attitudes to the Soviet Union. He had written very little on this subject since producing a very naive pamphlet entitled *Law and Justice in the Soviet Union*, soon after his trip to Moscow in 1934. In this work he praised aspects of the Soviet legal system and even described Vyshinsky, the procurator-general, as a man 'whose passion was law reform', and compared him with Jeremy Bentham.[52] Since Vishinsky was soon to be demanding executions in the Great Show Trials, this hardly showed Laski's judgement at its best (!) and the text has often been used against him. However, in an introduction to a new edition of *Liberty in the Modern State*, written in 1937, he summarised his views on the Soviet Union as a whole. It was, he claimed, a 'pioneer of a new civilization', which had emerged from a terrible background of revolution, civil war and foreign intervention, and it had brought about immense achievements:

> But it remains, after twenty years, definitely a dictatorship; and this has, naturally enough, caused grief and disappointment to those who care for freedom all over the world. Not only is it a dictatorship: but the ruthlessness with which it has suppressed those hostile to its authority has been sombrely seen in the grim tale of executions since the assassination of Kirov. In the classic sense of absolute liberalism, freedom does not exist in the Soviet Union. There is no liberty to criticise the fundamentals of the regime. There is no liberty to found parties to oust the Communist leaders. A man cannot found a journal of opinion or publish a

book, or hold a meeting, to advocate views which, in the judgment of the dictatorship, would threaten the stability of the system. A citizen who sought to overthrow the philosophy of Marx, or to urge that Trotsky, and not Stalin, wears the true mantle of Lenin's tradition, would soon find himself on the way to exile or imprisonment. Art, the drama, music, the cinema, through all of these the dictatorship has sought to pour a stream of tendency, often with ludicrous, and sometimes with tragic results.[53]

In fact, he still made so many allowances for Stalin and was so insistent that there would be a revival of freedom once the Soviet Union felt secure, that the overall implication was positive. Yet he was obviously troubled by the purges and show trials, although at first he tried to deny this by reasserting his faith in the most dogmatic manner.[54] But he could not sweep away his doubts as easily as he pretended, and a relatively small incident appears to have tipped the balance at just about the time he was elected to the NEC.

In April 1936 the Russian Jewish husband of Freda Utley, a British journalist, was arrested and imprisoned in the Soviet Union without specific charges being made. She last heard from him in May 1937 and never knew what happened to him.[55] Laski, with other members of the Left, including Kingsley Martin, the Webbs and Bernard Shaw, tried to get the case looked into by the Soviet authorities. However, as Laski told Palme Dutt, one of the British communist leaders, they had 'not received even the courtesy of an acknowledgement'. He continued: 'This seems to me completely indefensible, and in the worst tradition of the Hitler Government.'[56] As a result, Laski told Dutt that he was no longer prepared to send twentieth anniversary greetings for the Russian Revolution to *Labour Monthly*, as he had previously promised. He reviewed the second edition of the Webbs' *Soviet Communism: A New Civilization* early in 1938 and it was clear that the Utley incident had played a major part in the evolution of his views.

When discussing the Webbs' assertion that the new constitution guaranteed freedom from arbitrary arrest, he thus wrote:

I myself know of cases where men and women have been arrested and detained for long periods without being brought to trial. Their relatives do not know of what (if anything) they have been accused. They do not know if they are living or dead. They do not know where, if alive, they are to be found; and persistent requests for information produce no reply. I cannot, with great respect to Mr and Mrs Webb, avoid being sceptical about a right of whose realization this can be said. If the answer is that it would not be safe to implement the right in practice, then the obvious reply is . . . that the inability of the Soviet Government as yet to realize it casts doubt upon the whole 'new set of the rights of men' of which Mr and Mrs Webb speak so eagerly.[57]

Nor could he now accept the Webbs' account of the show trials:

are not Mr and Mrs Webb disturbed (a) at the wholesale character of purges that have taken place; (b) at the sense of fear at the possible repercussions that affect some even of the most eminent Soviet officials so that they will not undertake the most elementary inquiries into the fate of arrested persons; and (c) whether creative work of an intellectual kind can be achieved in a civilization in which 'an ideological deviation' may so easily be identified with treason. I think these are important questions. I think that everyone who believes, as I believe, that the future of the world is bound up with the success of the Soviet experiment has got to confront their implications with great regret. I cannot say that I think Mr and Mrs Webb have seriously confronted them.[58]

Finally, he argued that Acton's famous dictum that 'power always corrupts and absolute power corrupts absolutely' was as true of the Soviet Union as anywhere else:

I am not, therefore, able to assume that tolerance will come automatically in the Soviet Union as security comes. Tolerance will come, and as elsewhere, because those who believe in the immense service that the Soviet Union can render (has indeed rendered) mankind are militant about the urgency of its coming. It will not come unless people with the authority of Mr and Mrs Webb urgently protest against any action that is arbitrary and unexplained. The Soviet Union owes to the socialists of the world a far more full and conclusive account than is so far vouchsafed us of the meaning of events that, despite Mr and Mrs Webb, remain baffling and obscure . . . for if the persecution of 'ideological deviations' is to wait until the 'imminent danger of foreign aggression' has died away, the rendezvous may be very long. Germany, imperialist Japan and quasi-fascist Poland must all be democratized. Can that be achieved without defeat in war? What would be the effect of war on the Soviet Union so far as the problem of liberty is concerned? The more I reflect on Mr and Mrs Webb's argument, the more inclined I am to suspect that a new dark age lies before us through which we have to pass before a recovery of tolerance becomes again a possible adventure.[59]

Laski's disenchantment with the Soviet Union inevitably affected his attitude to its loyal defenders – the CP. Even when he had been most supportive of the CPs' wish to affiliate to the Labour Party, he had been worried about its relationship with the USSR. He had therefore never suggested that the Labour Party should automatically *accept* the application. In November 1936 he had thus stated:

I think the Communist Party's affiliation to the Third International is a definite stumbling-block unless the Party agrees that, after admission to the Labour Party, it will accept the latter's decisions in preference to any made at Moscow. But I should myself hope that this situation would make an end of the present divisions of the international working class and lead to the creation of that world united front that is now an urgent matter.[60]

This was wishful thinking, for there was no chance that Stalin would relinquish control over the communist parties of the West. But it indicated Laski's continuing concern over the Party's lack of independence and 'overnight' changes of line. It is therefore very significant that, in his speech to the 1937 Labour Party Conference in defence of the Socialist League, and the right to appear on platforms with Communists, he actually made an attack on the CP:

I would like to remind the Executive of this Party that mechanical uniformity of opinion is the supreme vice of the Communist Party of Great Britain, and therefore I do not want to see it introduced into the Labour Party of Great Britain.[61]

The CP's response to Laski's intervention in the Utley case no doubt strengthened his suspicions of the Party, for Dutt simply defended the Soviet ability 'to judge correctly the necessary measures to defeat the capitalist enemy'.[62] And his reservations about the CP also affected his work in the Left Book Club.

As already noted, the overwhelming majority of the books that were chosen by the Club were 'reliable' from a CP point of view. In order to ensure this, in March 1937 Strachey and Gollancz invited Emile Burns, a leading Party member, to vet the texts with them before holding the formal editorial meetings at which Laski, Gollancz and Strachey were supposed to make the decisions. Laski was not a party to this arrangement, and was presumably unaware of what was happening.[63] Similarly, Gollancz wrote the overwhelming majority of editorials in *Left News*, and Strachey provided regular long articles, whilst Laski normally confined himself to book reviews. Even in these he occasionally infuriated his co-selectors and the CP by deviating from orthodoxy.[64] In general, he maintained a comparatively low profile in the Left Book Club and by 1937 he may already have been concerned about its closeness to the CP. Certainly, he wanted to increase its links with the Labour Party, and secured Attlee's agreement to write *The Labour Party in Perspective* . Similarly, it was at his suggestion that in July 1937 the selectors approached Dalton, then Chair of the NEC, to propose that two special issues of *Left News* could be devoted to the Labour Party and TUC conferences. Dalton refused, on the grounds that the club was a vehicle for United Front activity.[65] As Ruth Dudley Edwards suggests, Laski's account of the failure of the negotiations 'was written more in sorrow than in anger'. He argued that the selectors had a duty to put the unification of working-class forces above loyalty to the Labour Party leadership, but he exhorted the membership to discuss Attlee's book seriously.[66]

These incipient tensions within the Left Book Club also came to a head early in 1938. Two years earlier Gollancz had contracted H. N. Brailsford to write a book for the Club. Brailsford was an independent, radical-left thinker, and in September 1937 produced a text which included criticisms of the Soviet Union. He had already created a furore with the CP by condemning the Moscow trials and it was clear that his new work would precipitate a further conflict.[67] Gollancz therefore appealed to him to cut his criticisms of the Soviet Union, but Brailsford refused to do so. Gollancz turned to Emile Burns, the CP 'censor', who insisted that the offending chapter must not be published. Gollancz then wrote to Brailsford to reject the book.[68] At this point Brailsford appealed to Laski.

The two men had known each other since 1920 and had considerable mutual affection and respect. Laski replied that he regarded Brailsford's work as 'legitimate criticism' and would seek a *modus vivendi* with Strachey and Gollancz.[69] Laski then threatened resignation unless a compromise was effected and, faced with this prospect, Gollancz chose the lesser evil and published the book (*Why Capitalism Means War*).[70] The whole episode must have reinforced Laski's growing doubts about the CP (even though he was probably unaware of the fact that Gollancz had referred to Burns before making his decision).

By the end of February 1938 Laski was therefore, once again, in a state of transition. On the one hand, he remained deeply critical of the Labour leadership and continued to believe that Chamberlain was effectively pro-Fascist in his domestic and foreign policies.[71] All this implied the need for a continuation of the United Front strategy. On the other hand, by now he had tacitly accepted British rearmament and was suspicious of the communist movement. He could not reconcile these contradictory pressures for long, and the 'crunch' came in May 1938.

AWAY FROM COMMUNISM, TOWARDS WAR

Laski had spent the Easter vacation in the USA. He noted that, while much American opinion was appalled by Chamberlain's refusal to give any guarantees to Czechoslovakia, it also used this fact to justify American non-involvement in European affairs.[72] In other words, British refusal to take a strong stand against Nazism was used to reinforce isolationist pressures in the United States. He also conducted a 'round table' in Washington for writers, economists and senior civil servants on the future of American government and saw Roosevelt again.[73] From all these discussions, he may have concluded that the President had little room for manoeuvre against the isolationists unless the British took a lead. In any case, the visit probably strengthened his conviction that further pressure must be mounted to end the appeasement policy. On his return to Britain he found that the proponents of the Popular Front were mounting a new campaign. His initial sympathies were naturally with this movement, and he reported to Frankfurter:

I gather from Stafford [Cripps] and the others that the Labour Party is all at sixes and sevens – no appreciation of the depth of the crisis, a chance to give a great national lead against Chamberlain by demanding a national union of progressives against him and a refusal to contemplate it for fear of the Communists.[74]

He therefore endorsed a memorandum entitled 'The International Situation' which was submitted to the NEC in the names of Cripps, Ellen Wilkinson, Pritt and himself. This argued that the foreign policy of the government was effectively pro-fascist, that the Labour Party was unlikely to win an election on its own, and that it should therefore form an alliance with Liberals, communists and others. This popular movement would campaign for 'peace versus war or democracy versus fascism'.[74]

There were two points about this statement which must have troubled Laski despite his apparent support for it. First, it was a full reiteration of the Comintern's peace policy, while Laski now accepted that the price of firm resistance to fascism might be war. Secondly, he had long opposed the CP's drift towards an alliance with non-socialists, and the statement went further than ever in this respect.[76]

The Popular Front campaign led to a major fight inside the Labour Party. The leadership remained unreservedly hostile to the proposal and sought to persuade the rank-and-file that support for the Labour Party was the only effective way of opposing the National government. The NEC therefore established a sub-committee to prepare an appropriate statement. Laski served on this committee, with Dalton, Morrison and Greenwood, and it was now that his decisive break with the CP took place. He prepared the first draft of the response. In this, he argued against uniting with the Liberals, since they were a diminishing force which offered no advantage to Labour. But the thrust of his argument was against the CP:

> The Communist Party is subject to political direction from abroad and to this extent is not allowed to determine its own policy. Both the Labour Party and the Liberals would be distracted from the main purpose of the proposed combination by the need to protect themselves against Communist manoeuvres . . . .
>
> Their policy is devoid of any certainty. They are committed rather to maneouvre than to principle. They would be capable of stabbing us in the back or of committing us to responsibility for their grave indiscretions for which we might have to pay a heavy price.[77]

There was, he claimed, an increasing probability of a Labour victory at the next election. It was therefore time to ensure that victory was achieved without compromising 'our socialist convictions' by building an artificial and ineffective combination.

It is evident that this involved a fundamental change in his attitude towards unity with the CP. Since 1933 he had believed that the
construction of some kind of United Front had been crucial and,
between 1935 and 1937, this had been a key element in his political
strategy. The decision in May 1938 to align himself with the leadership *against* the call for a Popular Front was therefore of enormous
importance. Nor would he ever again believe that there could be a
United Front with the CP unless a totally new relationship with the
Soviet Union had *already* been established. For he now realised that
the external control of the CP meant that, in the final analysis, the
interests of Stalin would prevail over any considerations of the
British party leadership. Whereas in August 1937, he had argued
that his first loyalty was to the ideas embodied in the Left Book Club,
henceforth the Labour Party would supersede the United Front.
However, there were also continuities in his position. First, he was
still on the Left of the Labour Party and remained highly critical of
the leadership. Secondly, he maintained both his 'Marxist' theoretical analysis, and his bitter and total opposition to the domestic and
foreign policies of the Chamberlain government. Thirdly, he continued to work in United Front organisations. Laski had therefore
moved back towards the mainstream of Labour Party politics without severing himself completely from his erstwhile allies in the
pro-Communist Left.

This tortuous position was made evident immediately. While
rejecting the Popular Front campaign, he thus took up the demand
of the Left for a special party conference on the international situation.[78] But the way in which he called for the conference was now
restrained and careful. It would, he argued, enforce and strengthen
the Party's opposition to the government:

> Above all, we could make it clear how firmly opposed the
> workers . . . are to a policy of consistent surrender to Fascist
> dictators. We have no sympathy for an imperialist war; but we
> cannot, as a movement, stand helplessly by and see Mr Chamber-
> lain connive at the slaughter of what remains of European demo-
> cracy to add prestige to the moral vandals of Berlin and Rome.[79]

Moreover, he now maintained that there was no need for Labour to
oppose the arms estimates. This stance, he claimed, had previously
been a means of expressing opposition to the government's foreign
policy rather than to defence per se. However, the intensity of

Labour's condemnation of Chamberlain was now well-known. In fact, Laski was now trying to play a mediating role between the Labour leadership and the Left in the hope that the Party as a whole would unite against appeasement, even if this ultimately involved war. And it is significant that he also tried to convince the Left of the crucial importance of the USA. He thus claimed (optimistically) that a British stance against fascism would push Roosevelt towards an effective form of collective security against Hitler.[80]

By now the Czech crisis was in its final stages and there seemed to be a real possibility of war. Laski still believed that Hitler might draw back from the brink if the British government gave a clear warning, and he was a member of an NEC delegation to the Foreign Office which presented this argument in early August.[81] He was also involved in the drafting of the statement issued by the Labour Party and the TUC on 8 September. This stated:

> The time has come for a positive and unmistakable lead for collective defence against aggression and to safeguard peace. The British Government must leave no doubt in the mind of the German Government that they will unite with the French and Soviet Governments to resist any attack upon Czechoslovakia. The Labour Movement urges the British Government to give this lead, confident that such a policy would have the solid support of the British people.[82]

However, he left for his sabbatical year in the USA before the denouement at Munich. Ten days later he told Frankfurter that 'something has gone out of my life since Munich' and that, when Frida had distributed gas masks in a factory there was 'a deep sense among the men that Chamberlain was letting down the whole status of democracy'.[83] In March 1939, just before Hitler tore up the agreement by dismembering the rest of the Czechoslovak state, he insisted that:

> Czechoslovakia . . . went on the sacrificial block in vain. The Munich pact was suicidal . . . .
>
> The democracies now will have to fight the fascists on infinitely more unfavourable terms than previously. . . . Had the democracies stood firm and Hitler fought, the Nazis might have been crushed both by military opposition on the battle front and social revolution in Germany.[84]

Laski was now at the height of his reputation in the United States, although he remained a controversial figure. Thus while some organisations in Seattle denounced the University of Washington for engaging him as a visiting professor, his lectures attracted capacity audiences and, on one occasion, 3500 people were turned away.[85] Apart from teaching, he used his considerable influence to alert liberal opinion as a whole to the dangers of the European situation. He also made several appeals to Roosevelt.

In January, when the President spoke to Congress of measures 'short of war, but stronger and more effective then mere words',[86] Laski immediately wrote:

> You cannot easily imagine the exhilaration an Englishman feels in recognising in your words the spirit he had hoped to find in his own rulers.

But he also warned him about the pro-appeasement stance of the American ambassador in London, Joe Kennedy:

> If I may say so, it is very important, from the angle of our common hopes, that Joe K be made to understand that his speeches in London, after his return, may, unless he is very careful, be turned to the service of the worst elements of reaction in Great Britain. There is, I fear, little doubt but that his speech of last October was interpreted to mean that you were solidly behind the Chamberlain policy.[87]

In mid-April, as the Nazi threat to Danzig and the Polish corridor mounted, and Roosevelt made a last appeal to Hitler and Mussolini to avert war, Laski again coupled expressions of gratitude with a plea:

> I hope that you will press the British Government to hasten the completion of the Anglo-Soviet arrangement. That will have immense influence in building unity with Labour in England; without it, there is bound to be deep suspicion of Chamberlain's motives, and I hope, too, that you can make them begin *now* to think out the terms of possible accommodation, a definition of aims, war or no war. For I fear, as I fear nothing else, the coming of an imperialist war on the old model in which there emerges an unbridgeable gap between the Tories and ourselves out of which

there comes the grave danger, above all if there is to be a war, of internal civil dissension.[88]

His letters to Roosevelt were, of course, unlikely to carry much weight on such momentous issues. But Laski's lectures and articles probably had some impact in alerting American opinion to the dangers of fascism. He was also convinced that, in the event of war, Britain would need the support of the USA, and urged Anglo-American 'friendship' as well as an Anglo-Soviet pact.[89] On his return to Britain, he also continued to stress the importance of American support for Britain. He may therefore be given credit for having perceived the potential significance of the United States and having used what influence he possessed to try to establish the 'special relationship'. It is ironic that he became appalled by its nature after the Second World War.

Once back in Britain in the early summer of 1939, he found the Labour Party bitterly divided. During his absence a new crisis over the Popular Front campaign had erupted when Cripps had circulated an appeal to local parties despite its rejection by the NEC. This had led to his expulsion, followed soon afterwards by those of Bevan, George Strauss, and Charles Trevelyan. Given Laski's decision the previous May, it is very unlikely that he would have supported the campaign had he been in Britain at the time. But he now believed that Party unity was the most crucial objective and moved a resolution in the NEC, which was defeated by twenty votes to four, for the immediate reinstatement of Cripps.[90] He also tried to use his influence over Labour Party members in the Left Book Club by persuading them to accept the Conference decision against the Popular Front, and to unite within the Party for the fight against the Chamberlain government and appeasement.[91]

Since he had already distanced himself from the CP, the Nazi-Soviet Pact of August 1939 was less traumatic for Laski than it was for many others on the Left. He viewed the Soviet decision as a 'tragedy', which 'provided Hitler with his assurance that the gamble was worthwhile'.[92] However, it did not affect his belief that war must be declared if the Nazis attacked Poland. Indeed he threatened to resign from the Left Book Club if it deviated from Labour's line over the pact.[93] Of course he still hoped that Hitler might back down or be overthrown if the British and French stood firm. But, as far as he was concerned, the die had been cast. When Hitler defied the British ultimatum on 3rd September, Laski was certain that war was justified.

In 1935 he had believed – or hoped – that a United Front might simultaneously both preserve the peace and defeat fascism. Now he supported war as the only means of defeating fascism. This change had been accompanied by an apparent return to the mainstream of the Labour Party and a definite separation from the CP. However, there were – as always – important continuities in his position.

He had not become a conventional patriot or social democrat. He still believed that capitalism was responsible for both fascism and war, and that appeasement had been a defence of class interests. He maintained that socialism was an urgent necessity, and that Roosevelt must play a critical role in the creation of a new world order. It was imperative to fight and win the war. But it was equally vital to construct a peace in which 'the common people . . . for the first time, assume control of their own destiny'.[94] His insistence that this was the cause for which the allies must fight would bring him into new and bitter conflicts.

10

Laski's War

During the Second World War, Laski drove himself almost beyond endurance. At best his life was divided between three centres. In London he attended an endless round of meetings mainly, but not solely, connected with Labour Party work, and he broadcast regularly on the BBC. In Cambridge, he often taught for twenty hours per week, and helped to run an understaffed LSE, which was evacuated for almost the whole of the war period. And he spent as many weekends as possible in the country cottage in Little Bardfield. Many of these journeys were through the blackout and he also travelled the length and breadth of the country, addressing local Labour Parties and speaking to army education groups. Several times he narrowly avoided death or serious injury from bombs, and even Little Bardfield was no haven, for Frida was in charge of evacuees and village social life, and still commuted regularly to London, where she continued to work as a councillor and JP. Yet Laski, who was often ill, occasionally frightened, and always physically weak, went on relentlessly, producing a constant stream of articles, pamphlets, and books. Moreover, he carried an enormous burden of work within the NEC, of which he became deputy Chair in 1944 (often acting as Chair while Ellen Wilkinson was ill) and Chair in 1945. He also played a pivotal role in Labour Party Conferences, where he was immensely popular with the rank-and-file and he was elected at the head of the poll in the constituency section every year of the war (a unique record for someone who was not an MP).

No-one has disputed the prodigious amount of work carried out by Laski during the war. However, its nature and impact has more often been criticised than praised. At the time, he infuriated· most political leaders, including those in his own party, by his outspoken criticisms of their policies, and he was the subject of vicious personal attacks by the Right in both Britain and the USA. Nor have historical accounts of his role been any more favourable. In general, he has been seen as an impractical doctrinaire socialist, who needed to be put in his place by Attlee, and he has also been portrayed as a publicity seeker who could not resist an opportunity to 'plunge into the limelight'.[1] As usual, Deane is even less sympathetic, arguing that:

> Since he had neither the time nor the will to undertake a fundamental reassessment of his political beliefs, he went on repeating the old formulas and hypnotizing himself and his audience by the use of a series of resounding phrases. Reality receded farther and farther from his grasp, but the words he uttered were so familiar and persuasive to him that he was not aware that he had, to a large extent, substituted a world of fiction and shadows for the world of facts.[2]

And:

> He seems to have been so enamored of prestige and the sense that he was close to the seats of power that he was never willing to break with the Party leadership.[3]

Overall, the impression that has been created is that Laski's efforts were misguided and that his political activity during the war was almost frivolous.

This chapter presents a 'revisionist' version of 'Laski's war'. This does not mean that he will be spared from criticism, for some of his interventions were counter-productive and based on errors of judgment. But it will be shown that he was driven by a sense of purpose which was intensely serious, that his campaigns brought him almost unbearable personal suffering, that some of his insights into the situation were remarkable, and that his influence over subsequent British political development has been underrated.

GENERAL ASSUMPTIONS ABOUT THE WAR

Laski was adamant from the beginning of the war that Nazism must be completely defeated and destroyed and that there could be no compromise peace.[4] Indeed, he was so convinced that this was an ideological war that he was also opposed to the attempt to separate Mussolini from Hitler, for he wanted the destruction of Italian fascism as well. But he was always sure that victory was dependent upon political factors, as well as military strength and, in the early stages of the war, he used his influence to help create the political prerequisites for the defeat of fascism. He was convinced that this required the establishment of a strong national consensus behind the war effort and that it was therefore necessary to undermine the propaganda of the communists on the Left (until June 1941) and the 'appeasers' on the Right.

He tried to persuade communists and their potential allies that it was not an 'imperialist' war, and that the CP line was helping Hitler. Given his Popular Front past, his continued association with the Left Book Club, and his ability to argue in Marxist, and even Leninist, terms, he was undoubtedly one of the most effective propagandists of this type. This was not only recognised by the Labour Party, which published his pamphlet *Is This an Imperialist War?* early in 1940, but also by the American government, which ordered 25,000 copies of it (through the British Ministry of Information) so as to counter the arguments of the American Left.[5] However, his condemnation of the CP did not mean that he adopted a 'right-wing' position in the Labour movement. On the contrary, his criticisms of CP arguments, organisation, and tactics were coupled with an insistence on the need to press ahead with domestic and international transformation. This was related to the other aspect of his search for national unity in 1939–40: opposition to the Chamberlain government.

Laski remained convinced that the 'appeasers' had favoured fascism and had become involved in the war reluctantly and half-heartedly when there appeared to be no alternative. He was therefore totally opposed to any suggestion that the Labour Party should join the Chamberlain government, which he believed could be overthrown if Labour showed more determined leadership. As he told one of his American friends:

> we leave the initiative to the other side when I believe vast numbers wait for the kind of new direction we could give to things, the new purposes we could announce, most of all the new hopes we could arouse. To fight for our lives with Hoare and Simon and Burgin and Kingsley Wood – it makes me sick in the stomach.[6]

However, even before May 1940 he supported Churchill, and had no doubts about Labour joining a coalition under his leadership. Indeed, once Churchill and Attlee formed a genuinely national government, he felt 'serene confidence' about winning the war.[7]

There was one further prerequisite to military victory to which

Laski devoted considerable efforts in the early stages of the war: the securing of American support. He was aware that Roosevelt's sympathies were with Britain, but that there were strong isolationist and Right-wing forces intent on keeping the United States out of the war. He was therefore careful not to call for American military intervention. But in a series of articles in the American press and in a short book particularly aimed at US students, he tried to persuade opinion that Britain should be helped.[8] In such writings he did all he could to demonstrate that this was a war for democracy against dictatorship. He also wrote sincere but emotional letters to his influential American friends – as well as to Roosevelt himself – emphasising the determination of the British people to endure any and all sacrifices in the fight against Hitler.[9] It is impossible to assess the impact of his private and public propaganda, but Laski was still an influential figure in American liberal circles. Certainly, some of the American Right believed that he carried far too much weight and, even before the US had joined the war, he was denounced as the 'intellectual switchboard' of a group advising Roosevelt and working to deliver the American state to socialism.[10]

In the early stages of the war, Laski thus played his part in trying to create the domestic and international pre-conditions for military victory. But he never saw the defeat of Hitler as a *sufficient* aim and, as he became increasingly confident about the ultimate result of the war, his emphasis on the political aspects of the struggle became ever more pronounced.

Laski felt, with intense emotion, that war was a catastrophe. It not only implied the destruction of reason and compromise – his fundamental values – but it made him feel deeply guilty because of his inability to fight. However, he believed, with equal fervour, that the Second World War presented a golden opportunity. To make sense of this paradox we need to recall the impasse that he had reached in his thought and practice between 1933 and 1939.

During those years Laski's political outlook had been primarily defensive. He had tried, without any real confidence, to maintain his optimism that successful resistance to fascism would lead to social transformation, but he could define no method for political advance. He remained non-revolutionary because he believed that violence was incompatible with liberal values, but his hopes for peaceful change had largely evaporated. Similarly, in the international arena, he could see no way that peace, prosperity and co-operation could be brought about while capitalist interests pressed the state into expansion, imperialism and ultimately armed conflict. In general, his pessimism had been disguised by his sustained political activity and his 'Marxist' commitment, but neither really compensated for the fact that he could see no way to bring about change while maintaining liberal democracy and peace.

This impasse had been even more marked in his theoretical work. He was able to elaborate his quasi-Marxist doctrine, but he did not know how to apply it to the present and future. *The Rise of European Liberalism* (1936) was thus a stimulating essay which used a form of historical materialism to discuss the origins and development of liberalism, but it offered few recommendations about the way in which this could now be transcended. And *Parliamentary Government in England* (1938) was an exact reflection of Laski's dilemma: it provided a reverential account of the virtues of a parliamentary system while simultaneously demonstrating that these were impossible to achieve in a society characterised by class inequality. It was a reflection of Laski's own state of mind that this work ended without any conclusion. He therefore saw the struggle against Nazi Germany as an *opportunity*, because it appeared to offer a way of resolving the problems that had appeared intractable in peacetime.

War at last appeared to provide a means by which socio-economic transformation could come about within the framework of the British parliamentary system. For military supremacy would depend on the full co-operation of the Labour movement, and the more 'total' the war became, the greater would be the extent of the necessary collaboration. But this meant that the Labour movement was provided with more effective bargaining power than it had ever secured in the inter-war period, for the privileged interests needed the working class if they were to defeat the external threat. Similarly, Churchill was dependent upon the co-operation of the Labour Party as the main representative of the working classes. It was therefore possible to take substantial steps *immediately* to eliminate the ills of the inter-war years.

Stated in this stark manner, Laski's demand for significant socio-economic change during the war might appear opportunist or even cynical. Was this not to take advantage of a national crisis so as to press for partisan and sectional interests? Laski justifiably denied this. In the first place he never suggested or would have accepted any weakening in the commitment to defeat Hitler militarily. On the contrary, he genuinely believed that enthusiasm for the war effort would be far greater if ordinary workers were convinced that they were fighting for a new world rather than the privileges of the elite. He therefore felt that concessions to the working classes would aid the war effort. Secondly, he rightly believed that privileged interests and the Conservatives were still defending their socio-economic position while fighting against Hitler.[11] It was therefore untrue to pretend that class and political conflict had been suspended for the duration of the war and that it was only the Left that was raising sectional demands. This leads on to the third, and most crucial, point in his argument. That is, it was *because* class conflict was an endemic feature of capitalism that it was vital for the Labour movement to press some of its claims while it was in a relatively strong position to do so. Once Hitler had been defeated, capitalists would want to restore the old order and would no longer have any incentive to reward the workers for their efforts. If the concessions were confined to promises for a better post-war world, they would prove no more enduring than similar pious hopes expressed during the 1914–18 conflict. It was therefore vital to secure genuine commitments for the post-war world and to demonstrate their validity by concrete measures during the war itself. If this were achieved, Laski's long-term goal of peaceful change within a democratic system would finally have been realised. The war therefore provided a unique opportunity to bring about a 'revolution by consent'.[12]

Once the war had begun it was obviously impossible for Laski to argue that international change could also come about without violence. But he believed that this conflict could be used to eliminate the seeds of future wars. It was, he argued, vital to recognise that this was a revolutionary war. Since international conflict was embedded in the capitalist system, domestic transformation should take place throughout Europe. The British and American governments must therefore use their influence to facilitate the process of revolutionary change so that it could be as peaceful and democratic as possible. Similarly, they must abandon imperialism. But, he argued, they would act in this way only if they themselves were intent on pursuing domestic change. Internal and external developments were therefore totally interconnected, and future international harmony was dependent upon the maintenance of the New Deal in the USA and thoroughgoing reform in Britain. In these circumstances, it would also be possible to resolve the final acute problem of the inter-war era: the relationship between the Soviet Union and the capitalist powers.

Laski's degree of enthusiasm for the Soviet Union varied during the course of the war.[13] But he consistently believed that rapprochement between the 'west' and the Soviet Union was crucial if the defeat of Hitler was to lead to an enduring peace. Since he continued to believe that 'appeasement' had reflected capitalist anti-communism, he argued that it was the responsibility of the British and Americans to demonstrate to the Soviet government that it had no need to feel threatened. For once the Soviet Union felt secure, he thought that it would be possible to secure East-West co-operation. He firmly believed that the Grand Alliance against Fascism provided a real opportunity for the Western powers to provide such assurances. However, he also maintained that they, could do so only if they abandoned expansionist capitalism and implemented progressive policies at home.

For Laski, domestic and international issues were thus inseparable and this led to the final element in his overall conception. If the requisite transformation took place during the war, he believed that it would also become possible to begin to attain another of his long-term goals: the establishment of a peaceful and co-operative international order, based on the gradual erosion of national sovereignty. For he still saw the nation-state as a barrier to peace, but no longer thought that it could be superseded while wedded to capitalist interests. He did not think that rigidly defined federalist schemes – of the type that were being propounded in the early stages of the war – were practicable.[14] But if capitalist expansionism were curtailed by domestic transformation, and the capitalist/Soviet division was ended, he hoped that it would be possible to move towards a world in which supranational institutions would develop progressively over time. Laski believed that his ideas were realistic and practicable. For the first time since the 1920s his theory and his emotions were therefore integrated. This meant that there was no contradiction between his thought and his action, and he could devote his vast energy to the attempt to transform his vision into reality. But his frenetic activity stemmed from something more fundamental than theory alone.

During the Second World War he was certain that he understood the requirements of the era. The war provided an opportunity for fundamental domestic and international change. But if political leaders failed to seize this opportunity, it would not simply be a regrettable error: it would be catastrophic. For it would mean the restoration of the old order, with all its attendant evils. The masses would not and should not accept this, but their attempt to overthrow it would lead to a new threat of violent social conflict or new forms of fascism. And, in the international arena, there would be still more terrible wars in the future.

Laski thus possessed an overall conception of the world, which was based on a theoretical perspective. But his attitude towards it was also deeply emotional. This meant that his political activity was driven by the most powerful forces of all: the belief that success would lead to a brave new world and failure would bring about Armageddon. This state of mind must be appreciated as we now examine his political role.

THE BATTLE FOR DOMESTIC REFORM, 1940–2

Since Laski was so intent on securing immediate domestic reforms this soon caused serious conflicts with the Labour leadership. Of course Attlee and his colleagues also wanted to establish the basis of a 'welfare' state. But they were less radical than he was, they did not possess his overall theory or vision, they were driven by a lesser sense of urgency, and they were operating within the narrow boundaries set by the dictates of coalition politics. These differences caused inevitable tensions which soon became apparent.

Laski had worked with Attlee on defence issues before the war, and this relationship was strengthened in 1940, when he began to act as one of the party leader's unofficial advisers. However, Laski's determination to force the pace meant that the relationship would not remain harmonious for long. Indeed, even before Labour joined the coalition, he was privately critical of his leader, telling one of his American friends that, although Attlee was 'admirable in simplicity and integrity', he 'hasn't got an ounce of leadership in him'.[15] However, the tensions really developed once Labour joined the coalition for Laski maintained – with justification – that people felt that it was the Labour Party which had injected a new sense of urgency into the situation and that it was necessary to exploit this popular mood by pressing forward immediately.[16] The conflict with the leadership over domestic policy began to take shape.

On 26 June 1940 Laski submitted a draft pamphlet, 'The Road to Power', to the NEC and proposed that the Executive should suggest to the Labour ministers that one or two socialist measures should be brought into operation. The pamphlet was referred to the Press, Publicity and Campaign sub-committee, which decided that it should be kept in reserve.[17] He therefore now took his main proposal to the NEC in the form of a resolution:

> That this executive places on record its deep appreciation of the new spirit infused into the conduct of the War by Labour ministers. It urges upon them the importance of adding to their achievement the enactment of at least a number of those definitely Socialist measures approved by the Bournemouth Conference as a method of maintaining the present high morale of the civil population.[18]

After discussion, it was agreed that his proposals should be referred to the policy sub-committee. When this met on 16 August to consider the resolution (and a memorandum that Laski had submitted), it was decided that Dalton, now Minister of Economic Warfare, should convey the views expressed to Attlee and Greenwood (the Minister without Portfolio) and arrange for them to meet the committee.[19] This meeting was supposed to take place at an 'early date', but no action appears to have been taken.

Laski obviously found the delays deeply frustrating and this feeling intensified in the autumn, when Churchill refused to agree any statement of war aims – something to which the Labour party had attached particular importance. This led to Laski's first conflict with the leadership for, on 21 October, he wrote an 'Open Letter to the Labour Movement' in the *Daily Herald*, asking readers to 'Demand War Aims'. The result was that the Party's Emergency Committee – which was dominated by the leadership – called a special meeting when both Attlee and Laski could be present.[20] When this took place, on 5 November, Laski:

> agreed that, in all the circumstances, he now felt that probably the publication of the article in the *Daily Herald* was unwise, and liable to misunderstanding considering the relation he held to Mr Attlee as Leader of the Party.[21]

In theory, the incident was then closed. In practice, Attlee no doubt now regarded Laski as 'unreliable', while Laski felt that attention had been focussed on his 'indiscretion' rather than the fundamental issue of whether Labour was prepared to press for its own policies within the coalition. The conflict therefore soon reemerged.

In January 1941, the Party Secretary suggested that, in view of the

possibility of invasion and problems of transport, it might be difficult to find a venue for the Party's annual conference that year. Laski
probably suspected that this was a leadership ploy to evade awkward discussions and insisted that the conference should be held.
He also proposed that ministers should give reports on the work
they had done and that the NEC should submit policy resolutions
for discussion. These proposals were subsequently accepted, but by
then the tensions had become still greater.[22]

On 27 January Laski had submitted a new memorandum to the
NEC. This was, he argued, a turning-point in the war. In the next few
weeks or months, 'we shall feel the full strength of the Nazi assault'
and this would lead to a point where Hitler would either break
British resistance or be 'doomed to certain failure'. Laski assumed
that Hitler would fail. In these circumstances, Britain would be
called upon to find the conditions of effective reconstruction and the
way to an enduring peace. But neither would be possible unless,
before hostilities ceased:

> we have found the conditions in this country which make our
> whole energies available for the leadership which destiny will
> then have placed in our hands.[23]

His general argument was that the opportunity for change must be
taken immediately because, after the armistice, 'it is practically certain that the forces of privilege will forget the obligations owed . . .
to the workers'.[24] Two additional points should be noted. First, he
complained – as tactfully as possible – about the role of the Labour
leadership. The decision to join the coalition government had, he
argued, 'saved European civilisation from the Fascist threat'. But, in
return for that contribution, the Labour leaders had secured nothing
more from their Conservative colleagues than would have been
achieved had they remained in opposition:

> I am not prepared to accept as satisfactory the fact that Mr Green-
> wood has been charged with a vague commission about recon-
> struction. I must point out that certain pivotal aspects of his
> problems are in the keeping of Sir John Anderson, others are in
> the keeping of Lord Reith; and the whole turns upon an agree-
> ment about principles which have not been seriously discussed in
> the Cabinet, let alone agreed upon. We do not even know that our
> own Ministers agree upon them. Even if they did, and acceptance

of them were postponed until victory, with three members out of eight in the War Cabinet, we have no assurance of their accept-ance. And if they have to wait on victory before they are pressed forward, all past experience points to their probable rejection.[25]

He therefore proposed that a joint NEC, PLP and TUC committee of ten members should be set up to act in conjunction with Labour ministers. This should immediately formulate 'our proposals for reconstruction so that our Ministers are made fully aware of the principles by which we expect them to be guided'. This, he argued, would strengthen their position in the War Cabinet and enable them 'to ask with authority that the Prime Minister and his Conservative colleagues should face up to the domestic problems of the post-war world' and the workers' needs.

The second notable aspect of his memorandum was its emphasis upon the crucial importance of *national* agreement:

We have to find a plane of relationships which enables the vast majority of citizens to feel with conviction that they have the great ends of life in common . . .

. . . unless we use *now* the widespread feeling that what, as a nation, we have in common goes far beyond the differences which divide us, when peace comes, it is our differences, and not our identities that will emerge as important. That situation may easily make an unbridgeable abyss between classes.[26]

Before the NEC met to consider the proposal, Attlee sent his per-sonal reply to Laski:

I cannot explain to the Party the steps which I am taking which will, I believe, result in getting a great deal done in the only possible way in existing circumstances – namely by consent. To do so would destroy the efficacy of the steps which I take. I am sufficiently experienced in warfare to know that the frontal attack with a flourish of trumpets . . . is not the best way to capture a position.

No single one of the points which you suggest as matters requiring attention such as Banks, education etc are out of mind or neglected in action, but the occasion and method by which that action is achieved are not necessarily the obvious ones.[27]

On 4 February, the NEC deferred consideration of Laski's memorandum (with his agreement) to the next meeting. In the meantime, he took a very surprising step: he made a direct, private appeal to Churchill.

Later Laski would condemn Churchill's domestic policy mercilessly but, in the early stages of the coalition, he was still prepared to give him the benefit of the doubt. In October 1940 he had told Roosevelt that Churchill had yet to prove himself a great Prime Minister and would only do so 'when he sees that the condition of a real victory is a New Deal for Britain'. Nevertheless, he thought that he had 'the imagination and the courage' and only needed 'the understanding'.[28] By late November he was becoming more sceptical, but thought that his faults as a Prime Minister were 'accentuated by the fact that no one in his entourage stands up to him'.[29] He coupled this latter criticism with a general assessment of government ministers:

> The failures, I think, are Greenwood, Dalton, K. Wood (a mean little reactionary) and, to some extent, Attlee; the successes are Bevin, Morrison, and A. Duncan. There isn't a sufficient team-spirit in the Labour ministers to make them act as a unit . . .

This was a significant comment for Andrew Duncan, the Minister of Supply, was a Conservative businessman. In other words, Laski was more favourably disposed to some ministers who were outside the Labour Party for he feared that the Labour leadership was not prepared to *insist* on the implementation of the necessary reforms. Attlee's response to his pressure in January 1941, and the signs of further procrastination, clearly reinforced this impression. It was presumably for this reason that he now decided to make a direct appeal (over the heads of the Labour leadership) to Churchill himself.

On 10 February he therefore wrote to the Prime Minister enclosing a secret memorandum which specified a programme. He suggested that, if Churchill accepted the proposed measures, he should continue to lead a National government on this basis after the war. His proposal was, he claimed:

> based on two simple principles which I feel are fundamental: (i) that if the parties separate on victory, our dangers are enormously multiplied with the prospect of disaster and (ii) that you,

on such a programme as I have here set out, could hold the elements into a cohesive unity which may save the world.[30]

The memorandum articulated his fundamental assumptions:

If war-time unity is to continue after the cessation of hostilities there are two indispensable conditions for its success. (1) It must be made possible now, so that public opinion may be fully prepared for its consequences; (2) it must be made possible on a basis which creates a wide atmosphere of hope and exhilaration among the masses whose endurance will have been so large a cause of victory.[31]

Such programme must aim at 'an economics of abundance instead of an economics of scarcity'. It must therefore prevent mass unemployment and the distressed areas, and this necessitated 'a socialized area in industry'. In particular, this meant state control over the mechanism of credit, the mines, electric power, transport, land, and housing. It must also offer assurance 'that the massive inequalities of our society are being seriously tackled'. This required a great extension of the education services, public health services, and an extension of social insurance.

If the constituent parties in the National government agreed to such a programme it would, he argued, be very difficult for the Labour Party to resist an invitation to continue the present experiment. But without such a programme, 'its membership would be deeply hostile to its continuance; and its leaders would be repudiated if they attempted to do so'. In his covering letter, he added: 'I believe that I could carry it through the Labour Party Executive if you would lead the nation on its basis'.[32]

Although this was an extraordinary intervention, three points should be borne in mind. First, there was the apparent unwillingness of the Labour leadership to build upon the more radical mood which had been evident since the downfall of Chamberlain. By late 1940 there was considerable public feeling against the 'old gang', and the power of vested interests. There appeared to be support for the idea of a 'people's war' and equality of sacrifice.[33] The rank-and-file of the Labour Party naturally voiced such sentiments, but Attlee had done little to *demonstrate* his support for them. In this respect, Laski could claim to be expressing Party views (even though he had no mandate to do so in this way). Secondly, Churchill was not yet seen to represent the Conservative Party. In May 1940 he had been far more popular with the Labour Party than with Conservatives and the mutual suspicion between himself and the 'appeasers' remained even after he became the party leader in October 1940. Laski's hope that Churchill might accept his ideas was therefore less bizarre in early 1941 than it would become later. Thirdly, the initiative was quite compatible with his goal of a 'revolution by consent', and with the arguments that he had just put to Attlee and the NEC. He fervently believed that the continuation of democracy in the post-war period depended on the establishment of a new consensus about social policy and the role of the state in the economy. Indeed, he had always insisted that peaceful change would be possible only if the privileged classes accepted a new settlement on such terms. Of course, he had generally expected the Labour Party to play the primary role in its introduction and often feared that conservative forces would resort to violence to defend their interests. But he would obviously welcome acceptance or even initiation of the process by non-socialist forces. This, after all, was the basis of his support for Roosevelt. Nevertheless, the direct appeal to Churchill revealed some naivete and an over-estimation of his own influence. In his reply, the Prime Minister simply assured him that the letter would be studied.[34] Laski therefore now resumed his efforts to pressurise the Labour Party into adopting a more radical stance.

Once again his proposals were tossed backwards and forwards between committees without any decision being taken. On 26 February the NEC referred his latest memorandum to the Policy Committee; when this met on 21 March, Greenwood objected to it, but it was agreed that, in view of the forthcoming annual conference, the office should prepare a new memorandum. However, Laski was critical of the result, and it was decided that he should collaborate with the Party's officers to amend the document for presentation to the subsequent meeting.[35] On 10 April the Policy Committee then agreed the document, with further amendments, and referred it back to the NEC.

The pace of progress was painfully slow and, at the beginning of April, Attlee also made it clear that he wanted no further official connection with Laski, who wished 'to continue propaganda of various kinds'.[36] Laski, feeling that his original suggestions had been diluted beyond recognition, and that Attlee was unwilling to do anything, probably now appealed to Herbert Morrison (the Home Secretary) to inject some urgency into the process.[37] As a result of his status as a potential rival for Attlee's leadership, this intervention was effective. The matter was now referred to a meeting of the Policy Committee on 23 May, chaired by Dalton and with Morrison in attendance. It was agreed to recommend to the NEC:

(1)   That a special committee on post-war Economic and Social Reconstruction be appointed to consider and make recommendations to the Policy Committee on problems likely to arise in the immediate post-war period.

(2)   That Mr Harold Laski be invited to become honorary secretary to the special committee in association with Head Office.

(3)   That the Committee (after consultation with Mr Harold Laski) be invited to select the personnel of the special committee, and be empowered to include persons not members of the National Executive Committee. That the special committee be authorised to appoint sub-committees from outside as well as inside its own membership.[38]

A week later the NEC confirmed this and Laski, having agreed to act as secretary, was asked to prepare a schedule of preliminary work for the committee.[39]

Almost a year after he had first raised the issue of the Labour ministers bringing some socialist measures into operation, Laski finally appeared to be getting somewhere. He now threw himself into his new task and, within a fortnight, proposed sixteen committees on reconstruction, suggesting the personnel of each. The composition of the Central Committee was approved, although Party control was strengthened by the insistence on additional membership from the NEC, PLP, and TUC General Council. Consideration of the membership of the sub-committees was deferred. A week later, the membership of the sub-committees was approved, and the whole amended document, with a memorandum by Laski, was referred back to the NEC.[40]

In terms of the scope of the enquiry and the expertise involved, this was clearly one of the most ambitious planning projects that any British political party had ever mounted. However, Attlee was not completely satisfied and, as a result of his intervention, NEC control was further strengthened by the decision to make all members of the Policy Committee members of the Central Committee. Shinwell was then elected as Chair of the new committee, with Laski as Secretary.[41]

The first meeting of the Central Committee took place on 30 July, with some further changes including, at Morrison's suggestion, the establishment of a further sub-committee on 'Social and Economic Transformation'.[42] After this, the work could finally start. But it was now summer and the first product of the committee was a long memorandum on 'The Labour Party and Domestic Reconstruction' written by Laski himself and submitted to the second meeting on 17 September.[43] This translated Laski's general theoretical position into the language of a party manifesto, and explained the rationale for specific reforms. Although his insistence on the need to begin domestic transformation *immediately* might have been controversial, the committee accepted his memorandum, with very minor amendments, although it stipulated that 'as a matter of courtesy the document should be sent, before publication, to the National Council of Labour' (the joint committee of the TUC, PLP, and NEC) and that consultations should take place with Greenwood with regard to the government's own post-war reconstruction survey.[44] The meeting also restructured the sub-committees, with Laski becoming Chair of the Committee on Scientific Research, Secretary of the Committee on Social and Economic Transformation and the Machinery of Central Government, a member of the International Relationships committee, and overall secretary. He was clearly the person with the greatest influence over the drafting of the report.

It was, as he said a 'big job' but, in his view, this was not simply because of the sheer amount of work involved but also because:

I foresee that a moment will come when the party has got to be made to stand up for certain vital principles even against the loyalty of its leaders to Winston. The latter is a grand war leader – really grand. But nothing leads me so far as to suppose that he is the right man for the peace.[45]

By December the committee's work was sufficiently advanced to prepare a preliminary report to present to the annual conference and Laski, in association with the officers, was called upon to draft it.[46] He produced this by 20 January and it was accepted by the Central Committee and forwarded to the NEC in early February. Shinwell presented the report – now known as *The Old World and the New Society* – and it was agreed that, subject to unspecified amendments, the document should be printed and issued. Shinwell also pointed out that, during the passage of the document through the committee,

Laski 'had performed extensive and unremitting work' and the NEC formally thanked him.

The specialist committees had only just begun their detailed work, so *The Old World and the New Society* was published as an interim report. It is notable that in various crucial respects the document was less radical than Laski's memorandum of the previous September. In particular, he had specified the need to nationalise the banks, land, the means of transport, and the supplies of coal and power and had envisaged a minimum wage. *The Old World and the New Society* was much vaguer on all these points. Nevertheless, it was an impressive document which outlined Labour's thinking and specific policy proposals on the whole range of domestic and international policy. It argued that to secure the fulfilment of Roosevelt's 'Four Freedoms' (freedom of speech and expression, religious freedom, freedom from want, and freedom from fear), it was necessary to organise immediately to provide full employment, social services to secure adequate health, nutrition, and care in old age, for everybody, and to provide full educational opportunities for all. It also dealt effectively with the problems of transition from a war-time to a peacetime economy; the necessary reforms in local and central government, and the machinery of justice; and the implications of Labour's programme on international and imperial policies. But the real quality of the document lay in its explanatory skills. In a succinct and forceful way, it traced the responsibility of capitalism for the failures of the past, argued that it would be equally catastrophic in the future, and explained the rationale for each of Labour's proposed reforms. And this was due to Laski, for the whole work was imbued with his outlook and style. Indeed he was incorporating his 'revolution by consent' into the party programme. But this meant that it reiterated, more than once, his fundamental assumption about the necessity for immediate change:

It is widely recognised . . . that the changes in our economic and social structure which the war-economy has exacted, while, if they are widely used, may lead to a strengthening of the democratic principle, cannot less surely lead, if they are unwisely used, to its destruction. It is certain that, at the end of this war, the economic system will have to lean heavily upon the support of the State. The central question this raises is whether this support is to be operated by the few in the interests of the few, as in the past, or by the organised community in the interests of the community.

One or the other is the choice we have to make. If we choose the first, a war for Democracy and Freedom will end in their destruction; if we choose the second, we can enter upon an epoch richer in fulfilment in ordinary men's lives than any past age. The choice cannot be postponed. It has to be made now.

We have to choose now because the character we give to the remaining period of this conflict itself determines the character of reconstruction, domestic and international. If we try to retain in being the foundations of the old system and regard reconstruction, as we regarded it in the last war, as a collection of pious maxims to be discarded when victory comes, it is quite certain that the after-war period will be one of frustration deepening into internecine conflict. If, on the other hand, the nation begins now the task of permeating its war-economy with the principles here affirmed, as peace comes, the minds of men will become accustomed to their acceptance and enlargement. By embarking now on a necessary readjustment, we shall make possible, in the post-war period, that unity of mood and purpose which enables the citizens of a community to keep the great ends of life in common, and to attain them stage by stage by the methods of democracy.[48]

Laski had now worked to excess to provide a programme and a rationale, which could rally the Party and exercise a power of attraction over the wider electorate. He also did his best – through another personal campaign within the NEC – to ensure that it was given some coverage by the BBC. But, of course, his real purpose was to make the leadership take the message about immediate implementation seriously. And it was on this issue that his conflict with Attlee escalated in February 1942. However, before examining this, it is necessary to consider two other issues in their disagreement.

INDIA

Throughout the 1930s Laski had become increasingly committed to the goal of Indian independence, despite his continuing qualms about the likelihood of inter-ethnic violence. In June 1938 he had participated, with Cripps and Attlee, in six secret meetings with Nehru, where they had discussed the terms of a treaty by which power would be transferred to India once a Labour government assumed control.[49] However, this appeared relatively academic in September 1939, and in India there was now a strengthening movement to refuse to support the war effort unless Britain made a categorical statement recognising the right to Indian self-determination. In October the Congress resigned from government in the seven provinces it controlled when the Viceroy failed to meet these demands.

Laski now favoured the issuing of an immediate British pledge on Indian independence. He therefore urged the Labour Party to take a far more active stance trying, unsuccessfully, to persuade the NEC to make a statement which would condemn the inadequacy of government policy. He also called upon NEC Shadow Cabinet members to indicate to Attlee and Wedgwood Benn the desirability for 'plain speaking' on government policy.[50] The next month he submitted a memorandum to the party leadership, in which he argued that there was a widespread threat of civil disobedience in India and that this would lead the Viceroy to resort to repressive measures. The government's Indian policy was being exploited by Germany and the Soviet Union to harm the British cause in neutral countries, and also made Labour supporters susceptible to the charge that this was an 'imperialist' war. And:

> The vague statements made on behalf of the Labour Party in the recent House of Commons debate have led to widespread suspicion in India of our *bona fides* as a Party about the future of India. It would be disastrous for us not to have the goodwill of the most effective Indian public opinion on our side, especially if circumstances made it desirable for us to enter a Government. It is certain that this would intensify Indian demands. We are already on record at Conference as being in favour of Indian self-government. I suggest that we should make our policy concrete *now* as a safeguard against future difficulties.[51]

He called for a pledge to grant full Dominion status to India within three years of the end of the war, and to adopt transitional measures immediately:

> A strong declaration by the Labour Party *now* would have a profound influence over the world. We simply cannot afford to appear either favourable to, or vague about, the reactionary attitude of the Government. Nothing so far said by or on behalf of the

Party has convinced people like Nehru and those in the Congress who are anxious to be our friends that we really care to join with them in a just and peaceful settlement of our relations.[52]

There was, however, no response by the leadership, and early in 1940 Laski (backed by Ellen Wilkinson) tried to secure a reference to India in Labour's statement on the war. Once again he was defeated, but it was agreed that a document specifically on India should be prepared by a sub-committee, on which he was to serve.[53] However, by April Attlee's position appeared to be little more than an endorsement of an appeal to Congress not to threaten civil disobedience.[54] In August the government made an offer to the Indians, but it was without concrete commitments, and was rejected, leading to further British repression.[55] In November 1940 Laski therefore took up the issue again, proposing that Labour should urge a new attempt at mediation. Attlee's response was non-committal.[56]

By now Laski was deeply critical of Churchill's 'blindness' on the issue of Indian independence, and of Labour's apparent acquiescence in this approach.[57] As Attlee had still not responded to the suggestion of mediation after two months it was agreed in the International sub-committee that Laski should approach him on the issue.[58] Nevertheless, when the Party Conference met in June 1941, no progress had been made, and three powerful pro-Congress speeches were made by delegates.[59] Soon afterwards Laski again took the issue up in a joint meeting of the Emergency Executive Committee and the International sub-committee. He pointed out that the Indian deadlock was so important that Attlee should be present and, in a later meeting the same day, it was agreed that five members of the NEC (including Laski) should see the Secretary of State for India (Amery) for a report of the latest situation.[60] This took place on 18 July but did not provide any real reassurance.

During the summer the Viceroy's Executive Council was enlarged to contain a majority of Indians for the first time, but the Viceroy retained his special powers and no Indians were given ministerial posts. Under pressure from the Cabinet – including Attlee – Churchill was forced to agree to the release of Indians who had supported Gandhi's campaign for civil disobedience. But he also insisted that the Atlantic Charter did not apply to India.[61] In October Laski therefore called for a further meeting and proposed constitutional progress on the model of Canadian and Australian negotiations. It was agreed that these ideas should be put to the NEC.[62] However, he was not able to be present at the meeting (because of the death of his father) and Attlee was in the USA, so the matter was referred back to the International sub-committee. Laski then had to make a special request to ensure that the matter was placed on the agenda for the committee's meeting in December.[63] At this he called for a further deputation to Amery, to propose that a high-level personality should be sent to India to make a new offer to Indian political parties. He also urged the rapid Indianisation of the Viceroy's Council and the subordination of the Commander-in-Chief of the armed forces to an Indian.[64] It was agreed that a special sub-committee meeting on India should be held, to which Attlee should be invited.[65] At this point Attlee, chairing the Cabinet in Churchill's absence, concluded that a further general discussion on India was necessary.[66] The issue had been raised by Bevin, and it is probable that both he and Attlee were responding to pressure from Laski and others in the party.[67]

The special meeting met on 19 January and Laski reported the results to Frida:

> Yesterday we got somewhere after a long struggle. Clem opposed it all; but they all backed me except George Ridley and he was shaken. So at 6.30 . . . we carried the resolution unanimously (i) that we re-affirm the right of India to self-government (ii) that the British government announce *now* that this is pledged to India within 3 years of the end of hostilities; and (iii) that a high personality be sent out to India pledged to faith in this to negotiate with political parties with a view to securing full co-operation on this basis at once. We have Stafford in mind. We meet next Friday to hear from Clem whether he will back it or not. And I think the group was clear that it would act independently of him if he refused. I made an attack on him there which had useful results.[68]

This may have been effective for, on 24 January, Attlee wrote to Amery suggesting that it was worth considering whether someone should be charged with a mission to try to bring the Indian leaders together.[69]

Laski then submitted a draft for a joint statement on India to be made by the NEC and the Parliamentary party, which would then also be put to the TUC. However, his proposal was diluted in a subsequent meeting. Whereas he had called for a high personality 'who fully accepts the idea of Indian self-government and is prepared to give all his energies to its successful initiation', the reference to a political commitment to independence was omitted from the final draft. Similarly, the following passage was excised from the final statement:

> In order that his mission (i.e. that of the high level personality) should be a success, his instructions should empower him, if he finds it necessary,
>
> a) to agree to the full Indianisation of the Viceroy's Council forthwith.
> b) to agree that the Viceroy's council should at once take measures to draft an Indian Constitution for negotiation with His Majesty's Government.
> c) to undertake . . . , after such negotiation, to pledge the word of His Majesty's Government to agree to submit the Constitution to Parliament for its acceptance.
> d) to offer all assistance to the Government of India, personal and otherwise that may aid in the achievement of 2) (i.e. the attainment of Indian self-government within three years of the armistice) above.[70]

Attlee took an even less specific proposal to the Cabinet. Lord Linthingow, the Viceroy, had just sent a dispatch effectively rejecting any concessions,[71] and on 2 February Attlee presented a memorandum on the Indian political situation to the War Cabinet, which challenged the Viceroy's conclusion that nothing could or should be done. Denouncing Linthingow's language as 'crude imperialism', Attlee proposed a renewed effort to get the leaders of Indian political parties to unite. His preference would be to send a person of standing with wide powers to negotiate a settlement in India, either as a special envoy or in replacement of the present Viceroy.[72] Churchill was now forced to compromise but an impasse on party lines remained until Cripps (now in the Government) offered to go to India himself to discuss an agreed Cabinet scheme with Indian leaders. In the event, Cripps's mission, which left on 30 March, was unsuccessful: civil disobedience again erupted and, in August 1942, the Congress leaders were interned.

In fact, it may well have been impossible for Attlee and the Labour leadership to have much impact on the Indian situation. Given the hostility of the Conservative ministers in the Cabinet, the attitude of the Viceroy, and the divisions amongst the Indian leaders, progress would have been extremely difficult.[73] Nevertheless, by early 1942 Laski had good reason to feel that Attlee was, once again, dragging his feet on an issue of crucial importance. Because of his intimate contact with Indian nationalist opinion, Laski was well aware that *immediate* changes were necessary, while Attlee appeared to believe that the future was more important than the current situation.[74] Moreover, at each stage he had seemed reluctant to raise the issue, and it was only when the India lobby within the Party exerted pressure that he appeared to act. Even then he used his influence against the commitment to a more radical stance on independence, sometimes appearing more anxious to defend his record on the Simon Committee in the 1920s than to discuss the immediate issues.[75]

By February 1942 the Indian issue, like that of domestic change, had made Laski extremely frustrated with the leadership. However, he viewed one other external question as still more crucial: the relationship with the Soviet Union.

THE SOVIET UNION AND THE SOCIALIST INTERNATIONAL

Laski had been deeply critical of the Nazi-Soviet pact and the attack on Finland.[76] Nevertheless, he was also alarmed by the warlike response of both the British government and the Labour Party to the Soviet action in Finland, for he had no doubt that Nazism constituted a far greater evil than Stalinism, and he continued to view the Soviet Union as a potential ally. Soon after the defeat of Finland, he therefore put forward a motion within the NEC, urging 'the Government to explore without delay the possibility of rebuilding effective relations with the USSR'.[77] However, his colleagues were not ready for this step and he could do nothing to change Party policy before June 1941. Almost immediately after Hitler's attack on the USSR he took his opportunity.

In July it was agreed in the party's Press, Publicity and Campaign committee that he should write a pamphlet on 'The Labour Party and the Soviet Union'.[78] This took a little longer than he had intended because of the death of his father. When he finally produced it in December 1941 – just after the USA had also entered the war – it precipitated a major new conflict between himself and Attlee.

Laski's draft pamphlet both summarised his view of the history of the Anglo-Soviet relationship since 1917 and proposed the direction of future policy. It was also a *cri de coeur* which elaborated some of his deepest feelings on the subject. In general, he argued that in international policy, the Soviet Union had been more sinned against than sinning, as Bolshevism had provided privileged interests with an excuse for counter-revolution. The British government had thus attempted an accommodation 'with Hitlerite Germany in the West which would direct the ambitions of its evil and restless leader against the Soviet Union'.[79] Although Stalin had been guilty of illegitimate policies between 1939 and 1941, Hitler's attack on the USSR had brought about a new Anglo-Soviet partnership which 'laid the foundation of a new world for the building of which the Labour Party had been fighting without cessation ever since 1917'.

Laski then proceeded to outline, in some detail, the necessity for a full partnership between Britain, the Soviet Union, and the USA in the post-war world on the basis of their continuing commitment to Roosevelt's 'Four Freedoms'. He predicted that it would be difficult to maintain unity between them because the armistice would probably lead to revolution over the greater part of Europe and, in many countries, the only effective revolutionary force would be communism. However, such disputes could be avoided if the three powers jointly assisted any government which accepted the Four Freedoms and if Britain and the USA agreed not to refuse aid to countries which combined constitutional democracy with socialist economic forms.

This was a simultaneous attempt to ensure Western acceptance of socialist regimes and the establishment of democratic, rather than dictatorial governments. However, he was equally insistent that the only way in which the 'four freedoms' could be effective would be in a world in which the 'principle of abundance' replaced the 'principle of scarcity' as the foundation of economic life. Since this was not possible under laissez-faire capitalism, he saw the solution in the West as a form of mixed economy in which considerable areas of production remained in private ownership. In these circumstances, he believed that harmonious relations between the Soviet Union and the West would be possible.

All this was controversial, but it was coupled with a further proposal which was even more problematic from the point of view of the Labour leadership: the suggestion that the Labour Party and the Soviet Union should attempt to reach agreement on the establishment of a new Socialist International.

In Laski's view the founding of the Communist International had been a disastrous mistake. Bourgeois statesman had seen it 'as a ghostly hand stretched forward everywhere to destroy' and had used it as a pretext for anti-Soviet actions. But it had also had a catastrophic impact on the Labour movement. The tragic past errors of the CP, including its persistent vilification of the Labour Party, had done much 'to destroy any prospect of a united working-class front in Britain'. All of this had come about because communists had placed their ideas under the patronage of Moscow and had therefore allowed their policies to follow the twists and turns in Soviet policies. Any repetition in the post-war world would be equally disastrous. Indeed, if the CP continued as before, it would 'do more to poison Anglo-Soviet relations than any other factor . . . '. This meant that the possibility of creative reconstruction in the post-war era depended 'very largely on the achievement of a full understanding now between the Soviet Union and the British Labour Movement'. Since this was extremely unlikely while the USSR maintained the Third International in its present form:

> The clear need is to rebuild . . . a single Socialist International, in which the Russian workers have their full share, able to mobilise, in an integrated way, the Socialist forces of Europe.

He maintained that this was a practical necessity since the problems would be on an international plane and only an organisation which could build 'the Socialist forces of the world into an unbreakable unity' would be able to meet them with confidence. But the construction of such unity would require a supreme effort from both British Labour and the Soviet Union:

> On the side of British Labour it means the recognition that isolation from the revolutionary forces of the Continent is disastrous, and that these forces are bound, in large degree, to look to a victorious Moscow for their inspiration; on the Russian side, it means the substitution of co-operation for domination, and the recognition that to elevate the methods of bolshevism to the status of a universal is to unite against a common understanding much that, with a greater elasticity of outlook, could provide it with important sources of strength.

Laski's pamphlet was perhaps too optimistic about Stalin's foreign policy, and was reductionist in its explanation of imperialism and expansionism as purely capitalist drives. Nevertheless, the main arguments were extremely powerful and there was an almost uncanny accuracy about its predictions of the dire consequences for the post-war world if no agreement was reached with the Soviet Union. But it was also an attempt to 'bounce' the party into adopting a particular policy, based on an overall perspective.

The Press and Publicity Campaign committee was divided when it discussed the pamphlet on 21 January 1942. But the only outright opposition to it came from Attlee who 'expressed the view that the pamphlet was not suitable for publication'.[80] He declared:

> I regard the pamphlet as one written for the intelligentsia rather than for the rank and file of the Party. I should prefer something written in more simple and homely language.[81]

He made some fair criticisms, arguing, for example, that Laski had overemphasised economic factors and that the danger of the enforcement of communist ideology by the Soviet Union was just as great as the enforcement of capitalism by Britain and the United States. But he also claimed, quite falsely, that Laski had not mentioned communist 'endeavours to destroy democratic socialist parties', and he ignored the main thrust of the argument. Overall, it was clear that Attlee's real objection was that the pamphlet was too sympathetic to the Soviet Union. This was hardly surprising as, within the Cabinet, Attlee was often more hostile to Soviet claims than many Conservatives.[82]

In view of Attlee's position, the Press and Publicity Committee decided that the pamphlet raised issues of policy and should be referred to the NEC as a whole. In fact, no further discussion was to take place on it until the end of March. Laski thus found that, on another crucial policy area, he had been blocked by the party leader.

LASKI VERSUS ATTLEE (1942–3)

By February 1942 Laski's impatience with Attlee was about to erupt. He had found him deeply reluctant to press ahead on any domestic reforms which might precipitate a major conflict with Churchill; his attitude to Indian independence appeared complacent; and he was blocking the suggestion of a new initiative towards the Soviet Union. Laski had also experienced rank-and-file dissatisfaction with the leadership while speaking in constituencies around the country.[83] Moreover, in December 1941, there had been the biggest backbench rebellion thus far in the war, when forty Labour MPs voted for an unofficial amendment which called for immediate public ownership of all industries vital for the war effort as a *quid pro quo* when the government tightened the regulations on National Service. Attlee, who had threatened resignation unless the party backed the new legislation, then tried to get NEC support for the disciplining of the dissidents.[84] However, Laski had obtained a majority for an amendment which refused to discuss the internal discipline of the PLP, unless the issue was brought to it by the parliamentary Party itself.[85] At the end of 1941 he was already beginning to feel that no progress could be made 'until we blow Attlee up'.[86] But the real crisis came in February 1942 when Churchill shuffled his Cabinet, and sacked Greenwood, who had been in charge of post-war reconstruction policy.

It is possible that, in the long term, the Cabinet changes strengthened Labour's position in the government, for Dalton was now promoted to President of the Board of Trade, Cripps (who did not rejoin the Party until March 1945) was brought in as Lord Privy Seal and Leader of the House, and Attlee became Deputy Prime Minister. However, Conservative ministers dominated education, health and housing, and there was no sign of any impetus towards post-war reconstruction. Since Laski, with considerable NEC and rank-and-life support, had been arguing that it was time for significant changes to be made *immediately*, the dismissal of Greenwood appeared to indicate a *weakening* of Labour's influence and the negation of the arguments of the *Old World and the New Society*, which the party had just published. A special meeting of the NEC was therefore called for 6 March to discuss the issues with Labour Ministers.

For Laski the reshuffling of the Cabinet was the final straw and he took the opportunity to try to topple Attlee as leader. Bevin was widely seen as the most dynamic and powerful Labour minister and, on 1 March, Laski told Frida that he wanted to persuade him to stand for the leadership.[87] He therefore consciously planned to undermine Attlee at the forthcoming NEC meeting, and wrote urgent letters to seven members of the Executive, including Morrison, to try to get them to fight hard.[88] In addition to this attack on Attlee, he hoped to secure agreement that a deputation should see the Prime Minister:

so that before the Conference we know where he stands. If he is hostile that gives me a chance of fighting there for our exit from the government.[89]

At the NEC a two-hour discussion took place. The only point which was minuted was the hope that similar meetings would take place in the future. But Laski continued his campaign, writing to Bevin on 9 March to urge him to take over the leadership, as it was time for a fighting leader.[90]

Although Laski's attempt to remove Attlee failed, there was certainly considerable discontent within the NEC. A joint NEC/PLP meeting on 26 March was a stormy occasion in which the leadership was critical of dissidents for rocking the boat, while the party chair pointed out that, at the NEC meeting the previous day, 'grave misgivings had been expressed regarding the changes in the Cabinet and the method by which these alterations had been brought about'.[91] The meeting broke up with a decision that further joint meetings should take place, perhaps also with the TUC General Council.

While the internal conflict within the Party had been mounting, Laski made a further direct private appeal to Churchill himself. On 25 March the Prime Minister sent a decisive reply:

> It is entirely beyond my share of life and strength to deal with all the issues which your letter raises. In my view, we ought to win the war first, and then in a free country the issues of Socialism and Free Enterprise can be fought out in a constitutional manner. I certainly should think it very undemocratic if anyone were to try to carry Socialism during a party truce without a Parliamentary majority. I have always accounted you a friend rather than a follower. I think it would be a pity to break up the national unity in the war and that I believe is the opinion of the mass of the people.[92]

Two weeks later the NEC held a special meeting, with Attlee in attendance, on the position of the Labour Party after the removal of Greenwood. Having received a final rebuff from Churchill, Laski now tried to exert more pressure on the party leadership by submitting a memorandum, 'The Party and the Future'.

The rank and file were, he argued, gravely perturbed by the drift of events because of the belief that:

the Labour Party is being dragged at the tail of the Conservative Party, that, in return for a handful of social reforms, none of them fundamental in character, we are assisting the vested interests of this country to strengthen their hold upon the state-power, and that, when the War is over, they will be able, as things stand, to preserve their privileges at the expense of the workers. Not a single measure has been taken by this Government which offsets this belief; and it appears that some measures have been taken – without any reference to this Executive – which prejudges the post-War position e.g. shipping, to the advantage of the vested interests.

Nor was it an answer to say that coalition government was a process of give and take:

I suggest that on all fundamental matters we do the giving and the Tories do the taking. No doubt in things like the Means Test and Old Age Pensions there have been improvements; my own belief is that Mr Churchill has conceded very little to us that he would not have been compelled to concede had we remained in Opposition.

It was, he argued, misconceived to say that Labour was not entitled to ask for Socialist measures. The war was a dynamic one which would inevitably lead towards a planned society:

Is it to be planned for privilege or for the people? Public opinion, not least the armed forces, asks that question insistently. We have ourselves answered it by implication in the Interim Report on Reconstruction [*Old World* . . .]. We have there said that steps must be taken along its lines *before* the cessation of hostilities if we are to avoid the tragedies of the inter-War years. If the Conference approves the resolutions we are submitting to it, then we must press for the steps to be taken *now*. The question we have, as an Executive, to ask ourselves is whether we mean seriously to demand action from the Government along the lines of our Resolutions – if the Conference accepts them – and if so what action we are to demand.

He then made a definite proposal:

I submit to my colleagues . . . that our solemn duty to the great Movement we represent is to make up our minds about the minimum programme of measures we must demand from the Prime Minister and stick to that programme at all costs. If it be said that this risks the break-up of the Government we must take that risk.[94]

This was a powerful argument for, as Laski claimed, party policy was to press for changes to begin during the war itself. Of course, one of the reasons that this had been stated explicitly was because of Laski's insistence upon the point and his primary role in drafting *The Old World and the New Society*. Nevertheless, it reflected much rank-and-file feeling, and Laski's report had presumably been allowed to go ahead because the leadership had wanted to rally morale in the movement at the annual conference. If so, Attlee was now facing the consequences of a somewhat disingenuous approach to the party. However, he defended himself vigorously, though in terms which hardly differed from those of Churchill.

Laski's memorandum, he argued, ignored the fundamental facts of the situation, since there was no majority in the House of Commons for a Socialist policy or for a fundamental change in the economic organisation of the country, and it was impossible to hold a fair General Election at present. He and his colleagues in the government held that the Party should not try to get socialist measures implemented under the guise of winning the war, but Laski was prepared to insist upon a minimum programme, even at the risk of breaking up the government.

What would be the effect on the Party if it left the Government? He [Mr Attlee] thought that by going into Opposition it would be held that the Party had slipped out of responsibility when things looked black. If, in such circumstances, the War went against the country, everybody would go down. If it went in favour of the country, the Labour Party, politically, would be in a poor position, and the result of a General Election would be disastrous. When victory came, we should be out of it.[95]

He also claimed that party criticisms of the government were having a damaging effect upon opinion in the USA and the Dominions, and could undermine morale in the armed forces and civilian population. Victory could be attained only by unity and it was not true that

Labour was doing all the 'giving' and the Tories all the 'taking' – the Tories felt the opposite. The government would be willing to take any step which could be shown definitely necessary or desirable for winning the war.

Having said this, Attlee left the meeting for another engagement, intimating that he could return later if so desired. However, he had failed to convince the NEC and, on his return, he was informed that the general opinion was that:

> any action leading to the break-up of the Government would be disastrous, but the view was held by a large number of people inside and outside the Party that the measures regarded as essential for the better prosecution of the War were not being implemented as political reasons and political prejudice prevented their fair consideration.[96]

Attlee tried to ward off the criticisms but was still unable to carry the meeting, which resolved that the Prime Minister should be asked to receive a deputation from the NEC so that he could personally hear the views which had been expressed. Since it was also decided to try to arrange a further joint NEC/PLP meeting (perhaps also with the TUC) before the end of April, there were clear signs that the pressure on Attlee would continue, and that Laski's views had considerable support.

Laski himself appeared certain about the position. On 6 April he told some of his American friends that he was prepared to go into opposition to fight for the Labour Party programme:

> I know that the PM has done great things for us, but not even he must be allowed to use his great authority to prevent the organisation of the postulates which make social peace possible in the post-war world. At present he is an obstacle. I cherish the hope that, after our conference in May, he may see that the alternative is some such changes or Labour in opposition and that he will choose the changes. But if he wont I have no sort of doubt that our job is to act on the principles we have set out in our report.[97]

He wrote to another American friend, Max Lerner:

> I hope we shall get a directive from the Party conference next month which will clarify the direction of events. At least I have

my programme through, and all the evidence suggests that the big unions will back me on its implications against Attlee and the other standpatters.

However, he also expressed a note of caution:

Whether, at the crucial moment, they will go as far as I would go I am not certain; the fear of embarrassing the government is deep, though I am certain that mass-opinion is literally ten years ahead of its leaders. Anyway a great drama is in the making, and the lines I have to speak are quite clear to me.[98]

In fact, he was overconfident. On 16 April, the decision to seek a meeting with Churchill was referred back to the NEC by the Emergency Executive Committee.[99] However, at the end of the month Left-wing Independents overturned large Conservative majorities in two by-elections, and Laski now cited these results in support of his campaign.[100] It was, he argued, clear that there was an anti-Conservative mood in all urban seats and that the political truce was driving would-be Labour voters to support Progressive independents. This could lead to a dangerous atomisation of political opinion, and it was vital to rally Labour supporters. He therefore again called for an interview with Churchill before the Party Conference. He also resumed his proposal, on which there had so far been procrastination, that a Labour Party delegation should be sent to the USSR and that this decision should be reported to the forthcoming annual conference.[101] His call for the meeting with Churchill was defeated, but it was now agreed that a general reference to the intention to send a delegation to Russia could be made. A divided NEC agreed that Laski should make a statement on this to the Conference.[102]

Laski's speech on post-war reconstruction, and his statement about the delegation to the Soviet Union, were both popular with the Labour Party Conference. A few weeks later he told Frida that there had been some great party meetings, almost like election time:

But the plea of all the questioners was – can't you give us a lead? So I sat down and wrote to Clem and told him what the universal impression was; and I said quite bluntly, if you don't want to lead, get out and give way to someone who will.[103]

In fact, Attlee's position was relatively secure. Even at the Conference there was little support for Laski's idea of withdrawing from the government if Churchill made no gesture,[104] and he was unable to make much headway either in policy terms or in his campaign against the party leader. He was heading for a new conflict which would weaken his own position.

By the summer of 1942 Laski was totally frustrated by the impasse that had been reached. At the same time his own constant attacks were naturally causing intense irritation in leadership circles and, of course, he had made no secret of his wish to topple Attlee. There were no doubt many who were anxious to cut Laski down to size, and he himself now precipitated the onslaught by a series of articles in *Reynolds News* between July and September which were openly critical of the Labour ministers for their acquiescence in Churchill's policies.[105] The anger of the leadership was exacerbated by the fact that it was also facing increasing opposition within the PLP. In July, for example, fifty Labour backbenchers tried to secure further increases in pensions by voting against the government. Since Laski's first article had effectively supported the rebels, the leadership used the opportunity as part of a wider attempt to clamp down on dissent.

On 12 August, Walter Halls, an ex-Labour MP, wrote to the Party secretary complaining about Laski's attacks on the leadership. The matter was immediately referred to the organisation sub-committee. This agreed that the articles were 'most reprehensible and deserving of censure' and unanimously resolved that the case should be referred to the NEC.[106] When the confrontation finally occurred on 12 October there was a two-hour debate, in which both Attlee and Bevin called for loyalty, with the latter stressing the gains made by the working class as a result of Labour being in office.[107]

It is difficult to adjudicate between Laski's argument that Labour's participation in government had led to no significant advance, and the leadership's insistence to the contrary. Certainly, the wartime economy was quite different from that which had existed in 1939. There were now government controls over capital and industry, direction of labour, conscription of both men and women for war work, regulation of civilian consumption through a comprehensive rationing system, and elaborate planning mechanisms. There was also higher taxation, price fixing, strict control over non-essential goods, and full employment. It is also true, as the Labour ministers maintained, that the Conservatives felt that they were on the defensive. As Jefferys puts it:

in the interests of national unity, Tory supporters had acquiesced in a whole range of measures that had hitherto been anathema. Higher rates of income tax; excess profits duty at 100%; increased wage rates in industry and a rationing system based on 'fair shares for all – all these could be taken as signs of 'creeping socialism'.[108]

Nevertheless, Laski's view was justified in two fundamental respects. First, it seems clear that the majority of the changes had come about almost entirely as a result of the exigencies of the war, and the 'battle for production'. The government had paid no real attention to social policy, and post-war planning had a very low status in the Cabinet's scale of priorities. Secondly, Laski – rather than the leadership – was certainly voicing the feelings of the rank-and-file and much of the electorate.[109]

In any case, Laski defended himself vehemently, claiming that:

having endeavoured, without success, to interest the NEC in criticisms he had brought to bear upon our leaders in the Government, he claimed that he had a right to make an appeal thereon to the Movement outside.[110]

Since Attlee and Bevin had to leave the meeting, it was adjourned until 28 October. When it resumed, Morrison tried to conciliate both sides in the dispute, arguing that criticism was healthy, but that Laski's views had been made more public than was desirable. Laski then intimated that he was prepared to accept this 'on the understanding that he was entitled to criticise or raise the personal issue of the leadership within the National Executive Committee'.[111] His explanation of his position was then accepted by thirteen to four, and he immediately moved back to the offensive by suggesting that the NEC should ask the PLP to put further pressure on the government by moving a motion at the opening of the new parliamentary session. Instead it was agreed that a joint meeting of the NEC and PLP should take place on 10 November 1942. Laski had been reprimanded, but the internal conflict had not been resolved.

The November meeting was not minuted, but Laski told Frida that he thought that Attlee would soon be forced out, since he had made a poor speech and had been attacked as soon as he had left.[112] At the NEC on 25 November, he tried to force the pace again by putting forward a motion 'that steps be taken by the Officers to arrange an early meeting between the Prime Minister and the National Executive Committee with a view to discussing the direction of policy'.[113] He then agreed to withdraw his motion when it was resolved that a meeting should first be held with the Labour minister (Sir William Jowitt) who had just been made responsible for government post-war reconstruction policy, and subsequently with the Labour members of the War Cabinet. He was clearly not isolated in the NEC – despite his 'indiscretions' – and Labour ministers continued to be put on the defensive, with manifestations of deep dissatisfaction over the government's record.

Then, in December, the inter-departmental committee on Social Insurance and Allied services, chaired by Lord Beveridge, produced a far more radical and extensive report than had been envisaged. The Beveridge report, proposing a system of social security for all citizens 'from the cradle to the grave' was immediately welcomed by the NEC, without any record of dissent and, on 17 December, this stance was confirmed by the National Council of Labour (representing the NEC, PLP, and TUC).[114] However, when the report was debated in Parliament in February, it became clear that the bulk of the Conservative Party was negative about it and that the government compromise was to procrastinate. This outraged the majority of the PLP, leading to an amendment calling for immediate implementation, and the biggest anti-government vote of the war period. On 24 February Attlee told the NEC that it was impossible to obtain support for the full Labour Party position within the government, and that its position there was weakened by disunity within the PLP. However, a motion moved by Laski, reaffirming the attitude towards the Beveridge Report which had been adopted on 17 December, was carried *nem con*, while a loyalist addendum expressing confidence in Labour Members of the government was defeated by thirteen votes to four.[115] The future of the coalition government appeared to be in doubt and, although it survived, there were to be further explosions of discontent during the year. In particular, Churchill's adamant refusal to repeal the Trade Disputes Act (enacted after the General Strike), led to further major conflict between the TUC, NEC and PLP on the one hand, and the Labour ministers on the other.[116] As always, Laski was at the centre of the disputes and, at a joint meeting of the three organisations on 8 June, he suggested a joint deputation to Churchill, asking for the repeal of parts of the Act so as to give masses of trade unionists 'a sense of hope and exhilaration, a gesture and return for the effort they had made'.[117] However, he failed to secure support for the proposal, and eventually the movement acquiesced in Churchill's refusal to budge on the issue.

By now Laski was completely alienated from the Labour leadership and saw his function as helping 'the Labour Party . . . to understand that it is better to fight alone for your socialism than to be a junior partner in a capitalist enterprise'.[118] However, few shared his belief that, in the final analysis, Labour should risk withdrawing from the coalition, and his attempt to unseat Attlee had failed.

In fact, his attempted 'coup' against the party leader had been unwise. Apart from any other considerations, Attlee's position was obviously far more powerful than Laski's. His public attacks on the leadership in the summer of 1942 also presented Attlee with a golden opportunity to weaken him within the NEC. This again reflected a lack of political judgment on Laski's part. Finally, as already noted, the idea of withdrawing from the coalition was unpopular in the party but, without this ultimate threat, its leverage over the government was inevitably limited. But if Laski's position is open to serious criticisms, it can also be defended. First, he reflected the genuine concerns of the rank-and-file. Secondly, on numerous occasions, other members of the NEC obviously supported him, but were content to shelter behind his lead. And it was this kind of pressure which at least induced Attlee to raise the issues with Churchill. This has already been shown on the Indian question. In the same way, it was no doubt party outrage over the Conservative attitudes to the Beveridge report which led Attlee to send an ascerbic private memorandum to the Prime Minister on the subject.[119]

Laski's campaign against Attlee was based on the fear that, instead of bringing about the 'revolution by consent', the leadership was buttressing the old order. He therefore believed that he had a duty to continue the pressure despite constant rebuffs. In June 1942 – at the height of his attempt to oust Attlee – he told Frida:

I suppose I must go on doing my job, but I wish I felt that I was serving a movement whose leaders were worthy of its followers.[120]

. . . I get to the wish that I had less of a conscience. It would give me more of you.[121]

In November 1942, just after he had been reprimanded by the NEC, he wrote her a still more significant letter:

> Don't be angry or distressed at my labour articles. It may well be that I accomplish nothing, as you say. . . . But even if I fail it is important to me to try and do the thing I believe to be right; I think that is a duty. It is something you taught me long ago, and I cannot now try to put my comfort first and my principles second. And I don't think you would really want me to try. I feel this the more because in these two wars I have had so much ease when others have had the pain.[122]

He genuinely believed that he had no choice but to act as he did, and that he was serving the interests of the ordinary peoples of Britain and the world. His unceasing battles were already causing him intense strain, which would soon become far worse.

FADING HOPES IN AMERICA, 1940–3

During the thirties Laski's faith in Roosevelt and the New Deal had been a solace when he felt generally deeply pessimistic about the political situation in Europe. During the early stages of the war, there was no change in his outlook. He celebrated Roosevelt's third term victory in 1940 and placed many of his hopes for the post-war world on liberal America. Once again, he also called on Roosevelt to pressurise the British government – and even the Labour Party – into a more radical stance on international and domestic issues.[123] His constant insertion of Roosevelt's 'Four Freedoms' in Labour Party statements was not simply propaganda: it reflected a genuine belief that an international New Deal provided the basis for post-war harmony. However, once the USA actually entered the war his hopes began to fade.

At best he soon found that Roosevelt, like Churchill, believed that military victory was the sole concern, and that there was no need to become involved in controversy over the post-war social and economic structure. At worst he saw that the US government preferred to deal with reactionary forces – such as the Vichy regime – than to side with 'European revolution'. During 1942 and 1943 he therefore realised that Roosevelt had feet of clay. Perhaps even worse, it soon became apparent that Felix Frankfurter also differed from him, sharing the conventional faith in military victory as the sole goal.

In the summer of 1942, in the midst of his conflict with Attlee, a new and profound disappointment befell him in relation to the USA.

The organisers of an International Student Conference invited Laski to be the principal speaker at the plenary session on 'The People's Century'.[124] Eleanor Roosevelt was to preside at this session and invited him to stay at the White House, saying that she and the President would get 'a great deal of pleasure to have an opportunity to see you.'[125] Laski was extremely keen to go and would obviously have taken the opportunity to try to convince his American friends that they should adopt progressive policies and exert maximum pressure on the British government to do the same. But he immediately sought Churchill's permission:

> Mr and Mrs Roosevelt are old and dear friends of mine and I should not like to miss the chance of a talk with them . . . But I do not want to accept . . . if, by any chance, you would feel that a speech of mine in Washington would be an embarrassment to you. Deeply as I differ from your conception of the meaning of the war, I am too keenly aware that you are the necessary leader of the nation at this time to be willing to add to your burdens by pushing a point of view about the political strategy of the war which, alas, you do not accept.[126]

This gave Churchill a chance to veto the visit, which he was determined to do, provided he did not offend the President. The Foreign Office had no doubts. Laski, an official argued, was still 'contentious' in the United States because of the Boston police strike (!), and his recent speech to the Labour Party conference:

> We do not want in the United States, just before the election, contentious figures who make timorous but friendly Republicans think that Great Britain is going Red.[127]

He argued that Eden and Beaverbrook were also convinced that Laski should be 'headed off', but that Halifax (the Ambassador in Washington) thought the worst possible solution would be if Laski was seen to decline because of Churchill's objections. However, Eleanor Roosevelt was also working through the American ambassador in London (John Winant) who took it up with Eden. He claimed that he had twice approached Churchill, but had received no indication of the Prime Minister's attitude. At this point Winant thought that he would still be able to secure his assent with a little more time.[128] However, the Prime Minister's office had already informed

Laski that, having consulted Halifax, Churchill would 'deprecate' the visit while an American election campaign was underway. This was a real blow to Laski. As he told Eleanor Roosevelt; 'a sight of America – a glance at the President, talk with Felix, these would been new life to me'.[129]

The next day she made a direct appeal to Churchill to allow Laski to come. This led to further subterfuge, with an unsuccessful attempt to pretend that the Prime Minister was only acting on advice.[130] However, on 7 August, an official in the British Embassy in Washington revealed a significant sidelight on the episode. He reported that, during a lunch with the President, Eleanor Roosevelt had expressed regret that Churchill had not wanted Laski to come to the USA. She presumed that he had felt that Laski's opinions about the British government might do harm, but she was disappointed. The dispatch continued:

> The President chipped in to say with emphasis that he, the President, had said he would not and could not have him here before the Elections in November. Didn't we think he was right in this? He would of course like to see 'dear Harold' and talk with him very much, but he was sure he was right. Mrs Roosevelt said she wished the President had told her.[131]

And on 13 August Churchill expressed his true feelings in a cable to Harry Hopkins:

> Laski has been a considerable nuisance over here and will I doubt not talk extreme left wing stuff in the United States. Although I liked his father and have maintained friendly relations with the son he has attacked me continually and tried to force my hand both in home and war politics. Unless therefore Mrs Roosevelt makes a personal point of it I should be glad if the invitation were not pressed.[132]

This ended the episode.

The truth was that Laski was now becoming very isolated amongst the political elites in both Britain and the USA. Churchill would not give him a platform in the USA, and there were many people in Washington who would not have welcomed his visit. The FBI was collecting a file of his statements, and some of the Right were arguing that he was the centre of an international communist conspiracy, which fed information to Eleanor Roosevelt and Felix Frankfurter.[133]

Churchill's action (perhaps connived at by Roosevelt) deprived Laski of an opportunity to see some of his closest friends and to try to influence the situation in Washington. From then on he attempted to work through Winant, newspaper articles, and radio broadcasts with the American correspondent, Ed Murrow. Naturally, he was unable to make any substantial impact on American policy and, by 1943, was beginning to despair about the situation. A message to him from Frankfurter (through Winant) to stop attacking Churchill no doubt reinforced his sense of isolation.[134]

In April 1943 Laski's frustration with American policy led him to voice his criticisms in public, with an Open Letter to Roosevelt in the *New Statesman*, which bitterly criticised American foreign policy.[135] Winant was furious and told him:

> it is a mistake to set up conflicting ideologies in the United States that have the appearance of pulling away from the men who are trying to prosecute the war by finding fault with them because you are not satisfied with the tempo or the manner in which they prosecute the peace.
>
> The need to fight the Nazis and the Fascists was plain to you. I believe men like Churchill and Eden and Roosevelt, Hull and Stimson were quick to recognize the fundamental implications in this conflict. Yet in the popular mind you align yourself against them before the battle is won. In so doing you not only weaken your influence as a liberal but you also weaken men like Frankfurter and others at home who are deeply sensitive to the issues involved and whose liberalism in the war period is of value to both our countries.[136]

Laski was, of course, unrepentant:

> You, like Felix, do not emphasise as I do the vital importance not only of winning the war, but of winning the war in the right way for the right ends. There is a deep ideological conflict in the US over the war as there is here.

He acknowledged that Churchill and Eden wanted to win the war against Hitler:

> But . . . I do not think the war they want to win is the war I want to win in the sense that, for them, the victory is a fulfilment while for me it is only a stage in a far vaster process than the fighting

itself defines. And absorption in the victory as fulfilment to the exclusion of the means of winning it, and the end for which it is won, may easily and quickly mean that we defeat Hitler and establish Hitlerism after his defeat.[137]

Laski and Winant – who had mutual affection and respect – remained friends, just as Frankfurter had sent Laski a message of his 'abiding and enveloping affection for him'.[138] But Laski was feeling increasingly isolated in his conviction that the future of the world depended upon Britain and the USA pledging themselves to social and economic transformation.

BREAKDOWN

In the middle of 1943 – probably sensing his relative impotence – Laski reneged on his undertaking to refrain from public attacks on the Labour leadership. At first he was comparatively subtle. For example, he used an article on J. S. Mill as a vehicle for condemning the Labour Party for holding back the moral and social revolution which it should be leading.[139] But in May 1943, in a Fabian pamphlet entitled *Marx and Today*, he launched an open attack.

This was a powerful reaffirmation of his general theory, which Marx used to buttress his own ideas. The general theme was again the need for immediate domestic progress, and an attempt to secure an understanding with the USSR. His critique of the leadership for subordinating the Labour Party to Churchill's fight to preserve 'traditional Britain' was forceful and, no doubt, resonant with much of the rank and file. But it was vitiated by some unnecessary personal attacks. In particular, he could not resist a snide allusion to Attlee's past policy on India, and a claim that the Labour Party's *raison d'etre* seemed to be 'to keep its ministers in the War Cabinet on Mr Churchill's terms'.[140]

Nothing was said about this in the NEC, but the pamphlet was probably noted for future reference as ammunition against Laski. And he continued to push his policy proposals within the Executive, even when they were clearly unpopular with the leadership. In the spring of 1943 the issue of the Soviet Union became prominent once again as the party conference approached, and Laski was allowed to open the debate. This was perhaps designed to balance the party's bitterly anti-communist statement, which accompanied the rejection of a new application for affiliation by the CP.[141] But although the NEC reaffirmed the previous conference decision to send a delegation to the Soviet Union, it would not accept a commitment to try to establish a new International.[142] Laski's frustration and anger were apparent when he subsequently wrote a memorandum on the issue. This began with the ascerbic comment:

> I assume that the Executive Committee does genuinely intend to carry out its pledge to Conference to send a *party* delegation to the USSR and will not regard a joint All-Party Parliamentary delegation as a substitute for its pledge.[143]

On this assumption — about which he was justifiably dubious – he proceeded to set out seventeen issues for discussion with the CPSU. There was no chance that Attlee would accept such proposals, which resembled the ideas that he had blocked in Laski's pamphlet eighteen months earlier. At the same time, yet another difference between Laski and the leadership came to a head: the German question.

Laski's consistent view was that it was necessary to find a middle way between Vansittartism, which sought a vindictive peace on the basis of alleged inherent expansionist drives in the German psyche, and the sort of sentimentalism 'which thinks that the day after the holocaust is over we and the Germans can meet in affectionate embrace'.[144] His approach was based on his theoretical perspective, which regarded Nazism as a product of a particular socio-economic system rather than of national characteristics. He therefore saw the solution as the elimination of the social structure which had produced the aggressive drives, and the establishment of a democratic socialist system in a new co-operative order in which national sovereignty would be superseded.[145] He believed in the unilateral disarmament of Germany, but rejected any implication of national stereotypes or national guilt.[146]

Ever since May 1941 he had been working with a grouping around the Austrian Socialist, Julius Braunthal, to counter 'Vansittartism' in the Labour movement.[147] He had written an excellent pamphlet on the subject (*The Germans – Are They Human?*), and had been involved in a major conflict over Germany within the NEC. His primary opponents were James Walker, MP, William Gillies, the Party's International Secretary, and Dalton, who wanted to ensure that all Germans were viewed as nationalists who shared responsibility for Hitler's aggression.[148] On this basis, they also sought to justify a peace settlement which would lead to a decisive weakening of Germany. In 1942 Laski had ensured that *The Old World and the New Society* expressed his views, which reflected the position that the Party had held at the beginning of the war. But by 1943 the anti-German line had gained ascendancy and, under Walker's lead, the conference moved, for the first time, towards identifying the German people with the spirit of aggression.

Laski might have been expected to share the anti-German emotions, for he was now aware of, and deeply affected by, the extermination policies.[149] However, he resisted this temptation and saw the party's new German policy as yet another indication that it was abandoning international socialism. In August 1943 he therefore wrote a devastating critique of a draft circular by Gillies, which had argued that the Germans were a 'guilty nation' and should be treated as such.[150] Gillies defended himself vigorously and his views were closer to those of the leadership than those of Laski.[151]

By the summer of 1943, the gulf between Laski and the leadership had therefore widened on almost all major aspects of policy, and his criticisms were a major irritant. In August he presented his opponents with a golden opportunity to isolate him within the NEC, when he wrote an article for an American newspaper in which he described Attlee as uninspiring and uninteresting.[152] Three weeks later the NEC, by fifteen votes to two, passed a motion dissociating itself from Laski's statement and, later in the day, released a press communique to this effect.[153] However, before this meeting had even taken place, Laski had collapsed with a nervous breakdown. Exhaustion was partly responsible. He had always been physically frail, with acute bronchial problems, and his current rate of activity would have been beyond the endurance of most people. Kingsley Martin recalls seeing him in this period at Cambridge when 'he had just – and not for the first time – had a blackout and fallen downstairs . . . So weak was he at this period that he was seen clutching the railings by the University Library to lever himself along'.[154] Yet even Laski, who tried to make light of the collapse, confessed to one friend that it had begun with an unhappy mind, as well as a tired body.[155] In fact, it is probable that psychological factors were a *primary* cause.

Some of the problems involved his personal life. In October 1941 his father had been killed, when hit by a car while crossing the road. This had been a profound shock to Laski, which was exacerbated by the fact that his mother subsequently suffered a series of heart attacks. His past conflicts with his family, and the associated guilt feelings, probably made this tragedy still more difficult to face. But he allowed himself no time to grieve: having sent his apologies to one NEC meeting, he was back for the next. In addition Frida, on whom he relied so totally, was able to give him less support than usual. They were separated during the week and, even when together, she was extremely busy herself, was often exhausted, and occasionally had other personal worries. In particular, she was giving a great deal of support to Diana, who had her first child in 1941. And even Frida was critical of some of Harold's political interventions, clearly believing them to be ineffective and counterproductive. However, these strains cannot be detached from his political life.

Since his driving force had been optimism about the post-war world, it was always likely that hope would be replaced by despair if he felt that the opportunity to make the necessary changes was not being taken. It was this feeling which gripped him by the summer of 1943. Indeed, there had long been signs of this. In January 1942, for example, he had told one of his American friends that he could not separate the two processes of peace and victory:

> if I don't think first and last not merely of the fight but of trying so to define the ends of the fight that the next generation has not got to go again into this hell, I don't see that life is worth living.[156]

By the middle of 1943 he had become more desperate. When Winant, the American ambassador, complained about one of his articles, Laski thus replied:

> I think Anglo-American policy, at present, is laying the foundations for a vast betrayal of the common peoples of the world. . . .
>
> I love F. D. R. with all my heart; I care for America as that land of promise which first gave democracy its letters of credit. And I feel none the less that the implications of these last months have already gone far towards losing the peace. When I think that another generation may go to the shambles ten or fifteen years from now I almost regret I was ever born. . . . I don't regret what I wrote. My regret is that I have no means of making what I said clear to the millions who hope for the four freedoms and will find that they are slowly left to drift into a new feudalism.[157]

Laski's collapse was no doubt brought on by excessive work. But the workload itself stemmed from his sense of guilt about young people dying while he lived in relative comfort, and his belief that he *knew* what would happen in the post-war world unless a new social order were constructed. And his fear of failure was reinforced by his sense of isolation. Frida therefore attributed his collapse to 'going too hard all the war' and also because:

> The fight over here is hard and . . . [he] is taking more than his share and is very *alone* in all he does. Things affect him just now; not the least that . . . [Felix Frankfurter] is so far away intellectually.[158]

The NEC's public dissociation from him no doubt also hurt because he was always vulnerable, despite apparently courting conflict. But the real pain came from the feeling that a war:

> which should work a great revolution in the spirit of man will end by safeguarding the very traditions and persons who are so largely responsible for its outbreak.[159]

The breakdown was extremely serious and he aged very considerably during the war. Indeed, he probably never recovered sufficiently to be able to withstand his later confrontations with the resilience that he needed. Certainly in early 1944, when he claimed to have recovered, he still often sounded deeply depressed. In January he told Max Lerner that he felt very lonely after his long years of separation from America, never having realised how large a part a dozen of his friends in New York and Washington had played 'in making my world seem livable and happy'.[160] And the next month he confessed to Winant that it was almost unbearable to be alive while young people died: 'It leaves one with a sense of failure that is absolute and beyond forgiveness'.[161] On 12 October (less than two months after the collapse) he attended a Labour Party subcommittee meeting and in late October 1943, at his first NEC meeting after the breakdown, he immediately put down a resolution:

> That this Party, in view of the developments in the War-situation, expresses its strong sense of the need for swift and decisive action by His Majesty's Government in the field of Reconstruction, and that facilities should be sought to discuss the whole position with the Labour members of the War Cabinet.[162]

It must have taken a superhuman effort, in his state of mind, to have taken the lead once again in trying to put pressure on Attlee. But Laski was still determined to do his best to bring about a 'revolution by consent'.

TOWARDS VICTORY

The battle with the leadership continued unabated, with Laski frequently defeated during 1944. In April he only secured four votes (against seventeen) when calling for NEC representations to Bevin over the notorious Defence Regulation 1AA, which limited the right to strike.[163] Almost immediately afterwards, Attlee rejected his attempt to insert a paragraph in the Annual Report, which would highlight the government's failure to implement major issues of party policy.[164] On this occasion the party leader also wrote a very long letter to Laski, defending his position.[165] Subsequently, he again courted unpopularity with sections of the leadership by playing a mediating role when Bevan faced the threat of expulsion from the Party for his opposition to Defence Regulation 1AA.[166] For his pains, one of the most vindictive of Bevan's opponents amongst the trade union leaders blamed Laski for inciting opposition to the regulation, and called for tighter control over NEC members as well as MPs.[167] Bevan survived and this was of great importance to the Left of the Party. But, for the remainder of the year little headway was made on domestic reforms and the NEC as a whole supported Laski's resolution expressing profound dissent with the government's Town and Country Planning Bill, which was much less radical than had been expected.[168]

Nor was there any clear progress on Laski's most important concerns in foreign policy. The memorandum which he had submitted in August 1943 on the delegation to the USSR had not been discussed during his absence (when suffering from the breakdown). It was only in December of that year that the NEC resolved that a delegation should be appointed in accordance with the pledge to the party conference, but there was no commitment to seek the establishment of a new International.[169] Six months later the members of the delegation were chosen (with Laski as the first choice).[170] However, nothing materialised from this for, although Eden subsequently recommended that the War Cabinet should allow the delegation to go, this was rejected on the grounds that it would be more desirable to arrange for an all-party delegation to visit the Supreme Soviet. None of the Labour ministers appear to have dissented from this decision,[171] and when Morgan Phillips and Ellen Wilkinson reported that Eden had told them that the first delegation must be an all-party one, the NEC agreed that the visit should be deferred.[172] In other words, the Labour ministers had done exactly what Laski had feared that they might do the previous year: they had indeed regarded 'a joint All-Party parliamentary delegation as a substitute' for the NEC's pledge to the Conference.

Party policy towards Germany was just as depressing from Laski's perspective. In April 1944 'The International Post-War Settlement' had been adopted and this had gone far towards holding the Germans as a whole responsible for war crimes. Laski and Noel-Baker had succeeded in toning down Dalton's original draft, but the statement, which was accepted by the Party Conference, still represented a major step towards 'Vansittartism' in the Labour movement. Laski continued to propagate his socialist perspective on Nazism – even holding a debate with Vansittart himself in September 1944 – but his position was now the minority view within the party.[173]

Nor was he any more optimistic about the international situation. He continued to appeal to Roosevelt to support the masses.[174] But he now seemed pessimistic about *all* the great powers. Late in 1944, for example, he wrote a pamphlet, entitled *Will the Peace Last?*, in which he criticised Britain and the USA for supporting vested interests in France, Greece, Spain and Italy, and the Soviet Union for adopting a nationalist rather than a socialist policy, particularly in Poland. He feared that there would be a recurrence of hatred and war and still saw the ultimate hope as a world community on socialist foundations. The duty of socialists was 'to clear our own minds of cant and our own hearts of hatred', and to establish a great coalition of progressive forces which would rebuild democratic and civilised values.[175] But he hardly sounded hopeful.

And yet the tide was finally beginning to turn, at least in the domestic sphere. In December 1944 the Labour Party Conference, chaired by Laski in Ellen Wilkinson's absence, was significant in three respects. First, it bitterly criticised the government's Greek policy, thereby indicating a real break from a bipartisan approach on foreign affairs. Secondly, it adopted an amendment moved by Ian Mikardo, against the wishes of the leadership, which called for a commitment to extensive nationalisation. Thirdly, it elected Bevan to the NEC, thereby reinforcing the Left and providing Laski with a powerful ally. This must have given him some real comfort, after feeling isolated for so long. Unfortunately, early the next year his new hopes were offset by sadness in his personal life.

In February his mother died. Their relationship had been complicated by the fact that Frida had never liked her or forgiven her for the role that she had played at the time of the marriage in 1910.[176] He had therefore probably tried to distance himself from her emotionally. However, he had found it heartbreaking to see her decline in strength during the war,[177] and was present when she died. He told Frida:

> I feel it rather keenly; more than I can say on paper, and it makes me grateful to have you and Diana. I never knew it could hurt so much.[178]

His grief was intensified by the fact that he and Neville also had to sort out the future of their sister, Mabel. She had never left home and may always have been simple-minded. As it became clear that her mother was dying she became 'lost in bewilderment' and Laski told Frida that she was 'a quite tragic sight which it isn't easy to endure'.[179] Subsequently, he was deeply concerned about Mabel's future.[180]

By the spring he was back in action on the Executive and with victory in Europe in sight he shared in the mood of growing optimism. As he absorbed himself in such issues as the possibilities of change in India and the future of Palestine, he became less preoccupied with the threat of a new world war. Above all, of course, he looked forward to the election of a Labour government, and became Chair of the NEC just as Germany was defeated. Since he was determined to end the coalition immediately, while Attlee wanted to continue it, the two men ended the war on different sides once again. Such differences had characterised their relationship since late 1940, and must now be considered in an assessment of 'Laski's war'.

FICTION, SHADOWS AND FACTS: LASKI'S WAR ASSESSED

The examination of Laski's political role during the war should have shown that two of the charges against him are quite false. First, it is surely evident that his interventions were far from frivolous. On the contrary, he was motivated by an intense – indeed overpowering –

seriousness of purpose. Secondly, it is also clear that if Laski 'had, to a large extent, substituted a world of fiction and shadows for a world of facts'[181], he shared this fantasy with an enormous number of other people. As we have seen, he often commanded support within the National Executive and represented the views of the Labour Party Conference and much of the rank-and-file. His influence also extended far beyond such circles, and he still maintained a following in the USA. Yet it is, of course, possible to be both serious and influential without being right. It is therefore necessary to consider how much validity there was in Laski's viewpoint. Although his outlook on domestic and international affairs were inextricably linked, I will consider them in turn.

The charge against Laski was expressed very cogently by Attlee himself in his letter of 1 May 1944. On domestic issues, this made three substantive points. First, the Executive had 'voted strongly for continuing the present Government in power'.[182] This meant that policy would inevitably be a compromise. Secondly:

Whether the post-war Government is Conservative or Labour it will inevitably have to work a mixed economy. If it is a Labour Government it will be a mixed economy developing towards Socialism. If a Conservative Government it will be an economy seeking to retain as much as possible of private enterprise, but both Governments will have to work with the world and the country as it exists. There are limits to the extent to which the clock can be put forward or back.

Thirdly, there had been a fundamental change in conception 'by all the leading politicians . . . and all the economists of any account'. All now accepted full employment, state planning and the government control of finance. In other words, Attlee was arguing that 'consensus politics' had arrived.

On the first point, Attlee was on strong ground. As has already been acknowledged, the constraints of coalition *did* limit the extent to which Labour policies could be advanced. Attlee and his colleagues often fought against the Conservatives within the government, and Churchill certainly feared their dominance.[183] On the other hand, as has also been shown, the Labour leaders often raised issues within the Cabinet *because* of rank-and-file pressure, often represented by Laski. It is unlikely that they would even have been this combative without such expressions of party feeling.

Attlee's second argument – about the necessity of recognising that the postwar settlement would be based on a 'mixed economy' rather than socialism – missed the point. Laski did not believe that the measures that he was demanding were 'socialist'. As far as he was concerned full employment and greater equality were possible only if there was substantial public ownership and the full implementation of the Beveridge Report. He did not therefore see his demands as necessitating an acceptance of *socialism* by the government. Rather he believed that liberal democracy could continue on a basis of consent only if both parties ultimately accepted the necessary reforms. However, Attlee was implying that there was no difference between himself and Laski on their ultimate goals. This was not so and the difference was not confined solely to the *pace* of change. One example from the beginning of the war and one from the end may illustrate this.

In October 1939 Keynes had suggested a capital levy and compulsory savings to pay for the war. He sent his proposal to Attlee with a covering letter which explained that he saw it as 'the only way of handling the financial end of the war in a way which is at the same time just and advantageous to the working class'.[184] Keynes reported Attlee's reply to Laski as follows:

> the main up-shot of his letter was that my scheme would impose on persons like himself, who presumably have more than £2,000 a year 'an amount of compulsory saving which would be crushing'. No comment whatever on the relation of my scheme to the working class.[185]

Laski was in general agreement with the scheme and subsequently had discussions with Keynes in an attempt to facilitate its progress in the party and trade union movement.[186]

Similarly, towards the end of the war, when discussions were taking place over the nature of the party manifesto, Attlee's views were highly orthodox. He argued that the workers were now concerned about their property rights and Labour should therefore state, with the upmost emphasis, that the party would stand absolutely against inflation and that the savings of the people would be inviolate. His main fear was that someone on the Labour-Left would make a 'silly' Marxist speech and lose the election.[187] His whole tone was 'centrist' and quite distinct from Laski's position.

There was also a fundamental difference in their views as to how change came about. Attlee now expressed the classical Fabian belief that there had been a gradual change in the 'assumptions of the ordinary man and woman' and that this was a measure of the progress that had been made. But Laski's view was that the reforms – and changes in assumptions – came about only if there was constant pressure. There was nothing inevitable about the process. This leads to Attlee's third argument: that there was now substantial agreement between the parties. Was he justified in his belief that the Conservatives had accepted such doctrines as full employment and state planning?

Until recently the conventional historical viewpoint reflected the case that Attlee was making and, until the Thatcher years, this belief was also fostered by the Conservative Party. However, the latest research suggests that by 1945 there had been no transformation in majority Conservative attitudes, and that it is unlikely that a Churchill government would have implemented the reforms that became known as 'the welfare state'.[188] It is possible that the Conservatives would have been forced to adopt such a programme by the constraints of office and popular pressures. But the historical evidence supports Laski's contemporary argument that they were resisting fundamental reforms and seeking to restore the pre-war order. The relatively smooth transition to the 'welfare state' was therefore probably dependent upon the election of the Labour government.

It is also likely that the seeds of the Labour victory were sown much earlier than 1945. Jefferys argues that the leftward shift, which was already apparent when Chamberlain was forced out of the premiership in 1940, became irreversible when the Conservatives prevaricated on the Beveridge report.[189] Thereafter the Labour Party became associated with favouring necessary change, while the Conservatives were seen to stand for a discredited old order. In one sense, this might appear to favour Attlee's complacency rather than Laski's dire warnings of potential catastrophe. However, Laski (and others on the Left) contributed to the establishment of these perceptions amongst the electorate. He played a very considerable role in ensuring that Labour had a distinctive programme, in rallying the Party faithful and giving them self-confidence, in publicising socialist arguments amongst the public at large, and in cajoling the leadership into the adoption of a more active role. Laski was certainly guilty of serious misjudgments. But there is little doubt that, over a long period, he helped to create a climate of opinion which was ultimately beneficial to the Party's electoral fortunes. He therefore played a role in creating the intellectual and political context which was to lead to the establishment of the welfare state.

The differences between Attlee and Laski over foreign policy – particularly regarding the Soviet Union – were even more stark. Russia, Attlee argued, was:

> a great continental power with an immense heritage in Asia to be developed, but with ambitions in Europe which are essentially imperialist, whether ideological or territorial, whether derived from Lenin or Peter the Great.[190]

Perhaps Laski sometimes went to the other extreme in implying that the existence of capitalism was a necessary and sufficient explanation for imperialism and war. Yet his prescience was sometimes extraordinary.

In the pamphlet 'Great Britain, Russia and the Labour Party', which Attlee vetoed in December 1941, Laski predicted the consequences if the three Great Powers failed to agree on the post-war order. In these circumstances:

> There is the danger, first, that the power of the United States and Britain to provide relief for the peoples of the occupied and defeated countries may be restricted by doctrinal considerations; and out of this there is the further danger that governments may be imposed on Europe less with a view to the natural evolution of social and political forces in each of the constituent countries than with a view to the receipt of Anglo-American aid; and that aid may be conditioned by a desire to make certain that the future of capitalism is not seriously jeopardised.

This could mean that:

> immediately the prospect of Nazi defeat becomes imminent, there will be competitive manoeuvring all over the territory in enemy occupation to secure that the successful overthrow of the German and Italian governments, and their quisling satellites, is accompanied by a group whose purposes can be patronised by London and Washington, on the one hand, or by Moscow on the other. It means an immediate divergence of interest between the major partners in the victory that will have been won; at the best, it will be a divergence sufficiently grave to postpone recovery by the

insecurities it will involve, and, at the worst, it may mean a return to power politics in a new and grim form, in which the main purpose of Britain and the United States will be to prevent, wherever and however they can, the spread of Bolshevik ideas, while it is the main purpose of the USSR to promote that spread.

In this situation, the Communist Parties would have a crucial role and:

> the Third International will become a political influence of exceptional importance, a new Vatican . . . deploying the policies Moscow is prepared to approve, where it is judged they may exercise authority. That, in its turn, will mean repressive legislation on a massive scale. The hope of realising the Four Freedoms will be stricken into impotence.

This insight into the Cold War, which was written just after Pearl Harbour, is of almost visionary accuracy. Perhaps there was some over-simplification in his theoretical position, and no doubt he was too optimistic about Stalin's intentions. But it was his understanding of the relationships between domestic and international policy, which enabled him to predict the probable future, and to do all in his power to avert it. Attlee neither had the vision nor the theoretical insight to transcend the orthodox interpretation of foreign policy and of 'communist imperialism'. This, of course, has generally been praised as 'realism'.

Laski pushed himself relentlessly to persuade the public and the political elite that fundamental change was necessary if military victory over Nazism was to be followed by a world of peace, justice, and stability. He made some serious errors of political judgment and, at one point, he lavished excessive praise on the Soviet Union.[191] But his theory and practice were in harmony once again, and he was prepared to court unpopularity and personal hardship in the attempt to translate his vision into reality. The war had also eliminated the elitist strain which had often been evident in his attitudes in the past. He constantly expressed the fear that political leaders were unworthy of the masses who had 'earned their inheritance',[192] and he devoted himself to the effort to ensure that they were not betrayed. During the Second World War he was therefore what he most wanted to be: 'a soldier in the liberation army of humanity'.

11

Political Trials

When he became Chair of the Labour Party in May 1945 Laski appeared to have fulfilled the personal ambitions that he had held as a young man. He was close to the centre of political affairs, he enjoyed a world-wide reputation as a Socialist theorist, he had a vast international circle of acquaintances, he was an influential populariser of Left-wing causes, and he was secure in his academic role. He was also confident that the Labour Party would win the forthcoming General Election and that there was, at the very least, a good chance that it would implement the 'revolution by consent' that he had urged throughout the war. Four years later, when he finally left the Labour Party National Executive the position seemed quite different. He was, of course, still a well-known figure and he was generally satisfied with the domestic achievements of the Labour Government. But he no longer carried any influence with the leadership, his public image had been undermined, his academic contributions were often attacked or ignored, and even his following amongst the Labour Party rank-and-file was greatly reduced. This dramatic decline in prestige was tragic. In the first place, it dealt a crippling blow to Laski's own self-esteem and certainly contributed to his early death in 1950. Secondly, it meant that his views at this time have never received the attention that they deserve.

This chapter has two sections. The first part examines the major stages in the process by which Laski was weakened and discredited. The second part examines his thinking on some of the crucial issues of the era. A brief conclusion then deals with the relationship between the two parts, arguing that the 'Cold War' was the key cause of the negative attitudes towards Laski in the last years of his life.

NOTORIETY

The 1945 Election

Laski had been well-known in political circles for years, but he became a 'household name' only during the General Election campaign in June–July 1945. This really began with a notorious broadcast by Churchill on 4 June, when the Prime Minister made a sensationalist attack on socialism. The phrase which is always recalled is that in which he claimed that a Socialist government 'would have to fall back on some form of Gestapo, no doubt very humanely directed in the first instance'.[1] However, the whole speech denigrated socialism as a creed which was incompatible with British notions of freedom since it inevitably led to bureaucracy and totalitarianism. Laski was not mentioned by name, but Churchill drew a distinction between the 'reasonable' leaders of the party and the doctrinaire socialists of the National Executive whom he viewed as the real threat. It is generally agreed that the speech was counterproductive in electoral terms, for few took such absurd claims about the Labour party very seriously. However, it was significant for Laski, both in relation to events which had already occurred, and to those which would take place in the near future.

On 18 May Churchill had written to Attlee, suggesting either an immediate election or the continuation of the coalition until after the defeat of Japan. The Labour leader – unlike the party's rank-and-file – had long favoured the postponement of the election until a reasonable time had elapsed after military victory, and immediately called upon Churchill to suggest an amendment in the letter which would make the NEC more likely to accept the continuation of the coalition.[2] This involved a new sentence which stated:

> In the meantime we would together do our utmost to implement the proposals for social security and full employment contained in the White papers which we have laid before Parliament.[3]

In other words, Attlee was revealing to Churchill his wish to continue the coalition by suggesting a means of making this more acceptable to the Labour Party. And because Churchill also wanted to continue the wartime collaboration he acceded to Attlee's request. According to Dalton, he and Bevin were inclined to agree with Attlee, but doubted whether the Labour Party conference, which was now meeting, would accept the idea.[4]

The crucial meeting of the NEC was held on Sunday 20 May, but Attlee was only able to get three members of the twenty-seven strong executive to accept his proposal that the coalition should continue until the end of the Japanese war. It was therefore agreed that a letter should be sent to Churchill rejecting the offer, but agreeing to continue in coalition until October (which was seen as the most favourable time for an election), and this proposal was subsequently approved by Conference with only two dissenters. However, it was rejected by Churchill: the coalition was dissolved on 23 May, and the election set for 5 July.

There were two issues in this episode which were to be of central importance in Laski's subsequent propulsion into the limelight, although neither was a matter of public knowledge at the time. First, there was a new controversy over Attlee's position. Laski's dissatisfaction with Attlee as Party leader was, of course, hardly new. But it was shared by others – above all by Herbert Morrison, who now sought the position himself, and by Ellen Wilkinson, the outgoing Party Chair who openly favoured Morrison's candidature. Attlee had little electoral appeal and his attempt to continue the coalition (which Morrison opposed), demonstrated the gulf between his ideas and rank-and-file sentiments. As new Party chair, Laski took it upon himself to express his view of the situation quite openly to Attlee:

My Dear Clem,

This is a very difficult letter to write, as it involves the hard work of reconciling private regard with public obligation. But you and I have known one another, I hope, for enough time for you to recognise that I have no motive save public duty in writing to you.

I have been acutely aware for many months but especially during the Blackpool conference of the strong feeling that the continuance of your leadership in the Party is a grave handicap to our hopes of victory in the coming election. This is a wide feeling. It is felt by a majority of our own executive. It is felt by the outstanding trade union leaders. It is felt by many of the candidates, not least by the very able young service candidates who made the conference so notable. And the rank and file, whether agents or ordinary delegates . . . share this view profoundly. So, as I found, do many of your Parliamentary colleagues, above all, the colleagues who are most active in the House of Commons. This discontent has reached the point of procedural discussions about a new and immediate test of the opinion of the Parliamentary party in order to enable the campaign to have a new leader.

No one, to my knowledge, has anything but respect for your

character and high integrity. No one but admits your real power as a committee-man and your devotion to the movement. It is agreed universally that you have worked with generous unselfishness for our whole nation as Deputy Prime Minister. But it is not less strongly agreed that the peculiar personal qualities which the leader of the Party now requires, the sense of the dramatic, the power to give a lead, the ability to reach the masses, the maintenance of an intimate relation with your immediate followers, the definition of great issues in a great way, – that these require a different personality from yours.

As chairman of the Party at this critical moment, not only in the history of the movement but also in the history of the nation, I should be failing in my obligations if I did not set these considerations before you and ask you, regretfully, but with a grave sense of my responsibility to draw from the inference that your resignation of the leadership now would be a great service to the Party . . .

Attlee ignored the letter, but obviously felt bitter towards Laski, particularly after their accumulation of conflicts throughout the war.

When Churchill made his 'Gestapo' broadcast on 4 June, the following crucial factors were therefore already affecting Laski's future. First, the NEC had overruled the wishes of Attlee (shared by Dalton and Bevin) that the coalition should be continued. Secondly, Churchill knew that this had happened. Thirdly, Laski had tried to persuade Attlee to resign from the leadership. Now the second episode occurred.

On 31 May Churchill had offered Attlee continued access to foreign policy papers, and on 2 June he invited him to accompany him to the Potsdam Conference, although the coalition had been dissolved.[6] Attlee was already worried by Soviet policy and was keen to maintain a bipartisan approach to the crucial European issues arising from the defeat of Germany.[7] On 8 June he therefore accepted both invitations, telling Churchill that he had discussed the proposal with his colleagues and:

There seems to me to be great public advantage to preserve and present to the world that unity on foreign policy which we maintained throughout the last five years. I do not anticipate that we shall differ on the main lines which we have discussed together so often.[8]

However, Attlee had not discussed the invitation to Potsdam with the NEC, which only learned of it on 14 June when Churchill publicly announced the idea in the House of Commons. Laski immediately wrote to Attlee:

> I observe that the P.M. has asked you to accompany him to the Three Power meeting in July.
>
> I assume that you will take steps to make it clear that neither you nor the Party can be regarded as bound by any decisions taken at the meeting, and that you can be present for information and consultation only. I do not think we can accept the doctrine of the 'continuity' of foreign policy since it assumes that the international relations of this country are not closely connected with the character of the purpose each of the parties seeks to fulfil. I should, therefore, like an assurance that, if you accept, we shall, with the knowledge of the P.M., Marshal Stalin, and President Truman, remain unbound by commitments which, if we form a government, we are free to reconsider.
>
> If you do not share my view, I think I must, as chairman, call a special meeting of the E. C. to consider the point. This is far too grave a matter to settle without discussion if expectation of acceptance is implied in your presence with the P.M.

This was, of course, a deeply-held view, for Laski had been expressing his fundamental opposition to continuity in foreign policy for years. He was also on strong ground in arguing that – particularly now that the Party was in opposition – this was a matter for discussion in the NEC. But even had he wished to do so Attlee could not now have acceded to Laski's request without again demonstrating to Churchill that he could be overruled by the NEC. In any case, he wanted to accompany the Prime Minister to Potsdam without any of the provisos that Laski was suggesting. There was therefore a fundamental conflict between the Chair of the NEC and the Labour leader. This immediately became more serious when Laski brought their difference out into the open.

According to his subsequent account to the NEC, he was unable to get into contact with Attlee that evening and had then been asked by the press to give an opinion on Churchill's offer. He had refused to do so until an American journal had threatened to regard his refusal to express an opinion as denoting disapproval of the acceptance of the invitation.[10] At this point he gave the following statement to the *Daily Herald*:

It is, of course, essential that if Mr Attlee attends this gathering he shall do so in the role of an observer only.

Obviously it is desirable that the leader of the Party which may shortly be elected to govern the country should know what is said, discussed, and agreed, at this vitally important meeting.

On the other hand, the Labour Party cannot be committed to any decisions arrived at, for the Three-Power Conference will be discussing matters which have not been debated either in the Party Executive or at meetings of the Parliamentary Labour Party.

Labour has a foreign policy which in many respects will not be continuous with that of a Tory-dominated Coalition. It has, in fact, a far sounder foreign policy.

It is therefore essential that, though Mr Attlee should attend the Three-Power talks, Labour and he should not accept responsibility for agreements which on the British side will have been concluded by Mr Churchill as Prime Minister.

It is essential also that Mr Churchill himself, Marshal Stalin and President Truman should be fully aware of the position.[11]

Churchill immediately wrote a public letter to Attlee stating that he had wanted him to come 'as a friend and counsellor, and help us on all subjects on which we have been so long agreed' and that merely to come as a 'mute observer' would be derogatory to his position as Party leader.[12] Attlee publicly reaffirmed his original commitment, and endorsed Churchill's interpretation of the position. This meant that Laski had, in effect, been disavowed by Attlee. Since the NEC (and Laski himself) did not want to precipitate a major row with the leadership just before the General Election, Laski now stated that the exchange of letters had made the position 'entirely satisfactory', although he continued to make speeches against the notion of continuity in foreign policy.[13]

By now Laski 'demonology' was really under way. On 16 June, for example, the *Daily Express* headline was 'Socialists Split: Attlee Repudiates Laski Order' and the leading article attacked both Laski himself and the 'rule of the secret party caucus'. Similar articles were carried throughout the Right-wing press.

The momentum increased a few days later when the *Nottingham Guardian* published a letter from H. C. C. Carlton, a Conservative member of the Nottinghamshire County Council, which claimed, in effect, that Laski had supported violent revolution in a speech in Newark on 16 June. Laski immediately issued a statement denying that he had said the words attributed to him, and warned that he would take libel action against anyone who so reported him. But the *Daily Express* went ahead anyway with the headline: 'Laski Unleashes Another General Election Broadside: Socialism Even If It Means Violence.' He therefore issued writs for libel, which meant that the press soon dropped this particular allegation against him (although the *Newark Advertiser* repeated it on 23 June). However, the Right now used him as their 'bogey' for the rest of the campaign. As he himself put it, he was portrayed as the 'Himmler' of the 'Socialist Gestapo' in a bitter onslaught in which there were often anti-semitic undertones.[14] And on 21 June Churchill himself specifically mentioned Laski in a radio broadcast:

> It was my conception that I should enjoy Mr Attlee's counsels at every stage of the discussions . . . However, a new figure has leaped into notoriety. The situation has been complicated and darkened by the repeated intervention of Professor Laski, Chairman of the Socialist Party Executive. He has reminded all of us, including Mr Attlee, that the final determination of all questions of foreign policy rests, so far as the Socialist Party is concerned, with this dominating Socialist Executive.[15]

And he continued to raise this issue with Attlee right up to the Election itself. On 2 July he wrote:

> We have learnt a great deal more than we knew before about the powers vested in the National Executive Committee, of which Mr Laski is the undisputed Chairman. It certainly appears that they are very wide in their terms and, from your silence, very real. It would appear that a Labour or Socialist Government would be subject to the directions of this Committee and that matters of foreign affairs and, I presume, if they desired it, military affairs, would have to be submitted to them.[16]

Attlee replied immediately refuting the suggestion, but Churchill returned to the charge the next day, stating that:

> I do not believe that the controversy on these very important issues can be satisfactorily cleared up until the public has a statement signed jointly by yourself and the chairman of the executive committee regarding the use of these powers in the future.[17]

It has generally been assumed that the whole campaign against Laski was simply ill-judged Tory electioneering. Indeed Laski himself believed this, declaring on the eve of polling that he had been selected as 'scapegoat number 1' and that at about 10 o'clock the following evening 'he would be returned to the obscurity from which he had emerged.'[18] Yet there is good reason to suppose that electoral considerations were not the sole factor in the situation, for Churchill obviously believed some of his own propaganda.

The clearest evidence for this lies in the fact that, having previously wanted to hold the Potsdam conference as early as possible, after Laski's intervention he seriously considered its postponement until after the election.[19] On 20 June, he thus told the Cabinet that, although his previous anxiety about Attlee's position at the Conference had been allayed by their correspondence, Laski had persisted in the more serious suggestion that there would not be continuity of foreign policy between the Caretaker Government and a Labour administration, and Attlee had not disagreed about this. He could therefore not be sure about the extent to which a Labour government's foreign policy would be determined by the former ministers, or how far it would be dictated by the 'Executive Committee of the Socialist Party'. In fact, of course, he eventually went ahead with Potsdam. Yet the fact that he had considered postponement (no doubt on the assumption that he would win the election) suggests that he felt genuine anxiety about the Labour Party constitution, while Laski was Chair of the NEC.

Aware that the NEC had overruled the leadership on the continuation of the coalition in May, he was perhaps worried that it might force a Labour government to adopt a pro-Soviet foreign policy. Since the Labour Party in fact won the election and continued a broadly bipartisan approach to international relations, it might seem that Churchill's tactics and concerns are irrelevant to an understanding of subsequent events. But this is not so, for his interventions almost certainly affected the power relationships within the Labour Party.

Despite Attlee's curt rejoinders to Churchill's allegations of NEC control over the leadership, the Labour Party constitution was, in fact, far less clear than he maintained. As Dalton privately acknowledged:

The question of the relationship of the National Executive to the Parliamentary leaders is, in fact, slightly delicate, though there is nothing new about it. It is not a thing the public discussion of which brings any gain to us.[20]

Churchill's continued goading on the issue had already led Attlee to claim that the NEC was a subordinate body, and it almost certainly increased his determination to ensure that policy was entirely controlled by the parliamentary leadership. His persistent conflicts with Laski would probably have led him to take this course in any case, but the Churchill-Beaverbrook campaign obviously reinforced his determination to do so. Moreover, Laski exacerbated the tension by continuing to raise the leadership issue even after the Party's overwhelming electoral victory was declared on 26 July. In the afternoon of that day he tried to persuade Attlee not to go to the Palace, until the PLP had met and made their choice of leader.[21] He was not alone in this view of the Party's constitution, and Morrison was still hoping to become Prime Minister.[22] However, Attlee had no intention of being deprived of the position, ignored Laski's request and, having already seen the King, presented the party with a *fait accompli* in the evening. This episode must have strengthened Attlee's determination to cut the NEC – and its Chair – down to size.

By the time the Labour government was established Laski's position had thus already been severely weakened. He was the main butt of Right-wing attacks, a figure of notoriety in the popular press, and was regarded as an electoral liability by the parliamentary leadership.[23] Certainly, he had been *partly* responsible for this himself by making some political blunders. In particular, he was unwise to have made his disagreement over Potsdam public and, when already in an exposed position, he should not have questioned Attlee's leadership – particularly *after* the electoral victory. But if he was not a great political tactician, this does not mean that his overall position was unjustified. In essence, he wanted to maintain the role of the NEC in order to ensure that a Labour government adopted a policy – particularly in foreign affairs – which would differ fundamentally from that of the Conservative-dominated coalition. The weakening of his position, and the subordination of the NEC to the parliamentary leadership, would make this much less likely.

Laski, Attlee and the NEC, 1945–6

The clash between Laski and Attlee that had been evident over the Potsdam invitation was papered over during the election campaign itself, but reemerged as soon as the new government assumed office. It was even implicit in Laski's victory speech:

At long last we have made possible full friendship with the Soviet Union. At long last we are going to be in a position to do full justice to our Spanish comrades. And we shall give no help either to decaying monarchs or obsolete social systems.[24]

In other words, his emphasis was upon transformation in foreign policy, while the whole thrust of the Bevin-Attlee strategy was 'continuity', based on an acceptance of the notion that there were enduring British national interests that transcended party differences. Had Laski simply made an effusive speech and then left foreign policy-making to the government, the underlying conflict might not have come to a head, but he was not content to do this. Instead he immediately tried to use his position to define government strategy.

During the next few weeks, he represented the Labour Party at a series of socialist party conferences on the continent. On the crucial issue of fusion between socialist and communist parties, he was effective in promoting the line which the Labour government favoured.[25] However, he was also reported as making a series of statements claiming that Labour would follow a socialist foreign policy. According to the French press agency, on 12 August he gave an interview in which:

He emphasised the complete change in the British Government's attitude towards Greece. The aim, he said, was to have elected, a truly democratic Government, even if that meant the rise of E.A.M. and E.L.A.S. to power. In no circumstances would a Labour government help to uphold royalist or other regimes that did not enjoy the support of the people. Spain, in her turn, must be free from the Franco regime or any imitation of it. He added that it would be most unfortunate if France maintained commercial or economic relations with General Franco, since they might strengthen his Government.[26]

According to Reuter, he also told press representatives that:

The British Government will keep its promises made during the election campaign regarding aid for Spanish republicans. One of the purposes of my coming to Paris was to discuss the question with the Spanish Socialist delegates.[27]

A few days later, in a signed interview published in *La Tribune Economique*, he followed this up with the statement that the Labour government would, if necessary, bring economic pressure to bear in Spain so as to bring about the political unity of republican forces.[28]

In fact, the Labour government had not yet defined its policy and, when it did so, it followed the line of non-intervention in Spain and support for anti-Left forces in Greece. Laski was therefore either consciously trying to force it to adopt his own ideas (and those of the party rank-and-file) by a pre-emptive statement, or was simply assuming that it would share these views. In any case, Attlee immediately wrote a note to him:

> I am . . . bound to point out to you that the constant flow of speeches from the interviews with you are embarrassing. As Chairman of the Labour Party Executive you hold an important office in the Party and the position is not well understood abroad. Your utterances are taken to express the views of the Government.
>
> You have no right whatever to speak on behalf of the Government. Foreign affairs are in the capable hands of Ernest Bevin. His task is quite sufficiently difficult without the embarrassment of irresponsible statements of the kind you are making. . . .
>
> I can assure you there is widespread resentment in the Party at your activities and a period of silence on your part would be welcome.[29]

Attlee did not succeed in silencing Laski, but he forced him to make it clear that he was not representing the government. For example, on 24 September, when Laski broadcast to the USA and launched a blistering attack on the present and past policies of the British and American governments towards Franco, he emphasised that he was speaking in a personal capacity only.[30] Attlee was, of course, constitutionally quite correct in rejecting any notion that Laski was entitled to speak for the government – if indeed he had ever really made any such claim. But the position with regard to NEC/government relations was less obvious.

In his major study of the post-war Labour government, Kenneth O. Morgan demonstrates that, throughout the period, the NEC was easily controlled by the parliamentary leadership, with assistance from its trade union allies, and Morgan Phillips, the General Secretary. Leading government ministers dominated the Executive and its sub-committees, working closely with loyal trade-union 'giants'.[31]

By late October 1945, Laski was already aware of the extent to which the NEC had been taken over by government ministers. He therefore raised the issue of whether ministers should be allowed to chair its sub-committees. It was resolved – against his wishes – that this should be permitted, although a sub-committee was also established to make recommendations on the matter.[32] Laski initiated this discussion of the party constitution partly because of the pressure to which he was being subjected to refrain from statements which might 'embarrass' the government. As he told one of his American friends:

> I take the view that until the Annual Conference next May I am the guardian of party policy whatever the government may do, and that I must see that this is stated without fear as a body of socialist doctrine. So it follows that everything I say and write is 'not helpful', and I have had frankly to insist that I am not a member of the government and that I must go on doing my duty even if they are embarrassed, and that their obvious remedy is to ask the Executive to compel me to resign. So far . . . they have not had the courage to face that issue, and we merely have angry discussions and angrier letters.

In a speech to a Fabian conference at about the same time, he referred explicitly to the problem, and advocated reform of the party constitution. It was, he suggested, likely that:

> a National Executive Committee which contains, apart from junior members of the Government, no less than nine Ministers of Cabinet rank, may feel less ardour than I do for its need to be active and resolute and daring, above all the unbreakable custodian of those socialist principles upon which we fought and . . . won the general election.[34]

He then pinpointed the essence of the problem, which was to resurface as a major issue in the 1970s.

> All of us agree that the vital responsibility of a Labour government is, like that of any other government, to the House of Commons. Yet that does not mean, and, indeed, cannot logically mean, that the Labour Party, as a national organisation, ceases to have meaning when a Labour government is in office. For, first of all, a

Labour government owes its existence and its power to live, to the support of Labour members in the House; and these, in their turn, owe their place, as Labour members, to their adoption . . . as candidates who are endorsed by the National Executive of the Labour Party. Endorsement carries with it an obligation in the candidate, both before and after election, to support the principles and policies which the annual conference of the Party has approved. Since, moreover, it is the duty and the express function of the National Executive Committee to act, between annual conferences, as the guardian of the party's principles and policies, neither the decisions of the Parliamentary party, nor, indeed, those of the Labour government, can be a matter of indifference to the National Executive Committee. It has, quite obviously, neither the right nor the power to exercise supervision, much less control, over the acts of the party in Parliament, or of the government; for, once these have been chosen, their authority is constitutionally independent of any external control.

But constitutional independence is not the same thing as moral independence. Political parties are the spinal column of representative democracy. They define the general and large-scale choices between which the electorate decides.

Since the NEC, between annual conferences, was the guardian of the general principles which were the party's raison d'etre, it had the duty 'to advise, to encourage, and to warn, both the Government and its supporters in Parliament' in the light of what was happening. This ought to be done in a spirit of sympathetic understanding. But its paramount duty was to the 'party as a national organisation striving to secure the building of a socialist commonwealth'. This meant that its function was also one of criticism and judgment. Recalling the party's history – most notably the MacDonald 'betrayal' – he emphasised that the NEC's guardianship of doctrine must be active and not passive. This meant that 'if the gap between the government's plans and party policy begins to widen dangerously', and reasoned discussion proved ineffective, in closing the gap the NEC 'must always remember that its primary allegiance is to principles and not to persons'. Its main objective was 'not simply to put a Labour government in power, but to see, when it gets there that its members use their power for socialist ends'. But, he argued, the great problem in all this was governmental and parliamentary domination of the NEC: 'An appeal to the National Executive thus becomes almost like an appeal to the Cabinet itself.' He ended by calling on the Fabian Society to devise a new constitution to overcome the problem.

The Fabians did not take up his challenge, and he made no impact within the NEC itself. On completion of his year of office as party chair, he returned to the issue in an article in *Tribune*. However, he had no chance of making any headway on the issue. Attlee was quite content with a docile Executive and later expressed the view that 'If you begin to consider yourself solely responsible to a political party you're half-way to a dictatorship'.[36] Of course, Laski had, never proposed anything resembling *sole* responsibility to the party, but it was convenient for Attlee (as it later was for Wilson and Callaghan) simply to deny the claims of the NEC by asserting the constitutional position of the government. The only minister who showed any sympathy to Laski's argument was Morrison, who offered to resign from the NEC, but was dissuaded from doing so.[37] When, in November 1947, a Labour councillor endorsed Laski's views and submitted a positive proposal to change the constitution, the Executive simply upheld Morgan Phillips' claim that the problem did not exist.[38]

During the war, Attlee had obviously disliked the pressure of the NEC in general, and of Laski in particular. By the summer of 1946, ministerial dominance had been asserted. Laski had remained prominent while he was Chair of the Executive, but his power base had already been eroded within a few months of the General Election. Now his influence was waning fast, and would be further undermined by a tragic event in his life: the libel action.

Laski in Court

The letter from H. C. C. Carlton in the *Nottingham Guardian* which had originally led Laski to issue the writ of libel, had stated:

Attending a meeting in the Newark Market Place on Saturday night I was horrified to hear Prof. Harold Laski, Chairman of the Socialist Party, when enumerating reforms he wanted to see, declare:

'If we cannot have them by fair means we shall use violence to obtain them'.

A member of the audience immediately challenged him and said; 'You are inviting revolution from the platform'.

Prof. Laski replied: 'If we cannot get reforms we desire we shall not hesitate to use violence, even if it means revolution'. I think the widest publicity should be given to this statement for I feel that electors all over the country should know what is really behind the Socialist mind.[39]

Laski's response, prepared in collaboration with Kingsley Martin and the Editor of the *Daily Herald*, was as follows:

My answer at the meeting was entirely different. What I said was: it was very much better to make changes in time of war when men were ready for great changes than to wait for the urgency to disappear through victory, and then to find that there was no consent to change what the workers felt an intolerable burden. That was the way that a society drifted to violence. We had it in our power to do by consent that which in other nations has been done by violence.[40]

These conflicting statements raise two immediate points. First, Laski's version of his words is exactly in line with the theory of 'revolution by consent' that he had preached throughout the war, while Carlton's version contradicts Laski's whole political philosophy. Since he was preoccupied with the need to reform so as to prevent any outbreak of violence, it seems inconceivable that he would have said that 'we' or 'the Labour Party' would use violence if unable to secure changes by consent. But, secondly, the distinction between *advocacy* of violence and *prophecy* in the event of a failure to reform was a subtle one. For a democratic socialist the difference between the two positions is of crucial importance. But someone who is unsympathetic to all positions on the Left, or generally indifferent to politics, might not perceive the significance of the distinction. Moreover, it was a difference which could easily be obscured by those who *wished* to discredit Laski. In the best of circumstances, it would be extremely difficult to prove exactly what had been said and, even if Laski's account of the actual words used was upheld, it would also be necessary to show that the other versions of his statement constituted libel. Laski had often discussed the problems faced by the Left in the courts. Why then did he issue the writs?

There is no reason to doubt his own explanation that 'I only undertook these cases to prevent the "Express" and others lying their way from the trap to a Zinoviev letter for the election'.[41] In other words, his fundamental aim was to protect the Labour Party from being labelled as a revolutionary organisation in a 'red scare' election, as had happened in 1924. And he was successful in this, for the issuing of libel writs made the matter *sub judice* and prevented coverage of the story for the remainder of the campaign. Once the election was over he could, of course, have withdrawn the writ. But there were probably two reasons why he did not do so. First, he no doubt felt that this would have been seized upon as proof that he had indeed stated the words attributed to him. Secondly, it would have been difficult for him to back out of the case after the Lord Chancellor, in an extraordinary intervention, predicted that he would do so.[42] Once he had taken his decision he thus initiated a process from which there was no escape.

By the time the case came to court, Laski faced at least three additional difficulties. First, he had been exposed to a prolonged media campaign, portraying him as a sinister influence. This might have prejudiced any jury against him. Secondly, the case was held before 'special jurors', which meant that they were all 'esquires', bankers or merchants whose houses had rateable values of at least £100. They were therefore even less likely to sympathise with a Left-wing socialist than ordinary jurors.[43] Thirdly, the chief counsel for the defence was Sir Patrick Hastings – one of the most formidable barristers of the era. The role of the Judge, Lord Goddard, the Lord Chief Justice, will be discussed below. The case has received considerable attention from a legal perspective. However, the technicalities of the judicial process are less significant in the context of this book than its political overtones. In theory, Laski was the plaintiff. In reality, it seemed that he and his form of socialism were on trial, and were eventually found 'guilty'.

The political motives had, of course, been present from the beginning. Laski was already the *bête noir* of the election campaign when he spoke at Newark on 16 June 1945, and the attack on him had been planned in advance. Wentworth Day, the questioner at the Newark meeting, was a publicity adviser for the Conservative candidate. He had previously helped Conservative governments with propaganda and, on this occasion, had used 'speaker's notes' supplied by Conservative Central Office. He had also worked for both the *Sunday Express* and the *Daily Express*.[44] He had expressed his intention of going to heckle Laski two days before the meeting and had rung the *Sunday Express* with a report immediately after it.[45] Carlton, whose letter had carried the original allegation against Laski, had known that Day was going to the meeting to attack Laski and had subsequently rung the *Nottingham Guardian* and allowed a journalist there to compose the letter on his behalf.[46] Moreover, the reporter of the *Newark Advertiser*, who had been present at the meeting, had not included the allegation about Laski's support for violent revolution in his shorthand notes or his original story, but the editor of the paper, the Conservative Deputy Mayor of Newark, had subsequently asked him to substitute a passage supplied by Wentworth Day himself. This article had not been published until *after* Laski had already taken out his first writs and it is likely that the *Newark Advertiser* carried the story only after having received assurances from the *Daily Express* that it would finance any subsequent legal action. Lord Beaverbrook, the proprietor of the *Daily Express* was a member of the Churchill cabinet and was heavily involved in the Conservatives' election campaign. It would seem reasonable to assume that he had authorised the *Express* to go ahead despite the fact that Laski had issued the writs.

It is therefore known that there was a premeditated attack on Laski by local Tories, and it is possible that Wentworth Day was part of a wider network which sought to discredit the Labour party by concentrating attention on Laski. Day himself was deliberately insulting in his approach. He implied that Laski had been cowardly or unpatriotic in his failure to fight during the First World War, and then claimed that on two previous occasions during the Second World War he had advocated violent revolution. His whole demeanour was deeply provocative and Laski probably sensed anti-semitic overtones.[47] Day's approach was designed to trap Laski into making an incriminating statement. This is not abnormal in political meetings, but the court hearing itself continued in much the same way.

In his opening speech, Laski's counsel had little difficulty in showing that the circumstances surrounding the allegation of violence were suspicious, and that there were several inconsistencies in the case put by the *Newark Advertiser*.[48] He also drew attention to Laski's own theory of 'revolution by consent' to demonstrate his belief in peaceful methods. A little later Laski himself stated that, as far as he was aware, no-one had ever accused him of advocating violence before. He also claimed:

> I have said, ever since I began to write, that if changes were effected in this country by violence, it would be disastrous, because it would result in the suppression of democratic govern-

ment and with it all the good things, religious toleration, freedom of speech, the security of the person, and so forth, that are naturally and logically associated with constitutional government.[49]

This was probably a mistake. It was quite true that he had devoted his adult life to the attempt to bring about change peacefully in the belief that the alternative of violent revolution would be disastrous. But Laski was implying that his writings *expressed* this sentiment consistently and explicitly. As has been shown, this was not so, for in the 1930s the dominant note of his writings had often appeared to be pessimism about the prospects of reform. In reality, even when he had appeared to prophesy fascism and dictatorship as the inevitable tendency of capitalism, the real message had been: 'reform now so as to avoid catastrophe'. However, it required a careful and sympathetic reading of the texts to appreciate his purpose. Sir Patrick Hastings' interpretation was naturally quite the opposite: it was deeply hostile and designed to denigrate Laski in the eyes of the jury.

Hastings succeeded in trapping and confusing Laski, who was forced to admit that he would no longer agree with some of the passages that he had written in *Democracy in Crisis* (1933) and *The State in Theory and Practice* (1934). His argument that they had been based on rational analysis of the conditions at the time probably failed to impress the jury and his flippant remark – after an episode of brow-beating by Hastings – that 'I am older and wiser now than I was' no doubt seemed like a confession of 'guilt'.[50] This did not mean that Hastings won the intellectual argument: Laski often demonstrated his meaning effectively and refuted Hastings' interpretations of his writings. But, as one of the best accounts of the case explains, while the transcript shows Laski fighting back spiritedly:

> the impression which many of those present in the courtroom have recorded, and which presumably the jury absorbed, is that, in the words of one commentator, 'Hastings, at his most subtle and incisive, made Laski look helpless and shifty'.[51]

However, Hastings' methods were extraordinary. Apart from subjecting Laski to extremely vicious questioning without allowing him to develop his answers, he also exploited political prejudices against him. He thus introduced aspects of Laski's beliefs, and made statements about him, which had no conceivable relevance to the case. He made sure that the jury knew that Laski believed that judges were often prejudiced against trade unions and the working classes, that he was anti-religious, and that he had believed in a General Strike to prevent war in 1914.[52] He then exploited all this in an overall attack:

> Look at him. He has said . . . [revolution] for years in safety. You know some people can be very rude to others . . . if they are not stopped. They can decry what to some people are the holiest feelings they possess. They can sneer at some of our old institutions which have been the glory of our Empire: Law, Justice, all that we hold dear. He thinks nothing of them. So be it: I do not suppose there is a person in the world who cares tuppence what Mr Laski thinks about anything. But rude as he is, if anybody says one word about him, so thin is his skin that he flies to the Tribunal of Justice which he so utterly despises. Look at him. He is the man who comes here and says: 'I come to my country for justice. For God's sake do not look and see what I have said about it before by any chance, but now let us forgive and forget. I come for justice, the justice I say I shall never get, the justice that I despise in this hopelessly effete country.' He says: 'away with all your religion'. Perhaps he has got none; I do not know; he is entitled to have none. I could not help noticing that he took an oath upon the Bible to tell you the truth. . . . He may have said: '*That* for the Bible. I do not care what oath I take; it makes no difference'. Has he a religion? If so, why does he want to go and hurt people by saying things like that? Oh, but he is so tender-skinned if anybody says anything about him![53]

And in his closing speech, he carefully distinguished between Laski and the Labour Party:

> Of course . . . it must not be thought that anyone in this Court on this side suggests that the Socialist Party believes in this rubbish. They are the last people to do so. But there are a few – perhaps people who have not got houses and want very little incitement to go and take them; a few who have not got comforts and who want very little incitement indeed to roar in the streets. Those are the people and the only people to whom he is dangerous.
> . . . A man of his attainments might well be ashamed of some of the doctrines that he scatters so recklessly to people who are in a

state of misfortune . . . There are great minds, advanced minds, perhaps you may think socialistic minds, at this moment working their best and achieving enormous results for those people who are in poverty and suffering; but they are not helped by a man who comes and decries the things they believe in and levels them into the mud. . . . I say he brings these things into the mud by advocating this sort of horror, shouting about Russian Revolution with all the horrors of that. . . [54]

Lord Goddard, the Judge, later expressed his unhappiness about the verdict and claimed that he disagreed with the jury. But his own summing-up was hardly favourable to Laski:

> . . . When you are using the words 'revolution' and 'violence', Members of the Jury, when you are making a public speech in the Market Square at Newark, where very likely there are young people of both sexes present [!!], it is at least desirable, is it not, to make it very clear what you do mean? Young people are often apt to be inflammable.
> . . . I feel sure you will agree that when you are dealing with such highly explosive material as revolution and violence in public speaking it is desirable to make it abundantly plain just what you mean.

Referring to the speech that Laski had made at Bishop Stortford during the war, he pointed out that only one word was in doubt: whether he had said that the choice was to begin social transformation by general consent now or 'do' it by violence after the war or 'have' it by violence after the war;

> Whether you think there is very much significance between the two words 'do' and 'have', whether you think that in making a speech to a public meeting, an election meeting, anybody would distinguish between the two words 'do' or 'have', or whether it would make any difference, is a matter entirely for you.[55]

The implication was surely that Goddard did not believe that there was a significant difference and that, in any case, it was much better not to use words like 'revolution' with young people of both sexes present(!).

The jury pronounced its verdict after only forty minutes, finding that the report in the *Newark Advertiser* was fair and accurate. Given Goddard's own interpretation in court this meant, in effect, that Laski was found 'guilty' of making a statement which called for sedition, breach of the peace and riot.[56] It is difficult to disagree with Laski's own subsequent argument that the real issue at stake was 'not what was said at some place on a definite occasion', but the fact that he held 'unpopular opinions which both judge and jury are convinced it is bad to hold and worse by far to express.'[57] In effect he had now been 'convicted' by the British Establishment both outside and inside the court.[58]

On the surface, the abortive libel action did not have any obvious effects. Laski took only one rest day before resuming work at LSE, and he continued to speak and write in academic and political circles at almost the same level of intensity as before (although his bouts of illness were now increasingly frequent). He remained on the NEC for another two and a half years and retained considerable popularity with the rank-and-file.

Yet if Laski's life *appeared* to continue in much the same way after the legal case, a subtle change had nevertheless occurred. For the process which had begun during the 1945 General Election campaign was now well on the way to completion: he had become a 'victim'.

During the Second World War Laski had been a major figure with considerable influence in the life and thought of socialist politics. Attlee had, of course, wielded far more concrete power within the Labour Party, but Laski had been a force to reckon with as a standard-bearer of the Left. As I have argued, this position had been eroded almost immediately after he became Chair of the party, but he had at least continued to play a prominent role throughout his year of office. However, the libel action symbolised defeat and effected a barely tangible – but highly significant – change in his position. Paradoxically, this was demonstrated even when the leadership was generous in the immediate aftermath of the court case.

One of Laski's first actions was to offer his resignation from the NEC, if his colleagues – and especially Attlee – felt that his continued presence might harm the Party and the government.[59] Noel-Baker, the new Chair, replied that it was 'very generous' of him to offer to resign, but 'this would be wrong in every way, and the P.M., with whom I have discussed it, agrees with this view'.[60] This was magnanimous, and an enormous weight was also taken off Laski's mind when Aneurin Bevan phoned to say that Attlee, Morrison and the leaders of the PLP would ensure that the court costs were met by public subscription.[61] But this very generosity also reflected a change in Laski's status: he was no longer a 'threat' but someone who needed sympathy and support. This may have been less apparent had Laski not taken the court verdict so badly himself. In fact, he was devastated by it.

Frida described his immediate reaction to one of their American friends:

> Harold bore up well till he got home and then wept as I have never seen a man weep, and it just made me feel useless.[62]

She may have felt 'useless', but three weeks after the case, he told her:

> But for you I could not have faced it, and I could not have borne the burden it seemed to put on me. You have saved my self-respect for me and made me able to face life even before this bitter blow.[63]

Yet almost a month later, Frida wrote to another friend, telling him not to expect to hear from Harold for a while:

> this business has hit him very hard. . . .
> Harold was a good bit under it for a time, now he begins to take a more objective view over the whole affair, and looks at it in its true perspective as a Labour Party incident. I could not get him to move out of the house for quite a while, then I thought of a New Year in Belgium where he would be away from it, in fact he got a fear of an audience and it made him quite ill, now however having taken two big meetings in Liege and Brussels where the subject was not mentioned he seems to have recovered, anyhow his students have been marvellous so that gave him a good bit of confidence, it seems to have humiliated him considerably, and he thinks it was an attack on his self respect . . . [64]

Even now Frida's optimism about his recovery was premature, for Laski himself was only able to express his feelings to Felix Frankfurter five months after the court verdict:

The simple truth is that, ever since my grim defeat in that libel action, all the strength and energy I have had has gone into keeping my head up, and convincing myself that I was not really a disastrous failure who injured those I love and all the principles for which I care . . .

. . . I went through a pretty dark cave from which only the infinite goodness of Frida first, and then literally thousands of friends, known and unknown, helped me to emerge. It has been a hard effort, but it is over, and I have peace within myself. If I have learned how petty and malicious some really important people can be, I have learned also that there is a kind of friendship the beauty of which is almost heartbreaking. So, if I can't say that I start all over again, I have had a kind of inner spiritual renaissance which seems to have rebuilt the proportion between my inner and my outer life. You will forgive all this egoism, but it is necessary to make you feel why I have shut myself so long into a world which had no window on any outer life.[65]

Perhaps he finally achieved this degree of tranquillity. Yet Frida always remained convinced that the libel action had shortened his life and that he died 'never having forgotten the case'.[66]

It is not immediately obvious why he was so crushed by the verdict for, as he told Frankfurter, his own philosophy 'ought to have taught me not to expect any other outcome'.[67] But he had obviously hoped that his powers of persuasion would be sufficient to convince even anti-socialist jurors that he would never advocate violence. He was therefore left feeling deeply humiliated at his failure. Yet this was not just a matter of wounded pride, for it went to the core of his being.

His whole adult life had been built around a quest for social justice through peaceful means. He had also seen himself as a kind of prophet, who could articulate the hopes of the masses and convince the powerful of the need to reform before it was too late. But in court he felt that he had been belittled by Hastings and made to appear a dishonest 'half-wit'.[68] It was not therefore simply the blow to the ego that most people might have felt in a similar situation. It was rather the overpowering sense of failure in his whole life and work. He may not have felt this so strongly had he not already been depressed about the international situation, and his declining influence over Labour Party policy. His resilience would also have been greater had he been more healthy. But as he was now prone to recurrent attacks of pneumonia and bronchitis, and had suffered from a nervous breakdown only three years previously, his strength was simply ebbing away. The defeat in the libel case, after the 'Gestapo' taunt in the General Election campaign, was simply too much for him.

If these episodes in Britain were the most devastating for him, it is worth noting that his final years in his second home, the United States, were equally depressing.

Laski Demonology in the United States

Despite his criticisms of Roosevelt during the war, Laski had retained a substantial following in the United States in 1945. As Robert Boothby said in the House of Commons:

> I have great admiration for him . . . but the influence he has in the American press is absolutely fantastic. His lightest word, his bed-time musings are headline news for every paper in the United States from coast to coast. He is regarded there not only as repre-senting 100% of the Labour government but also about 80% of this country as a whole.[69]

Naturally, this was an exaggeration, but Laski was certainly better known in the USA than any other comparable British figure. However, the attacks on him as a sinister influence had mounted during the war and in the Truman years he was rapidly transformed into a 'hate' figure. At the time of the British General Election in 1945, the popular press in the United States used the Beaverbrook-Churchill allegations – often in a still more sensationalist form. For example, when Labour's electoral victory was announced, the *New York Mirror's* headline was:

CLEMENT. R. ATTLEE MADE PRIME MINISTER OF ENGLAND BUT THE BOSS IS HAROLD LASKI A PRO-RUSSIAN FIGURE.[70]

However, the American press attacks on Laski were not only de-signed to point out the 'dangers' of socialism in Britain, but also to discredit him in the USA. By now the FBI was taking a lively interest in his movements and statements. Their agents were present in November 1945 when Joseph Kennedy (the former ambassador in London) told a Catholic college that his eldest son had become 'a completely devout Communist' when under the influence of Laski.[71]

When Laski spoke at a conference in New York in December 1945, urging international control over nuclear weapons, the meeting was picketed by Catholic war veterans, and he was again attacked in the American press.[72]

It is ironic that in August 1945 Laski had desperately wanted Attlee to appoint him British ambassador to the United States:

> I know I could do a good job in Washington and I care for that more than anything else. But at least I want the Beaverbrooks and the Brackens to know that my own Party does not regard me as a leper it would not touch.[73]

This was a naive hope. American press attacks on Laski were often sent over to Attlee, probably reinforcing his determination to ensure that Laski was not viewed as a representative of the Labour government.[74] In any case, American press vilification continued and Laski was often accused of speaking for the Kremlin.[75]

The British legal case gave new impetus to the campaign against him in the USA.[76] And it is extremely probable that the anti-Laski campaign in the USA, which was mounted during his lecture visits there in 1948 and 1949 was, at least in part, orchestrated by the FBI.

Before he left Britain to lecture at the Roosevelt University in Chicago in March 1948, the FBI section in the US Embassy in London informed J. Edgar Hoover that, 'upon instructions from higher officers in the Embassy', Laski had not been closely questioned when applying for his visa.[77] But, in order to demonstrate his political views, a copy of his centenary broadcast on the communist manifesto was sent to Hoover. It was too late for any retrospective action to be taken on this occasion and the talks took place without serious disruption. But soon after he returned to Britain the 'Sons of Liberty Boycott Committee' sent a report on Laski to Hoover.[78] It seems very likely that the FBI was involved in the events of the next spring.

Laski had been invited to lecture by the Sidney Hillman Foundation and a number of universities. However, two days after arriving in the USA, he received a special delivery letter from the Justice Department asking him to register as a foreign agent. He refused to do so and, after the Amalgamated Clothing Workers Union joined the protest, the Justice Department backed down.[79] This was no doubt a deliberate ploy to discredit him, but was only the beginning of a series of episodes.

US universities were then under extreme pressure from the Right with dismissals of liberal and Left-wing staff as a result of 'un-American activities' campaigns. As Kingsley Martin explained:

> When Harold began his travels, he found himself greeted at each halting place by a group of reporters, some of whom at least were anxious to secure statements from him which could be used to suggest that the local university, by permitting him to speak in its auditorium, was lending itself to some kind of 'un-American' activity.[80]

When he reached Los Angeles, he found that his lecture had been cancelled on an absurd pretext, because the university was already under investigation by the California legislature and the authorities did not want to risk provoking the Right. He was appalled by the cowardice of the university president, but experienced the atmosphere of intimidation and intolerance in many places, including Cambridge, Massachusetts, where the Mayor refused to allow the Harvard Law School to use a local auditorium on the ground that Laski was a Communist, hostile to all religions, and an enemy of Catholicism. This must have recalled his first major crisis in the same city thirty years earlier, and symbolised the eradication of the New Deal era.

After he left the USA (for the last time), he wrote an article in *The Nation* which included a bitter condemnation of the FBI. This provoked a new internal memorandum on him by the Agency. Not only did this quote from his works to demonstrate that he was a Marxist but, in a passage where he compared Marx with Abraham Lincoln, an FBI official commented that this was 'certainly blasphemy on Lincoln's good name'. The fact that Laski had dedicated books to Frankfurter was twice mentioned (with the obvious intention of also damning him by association). The conclusion was that Laski should never have been given a visa on the assumption that he was an anti-communist:

> it is disconcerting to realize that he was apparently allowed to enter this country under this assumption; an entry which gave him the freedom to tour our nation and to attack our American way of life in public lectures, contributing thereby to undermining the faith of the American people in their own institutions.[81]

Naturally, Laski did not see this memorandum, but it would not have surprised him. He knew that the situation was far worse for his American counterparts and that the attack on him was a relatively insignificant part of a far wider process. But it added to the torment and isolation of his last years.

Laski never gave up his struggle. In the final years of his life, he fought against his own ill-health and pessimism, in an attempt to impress his views upon the era. But circumstances had now changed, with the emergence of new orthodoxies in both political thought and practice. American ideologies, bewitched by the 'Red Scare', presented him as a danger while the Labour leadership and many academics, seemed to view him as 'yesterday's man'. It is doubtful whether Laski could have made a major impact in this situation even with his former vitality. Increasingly isolated, and with waning strength and self-confidence, he certainly could not do so. Yet both his views, and his attempts to influence political developments, remain very significant. It is these which must now be considered.

LASKI'S WORLD OUTLOOK 1945–50

Liberty, Democracy and Pluralism

It is absurd to portray Laski, in his final years, as an enemy of liberty and democracy, or as a defender of 'totalitarianism'. In fact, he reaffirmed his earlier values – in which he had never ceased to believe – far more explicitly than he had during the late 1930s. He constantly reiterated his fervent belief in tolerance, discussion, and constitutionalism as the basis for freedom and civilisation and, in a series of lectures that he delivered at Manchester University only six weeks before his death, he proclaimed that the real alternative to the House of Commons was the concentration camp.[82] Indeed, one of the many ironies of the libel case was that it came at a time when his faith in the possibility of peaceful change was higher than at any time since the early 1920s. Nor was this simply a pragmatic attitude, for his work extolled the virtues of constitutionalism, celebrating its historical and institutional intricacies.

This was not a stale repetition of platitudes, but a total commitment to parliamentary democracy as the *sine qua non* for liberty. Indeed his underlying preoccupation with 'liberty' as the basis of civilised life was as strong as it had been in his early pluralist phase, and permeated his work. Such values were manifest, for example, when he wrote about education. He thus argued that even non-academic pupils, who leave school early:

> ought not . . . to be given some special technique which finds its immediate sale on the labour market and is thenceforward a frame within which it is enclosed until retirement from work. Youth needs a rough map of the universe, a training in the art of living with other people, a realisation of what is meant by a world perpetually in flux, and an insight into the art of self-adaptation to the fact of change. Nothing is so ruinous either to mind or to character as premature specialization through an early emphasis on vocational training. Boys and girls are sent to school not to become bricklayers or shop assistants, clerks or typists, but men and women who can help to make democracy a living principle of action.[83]

In higher education:

> no teacher can attempt to teach adequately or to embark upon researches with a full mind and heart unless he can speak the truth that is in him without regard to the novelty or the inconvenience of the results he believes himself to have attained. His intellectual activities, therefore, must be unimpeded. He has the obligation, in return, to pursue his task in a scientific spirit; that is to say, he owes it to the university not to leap into utterance without the careful and critical examination of the facts upon which he bases his conclusions. But once he has made that effort, the university in its turn, can neither penalize him, nor permit his penalisation, without destroying the peculiar value upon which its whole value as an academic institution depends.[84]

The university teacher:

> must seek to convey the inescapable dynamism of life, the need to be ready for novelty and experiment, to refuse to confound the new with the dangerous or the traditional with the beneficent, and, above all in a civilization so dependent upon the division of

labour as our own, he must convince . . . [students] of the curse of specialization, the need for an ever-increasing number of minds able to co-ordinate, to build wholes and not parts merely, if we are to attain that balanced life in which human beings reach beyond frustration to fulfilment.[85]

This depiction of genuine education as fearless, free enquiry which could lead to fulfilled and rounded citizens is illustrative of Laski's attitudes to democracy and liberty as *living* forces. Similar values were apparent in his discussions of other features of modern life. In particular, it is significant, that when discussing the role of workers in nationalised industries, and the political rights of civil servants, he reverted to many of the themes that he had developed in his earlier pluralist thinking. Once again he stressed the need for participation and a role in decision-making as a vital part of citizenship.[86] Laski's concepts of freedom and democracy in his final years thus included both constitutional/institutional concerns, and a recognition of the need to generate vibrant political activity amongst ordinary people. It is clear that he was searching for a more positive concept than the model of 'democratic elitism' that would dominate Western conceptions of freedom in the post-war period. However, he was also aware of the difficulties faced by the masses in understanding 'the forces by which the world is moved':

Before them is the daily need to live, the exacting toil of work, the need for play and sleep and a brief hour of love. They are schooled to obedience by the rigorous discipline of their lives. It is no easy task to give them the sense of grave dangers to be arrested, of big ideas which need an army to fight for them.[87]

He therefore concluded that 'great leadership' was necessary and, despite all his criticisms, Roosevelt remained his model.

Laski never fully defined the synthesis between participation, constitutionalism, and leadership that he was seeking. But his commitment to such values was manifest throughout his post-war work. And he was quite explicit in arguing that these conceptions bore no relation to life in the Soviet Union. For example, in a lecture in memory of the Webbs on 4 June 1947, he maintained that, while various definitions of democracy were possible, none of them was applicable to Russia:

The real government of Soviet Russia is not the elected government, but the Communist Party. The constitution of 1936 permits no rivalry to that party. To put it bluntly, the Party is the state power; whenever, therefore the Party may choose, opposition to its line becomes at once sedition, and even treason. So that, in ultimate fact, the 'rights' granted to the Russian citizen by the Constitution are effective, or not effective, in terms of the will of the little group of men who form the executive committee of the Communist Party. They have the power of life and death.[88]

Later in the lecture, he developed his critique:

I do not think it is possible seriously to deny that Soviet Russia is still a police-state in which the individual citizen must move within a carefully defined area of thought and action, and moves outside that area only at grave risk of penalty to himself. If Russia were, in a full sense, a democracy, the right to opposition would be conceded. There would not be a religious veneration for the ruler, to preserve which his subordinates will even suppress his eulogies of his former opponents. There would not be so careful a conditioning of the national mind to one outlook, and one outlook only. There would not be the determined effort on the part of the Government to safeguard its people from contact with foreign ideas. There would be a profounder respect for the personal freedom of the citizen, and some serious institutional effort towards an independent judiciary which, in political cases, would give the defendant at least an equal chance with his persecutors, and, in each instance, make the process of trial public from the moment that alleged offences are followed by arrest. The government would not monopolise all the instruments of propaganda and publicity, and compel even the imaginative arts to be subdued by their practitioners to the momentary needs of the state power.[89]

Elsewhere he anticipated Orwell by talking of the 'one-party state' as a phenomenon in which rulers:

use words without relation to their meaning, so that servile obedience is hailed as freedom and the unity imposed by compulsion should be heralded as the fulfilment of democracy.[90]

In Laski's last years, there is therefore no doubt either of his commitment to the values of liberty, pluralism and democracy or of his belief that the Soviet Union remained a police-state. Yet is is not surprising that his stance was unpopular, for he was concerned with the translation of his ultimate goals into reality, not simply to avow them as propaganda. And his analysis of the current position, his interpretative framework, and his policy recommendations were all at variance with the new consensus.

THE GULF BETWEEN THEORY AND REALITY

Laski saw liberty and democracy as essential components of civilisation, but also maintained that they were dependent on some crucial prerequisites. The primary condition of liberty was an expanding economy. Only then would people have 'hope' – the basis for the respect for law, the sense of opportunity, and a society which had sufficient self-confidence to accept free discussion.[91] Indeed, an interest in liberty could begin only when people had ceased to be overwhelmed by the problem of sheer existence. Once they had a modicum of leisure, and the opportunity to reflect upon their situation, they could recognise that they need not helplessly accept the routine in which they had previously seemed to be immersed.

Economic sufficiency, and time for thought were thus the primary conditions for a free people.[92] But Laski believed – as strongly as ever – that capitalism was incompatible with the creation of such conditions for the mass of the population. In the final analysis it was therefore also an insuperable barrier to the establishment of liberty. Similarly, full democracy was possible only when people were able to participate and when they agreed about the fundamental goals of the system. But poverty and inequality precluded the full realisation of such conditions in the long run, and this again meant that democracy was threatened by the continuation of capitalism.

Laski regarded contemporary Britain as a 'democracy', and celebrated the post-war Labour government's success in establishing the 'welfare state' and full employment. This meant that the masses could believe that their rising expectations might be satisfied, and that there would be a progressive enlargement in their realm of liberty. However, the situation remained precarious, for mass unemployment (on the pre-war scale) was incompatible with democracy.[93] Since he believed that unemployment was inherent in capitalism, this also meant that democracy could be maintained only with the progressive establishment of socialism. This again raised the fundamental problem which had preoccupied him for so long: to what extent was it possible to transform capitalism peacefully? He was impressed both by the maintenance of the democratic system throughout the war, and under the post-war Labour government, but this had not altered his fundamental theoretical position:

> a socialist government which, even with a majority, takes office in a capitalist society the institutions of which are formally democratic cannot help but be aware of the fairly narrow limits within which it may successfully manoeuvre, and the danger to which it is exposed if it embarks upon measures which disturb the 'confidence' of men of property. . . .
>
> There is a point, never capable of exact definition, up to which the men of property are willing to buy off the opponents of capitalism by measures of social reform. But when that point is reached there is always the gravest danger that men of property, if they have to make their choice between their possessions and democratic institutions, will prefer their possessions, and destroy democratic institutions.[94]

Laski was now prepared to grant that there was greater room for manoeuvre within the system than he had believed during his more pessimistic moments in the thirties, but he also knew that the Labour government had not made any attempt to penetrate the 'citadel' of capitalist power.[95] In general, he accepted that progress was being made – despite occasional impatience about undue caution – but he remained agnostic about the ultimate prognosis.

If he was relatively optimistic about the future of British democracy, by 1945 he also realised that this was no longer of pivotal importance in world historical terms. Naturally, as a British citizen, Labour Party Chair, and a Professor at LSE, he continued to operate in, and offer extensive analyses of, the British situation. Yet he obviously sensed that the future of capitalist democracy was dependent more upon the politics of Washington, and he became increasingly preoccupied with American politics in his last years.

His most sustained analysis was contained in his final major work, *The American Democracy*. This was a study of monumental proportions – the most ambitious of all his books. He had begun it in 1937 and completed it ten years later. It ranged over the whole range of American society and history, encompassing education, religion, culture, business, and minorities as well as more explicitly political matters. Inevitably, the quality was uneven, but much of the analysis was magisterial and it offered insights into American society which are still instructive. Laski also visited the USA several times during his last years, and alluded to it in a vast number of speeches and articles. It is therefore possible only to summarise the essence of his views.

For Laski, the death of Roosevelt in April 1945 was a tragedy. Certainly, he had criticised him for abandoning the New Deal in order to secure the support of business for the war, and he had condemned much of his foreign policy as effectively 'reactionary'. Yet he still believed that he stood for the common people of the world and that American democracy was retrievable while he lived. He was immediately more pessimistic about Truman and, within a few months of the end of the war, he feared that Washington would be engulfed by anti-communist witch-hunts. All these fears were confirmed by his six week visit to the United States from August to October 1946.

Having yearned for America throughout the war, he was now bitterly disappointed. 'The outstanding impression', he told Frida:

> is one of their overwhelming consciousness of power . . . Put generously it is the conviction that other people ought to be pitied because they haven't the good fortune to be Americans.[96]

He was now struck by American materialism, lack of social consciousness, and deep anti-Soviet and anti-Labour feelings. He could no longer live there, and had become 'very English or very European'.[97]

> It isn't a country for foreign liberals. It has become harsh and acrid, and so conscious of its power and wealth.[98]

Such impressions were incorporated into his analysis of the United States, leading him to emphasise the total gulf that now existed between the theory and practice of its democracy. On the one hand, there were qualities which he still loved – hospitality, openness, a lack of marked social differentiation, and a vibrant quality of life. But he argued that the United States was now corrupted by the dominance of business over all its institutions and social organisations.

Indeed the argument of *The American Democracy* – reiterated in each chapter – was that there was an ever wider divergence between the democracy it proclaimed in its constitution and professed values and the reality of capitalist power. However, he did not simply *state* this: he demonstrated it in a meticulous examination of such phenomena as social and racial inequalities, the educational system, the materialist corruption of 'religiosity', and the use of hired thugs to intimidate workers in labour disputes. His overall argument was that capitalism now had exactly the same defects in the USA as in Europe, but that it was failing to take any of the remedial action that was being adopted by the Labour government in Britain. American democracy was not only flawed, but also fundamentally hypocritical in proclaiming support for 'freedom' abroad, while standing for corruption at home.

For example, in 1947 he agreed with American denunciations of the Soviet-controlled elections in Eastern Europe, but drew attention to the systematic purge of liberals in the US civil service, and the intimidation of black voters in the Southern states. How, he asked, could the US proclaim the virtues of freedom abroad while allowing its own system to deviate so totally from the liberalism, constitutionalism and democracy that it proclaimed?[99] And, as the witch-hunts mounted in the later forties, so that liberals in academic and cultural life were forced out of their jobs, he asked, with increasing bitterness, how such activities could possibly be reconciled with the principles of the constitution. By 1949 he believed that the USA was gripped by an irrationalism and intolerance comparable to earlier waves of religious persecution and that the fundamental tenets of American democracy were being eroded.[100] In his view, the transformation of capitalism was the key to change for, although the anti-Left hysteria had its own dynamics, it was rooted in the interests of the privileged classes. Having feared the comparatively mild measures of the New Deal, American capitalism was now reasserting its position through a denunciation of anything that smacked of liberalism, and the Soviet 'threat' provided it with an opportunity to do so. If, therefore, progressive forces could counteract the hegemony of big business, they would also be able to restore the traditional values. In his Sidney Hillman lectures he therefore tried to persuade the trade union movement to develop a socialistic political consciousness and to refuse to collaborate with the employers' anti-communist measures.[101] But by now all the hopes that he held for American democracy during the 1930s had been replaced by a deep pessimism.

None of this reduced Laski's commitment to the *values* of liberalism and democracy. It simply reinforced his view that the mere *profession* of the values was worthless. What was necessary was sincere commitment, an understanding of the conditions in which the values could be implemented in reality, and a determination to bring about the necessary changes. Indeed Laski was now so adamant that, in itself, the proclamation of values was a propaganda exercise that he sometimes even opposed verbal statements of this kind. For example, in 1947 he was appointed to a UNESCO Committee to draw up a Universal Declaration of Human Rights. Alone amongst the international team, he argued that there was no point in making any such declaration unless this was accompanied by other essential commitments: specification of the necessary socio-economic conditions which would make the implementation of such rights possible, and agreement by the United Nations to ensure that the transformation took place. Otherwise states would cynically disregard the Declaration themselves, while using it as a propagandist tool against their political opponents.[102] This was an accurate prediction of international arguments over human rights for the next forty years, although it is debatable whether this made the Declaration worthless.

Implicit in Laski's attitudes to all these issues was a form of Marxism, which meant that he would never accept professed ideals as equivalent to practical reality. What then was his attitude to Marxism and Communism in the post-war period?

MARXISM AND COMMUNISM

Having described himself as a 'Marxist' during the 1930s, Laski never renounced this 'label', and there was certainly a Marxist influence over his analysis of the contemporary world in the last five years of his life. Yet he was totally opposed to 'mechanical Marxism' and believed that it was a doctrine to be examined empirically in the light of evidence, rather than as an axiom or dogma. One of his last research students thus recalled him recommending a class to read *The Communist Manifesto* 'as a discourse, not an incantation, and in an armchair not on your knees'.[103] In fact his distinctive attitude to Marxism became far more apparent in the post-war period than it had been earlier.

For Laski, Marxism served a dual function. On the one hand it was an essential critique of liberalism, which exposed its class character both historically and in the current situation. On the other hand, he sought to absorb Marxism into the liberal tradition. His assumption was that the achievement of this synthesis would make it possible for liberalism to practise the values that it professed. In concrete terms this meant that he simultaneously urged the Labour Party to use Marxism to analyse and understand capitalist society, and urged Marxists to realise that constitutionalism, consent, discussion, and freedom were universal values which must not be jettisoned. This coexistence of liberalism and Marxism had, of course, been a feature of Laski's outlook even in the 1930s. However, it had then been masked by communist domination of the Popular Front movement and Laski's difficulties in differentiating his own position from that of the CP. Hence the unresolved contradictions in his thought. However, his break from the Popular Front in 1938, and his bitter opposition to the Communist Party between 1939–41, liberated him and led to a change in his thinking.

By 1939 he had already criticised the USSR and communist parties, but he now went much further. For he argued that *even in theoretical terms* Leninism was a deviation from Marxism.[104] The Bolshevik revolution may have been necessary and justifiable, but it was nevertheless a distortion which emanated from the Blanquist, conspiratorial tradition. In Marxism itself there was no basis for the single party either before or after the seizure of power. Leninist-communism was not therefore of universal application. Moreover, in any country with a strong democratic tradition it would be both retrograde and counterproductive to seek to emulate it or to base socialism upon it. For democracy was in advance of Soviet-style communism. It followed from this that communist and socialist parties were quite distinct entities, based on different ideological and organisational principles. This led him to adopt a firm stance against communism at the end of the war.

After the Nazi attack on the Soviet Union in 1941, communist parties had played a major role in the European resistance and had resumed the 'Popular Front' stance. In 1945 they advocated a reinforcement of this policy through mergers with socialist forces. Since they were more militant and disciplined than the socialists, it appeared highly probable that this could lead to communist domination of the working-class movement in many countries. Given his general analysis, and his experience of Soviet control of communist parties, Laski was as keen to prevent this occurrence as the Labour government itself. Since he had played a considerable role in facilitating consultations between the representatives of socialist parties in London throughout the war, and was well-known throughout Europe, he was well placed to exercise some influence on behalf of the Labour Party.

In August 1945 he attended the Conference of the French Socialist Party (SFIO) which was to discuss the PCF proposal for 'organic unity' between the two parties. This had some rank-and-file support, but was bitterly opposed by most of the leaders. Léon Blum, who had just returned from Buchenwald, mounted an influential campaign against it in a series of articles in *Le Populaire* just before the Congress. Laski had already been on friendly terms with Blum before the war and now obviously encouraged him behind the scenes in the stance that he was taking. Many of Blum's articles bore a very close relationship to Laski's views, and the successful resolution at the Congress cited the Labour victory in Britain, and the need for international socialist unity, as an argument against unity with the Communists at national level.[105] Attendance at the French socialist party was followed up in the same month with participation in the Danish and Swedish party conferences, where he also argued against mergers with the Communists.[106] But his most controversial intervention was in the Italian Socialist Party (PSI), for here he tried to counter the influence of the leadership rather than supporting it.

The Pact of Unity between the PSI and PCI had originally been forged between the two parties in exile from fascism, but was reaffirmed after the liberation. It is debatable how far Nenni, the PSI leader, saw it as a strategy to prevent the decline of his party, and how far he was a genuine convert to ideological convergence with Communism. But, in any case, he was committed to the principle of unity. However, Laski shared the view of the Labour leadership that PSI independence would be undermined by such a close relationship. He therefore wrote an article in an Italian progressive weekly, entitled 'My advice to Pietro Nenni', which warned him against an alleged tendency to Left-wing dictatorship in Italy. This, he argued, could follow from the formation of a unified party even if Nenni had no such intentions.[107] The PSI leader was outraged by this and replied in spirited terms on 2 September in *Avanti*. But this was only the beginning of Laski's involvement, for the question of unity with the Communists was to be discussed at the PSI Congress the following April and many of the opponents of the leadership line wanted Laski to attend.[108] Since Laski had great status in Italy at the time, the Labour Party reluctantly agreed to this request and sent him with

Denis Healey as the other delegate.[109] While there Laski handed Nenni a letter from Bevin (the contents of which are still not disclosed in the Public Records Office),[110] and he spoke publicly against fusion with the PCI 'which was run from abroad and was not democratic in method'.[111] The Labour attache at the British Embassy described the speech as 'magnificent' and in Whitehall an official commented:

> we decided not to preach against fusion ourselves, but I think from Professor Laski this line will go down well in Italy and give the Socialists the lead which their party bosses are unable to give.[112]

Laski also intervened against the Communist movement in Britain. In April 1946 he wrote a pamphlet for the Labour Party (*The Secret Battalion*), which was designed to expose the 'insincerity' of the latest CP campaign for affiliation. This was a bitter condemnation of the communists' tactics:

> They must . . . destroy the very parties with which they seek alliance in order to command their resources for their own ends. To do this, they must declare that they are at one with them, loyal to their principles, ready to accept their rules, prepared to serve under their leaders.
> But since none of these declarations are true, they must also, at the same time, deny those principles, manoeuvre round the rules, and do all in their power both to discredit the leaders they agree to serve, and, if possible, secure their places when they are discredited.[113]

The parties were likened to secret battalions because they were organised conspiracies, trying to get their supporters into key positions. They required from their members:

> the complete and unquestioning sacrifice of their consciences to the decisions their inner leadership makes. A refusal to make that sacrifice is the proof of a dangerous and rebellious personality for whom excommunication from the body of the faithful is the only possible remedy.[114]

Western socialists should reject organic unity with communist parties because they:

act without moral scruples, intrigue without any sense of shame, are utterly careless of truth, sacrifice, without any hesitation, the means they use to the ends they serve.

Labour leaders were thus bound to suspect that communist intentions, after entry, would turn the party into an instrument 'of subservient devotion to the dictatorship of the Communist Party in Moscow'.[115]

Laski's vehement and unqualified attack on communism led him into an immediate exchange of polemics with Harry Pollitt, the CP leader, and warm congratulations from Attlee.[116] His attitude – and the applause it elicited from the Foreign Office and the Labour leader – is difficult to reconcile with the popular portrayal of Laski as a 'fellow-traveller'. And indeed this view has little basis, given both his claim that communism was a distortion of Marxism, and his willingness to confront communist parties in practice. However, his attitude towards the Soviet Union was more complex than his negative view of the international communist movement.

THE SOVIET UNION

As has already been shown, he regarded the Soviet Union as a non-democratic police state. He also continued, in the post-war era, to criticise the signs of Soviet expansionism. In November 1945 he thus wrote a public list of 'Questions to Molotov':

Are there any more territorial adjustments desired by Russia? If so what are these adjustments and on what grounds are they sought? . . . If Russia is entitled to make a series of treaties, economic or political, with States which it regards as friendly to itself, why is not Great Britain entitled to make a series of treaties on a similar basis?

. . . Why is the formation of an Eastern bloc by Russia unexceptionable while the formation of a Western bloc is to be regarded as a threat to the peace?[117]

He was also worried about early signs that Stalin was intent on imposing the Soviet model on East European states. Socialists of the Left, he argued, had no more regard for one-party states imposed by Russia than they had for Western non-intervention in Spain and

Portugal.[118] Yet although he often viewed the Soviet Union as difficult, suspicious, demanding and provocative, he was categorical about the need for the Labour government to seek an understanding with Stalin. And he continued to believe that if the mutual mistrust could be dispelled, it would be possible to establish peace, good socialist/communist relations, and greater internal democracy within the Soviet Union. Indeed he maintained exactly the position that he had held during the war, and continued to argue that no new Socialist International should be created until a major effort had been made to secure co-operation with the USSR: 'Given Russian co-operation, I believe that the whole of Europe could be socialist within twenty years'.

On the other hand:

> Russian isolationism seems to me not less likely to make at least a large part of Europe the predestined victim of monopoly capitalism. When that stage approaches, the third world war will be at hand. It is both to avoid that catastrophe and to unite working men and women the world over against its dangers that I seek for friendship with Soviet Russia.[119]

He believed that the opportunity to play a role in achieving his goal had arrived when, in July/August 1946, he was one of the members of the Labour Party delegation to the Soviet Union.[120] The visit that he had been advocating ever since 1941 had finally come about. In fact, it was not likely to be particularly important. Foreign policy was kept firmly in the hands of Bevin and Attlee, and Morgan Phillips was the leader of the delegation. But Laski clearly hoped that a major breakthrough would result despite the subordinate position of the delegation.

His first letter to Frida from Moscow described a conversation with the Acting Foreign Secretary which grew increasingly heated and resulted in a meeting with Popov, the secretary of the CPSU:

> Until we have seen Popoff [sic] and get to the next stage I do not want to be too certain of the direction. There are clearly deep reserves, a good deal of suspicion, and yet, behind it, a desire for friendship. Whether we can discover the key to the lock I shall be able to tell you better . . . after tonight.[121]

However, Popov was a disappointment because he would not be drawn into general political discussions. Laski reported to Frida that, after an hour of questioning about his role as Mayor of Moscow:

> I told him with great sternness that this was not what we had
> come to Russia for; and that if we were not allowed to discuss
> urgent political questions at the highest level it was not worth
> our staying.[122]

This, he claimed, resulted in a meeting with Shvernik, President of the People's Council. According to his account to Frida, Laski opened by saying that it was futile to do sight-seeing and, after an hour and a half's discussion, Shvernik agreed that the delegation should see the Politbureau and Stalin.

> It is hard work, but now I feel we are moving – how far I would
> not guess. There are many interesting tit-bits – hatred of Church-
> ill, suspicion of Ernest [Bevin], fear and distrust of America. But
> the basic motive of everything is self-amazement at finding itself
> alive, and conviction that there should be no such risks again. I
> am convinced that this is the clue to everything.[123]

After discussions with the Minister of Education and the Head of the Trade Unions, he sent one more letter claiming that the trip was going well and that the Russians were impressed that the delegation insisted on arguing its case. But he ended by saying that the real discussion would take place later, and that: 'I have oceans to tell you, but I think it is wiser to wait till we can talk.[124]

This is tantalising, since a full account of the trip to Frida would have provided some fairly conclusive evidence to settle the disputes about subsequent events. As it is, the only real source is the official version written by the delegation as a whole on its return. In general, this was enthusiastic about the Soviet Union, and Stalin himself, who was described as follows:

> We were met by a man simply dressed, smaller and somewhat
> older looking than we had expected, but whose merry smile and
> twinkling eyes welcomed us before he had uttered a word. There
> was nothing formal about the meeting . . . and we talked in an
> easy conversational manner for 2 and 1/4 hours upon the tasks
> which confronted the people of our two countries.

After a general discussion:

> Mr Stalin said that he was gratified to know that two great coun-
> tries were travelling in the Socialist direction. In Russia they were
> travelling to Socialism in the Russian way, which he believed was
> shorter but more difficult, whereas in Britain we were going in
> what appeared to be the more roundabout British way – to which
> there was an aside that 'we had a habit of getting there'. He felt
> that in both countries we could reach the Socialist objective. As
> Marxists and Leninists the Russians did not think that theirs was
> the only road to Socialism. They recognised that though Socialism
> could be obtained by other methods than through Soviets, they
> believed that theirs was the shortest, even if the most difficult,
> way, and that it may be accompanied by bloodshed; by the British
> method, the change may be less violent but the process was much
> longer.[125]

Stalin then followed this with a more detailed analysis of the situation in the two countries. The Labour government, he argued, had
adopted the right line in dealing with the public ownership of basic
industries first, for the Soviet experience indicated that the State
could then direct its policy to reduce prices and raise real wages. In
the Soviet Union it had been a difficult task to win over the peasant
population and 'much care and thought had to be given to the many
problems which arose'. The problems relating to industrial workers
had been overcome, and women were now playing an important
role in the building of socialism. Great progress was now being
made in production and living standards, but 'things could, of course,
be speeded up if the armed forces of the State could be reduced'.
This could be achieved only if there were no further danger of
aggression, and this required suitable mutual treaties of defence. He
also expressed concern about the low level of culture amongst
the large peasant population, while Britain had a highly organised
working-class and a higher level of culture. Overall, he therefore
felt that there was the possibility of a more peaceful approach to
Socialist construction in Britain than in Russia. However, he referred
more than once to the dangers of reaction from the enemies of the
Labour Party in Britain and left the delegation with the impression
that this was a real fear in Russian minds.

Having discussed many other aspects of the visit in fairly positive
terms, the report concluded:

we saw all that we had asked to see and met everyone we expressed a desire to meet. We were lavishly entertained and both the informal and more formal discussions were carried on in the most friendly manner possible. From all quarters we received assurances of the desire of the Russian people for friendship with the people of Britain. We did not regard it as part of our duty . . . to discuss international questions. Nor did we discuss the relationship of the two parties except in so far as it had a bearing upon the development and maintenance of friendship between the peoples of the two nations. We should be foolish to assume that difficulties and differences do not exist or that all misunderstanding has been dispelled. We do, however, believe that as a goodwill mission our visit was well worth while. The publicity given to the delegation together with the response from the people we met justifies our saying that the mission was a successful one.

There is no doubt that the visit made a deep impression upon Laski. Stalin had, of course, said exactly what Laski would have wanted to hear. His elaboration of the possibility of different roads to socialism and the claim that a peaceful transition in Britain was feasible were totally in harmony with Laski's own notions. Similarly, the argument that the Soviet Union wanted to divert more expenditure to peaceful production and the raising of living standards rather than squandering it on arms production was in line with his own views.

Moreover, when the Soviet leader discussed the dangers of reactionary forces in Britain undermining the achievements of the Labour government he could almost have been quoting Laski himself. Finally, it would also have struck a chord with Laski when Stalin expressed the hope that there would be the fullest cooperation between the two peoples, and continued by indicating:

> that a delegation from the Supreme Soviet would visit England in response to a British invitation, and with an ingratiating smile, he expressed the hope that when they came, Mr Bevin would not 'scold them too much'. And in just the same spirit of light raillery Mr Clay responded, 'I know of no problem to which you and Mr Bevin would not find a solution.'

Laski was desperately keen to believe that there really was a basis for Labour/Soviet understanding if only the mutual suspicion were dispelled. This exchange – and its underlying implication that harmonious relations were possible if goodwill was shown on both sides – would therefore have strongly appealed to him. For Laski the visit was thus of great importance and he tried (unsuccessfully) to ensure that the final report carried a policy recommendation as a 'base for the next move'.[126] In fact, he was deluding himself if he really believed that the delegation or its report would have any impact on government policy. However, he saw the visit as crucially significant for it reinforced all his existing views about the Soviet Union: that its provocative policies were the result of insecurity, that it wanted peace and internal reconstruction, and that the West could achieve these results if it adopted appropriate policies.

The controversial aspect of the visit is that Laski subsequently told many people that he had a second meeting with Stalin, while the rest of the delegation were watching a film. The substance of this alleged conversation did not differ very significantly from the one recorded in the delegation report, except that Stalin was said to have told him that he found Molotov somewhat inflexible and gruff, and wished that Bevin would be more conciliatory.[127] However, it has generally been argued that this was a fantasy or lie on Laski's part, particularly as Morgan Phillips is said to have claimed that there was no opportunity for any such second meeting. Since all the members of the delegation are now dead, and it is unlikely that a record of the conversation would be kept in the Soviet Union, it is almost impossible to verify or disprove Laski's claim. I believe that it is quite likely that he was telling the truth.[128] Yet if he was guilty of fabricating the 'second interview', his motives were, no doubt, more complex than personal vanity. It is more probable that he might lie to achieve a political purpose. In other words, he was so convinced that Stalin needed and wanted peace that he *might* have resorted to 'faction' to reinforce his case. He might have been tempted to do so as the official report of the delegation – which implicitly supported Laski's views – was not publicised, but remained buried in the party archives. Given his conviction that the need to reach agreement with the Soviet Union was the task of paramount importance, he may have felt that a lie was justified. But whatever actually happened in Moscow in August 1946, it had no impact on the course of history. Despite his fervent hopes, East-West relations continued to deteriorate and by 1947 the Cold War had become the dominant feature of the age.

THE COLD WAR

For Laski the Cold War was a tragedy of monumental proportions. Since the whole basis for his hopes for the post-war world had been the maintenance of the wartime alliance, evolving into agreement about reconstruction and peace, the prospect of renewed conflict appeared literally catastrophic. He was dominated by an overpowering wish to prevent the breakdown in relations, and to refuse to accept the necessity for the Labour government to align itself with either side. His stance was not fully consistent, as he was buffeted by the contradictory pressures, but he attempted to take an independent position informed by his general interpretative framework.

He was deeply critical of US foreign policy throughout the period, but he believed that a decisive phase occurred with the promulgation of the Truman Doctrine in March 1947. Despite the rhetoric about freedom and democracy this was, he argued, designed to 'build a new empire'. Truman must know that the plan was:

> to make American money the safeguard of Greek reaction and American advisers the architects of its efficiency. He must know that he is, in fact, instructing Turkey to act as a barrier against Russian access to the Mediterranean and that he thus is not only asking his people to support a still partially feudal dictatorship but accepting on their behalf the traditional British folly . . . of backing the wrong horse. The peoples of the Middle East are to be pinned down in vassalage to obsolete regimes until there arises a power strong enough to rescue them from the dependence America will be driven to force upon them.[129]

Six weeks later he told Frankfurter that US policy was 'hateful' and backed reaction throughout the world.[130] He dismissed Frankfurter's objections, maintaining that the Americans had a covert alliance with the Vatican, and were prepared to support only Right-wing governments, and even ex-fascist industrialists, while stopping all help to Poles, Czechs and Hungarians on political grounds.

> in my judgment your policy towards Russia has involved you in a policy where you back every counterrevolutionary movement there is in Europe.[131]

While he believed that Roosevelt might have followed a more enlightened policy, he regarded the structure of the American economy as responsible for an expansionist drive based on support for capitalist regimes abroad. However, he was unsure as to how to interpret the Marshall Aid offer. There were, he said, intriguing possibilities in the speech, but if there were:

> unstated principles of exclusion in Mr Marshall's mind, the application of which is . . . intended to produce a 'divided Europe' or a 'Western bloc', then British participation should not be taken for granted.[132]

He was also convinced that the Soviet Union should accept the invitation to participate in the discussions. In private he claimed to be negotiating over this, and in public he argued:

> Russian statesmen owe this cooperation to their friends all over the world . . . If the Marshall plan is no more than a new road to American domination . . . much the best way to expose it is to present the American Government with a reasonable and well articulated plan on which European Governments are united. The test of American good faith then becomes the terms it asks for accepting the plan.[134]

Soviet rejection of the invitation was therefore a bitter blow, but he still believed that the USA bore the greater responsibility for the breakdown in relations:

> I wish I could share Bevin's ardent faith in the Marshall offer. But I think it was done in the wrong way, that it was badly timed, and that it has been set in a perspective which opens ugly horizons. I know as well as most people how difficult Russia is, but I think the psychological inability of American to understand Russia is almost as disturbing as the political immaturity of Moscow. I know with all the mind I have that Russia cannot make war, does not want to make war, would be broken by war. All that American policy does is to give an ever deeper impression of . . . making ideological conflict where there need be none, of a self-righteousness which is almost as infantile as the propaganda of Moscow. . . . I am more convinced than ever that you are on the wrong road . . . that the 'be tough' policy with Russia only gives the anti-Western influence in the Politbureau far more strength than they need to have . . . We and you are in fact halting recovery

everywhere by giving the old regime the same chance of staging a counter-revolution as we gave them after Versailles.[135]

Yet he never aligned himself with the Soviet Union and by the autumn of 1947 was still desperately trying to define a middle way between two 'Messianic philosophies'.[136] Thus when the Soviet Union established the Cominform, he tried to induce the Labour Party not to respond to this 'provocation'. He warned that 'we must expect a revival of the theme that social democrats are the 'lacqueys [sic] of capitalism' and the 'allies of imperialist warmongers'. However, he advocated taking the line:

> that this is the pathological expression of fear, that we regret its revival, and that we stand as ready to prove our friendship, as on June 22, 1941, as we always have been, and that we await the day when Russia realises that we can neither be cajoled nor bullied into any kind of subservience.[137]

A few weeks later, at an International Socialist Conference in Antwerp, when the division between Socialists in the Soviet-dominated sphere and those of most West European countries was intensifying, he tried to maintain the notion of a united continent and united movement. He 'vehemently opposed' an amendment put forward by Nenni which he saw as a one-sided denunciation of the USA.[138]

This was mainly a negative policy, but in 1947 Czechoslovakia still appeared to offer him some ground for optimism. Laski was on close terms with leading non-communist figures in the Czechoslovak government, including Jan Masaryk, the Foreign Minister and Benes, the President. In May 1947 he visited Prague to receive an Honorary degree from the university. On his return, he wrote:

> If I ever saw a really democratic commonwealth I saw it in Czechoslovakia . . . This . . . is a really free people . . . There is the fullest freedom of discussion . . . Religious freedom is complete . . . The mixed Government of Communists, Social Democrats and National Democrats works together surprisingly well.[139]

Similarly, he told Frankfurter that the situation in Prague demonstrated that there was 'massive room . . . for the compromises of commonsense'.[140] The 'coup' the following spring, when the communists mobilised their forces to eject the government and replace it with a one-party state, was therefore a crushing blow to him. He now wrote:

> A democratic community has been placed under the control of a dictatorship . . . There are purges in the universities and schools, in the army and the civil service; newspapers are suppressed; editors are dismissed . . . Even the boys scouts have been ordered to unite with the Communist youth.

The Soviet leaders were, he argued, direct accomplices in the assassination of Jan Masaryk:

> Blind with the fury of fear, they broke a free democracy to exhibit to those whom they deemed their enemies their power and the ruthlessness with which, should conflict come, they would defend themselves.[141]

Yet he still strove to understand what was happening in terms other than Cold War stereotypes. On arrival in the USA a few weeks later, he thus told the *Chicago Daily News* that Czechoslovakia 'was the victim of the conflict of the great powers' and that there could be no defence of the Soviet Union except to see it as the action 'of a foolish, frightened person'.[142] And he argued that the Soviet insecurity which led to such actions was rooted in its whole experience – past and present – of capitalist anti-communism.

As the situation steadily worsened, he attempted both to look at each event on its merits, and to maintain an overall interpretation of what was happening. He had no doubt that the West was right to take the stance that it adopted during the Berlin crisis of 1948–9,[143] but was totally opposed to the establishment of NATO and a capitalist West Germany. He loathed the trials and executions in Eastern Europe, but still believed that the USA, supported by Britain, was the parent of counter-revolution. Neither of them, he argued was concerned with peace so much as with 'the chance to conserve our power and prestige'.[144]

By now he was sickened by the general climate of intolerance, and obsessed with the fear that a Third World War was imminent. He argued that nothing was to be gained by the attempt to measure the degree of responsibility for the inception of the 'Cold War':

The 'cold war' was born of fear; and it has intensified fear as it has developed. Men who have to take decisions in the atmosphere where fear prevails are rarely capable of scrutinising their own activities with either disinterestedness or imagination.[145]

For Laski, the exponent of 'rationalism', the conclusion that 'reason' no longer accounted for the policies of any of the major powers was deeply depressing. Yet although he analysed the 'irrationalism' of both sides brilliantly, his interpretation was not simply even-handed or neutral, but contained a clear view. On the one hand he was categorical that the West was preferable to the Soviet bloc in terms of civil rights, political liberty, and democracy.[146] On the other hand, he was equally insistent that there was a capitalist, counter-revolutionary drive behind Western foreign policy which inevitably led to Soviet feelings of insecurity. And such fears heightened both the internal repression and the provocative external stance. He therefore maintained until the end of his life that the West – and particularly the United States – could make the decisive move to reverse the ever more dangerous cycle of action and counter-action, which was, by 1950, threatening the whole world.[147]

Even though the Cold War is now 'history', it remains true, as Laski stated at the time, that there is no 'standardised ethic . . . by which to establish which side is right and which side is wrong'.[148] He may sometimes have appeared dogmatic, but at least he made a supreme effort to transcend the banal contemporary orthodoxies on both sides, and to understand what was really happening in the world. As he put it in 1947:

> The proponents on either side begin to take steps to strengthen the principles of their policy, and to weaken that of their opponents. Each side may well proclaim that it has no interest save peace. It may advance arguments to prove that only by means of its policy can justice or liberty or the common well-being of nations be secured. *It is essential for us to understand that all this even when those who expound it are convinced of its truth, is above everything propaganda, intended to put the best face possible on the case for a given policy.*[149]

He maintained this position, striving to distinguish between reality and propaganda, as most of his contemporaries rallied to one or other of the two 'Messianic philosophies'. Even within the Labour

Party he was increasingly isolated as the majority of the 'Keep Left' group, around Richard Crossman and Michael Foot, adopted a pro-American stance, and other dissidents, such as John Platts-Mills and Leslie Hutchinson, were expelled as fellow-travellers.[150]

Laski did not write a full analysis of the 'Cold War' which was still unfolding as he died. His interpretations need to be pieced together from numerous sources including his private letters and the posthumous, unedited work, *The Dilemma of Our Times*. But the attempt to remain non-aligned, and to combine Marxist, liberal, and even social-psychological perspectives, meant that his insights had real originality and importance.

CONCLUSION: COLD WAR VICTIM

The first part of this chapter examined the process by which Laski was discredited, and the second summarised some of the most significant aspects of his political stance. In reality, the two parts were inextricably linked, for he was clearly a victim of the transformation that took place in this period.

After 1945 the reversal of alliances, and their ideological underpinning, took place with incredible rapidity. The new Western consensus, which was fully established by the late forties, was straightforward. It consisted of a world outlook in which democracy – epitomised by Britain and the United States – stood for freedom. In order to preserve this it was necessary to avoid 'extremism'. The enemy was totalitarianism, in which Nazism and Stalinism were perceived as virtually identical. Totalitarianism had been responsible for the Second World War, and was also causing the current tension between East and West. This time, however, it was possible to learn from the mistakes of the inter-war period by rejecting appeasement and by adopting a firm and resolute stance against the enemy. This also involved vigilance against the threat of internal foes who sympathised with totalitarian ideas.

Laski could not unconditionally accept a single one of these propositions. Neither Britain nor, still more, the United States was genuinely free and democratic; Marxism was not 'extremist', but an integral part of socialism; Nazism and Stalinism were wholly different phenomena; capitalist expansion and counter-revolution was a fundamental force behind the Cold War; 'appeasement' had been rooted in sympathy for fascism, and the 'firm stance' now provoked greater intransigence in the Kremlin. In fact, Laski's position was completely unorthodox. Moreover, he was not simply a writer or an academic theorist. He was trying to affect the course of politics and, in 1945 at least, he remained an influential figure in the Labour Party. The discrediting of Laski was therefore part of the process through which the new orthodoxy was established.[151]

This does not mean that there was a conspiracy against him (even though there may have been elements of this in the attacks upon him in the USA in 1949). It would be absurd to suggest that the British press, politicians, and law courts were working hand-in-glove with American journalists and academics to undermine his reputation. Nor was Laski so powerful a figure that it was necessary to discredit him in order to establish the new consensus. Laski's decline in reputation was the result of a semi-conscious shift in ideology rather than a concrete political strategy.

In 1945 the Churchill-Beaverbrook campaign against Laski was premature in *electoral* terms. But it foreshadowed the full Cold War thought categories that would emerge over the next few years. For this stated, quite unequivocally, that socialism was incompatible with freedom. Similarly, the libel action came about because Laski was equivocal about the future of liberal-democracy: he was suggesting that it could give way to violence unless fundamental changes were introduced. But by 1945 such ideas were no longer legitimate and the judge made it very clear that it was irresponsible even to use words like 'revolution'. The Labour leaders also believed that it was now 'silly' to talk in such terms,[152] and the whole idea that foreign policy should be based on 'socialist' rather than 'national' interests was seen as outdated and immature. Academic fashion followed the general political shift and was revealed most pointedly in the reception given to *The American Democracy*, when many critics focused on the 'dated' nature of the book. It is fairly obvious that the real objection was that Laski had continued to emphasise the negative domestic and international aspects of American capitalism, rather than singing its praises.

Yet there was a further reason why Laski was attacked with particular venom. Not only did he refuse to accept the new orthodoxy: *he condemned it in the name of the very values which it professed.*

As has been shown, he was constantly attacked – particularly in the United States – as a pro-communist, or fellow-traveller. However, many of those who made the charge were probably aware that it was groundless. Laski's real guilt was that he refused to accept the conventional categories of thought, and proclaimed Marx in support of the values of western liberalism. Similarly, whenever he condemned the Soviet Union, he also insisted in arguing that its excesses needed to be compared with its own history, the wars of religion, and even current witch-hunts in the USA. Had he been a communist or fellow-traveller who simply defended Stalinism and denounced capitalist-imperialism, his views would have been much easier to dismiss. As it was, he was a continual irritant, for non-communists were supposed to adhere to the consensus viewpoint. This was epitomised by the frustration of the FBI in 1949 that Laski had been allowed entry as an 'anti-Communist'. For it was no longer sufficient not to be a communist: it was now necessary to adhere to the 'American ideology'. Laski was never prepared to do this and insisted on portraying reality as he saw it in terms which were clearly comprehensible to those who accepted the liberal tradition. Some of the contempt poured upon him by his critics perhaps stemmed from their knowledge that much of what he said was true.

After 1945 Laski was therefore discredited because he refused to allow his convictions to be subordinated to the emerging new consensus. He would not view 'Communism as nothing but fascism in a different uniform',[153] and he would not accept that fundamental socio-economic change in the West was any less urgent than previously because Stalinist Russia was a dictatorship. His own indiscretions and political naivete may have made him a vulnerable target, but these are secondary considerations. The overwhelming factor in his downfall was the establishment of the bipolar world and its sustaining orthodoxies.

Now that the Cold War division has finally collapsed, it is surely time to recognise the contribution that Laski was trying to make in his final years. Perhaps it is now at last possible to escape from the orthodoxies of his era, and to assess his position on its merits.

12

Zionism, Jewish Identity and Socialism

Laski experienced disillusionment in a whole range of issues in the post-war period, but the most painful for him was the Labour government's Palestine policy. This was because it brought to the surface problems in his own identity which he had tried to evade for much of his life. Since the problem was so important to him, and raises wider questions about his character and beliefs, it is necessary to explore it at some length. The chapter begins by examining the evolution of his position up to 1945, and then deals in detail with the stages in his alienation from government policy. It ends by considering Laski's attitudes towards Jewish identity and Zionism, and the relationship between these issues and his wider beliefs.

THE 1930S

As was shown in Chapter Six, Laski had reversed his previous antipathy towards Zionism during the period of the second Labour government, and had become involved in the struggle to revoke or reinterpret the Passfield White Paper. Having once taken this step, he never reverted to his previously hostile stance. (Paradoxically, it was his brother Neville, the President of the Board of Deputies of British Jews, who adopted an anti-Zionist stance, even at one point offering to spy on the Zionists on behalf of the Colonial Office.[1]) Harold remained broadly sympathetic to moderate Zionism throughout the 1930s, met Zionists when they came to London and facilitated their access to the Labour leadership.[2] He also corresponded with Felix Frankfurter on the subject, complaining bitterly about British attempts to limit European Jewish immigration into Palestine, and urged an American 'explosion' of opinion to counteract any such policy.[3] He was at this stage deeply critical of the whole concept of partition, as advocated in the 1937 Peel Commission Report, and of the intimation by the Zionist Congress in the same year that it might be prepared to agree to limitations of immigration in return for securing a Jewish state. As he told Frankfurter:

> I hope American Jews will go on protesting against the folly of partition. I don't see why you should sacrifice half a million E. European Jews to Weizmann's ambition to be a President of a State.[4]

His own ideal seems to have been one of the unlimited immigration, land reform to break up the estates of absentee Arab landowners in favour of Arab peasants, and a revised educational system. He thus wanted a bi-national Palestine and persisted in the (convenient) belief that Arab nationalism did not really exist, and that the real problem was that 'H. M. G. merely wants to preserve its lines of communication and get rid of its Jewish obligations'.[5] The British White Paper of May 1939, which imposed highly restrictive limitations on Jewish immigration, following three years of Arab riots and protests, represented the antithesis of all his hopes.

Yet if he remained a supporter of Zionism during the thirties, this was not one of his priorities. Nor did he regard it as the major ingredient in any solution to the 'Jewish question'. He made this apparent in August 1938 when reviewing a book (*People At Bay* by O. Janowsky, 1938) which dealt with the condition of the Jews in Poland and Romania. The author argued that the main solution, particularly for the younger generation, was migration to Palestine. Laski disagreed:

> I wish I could feel that it was a realistic conclusion. Frankly, the notion that five million human beings can find a refuge there under present conditions seems, to me, fantastic, merely in terms of the time-factor involved.

More fundamentally, he argued that Janowsky's conclusion stemmed from his wish to minimise the significance of the Marxist interpretation of anti-semitism. This, Laski believed, was a mistake:

> It is notable, first, that the power to make successful propaganda against the Jews largely depends upon the ability of its exponents to find an economic misery to be exploited. Those, second, who do exploit it are usually linked to interests which are seeking to find a scapegoat under cover of which they may prevent attention

being drawn to privileges, the effect of which they wish to obscure. Anti-semitism, moreover, varies in intensity with economic well-being; its immense post-war growth in Germany was directly related to an economic misery accentuated by the undermining of self-respect by defeat. And it is notable that not only has depression developed a fertile soil for anti-semitism in Great Britain and America, it is notable, also, that growing prosperity in the Soviet Union has largely terminated its existence there. Socialism makes the Jew an ordinary and integral part of the general population. He finds no avenue of effort closed to him. He is farmer, soldier, artisan, engineer. The historic psychological difficulties which accentuate his difference from the rest of the population literally wither away. The power of propaganda to exploit those difficulties withers away at the same time. Professor Janowsky is, no doubt, right in insisting that anti-semitism is a complex phenomenon; that is because history is complex in itself. But the root cause upon which it is founded is the grim economic struggle for existence under a capitalist system vividly and rapidly in decay. Just as the conditions of the Jews improved under capitalism in its period of expansion, so will they improve in the degree that socialism makes possible the expansion of the forces of production by abolishing that class-structure of society which stands in the way of that expansion . . .

The vital thing is the understanding that here is a classic case of the exploitation of a minority in the effort to stave off the collapse of an outworn order. No amount of humanitarian sentiment or rational analysis will avail to prevent that exploitation. . . . The peasants of Rumania and Poland have painfully to be brought to see that their enemies are not those Jews who are their fellow-victims, but the owners of those privileges which stand in the way of the common good. The way to fight anti-semitism, therefore, is not to make the task of the oppressors more easy by palliatives but to strike at the foundations which make it possible. The fight for socialism is the fight against anti-semitism. The victory of the one is the defeat of the other.[6]

That this was not simply a polemical or propagandist view is indicated by a letter which Laski wrote to Frankfurter at the time of the Peel Commission report. For his immediate conclusion then was:

that 400,000 East European Jews have no hope for their future save in a revolutionary overturn in Poland, Rumania etc. Certainly I think it is the end of Zionism in any effectively creative form. . . .

My one concern now is to make poor Jews see that they are helpless in the confines of the present social order.[7]

During the thirties Laski had thus clung to a reductionist 'Marxist' view of anti-semitism. However, he had simultaneously become increasingly active on the Jewish question in practice. In addition to his work for academic refugees from Nazism, the majority of whom were Jewish, he was also worried about the growth of anti-semitism in Britain. In 1936 he had arranged a meeting between his brother, Neville, Herbert Morrison and Harry Pollit to discuss the issue, and he also urged the Labour Party actively to condemn signs of anti-Jewish measures abroad.[8] He was also scathing about Neville's attitude to Jewish immigration into Britain, telling Frankfurter in August 1938, that little could be done:

unless somehow Neville & co are stirred up to demand that Jews are allowed to bring out their property. But their main preoccupation is not to risk anti-semitism here at any price. That really means that they are fighting with their hands behind their backs.[9]

By 1939 he was thus sympathetic to moderate Zionism, without believing that it could play a major role in resolving the 'Jewish question'. Instead, he assumed that anti-semitism was bound up with capitalism and could be eliminated with socialism. The war was to bring about a major transformation in his attitudes – as it did for so many others.

THE IMPACT OF THE WAR

By 1942–3, news of the Holocaust was reaching Britain and presented the spectre of anti-semitism in a new and horrifying form. This also raised, as a matter of urgency, the issue of Jewish immigration into both the UK and Palestine. At the same time, however, there appeared to be a growth of prejudice in Britain. In the winter of 1942–3 this even led to anti-semitic riots in the East End but, more general, was the snide claim that this was a 'Jews' war'. In February 1943 Laski was moved to write a 'Note on anti-semitism' in the *New Statesman*. The theoretical argument – that 'the enemy of the Jew is the enemy of freedom' – was less interesting than the burning conviction of the article which, as he confessed, he had felt 'from inside myself':[10]

> The Jews are blamed for their failure to win outstanding military distinction. They are blamed because some Jews play a part in the Black Market. They are blamed because they fill the air with protest against their misfortunes. They are blamed because they have sought to evade the blitz in Manchester or Leeds or the East end of London by what, proportionately, has been a large-scale evacuation. They irritate Ministers because they complicate our relations with Arabs, and because our policy in Palestine leads to criticism from their friends in the United States. They irritate administrators because the intricate problems to which they give rise cause long researches in the Departments and constant trouble in Parliament. They irritate social workers because they do not fit into the formulae applicable to the general population, so that every issue to which they are relevant involves the need for fatiguing effort in a time of strain. They irritate business men because their quick commercial instinct leads them irresistibly to every newly profitable market. They irritate the landlady or the hotel keeper because their group-loyalty gives a special character to the boarding house or hotel where they congregate. They irritate all of these by their vivacity, their energy in defending themselves, the power they exercise of making their grievances known. It is felt that they deserve sympathy. It is agreed that they are outstanding proof of Nazi brutality. But it is also felt that they are over-insistent upon their tragic role in a time of supreme tragedy. They cause relentless and unceasing uneasiness by their inability to maintain a dignified silence in the presence of massive wrongs. Patriotic Jews would not force the full-scale horror of their sufferings upon the national attention. They would develop that sense of proportion which enables them to be seen and not heard.[11]

Shortly before his nervous breakdown he wrote a heartfelt letter to Churchill, which revealed some of his innermost thoughts about the plight of European Jewry:

I cannot but remember every day that if . . . my grandparents had not come to this refuge of freedom, I might myself, with all my family, either be dead or waiting eagerly for death in the grim horror of the new ghetto – so that because my life is haunted by the ghosts of these slaves, living or dead, I do beg you from the bottom of my heart to make possible some help beyond the boundaries now traced by our policy.[12]

The appeal to Churchill was not only significant as a testimony to Laski's feelings, but also in its consequences. For when he asked for a limited measure of practical help – the issuing of up to 5,000 visas for Jews in neutral countries – Churchill passed the suggestion to the Foreign Office, which sent a narrow bureaucratic response, rejecting the proposal.[13] Laski had already seen Zionism as necessary and, in his first letter to Churchill, he had called for an end to the policy of 'appeasement' of the Arabs in Palestine. But the apparent unwillingness of even Churchill to supersede officialdom in order to rescue the Jews of Europe inevitably led Laski to see Zionism as a crucial element in the resolution of the 'Jewish question'.

A few months later, he tied the plight of Jewry and Zionism still more closely together in an article in the *New Statesman*. Entitled 'On a Jewish Soldier's Letter', it was based on a letter he had himself received from a former student, and is a moving piece of writing.

The soldier, he explained, had been based at the Suez Canal and had just seen a group of Jewish orphans of between the ages of four and twelve arrive on their way to Palestine. None of them could cry:

But the soldier said that he had never seen before any agony of this kind. It was as though the stillness of these children was louder even than the shrieking of the ship's siren, or the roar of aeroplanes as they passed by. On their faces was written all the tragedy of all Jewry, of boys and girls who had seen the kind of thing which belongs not to civilisation but to the tiger in the jungle when it flings itself upon its prey.

There were children of seven and nine who had not only been compelled to watch their parents buried alive; but remembered what they had seen. There were others who had seen a whole community of Jews driven to the edge of a common grave into which they fell as they were machine-gunned. There were children who did not know what it meant to be spoken to softly, to be smiled at, who shrank away in fear when any of the troops offered them a piece of chocolate, who could not be made to understand that some little toy, a flag or a doll, was for them. There were others to whom the spoken word brought at once a look of terror; for over four years the spoken word had meant insult or cruelty or sometimes death.

The concluding section of the article was indicative of the extent of the change in Laski's attitudes. The soldier, he asserted:

sees no shame in being a Jew, though he is acutely aware that the temper of the British administration in Palestine is, generally, that a Jew, as such, almost owes an apology to the Government there for all the trouble he has caused. He feels a keen admiration for the history of his nation; to have survived catastrophe and tragedy of the order that it has experienced seems to him to justify one further effort to survive. And having seen the first children of exile from Nazi persecution become transformed in Palestine from tragic automata into human beings who learn, within a year, how to laugh and play, who lose the sense of fear and no longer carry in their eyes what seems like the sorrow of all the ages, he believes with passion that Fate has destined Palestine not to rescue a few here and there, but the hundreds of thousands of orphans whom kindness might similarly transform. And, above all, as he writes with firmness, there is no people nor Government in the world who, when the war is over, will feel the urgency of lifting the shadows of this terror from the memory of the Jews except the Jews themselves. He cannot forget those grim years from 1933 to 1939 when Hitler in Germany, the Governments of Poland and Hungary and Rumania, competed with one another to take from the Jew such brief moments of happiness as his life in Central and Eastern Europe made possible. He must fight for his rights as a human being; no one else is likely to fight for them if he is servile and indifferent.[14]

The 'Jewish soldier' was, of course, expressing Laski's own views. Nor did he attempt to influence only British opinion in this way, for he sent his article to John Winant, the American ambassador, expressing the hope that the American government would tell 'our government here that a Jew is not out of place when he is free, and still less, when he is free in Palestine.'[15]

He had become a supporter of Zionism in the sense that he now saw the Jewish struggle in Palestine as an important part of his own commitment. He explained his conversion to a Poale Zion (Jewish Socialist Movement) conference in May 1945:

> he said he felt like the prodigal son returning home, but a home of a special kind. As a student of history, he had no more interest in the Jewish religion . . . than in any other creed. He subsequently declared that as a Marxian Socialist, he held that religion was an opiate for the people. Until the outbreak of the war, he had been, he said, an advocate of assimilation who thought the best service to civilisation the Jews could render was to lose their identity. He was now firmly and utterly convinced of the need for the rebirth of the Jewish nation in Palestine. The need of the Jews could only find completion in a territory of their own, and no other country but Palestine could have any meaning for them. His boyhood and manhood friend, Dr Weizmann, had not been able to convince him in former years, but in 1939 events did, and he was still capable of revising his convictions.[16]

This did not mean that Laski himself would ever have considered emigration to Palestine. But it did mean that support for Zionist emigration was now an integral part of his political thought *and emotions*. Not only was Palestine essential as a refuge for Jews fleeing persecution, but he also now saw its existence as part of the antidote to anti-semitism itself. Soon after the war, he thus wrote of it in very much the same way as he had previously written of socialism as the solution to anti-semitism:

> After some two thousand years of exile, under highly special, and mostly tragic conditions, the Palestinian experiment has demonstrated that a community of Jews is no different from any other community. Given . . . favourable conditions, its members will distribute themselves into trades and professions in much the same way as members of any other community. They make good farmers. They undertake heavy manual labour. They become adept in a great variety of crafts which have lain outside their European experience. They make fine soldiers and trustworthy police. They take to the outdoor life of the countryside as successfully as to the indoor life of office or factory in the town. They can adapt themselves with ardour and goodwill to the socialist economy of a co-operative colony as to the individualist

economy of private enterprise . . . To have shown in this way that what are often called 'Jewish characteristics' in the typical economies of Europe and America are no more than conditioned responses to an imposed environment behind the compulsions of which there are long centuries of history is a matter of quite primary significance.[17]

In other words, Laski was now arguing that Palestine provided a means of counteracting 'stereotyping' of the Jew. In this way it was possible both to counter anti-semitic propaganda, and to bolster the self-esteem of its victims. And, of course, he himself remained a victim of anti-semitism, as was again shown during the press campaign against him in the 1945 General Election.

Yet if Laski's support for Zionism had much to do with his Jewish identity, this was not, in any way, detached from his socialism. In the first place, the Labour Party had adopted a strongly Zionist commitment during the Second World War. Indeed, in 1944 it had even embarrassed some Zionists by calling for population transfers to resettle Arabs away from areas of Jewish immigration.[18] As will be shown, some of the leaders had been lukewarm about 'excessive' commitments to Zionism but, against the background of Nazi bestiality to the Jews, the rank-and-file had seen an overwhelming case for Jewish emigration to Palestine. As the sympathies of most of the Labour Left were firmly on the side of the Jews in this period, there was no reason for Laski to believe that he was, in any way, committed to a policy which was out of step with that of his normal associates. Secondly, he reconciled his support for Zionism with socialist principles. This meant that he continued to advocate (probably long after it was practicable) a bi-national state in which Jews and Arabs would co-operate peacefully. He also wanted initiatives such as mixed collective farms, mixed trade unions, and a development commission, advised by equal numbers of Jews and Arabs.[19] His model of economic development was the kibbutz which, he argued, 'may be regarded as among the outstanding experiments in the post-war world' and his goal was the creation of a semi-socialist entity, with harmonious relationships between all the peoples of the area.[20] Indeed as late as January 1947, he saw the relations between the English, Welsh and Scottish as a model for Arab-Jewish relations in a bi-national state.[21] He identified two main threats to this vision of harmony. The first was British imperial policy with its anxiety to appease Moslem opinion in the Empire, maintain strategic defence links, and to preserve its future oil supplies. These, he argued, had been the interests which had led British governments to retreat on the Balfour Declaration in the inter-war period.[22] Secondly, there were the interests of rich Arab *effendi* (overlords):

This is the real source of the resistance to large-scale Jewish immigration. The Jew brings with him Western ideas, often Western socialist ideas, which cut right across a traditional historical pattern, the beneficiaries of which seek at any cost to defend their claims. They therefore mobilise both religious fanaticism and nationalist passion to arrest changes in which they see the threat to their privilege; and seek to use the dislike of the masses for change before they [the masses] see that the change is to their advantage.[23]

It may have been facile – and based on wishful thinking – to believe by 1945 that Arab-Jewish co-operation could be established if only the British were more enlightened and the Arab masses were detached from their rulers. Nevertheless, it was a vision which was compatible with his general perspective. In his own mind there was therefore no contradiction between his Zionism and his socialism.

The final point to note before considering the policy of the post-war Labour government is that Laski was not wedded to any particular settlement. Indeed, despite his general commitment to a bi-national state, he sometimes favoured continued trusteeship, and sometimes partition. What he wanted was a settlement, which would allow unlimited rights of immigration and land purchase for the Jewish victims of persecution. And, as usual, he hoped for a peaceful solution, based on compromise, so long as this goal could be attained. But he would not accept compromise on the goal itself, which he saw as a moral imperative and a firm Labour Party commitment.

THE FIRST PHASE, APRIL 1945–APRIL 1946

On 25 April 1945 the NEC approved a resolution on Palestine, put forward by Laski. This reaffirmed the commitment of the 1944 party conference, and called on the government:

to remove the present unjustifiable barriers on immigration and to announce, without delay, proposals for the future of Palestine in which it has the full sympathy and support of the American and Russian governments.[24]

The next month the annual conference endorsed this position. Shortly before the General Election, Laski was therefore optimistic and expressed confidence that a Labour victory would lead to a 'big new start' in place of the current tendency which he viewed as the sacrifice of Palestine to 'pan-Arabism'.[25] In fact, Labour's 'big three' were more ambivalent in their attitudes than the rank-and-file. Morrison, who had visited Palestine in 1935 and claimed to have been converted to Zionism,[26] had also chaired the Cabinet committee on the problem during the war and had admitted to Laski in 1943 that he was racking his brains to find another country for the Jews.[27] Bevin, who had been regarded as a supporter by the Zionists in 1940–1, had become more tentative by March 1944,[28] and Attlee had always adopted a very reserved position on the whole issue.[29] Although it was not yet apparent, there was thus a gulf between Laski's approach to the Palestine problem and that of the Labour leadership even at the time of the General Election. Instead of sharing his view that it was an overriding moral and political imperative to support Zionist goals, the principal members of the new government were far more likely to see it as one problem among many, to be dealt with pragmatically. A very early decision indicated the approach which it would adopt.

In August 1945 Ben Gurion led a Zionist delegation to the Colonial Office. They demanded 100,000 new immigration certificates and a declaration of Palestine as a Jewish State. In the same month, however, the Arab League (which had recently been established with British help), proclaimed that it would never accept Palestine as a Jewish homeland and that this could cause 'a new crusaders' war'.[30] On 25 August, Labour's colonial secretary, George Hall, proposed that the 2,000 immigration certificates remaining from the White Paper (which the Labour Party had previously regarded as illegitimate since it had not been accepted by the League of Nations Mandates Commission) should be used, and that Arab agreement would be sought for a further monthly immigration figure of 1,500. This caused an outcry in Zionist circles, backed by the USA, and on 28 August a Cabinet committee, chaired by Morrison, was established. This submitted its conclusions, subsequently endorsed by the Cabinet (with opposition from Dalton, Bevan and Greenwood) on 8 September. These were that, as an interim policy for six months:

(a) Jewish immigration should remain on the basis of the quotas in the White Paper;

(b) that the US Government should be informed that the British Cabinet was endeavouring to evolve a long-term Palestine policy to be submitted to the UN for approval;

(c) Military units in Palestine would be augmented to forestall any possible unrest there.[31]

The thinking behind this policy was still more significant than the proposals themselves. For the Cabinet had argued that, as any course involved risks, it was better to choose 'the possibility of localised trouble with the Jews in Palestine' than 'the virtual certainty of widespread disturbance among the Arabs throughout the Middle East and possibly among the Muslims in India'. Furthermore:

> The Middle East is a region of vital consequence for Britain and the British Empire. It forms the point in the system of communications by land, sea and air, which links Britain with India, Australia and the Far East; it is also the Empire's main reservoir of mineral oil . . . The attitude of the Arab states to any decision which may be reached is a matter of the first importance . . . Protection of our vital interests depends, therefore, upon the collaboration which we can obtain from these independent states . . . Unfortunately the future of Palestine bulks large in all Arab eyes . . . To enforce any such policy (to which they object) and especially one which lays us open to a charge of breach of faith, is bound seriously to undermine our position and may well lead not only to widespread disturbances . . . but to the withdrawal of cooperation on which our Imperial interests so largely depend.[32]

In other words, the first priority was the maintenance of British power in the Middle East. Since there were fewer Jews than Arabs, and they could make less trouble, it was preferable to confront Zionism than to risk the possibility of upheaval throughout the Moslem world. A further assumption was related to this: Zionism was a localised problem in Palestine, and there was no reason why the bulk of the Jewish refugees should not stay in Europe. However, this did not include Britain for, as the Cabinet minutes on 11 October recorded:

> The Home Secretary (Chuter Ede) drew attention to the increasing pressure for the admission of Jewish refugees from the con-

tinent into this country. So far he and his predecessors had been able to resist pressure of this kind, but it would become increasingly difficult to hold the position.[33]

Had it been left alone, it thus seems that the Cabinet inclination would have been to maintain strict controls on Jewish immigration to Palestine (and Britain), to have persuaded as many refugees as possible to remain in mainland Europe (and even Germany), and to have co-operated with the Americans in re-settling the rest elsewhere. This was, of course, exactly in line with previous British governmental thinking and hardly suggested that either the Holocaust or the Labour Party commitment had made any significant impact on policy preferences. However, the government would not be 'left alone' for it was to be subjected to counter-pressures. Some Zionists – particularly Weizmann and Poale Zion, which was affiliated to the Labour Party, would seek to persuade it to change its mind through diplomacy; others would exert pressure through direct action, including the organisation of illegal immigration on a mass scale; while the terrorist organisations, the Stern Gang (Lehy) and Irgun Zwei Leumi, would carry out violent attacks against British targets. In addition, American support for Zionism was already putting additional pressure on the Labour Cabinet, for on 31 August President Truman reiterated a view he had already expressed at Potsdam, when he wrote to Attlee suggesting that 100,000 additional immigration certificates should be granted.[34] All this would demonstrate to the Labour government that it was taking on more than 'localised trouble with the Jews in Palestine'.

Almost immediately Laski played a role in seeking to persuade the Labour leadership to adopt a more pro-Zionist policy. In late September 1945 the NEC (of which he was chair) agreed to a request to receive a Poale Zion deputation and, if desirable, to seek an interview with ministers.[35] He also chaired the meeting with this delegation, at which the Poale Zion speakers called for 100,000 immigration permits (as a first instalment) and the abrogation of a 1940 land law which restricted the area of settlement, and warned that the alternative might be a resort to terrorism.[36] Subsequently, a subcommittee of the NEC (including Laski) met Attlee, Bevin and Hall, and Laski wrote a note of this meeting immediately after it had taken place. This was carefully phrased so as to avoid the impression of any hostility to the leadership, but the tension was apparent. Attlee, he stated, had been unwilling to discuss government policy until a statement had been made to Parliament:

I therefore asked Mrs Gould, MP and Miss Bacon, MP to state their positions as Labour members who had given pledges to their constituents in the light of declarations of policy made by the Party Conference and by members of the Executive, most of whom were now Ministers of the Crown . . .

I myself emphasised the National Executive Committee's desire to be able to act in harmony with the Government. I said that the National Executive Committee had three anxieties: (I) to carry out the policy upon the White Paper which it had announced ever since 1939; (II) to do all in its power to relieve the suffering of Jewry in Europe; and (III) to undertake large-scale economic measures in the Middle East in general, and the Palestine-Transjordan area in particular to improve the prospects of settlement and development.[37]

Although the ministers replied at considerable length, they revealed no details of their proposals, so Laski informed Attlee that he would call a special NEC meeting after the government's proposals had been made public. The Prime Minister then authorised him to state to the NEC that the government agreed that the White Paper could not stand and that its proposals would be designed to ensure the fulfilment of the Mandate. This went beyond anything that had been agreed in Cabinet and was presumably designed to keep the NEC quiet. On his side Laski emphasised more than once that the Executive was not criticising the government, but was merely fulfilling its 'obvious duty to consider the relation of the proposals to our policy' and that the meeting was a 'family' discussion.[38] In private he was already afraid that Bevin was looking at the Middle East through the eyes 'of those foolish little would-be T. E. Lawrences' and that 'there is just ahead the betrayal of the Jews over Palestine'.[39] But he said none of this in public, and on 24 October the NEC simply empowered him to call a further meeting of the sub-committee if he thought this necessary after Attlee had made his statement in Parliament.

On 31 October the most serious Jewish attack thus far took place on British installations in Palestine. From Laski's perspective this was obviously unwelcome, because he wanted the question settled by negotiation and compromise. From the government's point of view it exerted contradictory pressures. On the one hand, it heightened its awareness of the seriousness of the situation, and the difficulty in containing the pressures. But as its general aims had not changed, it also strengthened its determination to resist Zionist pressure, particularly as it knew that the Haganah (the 'official' Jewish Defence Force) had been aware of the planned action by the extremist groups.[40]

However, the Cabinet had realised for some time that it was necessary to find some way of accommodating the various pressures, and in mid-November Bevin announced the establishment of an Anglo-American Commission of Enquiry, which would report to the United Nations, with two essential terms of reference: (1) To examine the political, economic and social conditions in Palestine as they bore upon the problems of Jewish immigration, and (2) to examine the position of the Jews in the countries of Europe where they had been victims of Nazi and fascist propaganda. In fact, there had been disputes over the terms of reference as the British had not wanted to give apparent priority to Palestine – still believing that the majority of Jews could stay in Europe – but, since they had wanted to secure American involvement, they had been forced to defer to their wishes.[41]

In general, the initiative was acceptable to Zionist opinion as it implied a move away from the 1939 White Paper[42] but, when justifying the policy in a Press Conference, Bevin made some offensive remarks, which led many Jews to regard him as a major enemy (see below). However, Laski tried to maintain an open mind. He told Bevin that his first impressions were that the House of Commons statement was a success and that if the government now gave an impression of urgency of action it would be possible to avoid the criticisms of extreme partisans on both sides.[43] But he also wrote a long note on British policy for the international sub-committee.

He acknowledged that Bevin's statement contained important advances in that it involved the USA and the UN, and insisted that Jews should have equal rights in any community in which they dwelt. He also valued the implication that the White Paper had now been by-passed. On the other hand there were disquieting features, in view of the urgency of the Jewish problem and the character of Labour Party pledges up to May 1945. He then itemised ten points on which the government needed to be interrogated, and concluded that a series of recommendations should be made to the NEC, including the following:

1. That the British government be asked for clarification of the obscurities in the Foreign Secretary's statement.
2. That the discriminatory restrictions on the sale of land be withdrawn forthwith.

3. That during the period between now and the report of the Anglo-American Commission 4000 Jews monthly should be allowed to enter Palestine, the Jews being responsible for their maintenance. This would (i) satisfy world-opinion on the condition of European Jewry in general, and of German Jews in particular; and (ii) it would avoid the impression that the White Paper is continued in another form. I think it highly likely that it would calm down the general acerbity of Jewish agitation.

In addition, he called for sympathetic attention to be given to Zionist schemes for economic development, assurances that the pro-Nazi Grand Mufti would not be allowed to return to Jerusalem, that the British authorities would not finance, arm or encourage former Arab terrorists, and that warnings should be given to the Hungarian, Romanian and Polish governments that the resumption of the anti-semitic atrocities would not be tolerated. He concluded:

On the basis of these clarifications and proposals, the NEC should announce to Poale Zion and similar bodies that it looks to them for their fullest support in aiding HMG both in Palestine and elsewhere to implement this policy. This aid involves co-operation with the authorities in preventing Jewish violence and such terrorism as that of the Stern gang.[44]

In other words, Laski was calling for a more pro-Zionist policy and, as a *quid pro quo*, for Jewish co-operation with the British authorities. However, it is not clear that he ever formally submitted this memorandum to the international sub-committee, as the minutes of the meeting do not mention it. Possibly he was persuaded not to do so after receiving some private assurances from the leadership. In any case, the sub-committee decided that there was no point in holding another meeting with Poale Zion, and agreed that it was better to wait for the Anglo-American Commission to report than to make any separate proposals.[45] Laski expressed some of his views in public, including his disappointment that the government had not unilaterally increased immigration quotas, but his criticisms were very restrained.[46] And although the situation in the Middle East was worsening, with an Arab massacre of Jews in Tripoli in November, Jewish terrorist action against the British in December, and the introduction of severe emergency laws in Palestine in January, Laski tried to maintain his optimism in the first few months of 1946. Moreover, in April an event in which he played a direct part restored his hopes that Bevin would still adopt a sympathetic stance towards Zionism.

Laski was in Italy as one of the Labour Party delegates for the Italian Socialist Congress, when a major incident erupted in the port of La Spezia between Polish Jewish refugees and the Italian authorities, acting in co-operation with British military forces. The refugees had commandeered thirty-eight British army lorries (with the help of three Jewish NCOs, belonging to a Palestine unit of the British army) and had been arrested when about to sail for Palestine.[47] They were now on hunger strike and were threatening that ten of them per day would commit suicide unless they were allowed to proceed. Local Italian opinion supported the refugees and workers in La Spezia were proposing a sympathy strike.[48] The case was receiving worldwide publicity and some Jews in Palestine were also participating in the hunger strike.[49] Laski (accompanied by the labour attache from the embassy) spoke to the refugees for two hours and, according to the British ambassador, handled an extremely difficult situation 'with tact and firmness':

> He made no promises and made it clear that he was acting as go-between. . . . The men were in ugly mood and among other things accused the British of being responsible for the death of some four million Jews. Mr Laski pointed out that if it had not been for the British none of them would probably be alive today. He told them that nothing definite could be done about large scale emigration of Jews until the result of the Anglo-American Conference was known and he, as an English Jew, would be the first to complain if he felt that the Jews were not to receive just treatment.[50]

However, he persuaded them to call off their hunger strike in return for a personal undertaking to present their case to Bevin. He also sent a telegram to the Foreign Secretary, asking to see him on his return so that he could send a message back to the refugees by the 19th at the latest.[51]

The incident caused the government a major dilemma. Immigration was still restricted by the 1939 White Paper and, according to official policy, any refugees from La Spezia that were allowed to proceed to Palestine should be taken from the current quota. But the Zionists had never accepted the quotas and desperate refugees – facing continuing anti-semitism in Poland – were prepared to die if denied entry to Palestine. The Colonial Secretary had no doubts about what should done. Fearing that Laski might be too persuasive, he sent a long memorandum to Attlee, Morrison and Bevin urging an unbending stance, even if the lives of the hunger strikers were endangered, and there was pressure from the Americans and Parliament. It would, he argued, be unjustifiable in itself to allow additional immigrants and the hunger strike was a 'political move designed to force our hands':

> I do not think we should allow ourselves to be deflected by such means from our declared policy. I believe that to do so would have disastrous consequences in the Middle East and would cause the Arabs to repudiate in advance anything which the Anglo-American committee may recommend, on the ground that they have no hope of obtaining impartial treatment from Great Britain in the face of Jewish pressure, whatever the recommendations may be.[52]

Both Attlee and Morrison agreed and the Foreign Office added its own endorsement of this position. In its view, the trouble was 'the result of a particularly flagrant flouting of our authority by the Zionists', and it argued that the Arabs would certainly accuse Britain of bad faith 'if we give way now'.[53]

The odds therefore seemed to be stacked against Laski when he saw Bevin on 18 April. However, he appears to have been confident that he would succeed and, following the interview, the Foreign Secretary took the view that the Colonial Office was adopting 'too rigid an attitude' and that it was not necessary to 'stick too strictly to the letter of the law'.[54] Quite unrealistically, he also suggested that all the Jews in La Spezia should be called together to a mass meeting at which they should admit their error, and if they did so they should be allowed to go to Palestine in 'driblets' of a hundred a time over and above the quota. This would have been quite unacceptable to the refugees who all wanted to sail together. In the event, they were allowed to go in two batches, but Laski had to send them a firm telegram on 26 April persuading them to call off their protests and accept this proposal:

> I think the British Government have dealt generously and with sympathy with your problem. Accordingly I strongly urge on you acceptance of their proposals. The delay between the two parties arriving in Palestine is short. The Jewish Agency wholly approve

this settlement. You only jeopardise the position of other refugees by this reckless attitude. You have a duty to other Jews as well as to yourselves. Do not therefore refuse an offer which is sensible and just.[55]

The official version was that the refugees were being allowed to enter Palestine against the monthly quota.[56] In fact, Bevin had obviously induced Hall to accept them over and above existing totals on the safe assumption that the Arabs would not be counting them (and Laski may have asked the Jewish Agency not to publicise the fact). Apart from succumbing to Laski's persuasive powers, Bevin had no doubt been anxious to avoid further embarrassment in a case that was already attracting so much publicity. But his action certainly increased Laski's optimism about the government's Palestine policy.[57] Moreover, his own behaviour indicates his continuing belief that the difficulties could be resolved by mediation and compromise.

THE SECOND PHASE (APRIL 1946–AUGUST 1947)

The Anglo-American Commission reported just after the La Spezia incident, recommending a bi-national state, with 100,000 immigration certificates to be issued immediately and further immigration to be facilitated. It also called for continued trusteeship and the prohibition of the exclusion of Arab labour in enterprises financed by the Jewish National Fund.[-58] However, although Bevin had originally intimated that he would accept a unanimous recommendation, and initially favoured this course when it was considered in the Cabinet Defence Committee on 24 April, Attlee believed that it was too conciliatory to the Zionists.[59] Although President Truman immediately accepted the proposal for 100,000 Jewish immigration certificates, Attlee therefore publicly criticised American intervention and rejected the call for increased immigration unless all the Jewish armies (including that of the Jewish Agency) were disbanded.[60] It is possible that he took this line partly because Stern gang atrocities against British troops (and counter-atrocities) had escalated just before the report was published. But a more fundamental reason was his continuing belief that the main importance of the Middle East to Britain lay in its oil supplies, and that the first requirement was therefore to come to terms with Arab nationalism.[61]

Laski still tried to maintain a middle position of loyal criticism of government policy, while continuing to support the Zionist demand for the immediate right to send 100,000 immigrants to Palestine.[62] At the Party Conference in mid-June he thus deplored the way in which the 100,000 should be made 'victims of timidity and hesitation' and spoke of the unsocialist policy of sacrificing 'the Jews who escaped from the tortures of Hitlerism to the Arab leaders'.[63] But he did not ask for a Jewish state in Palestine, on the grounds that the situation was too complex for so simple a formula.[64] However, the situation was deteriorating fast. In mid-June there were more incidents of Jewish sabotage in Palestine. This led to an increase in British repression, with the detention of 2,700 people, including Jewish Agency leaders, at the end of the month. And on 10 July the Chiefs of Staff submitted their views to the Cabinet on the Anglo-American report:

> All our defence requirements in the Middle East, including the maintenance of our essential oil supplies and communications, demand that an essential feature of our policy should be to retain the co-operation of the Arab states, and to ensure that the Arab world does not gravitate towards the Russians . . .
>
> We cannot stress too strongly the importance of Middle East oil resources to us both in peace and war. We consider that this factor alone makes the retention of Arab friendship essential.[65]

The next day the Cabinet rejected the proposals of the Anglo-American Commission.[66]

During July various alternative schemes were discussed and, at one point, it seemed that the Americans might accept a provincial autonomy scheme (the so-called Morrison-Grady plan), which would have allowed the British to maintain their strategic position in Palestine.[67] In return the British would support the commitment to allow the 100,000 immigrants into Palestine. However, at the end of July Truman rejected the plan.

This was not the only setback, for a few days earlier Irgun Zwei Leumi blew up a wing of the King David Hotel in Jerusalem – the headquarters of the British army – resulting in ninety-one deaths and forty-five injuries. Britain's Palestine policy had thus reached a crossroads. One possibility was an attempt to resolve the situation by total repression of Jewish forces in a tacit alliance with some of the Arab representatives. A second possibility was an attempt to find some kind of negotiated solution, offering something to moderate Zionists rather than allowing the terrorist organisations to gain support as the sole means of securing Jewish demands.

Naturally, Laski had no doubts about which of these policies was correct. When the repression of Jewish organisations in Palestine mounted in the aftermath of the King David hotel atrocity, he urged the government to encourage moderate Zionist forces. At the same time he called on Jewish leaders to persuade the Arabs that the establishment of a Palestinian state with equal national rights for both peoples would be in their own interests.[68] He also reiterated his rejection of the demand for the transformation of Palestine into a Jewish state.[69] This appeared to be in line with developments within the Zionist leadership, for Weizmann threatened to resign after the King David Hotel incident, and this led to a retreat from the position adopted by the Zionist Conference in 1942 (which had demanded a Jewish state in the entire area of Palestine). Jewish leaders now sought confidential diplomatic negotiations which would lead to partition.[70] There was therefore still an important (and perhaps irreconcilable) difference between the two sides, but a negotiated settlement appeared conceivable and direct talks were scheduled to begin at the end of the summer.

Laski was probably inclined to believe that the conciliatory wing was dominant within the British government, when he left for a long holiday in the USA in late August. There he experienced, at first hand, the deep suspicion of British policy in American Zionist circles.[71] This influenced him, and he was still in the USA five weeks later when a real crisis in Anglo-American relations over the Palestine issue occurred. This was precipitated on 4 October, the eve of the Jewish Day of Atonement, when Truman decided to make a statement supporting Zionism. Attlee begged him not to do so since Bevin was currently involved in negotiations with Weizmann, but he went ahead and effectively endorsed the Jewish Agency's Partition Plan and the demand for the admission of the 100,000.[72] Bevin was furious and the negotiations with Weizmann immediately broke down. Laski supported the American position and told Frida that 'Bevin's Palestine policy becomes ever more outrageous'.[73] The next day he and Frankfurter saw Dalton, who was in the USA at the time, and Laski gave the following account of the meeting:

Felix and I let him have it for over two hours with grand support from Inverchapel [the British Ambassador] on the damage that Bevin and Attlee are doing to Anglo-American relations, especially over Palestine. Hugh, I must say, took it very well and said frankly that the whole thing was a blunder. I told him that when I got back I should get on the warpath for a change and that if Attlee refused to budge I should resign from the E.C. and make public all I knew especially in the U.S. He goes home tomorrow so I hope that will prepare the grounds for when I come.[74]

However, he did not carry out his threat. On his return to Britain, he continued to condemn terrorism, while maintaining that the British could not expect the Jewish Agency to take part in suppressing it unless the government changed its anti-Zionist policy.[75] He also made private overtures to Attlee, but received noncommittal replies.[76] Yet even though both Jewish terrorism, and British repression and counter-terrorism, increased and threatened to escalate out of control, Laski still reassured Weizmann that a positive outcome was possible in the near future.[77] In public he argued that, as his ideal of a bi-national state was no longer feasible, the best option was an improved version of the Morrison-Grady plan, in which both peoples would be granted self-rule. The Jews should be given the right to absorb immigrants in their own area, to develop their economy, and to receive international loans. He still spoke of a 'Jewish homeland' rather than a 'Jewish state', but argued that this entity should be eligible for membership of the UN.[78]

The Jewish Agency was now also now prepared to 'forego mention of a Jewish State as the goal, and leave the outcome to time', on condition that Britain agreed to the full Jewish immigration programme and the removal of all restrictions on land-purchase.[79] But the Arab delegation to a final conference in London on the subject was intent on blocking all land sales and immigration, and both the Chiefs of Staff and Foreign Office remained adamantly opposed to any proposals which would jeopardise Arab goodwill.[80] In the Cabinet Attlee and Bevin, supported by the Minister of Defence, A. V. Alexander, opposed partition and, by 7 February, Creech-Jones, who had replaced Hall as Colonial Secretary in October, had also been brought round to this view, leaving Bevan and Dalton in a small minority.[81] On 7 February 1947 Bevin put forward a modified version of the Morrison-Grady plan, which accepted the prospect of almost 100,000 immigrants over a two-year period, but made subsequent Jewish settlement dependent upon consultation with the Arabs. Both sides rejected this offer, which had come far too late. On 18 February Bevin announced that the Mandate was to be referred back to the United Nations by the British government, without any specific recommendation for a solution.

It was from this point that British policy began to become increasingly complex and contradictory. The government was clearly beginning to think of withdrawal, although Bevin and Creech-Jones ruled this out as a 'humiliating course' on 13 February.[82] What was evident was the hostile attitude now taken towards Zionism and its supporters. In Cabinet, Bevin made dire forecasts about the Jews using partition as a springboard to take over the whole of Palestine,[83] and in the House of Commons on 25 February, he accused the USA of complicating his search for solutions because of domestic elections, and he sympathised with Arab objections to entrusting immigration matters to the Jewish Agency:

> Why should an external agency, largely financed from America, determine how many people should come into Palestine and interfere with the economy of the Arabs, who have been there for 2000 years?[84]

The British government had wanted to maintain control over Palestine and had hoped to maintain friendship with the Arabs while persuading them to make some concessions to the Jewish settlers. Instead it had, in effect, been forced to refer the matter to the United Nations because of Zionist pressure. Zionism was therefore viewed as a major threat to British interests – even as an enemy. It was now that the real parting of the ways between Laski and the government was to begin.

As soon as the London talks had failed, he argued that Britain should impose a solution on Palestine, reverting to the terms of the original Mandate. This meant immediate acceptance of the 100,000 immigrants, revocation of the restrictions on land purchase, and continuing immigration on the basis of Palestine's economic capacity.[85] Once it was clear that the government intended no such thing, he launched his most bitter attack to date. Coupling British policy in the Middle East with the Truman Doctrine, he argued that Bevin's policy was now dominated by anti-communism and the wish to ensure that the Soviet Union gained no foothold in the area:

> For the same reason Mr Bevin hurriedly evoked the unreal kingdom of Transjordan while the Anglo-American Commission on Palestine was still sitting. For the same reason Mr Bevin, backed by the officials of the Foreign Office and the defence chiefs, has

sought to bolster up the ugly feudalism of the Arab *effendi* in Iraq and Syria and Saudi-Arabia. . . . For the same reason we are ready . . . to evacuate Egypt, ceasing to use it to safeguard the Suez Canal.

For the same reason Mr Attlee and Mr Bevin have been able to persuade their Cabinet colleagues to throw overboard precise and unmistakeable pledges made by the Labour Party as recently as May 1945, to those Jews who seek to go on building their National Home; and not daring to declare full-scale war upon them, have now thrown the problem of the Mandate for Palestine back to the United Nations, in a rather Micawber-like hope that some way of escape may be found from the cul-de-sac into which Mr Bevin has led us.[86]

Coupling Palestine with Iran, he now asserted that Bevin was on the wrong side in the Middle East for:

Objectively our Middle Eastern policy makes Mr Bevin the ally of American Standard Oil on the one hand and of the Grand Mufti on the other. It makes him hostile to every interest which wishes to see economic progress in that area, whether it be Jews in Palestine or Communist-inspired reformers in Persia.[87]

Nevertheless, he still tried to remain optimistic while the issue was being considered by the United Nations, and probably played a mediating role between the government and Poale Zion during the early summer of 1947.[88] He was also encouraged by Attlee's role over Indian independence, which he described as 'superb'.[89] However, he was to be disappointed.

In July the vessel *Exodus 1947* (originally named the *President Warfield*) arrived in Haifa with about 4,500 Jewish refugees. Bevin was now in a quite different frame of mind from the conciliatory stance he had taken in La Spezia the previous year. The government decided 'to make an example of this ship by obliging her to return to a French port with all her passengers' and, when the refugees would not land in France, they were returned, with an appalling lack of sensitivity, to Germany.[90] When Laski appealed to Attlee about the incident, he received a curt reply:

while I can understand your feelings, I cannot accept your esti-mate of the situation or your judgment on our policy. The condi-tion of the unfortunate people on the *President Warfield* is not the result of the action of the Government, but of those who are directing this campaign of which they are victims.[91]

The gulf between Laski and the leadership was growing all the time, and there were further strains over the summer as Jewish terrorist atrocities on British soldiers increased, with reprisals against Jews. But the break finally occurred in the early autumn.

THE THIRD PHASE: LASKI'S ALIENATION FROM THE GOVERNMENT (SEPTEMBER 1947–DECEMBER 1949)

On 1 September 1947 the United Nations Subcommittee on Palestine (UNSCOP) issued a majority report recommending a partition scheme. This was accepted by the Zionist General Council, but rejected by the Arab organisations.[92] Laski called a meeting of the Labour Party International Sub-committee, which agreed unanimously to recommend the NEC to approve the UNSCOP majority report, and he subsequently wrote to the leadership to say that a heavy weight would be lifted from the party if the Cabinet took the same line.[93] His hopes were dashed, for Bevin had already written a paper describing the majority report as 'manifestly unjust to the Arabs' and recommending that Britain should decline responsibility for enforcing it.[94] On 20 September the Cabinet endorsed this view, without argument, with Attlee expressing the hope:

> that salutary results would be produced by a clear announcement that HMG intended to relinquish the Mandate and, failing a peaceful settlement, to withdraw British administration and British forces.[95]

For Laski this was a bitter blow. He explained his view of the situation to Frankfurter:

> [Attlee] turned up on Wednesday last at the Executive . . . The substance of his speech was (i) that the Majority report was 'fantastic', because it gave the Jews more than any other committee had ever suggested (ii) that if we accepted it we should be repudiating Bevin, and (iii) that there was no suggestion in the sub-committee's proposal that Great Britain should be aided in imposing the Majority plan. Then, to my astonishment, Phil Baker

[Noel-Baker] made a speech saying that the Jews had brought all this on themselves by terrorism, and that if they could not find terms of agreement with the Arabs, . . . the only thing to do was to clear out, recognising that Zionism was doomed. After a long and hard struggle in which Nye Bevan and Shinwell backed me superbly, Attlee revealed the Cabinet decision, which I denounced as nothing but a Foreign Office manoeuvre on behalf of the Arabs of which E. B. [Bevin] was now the passionate advocate since there was nothing left of 'the reputation he had staked' on his Palestine policy, and he was revenging himself on the Jews in consequence. . . . So there it is. I emerged completely convinced that our Government proposes to sell the Jews down the river . . .[96]

From this point he was completely alienated from the government's Palestine policy, and became deeply disillusioned. But was his interpretation of the Cabinet's decision correct: had the Jews been 'sold down the river'?

Even with the release of vast quantities of government documents, historians have interpreted the government's motives in different ways. Kenneth O. Morgan takes the same line as Laski:

There would simply be a deliberate vacuum, to be resolved by armed violence – in which, so the British thought, the tiny Jewish armies would be swept into the sea by superior Arab numbers.[97]

Similarly, Northedge argues:

It is hard to resist the conclusion that the British, after their long efforts to contain Jewish terrorism, and after seeing the General Assembly vote in favour of a pro-Jewish partition plan, were not disinclined to see the whole problem resolved by a blood-letting, in which they seemed to take an Arab victory for granted, a not unreasonable assumption in view of the fact that the Arabs in and around Palestine numbered some 30 million, as against 600,000 Jews.[98]

On the other hand, Bullock is sympathetic to the Attlee government's argument that it was unreasonable to expect Britain to carry the burden of enforcing a plan it regarded as unjust against the opposition of the Arabs. According to this interpretation, the hope was that British withdrawal – and the fear of chaos and war – would lead to more 'reasonable' attitudes and a negotiated settlement on terms which the Arabs could accept. He also maintains that the British were uncertain as to which side would win and quotes, for example, a memorandum from Bevin to Attlee on 22 October 1947 which suggested that the danger from the Arab armies had been much exaggerated and that the most likely action would be guerilla warfare, with support from the Arab states in the form of money and arms for the Palestinian Arabs.[99]

Bullock is probably justified in believing that the Cabinet did not *want* war, and it is quite likely that the British had no accurate information as to the military balance.[100] Yet it must have seemed highly unlikely that the Jews could achieve an outright victory if war did break out: indeed none of the Jewish leaders believed this when the State of Israel was proclaimed in May 1948.[101] The government was therefore surely hoping that British withdrawal would frighten the Jews into accepting something less than the United Nations' proposal. In other words, when Attlee spoke of the decision being 'salutary', he saw it as a means of putting pressure on the Zionists. The British government did not *want* massacres or bloodshed, but they no doubt anticipated that Zionist fears of military conquest would drive them back to the negotiating table to accept more 'reasonable' terms.

Nor was this preliminary decision to withdraw the worst blow for Zionist sympathisers. For British policy now became increasingly aligned with the Arab cause. At the UN the British delegate (Cadogan) did his best to dissuade other delegates from supporting partition plans, warning that Britain could not assist in their implementation.[102] And as soon the UN voted in favour of a partition plan (on less favourable terms to the Jews than the sub-committee's proposal) the anti-Jewish stance was clear. For the UN decision led to Arab attacks on Jews throughout Palestine, and anti-Jewish riots, with bloodshed in many Arab countries, but the British authorities in Palestine made no serious attempt to eject armed Arab invaders from neighbouring countries, while continuing to disarm the Jews.[103] Nor was British military assistance to any of the Arab states reduced, despite their threat to use their armed forces in Palestine, and despite the fact that the Jews were militarily very weak at this stage. Instead the British simply announced that they would withdraw all forces and administrative personnel by mid-May.[104] However, once it became clear that the 'salutary' warning was not inducing the Jews to abandon the partition scheme, members of the British government became more anxious about the threat of war. At the end of February 1948 the Chiefs of Staff expressed the fear that the Jews might align themselves with the Soviet Union, and suggested altering the UN plan by incorporating the southern and eastern parts of Palestine into Transjordan and the northern part into Syria/Lebanon, effectively leaving a Jewish enclave around Tel Aviv. In addition, the Arabs should be offered a regional defence pact and aid and, in return, should refrain from forcibly opposing the Jewish state.[105] This was just one of a number of such schemes which were being actively considered within the government.

The Cabinet and Laski were therefore now in totally different camps and, from late 1947, he attacked the leadership publicly and bitterly, as indeed did Crossman, Foot, and *Tribune*.[106] As far as Laski was concerned, the government's duty was actively to support the UN's partition plan, while the Cabinet saw its task as maintaining Arab goodwill, and seeking a new settlement.

Laski still tried to influence policy, but the gulf between his position and the government's was apparent in an NEC meeting in March 1948. Whereas he called for firm, public warnings to the Arab states that they would be expected to take full precautionary measures against anti-Jewish pogroms, the NEC instead decided that the Jews should again be told that the government's decision to withdraw from Palestine was irrevocable and that they should therefore consult the Arabs about a settlement.[107] He could now do little more than watch, in horror, as the anti-Zionist policy became increasingly pronounced.

The extent of the government's opposition to the formation of a Jewish state was indicated by Bevin the next month. On 21 April he told the American Ambassador that, although the Jews might win their first battles, the whole Arab and Moslem world would become inflamed and the real bloodshed would come later.[108] The next day he outlined an absurdly impracticable proposal to Creech Jones, then at the UN:

(1) Partition must be dropped in order to satisfy the Arabs; and
(2) there must be acceptance of the ultimate creation of a Palestinian State;
(3) there must be an assurance to the Jews that there would be a removal from Europe of a quarter of a million refugees – that is say 4,000 a month for Palestine for 18 months . . . The United

States should then take another 100,000 and so many to the British Commonwealth, and the rest to other parts of the world such as France.[109]

This was a bizarre suggestion. There was no indication that either France or the Commonwealth had been consulted, and it was notable that he specifically excluded Britain (on the grounds that it had already taken more Displaced Persons than any other state). France would have been a particularly unwelcome choice, given the Vichy regime's anti-Jewish policies. Nor was it conceivable that, having been promised a state, the Jews would now accept a dispersal policy. Bevin's plan simply showed that he had no conception of the appeal of Zionism in the aftermath of the Holocaust. And he was still hoping that a 'Britisher' might yet control some kind of Commission which would rule Palestine, with both the Arab Legion and the Haganah under his command.[110] The next day Creech Jones told a special session of the General Assembly that, in his government's opinion, the UN should aim at a more modest objective than partition. But there was no hope of such ideas now being accepted by the Jewish leaders.

When the British withdrew all their forces from Palestine in May 1948, Ben Gurion immediately declared the establishment of the State of Israel and the Arab armies invaded. The British government tended to view the establishment of the new state, rather than the invasion, as constituting 'aggression'. Indeed, Bevin was even prepared to reconsider an earlier decision not to allow British officers to fight with Abdullah's forces if the British ambassador thought that the existing policy 'would seriously injure our relationship with the Transjordan Government'.[111] Similarly, at the United Nations Cadogan subsequently opposed or delayed ceasefire resolutions in the early stages of the conflict when the Arab armies appeared to be winning, but later stood for firm action when the Jews assumed control.[112] As Bevin explained to the Lebanese Foreign Minister in October:

> we had to consider the Middle East in the light of the general world situation and of the overriding problem of Soviet expansion . . . We were collaborating closely with the USA and the only place where our policies tended to differ was Palestine. This was owing to the pressure put on the American administration by the Jewish population of the USA. I had done my best to support the Arab countries before fighting had broken out and I had sup-

ported the cease fire because our information did not suggest that the Arabs were likely to meet with much success.[113]

By January 1949, the Israeli forces had defeated most of the Arab armies, had expanded well beyond the frontiers originally agreed by the UN, and were advancing in the south. It now even seemed likely that the British would themselves become involved in the war in alliance with the Egyptians. Bevin appealed to the Americans to join Britain in restraining Israel. He argued that, if this chance were lost:

> I think it will be a victory not for the Jews but a great victory for Russia. Faith in us will be lost on the one hand, and on the other the Russians will have an open road through the Middle East.[114]

The Americans in fact used their influence with both sides to prevent an Anglo-Israeli war, the threat of which also led to a dispute in the Cabinet, with Bevan opposing government policy and calling for friendship with Israel.[115] Bevin then grudgingly accepted a *de facto* recognition of Israel in order to prevent a party split, but there was still a backbench rebellion against his anti-Zionist policy in the Commons debate on 26 January, with seventy backbenchers abstaining. But neither American nor party pressure led to any real shift in Bevin's attitude. On 24 January he had tried to persuade the Cabinet to re-supply arms (which had been suspended during the fighting) to Arab governments and on 3 February he expressed the view that the US attitude seemed to be not only 'to let there be an Israel and to hell with the consequences', but 'peace at any price and Jewish expansion whatever the consequences.'[116] The implication was that he still believe that war against Israel would be legitimate. Ultimately, he abandoned such thoughts but, when Morrison and Bevan went to an Independence Day reception at the Israeli Mission on 4 May 1949, Bevin remained conspicuously absent.[117]

This anti-Israeli stance had a devastating effect on Laski. In August 1948 he told Max Lerner, one of his American friends:

> E. B. [Bevin] is certainly a tragedy; and his colleagues who give him his own way over Israel are unpardonable. I can't put down on paper the things I know. But, between ourselves, it has made me decide certainly not to stand for re-election next year to the Labour Party E. C. and perhaps to resign before then. I have just about reached the limit of what is tolerable and I should think

myself a coward if I did not speak out in a position where I was free to say all I know. . . .

I am not sure whether E. B. hates Jews more than Communists; it must be a near thing – you can imagine what I feel after giving half my life to this Party and still feeling that its rank and file are the salt of the earth.[118]

In fact, he never really spoke out. Perhaps this was because the war was over by the time he actually left the NEC in 1949, and he did not want to be disloyal to the Labour Party with a General Election approaching. Or perhaps he found it too painful to express his feelings publicly. But Labour's Palestine policy continued to torment him.[119] Indeed in December 1949 he and Frida postponed a trip to Israel that they had intended to make the next year because:

the Labour Executive Committee decided to send out a 'delega-tion of friendship' at the same time, and as its members will be 3 people who consistently supported E. B. throughout, and in-clude two who go only to be sure of the Jewish vote in their constituencies I felt I could not bear to be there and hear them speak honoured words whilst that miserable Cadogan fought the last rear-guard action against Israel at Lake Success, so we decided to go later.[120]

He died without ever fulfilling an ambition to lecture at the Hebrew University and satisfying 'one of the profoundest inner emotions he possessed'.[121]

CONCLUSION

Why was Laski so upset about the Palestine issue? Why was it this, rather than British policy in the Cold War which finally led him to withdraw from the NEC? One reason was that support for a Jewish National Home had been a precise party commitment, while policy towards the USA and Soviet Union was inevitably more nebulous. Like Richard Crossman and Michael Foot, he also saw the policy towards Zionism as comparable with the betrayal of the Czechs in 1938.[122] However, for Laski even this comparison did not express the depth of his feelings. The trauma was still deeper because of his Jewish consciousness.

During the Second World War he had become more assertive about being Jewish and made a definite link between this fact and his support for Zionism. 'It is, I think, fitting' he told the Party Conference in 1943, 'that a member of the National Executive who is also a Jew should have the opportunity, on behalf of his colleagues, of accepting the resolution that is done in the name of the Poale Zion.'[123] But because Jewish identity and Zionism were now intertwined in his mind he also felt that there was a strong element of anti-semitism in its policy when the Labour government turned against Zionism. This was extremely painful for him and he tried hard to resist the belief. When, for example, he went to the USA in August 1946, he told Frida that Frankfurter had an unshakable conviction of Bevin's anti-semitism, but he did not endorse this view himself.[124] As he grew more critical of British policy during 1947, he vacillated in his attitude. In May he told Frankfurter that Bevin was vain, disastrously ungenerous and 'quite definitely anti-semitic in a brutal way', and that he had 'got to a stage of anti-semitism that is fantastic'.[125] But he did not really want to believe this and a month later – perhaps after Bevin had used him as an intermediary with Poale Zion – he reversed this opinion, telling Frankfurter that, 'in a curious way I like E. B. I even think he has odd moments when he likes me'.[126] However, after the British decision to withdraw from Palestine, he was no longer prepared to give Bevin the benefit of the doubt, believing that he was completely absorbed in hatred of all Jews.[127] Was there any justification for this view?

Bullock defends Bevin on the grounds that no-one had ever regarded him as anti-semitic before the summer of 1945 although 'he was widely known as a man with strong likes and dislikes which he made no effort to conceal'.[128] This hardly seems conclusive, for anti-Jewish prejudice (like other forms of racism) is not necessarily a matter of total absence or presence, but also of degree. It is no doubt true that anti-semitism was not a fundamental determinant of Palestine policy in 1945, for the primary consideration was simply the wish to maintain British power in the Middle East. But once Zionism was identified as the major obstacle to the realisation of this goal, latent anti-Jewish prejudices seem to have become activated as much in Attlee as in Bevin.

As early as 16 September 1945, Attlee responded to pressure from Truman to increase immigration into Palestine with the argument that Jewish refugees should not be put 'in a special racial category at the head of the queue'.[129] Given the frequent stereotyping of Jews as 'queue jumpers' (as, indeed, Laski had pointed out in his *New States-man* article in 1943), even this phraseology was offensive – particu-larly so soon after Auschwitz. Two months later Bevin used the same phrase publicly:

> I am very anxious . . . that Jews shall not in Europe overemphasise their racial position. The keynote of the statement I made in the House is that I want the suppression of racial warfare, and there-fore if the Jews, with all their sufferings, want to get too much at the head of the queue, you have the danger of another anti-Semitic reaction through it all.[130]

At the very least, such statements suggest that both the Prime Min-ister and Foreign Secretary were acutely insensitive to Jewish feel-ings from the start. As the conflict escalated, and Zionism was perceived as a threat to British interests, and Jews attacked British personnel and property, the latent prejudices became manifest.

This is apparent from the record of a meeting Attlee and Bevin held with the American ambassador on 28 April 1948. The discus-sion was heated because the Americans believed that an invasion of Palestine by Abdullah's forces would constitute aggression. Since Abdullah was Britain's closest ally in the region, Attlee and Bevin expressed vehement disagreement:

> were the Jews to be allowed to be aggressors on his co-religionists and fellow-Arabs in the State of Palestine while he had to stand idly by doing nothing?

The USA, they continued, would not allow Arabs to help their fellows anywhere but assisted Jews to crush Arabs without stopping the slaughter. The Jews appeared to be 'aggressive and arrogant', while the number of Arabs who had infiltrated was not large 'and any acts they had committed had been exaggerated. After all Pales-tine was an Arab country'.

> The Prime Minister asked what was aggression? Was it aggres-sion for Arabs to come into Palestine from their own countries, and non-aggression for Jews to come in by sea to the tune of thousands? The Ambassador said that the Jews were coming in unarmed and were not fighting men, but the Prime Minister

pointed out that this was just Hitler's method. He put people in as tourists, but they were soon armed once they got in.[131]

Even in the heat of the moment such comments surely demonstrate anti-Jewish prejudices.[132]

Laski was thus justified in his belief that anti-semitism had become a factor in British attitudes and, although he tended to focus on Bevin, he also identified Attlee as particularly hostile to Israel.[133] Since Laski had viewed prejudice of this kind as a phenomenon of the Right, this was a bitter blow.

In 1944, when introducing himself as Chair of the Party Conference he had stated:

> I represent something a little different from the past, British by birth, middle-class by origin, Jewish by inheritance – symbolic of the vital fact that the Labour Party knows no boundaries save those which are defined by faith in its principles and policies.[134]

Five years later he withdrew from the NEC because he was no longer so sure that this was true. His own experiences of anti-semitism, set against the wider backcloth of the contemporary history, had also led to a substantial change in his attitude to the 'Jewish question' as a whole. Just before he died he thus wrote an article for the *Daily Herald*, condemning the attempt of the CP to secure Jewish support to counter Fascism in the East End:

> I know few realms of political behaviour where the Communist tactics have been more dishonest and more irresponsible than this. They ask for support from Jews on the ground that they, the Communists, are the only people who really mean to give the Jews safety, to suppress Fascism in all its forms, and to punish anti-semitism with the severity its foulness warrants. . . . But they say nothing about the harsh treatment of Jews in recent years in Russia and the countries under its domination.
>
> They are silent about Communist hostility to Zionism as a faith and of Communist punishment of Jews who seek to emigrate to Palestine. There is silence about the skilful exclusion of Jews from leading political positions, silence about the stern discouragement of Yiddish . . . and silence about the failure of Russian attempts to make a Jewish national community within its own frontiers. In

seeking to subordinate all thinking to the Party line there has grown up an ugly type of anti-Semitism in the area of Soviet influence which is intended to discourage, and, where possible, to destroy the Jewish hunger for fulfilment as a Jew.

It is a change from the older policy of self-determination; and it is applied with the ruthless speed characteristic of the Communist in power. He is friendly to Jews in Britain because he has used that friendship as a stick with which to beat the Socialist Government. He is unfriendly to Jews in the Soviet area unless they submit to whatever line of policy Moscow decides shall be imposed upon them. With the emergence of 'cosmopolitanism' as a deviation, the Jews, whose eyes are cast with longing on Palestine, are already in a zone of danger.[135]

Gone was his easy assumption that a change in the economic system would eradicate prejudice, and that anti-semitism was simply a product of capitalist exploitation. Gone too was the belief in assimilation as the ideal, for his implicit support for 'the Jewish hunger for fulfilment as a Jew' and the eyes 'cast with longing on Palestine' were light years away from his earlier belief that the Jews could and should cease to have any separate consciousness. The experiences of his life had taught him that the problem was more complex than he had thought when he had written *The Chosen People*. At that stage he had assumed that his marriage to Frida would change his own identity and that other Jews should follow his example. Now he was more prepared to assert his 'Jewishness' and he knew that a simple act of renunciation did not solve the problem of anti-semitism.

Yet it is important not to distort the nature of his attitude either to Jewish identity or to Zionism. It is, for example, impossible to accept the argument of Yaakov Morris that, had Laski shared the 'Israel experience', 'he might have found more intellectual and spiritual harmony'.[136] This Zionist appropriation of Laski is, I believe, without validity. In the first place, it is difficult to imagine that Laski could ever have achieved 'intellectual and spiritual harmony'. He had sought this kind of solace in academic life, the Labour Party, the New Deal, and Marxism without long-term success. It is almost inconceivable that, as an atheist deeply attached to liberal, secular European intellectual values, he would, for long, have been satisfied by Israeli society. But in any case, this view misrepresents Laski's attitude to Zionism.

His ideal had been a bi-national state. He had also argued that Jewish immigration was beneficial to the Arabs, and that the two peoples had a common interest in modernisation and socialism as against the reactionary feudal landowners. In fact Arab-Jewish co-operation was probably never a real possibility after the Second World War, and the claim that the Arabs were deriving benefits from Jewish settlements was a rationalisation. Yet the assumptions behind his position were significant even if his position was based on wishful thinking or ignorance. Laski knew that there was continuing anti-semitism in Eastern Europe after the war, that neither the British nor the Americans would welcome increased Jewish immigration, and that the majority of the refugees wanted to go to Palestine. He therefore saw the Jews as victims and the creation of the National Home in Palestine as a vital element in the solution to the problem. And he felt particular solidarity with them because of his Jewish identity and his own experiences. Because he felt this so strongly he hoped, without too much analysis, that the Arabs would be reconciled to Zionism and he needed to believe that this was possible. He had not insisted on the necessity for a full state and would have welcomed a continuing UN presence and economic development plan for the region as a whole. But his support for the Jews in Palestine was rooted in the belief that this was part of the 'liberation war of humanity'. As he told Frankfurter, in a different context: 'My socialism comes before everything else in the making of political judgments'.[137] In the early post-war period, he believed that his socialism, as well as his Jewish identity, implied support for the creation of a National Home in Palestine. In no sense had he become a Jewish nationalist and it is inherently improbable that he would have adopted an uncritical attitude towards subsequent developments in Israel. Indeed his consciousness would never be exclusively Jewish or British. In a real sense he remained an international socialist.

13

'I Build my Policy on Hope'

When the Labour Party took office in 1945 and announced its legislative proposals, Laski wrote to Frida:

> in a real sense, it was our victory, for it was big ideas you and I had dreamed. . . . I think the King's speech is *fine*; and if they really fight for it and give India freedom I shall feel I have not lived in vain.[1]

Subsequently, he was generally fairly satisfied with the government's domestic programme. Occasionally, he criticised it for undue caution, and he was aware that it had not attacked the 'citadel' of capitalism. But he did not become deeply involved in the disputes about the pace of nationalisation, and believed that the establishment of the 'welfare' state was a very creditable achievement. After some early worries, he was also impressed by its Indian policy. At first, he had feared that 'there was still a marked absence of real will to help in the making of a free India',[2] but as it became increasingly clear that the government was committed to withdrawal, he defended its position enthusiastically.[3] Indeed he told Frankfurter in June 1947 that Attlee had been 'superb' over India and that:

> He has more than made up to me for the days, during the war, when his loyalty to Winston made every sub-committee of the EC a stand-up fight between us both.[4]

Yet despite his attempt to maintain his external image of ebullient optimism, neither the domestic programme of the Labour government nor Indian independence could offset his tendency towards increasing pessimism during the last years of his life.

It is not difficult to understand the reasons for Laski's despondency. The experience of victimisation, culminating in the libel case, had profoundly undermined his self-esteem, and this sense of failure was exacerbated by his physical ill-health as he struggled against debilitating chronic bronchitis, with recurrent bouts of pneumonia. His family life remained a source of contentment: his love for Frida was as strong as ever, and he was now happy as a grandfather. Frida tried hard to shelter him from external pressures so that their last years together were much quieter than they had been, with most weekends spent in their cottage in Essex. But even his exceptionally harmonious marriage could not counteract his pessimism, for his life had been so bound up with his sense of 'mission' that his personal circumstances could not be separated from it. And his despair about the the state of the world – perhaps reinforced by ill-health – now affected him deeply.

Almost as soon as the Labour government came to power, he had discerned a betrayal of international socialism in its foreign policy. He could not accept pragmatic justifications for the cautious policy towards Franco's Spain or the support for anti-Communist forces in Greece, let alone the anti-Zionist stance in Palestine. In February 1946 he told Julius Braunthal, the Austrian Socialist, 'How much grimmer the world grows every day; and how easy it seems for socialists to lose sight of principle in their search for the applause of privilege'.[5] But, above all, it was the Cold War which epitomised the failure of Laski's political project. His letters, and sometimes even his published work, provide eloquent testimony to the impact that this had on his morale.

In June 1947 he felt that Soviet acceptance of the invitation to discuss the Marshall Aid offer might provide the last chance to prevent the division of Europe and the breakdown of East-West relations. 'There is just a chance', he told Frankfurter, 'and I feel like someone clinging on to a cliff's edge by a hair-pin'.[6] Three months later, the door appeared to be closed and he now confessed to feeling 'that I am already a ghost in a play that is now over'.[7] The Prague coup was so distressing for him that he expressed his feelings publicly:

If the statesmen will not make an end of this twilight world in which hope is born to be broken, and victory won only to be thrown away . . . it is better to finish the fruitless effort of civilization which lacks the wisdom and the magnanimity without which life is indeed an idiot's tale, for all its fury still signifying nothing.[8]

From then on his anguish mounted. In February 1949 he told a friend that his latest bout of bronchitis and pneumonia had left him with an enlarged heart, high blood pressure and an inability to do any unusual exertion without being left 'flat for the rest of the day'. He admitted:

> I don't doubt that a good deal of it is psychological. A piece of it, no doubt, is the hurt vanity of a writer who thought he had said something significant and found from his critics that he was a poor kind of creature. Then another part is sheer horror at this drift, as slow and sure as it is unnecessary and wicked, to this third world war in which, win or lose, every candle of free thought and the rights of conscience will be extinguished. And a third part, I am sure, is an inner and growing horror that the Labour government, in the realm of foreign affairs, should have lent itself to this.[9]

His suffering increased as the purges on both sides of the new 'iron curtain' intensified. He was deeply upset when Alger Hiss, the head of the Carnegie Endowment for International Peace, was named as a communist and found guilty of espionage. Laski had known him first as one of Holmes's secretaries, and later as a State Department Official in the Roosevelt administration. In August 1949 he told Frankfurter that he was 'broken hearted' about the fate of Hiss and a few months later he wrote again:

> To tell you the honest truth, a grey, grim mood has settled on me, self-doubts, inner unhappiness, the kind of pain that is a perpetual crucifixion. I cannot bear much longer the kind of ugliness that rejoices in torturing either the living like Alger Hiss or the dead, like Harry Hopkins, or half a dozen men they have hanged in Hungary, and Bulgaria, and the other half-dozen they will hang in the next six months in Poland and Czechoslovakia, men whom I know, men of whose honesty of purpose I feel as certain as I do my own.[10]

Perhaps most depressing of all for Laski – the ardent rationalist – was the belief that persecution of dissidents and the threat of war, demonstrated the predominance of irrationalism and fear. To another friend he thus compared the Hiss affair with Dreyfus, and wrote:

Doesn't it make you see how those trials in Hungary and Bulgaria excite the sadistic appetite and make most people just afraid – then angry with themselves because they are afraid, then, out of self-anger, justifying themselves by accepting as truth what inside themselves they know to be untrue. This belongs with the Salem Witches. . . . I find it an unbearable thing.[11]

He confided in Frankfurter's wife, Marion, telling her that even the fact that Frida had been 'angelic' could not counteract his unhappiness. He now felt that the 'world is a jumble in which a poor, shivering thing called man wanders through with not much to hope for'.[12] Moreover, from about 1947 onwards the emotional pain was intensified because he was also troubled by his conscience.

Laski's political involvement was always determined by two drives: a zeal to create a better world, and the wish to influence the course of history. He had become a leading, active member of the Labour Party because it had seemed to satisfy both of these fundamental aspirations. However, by the late 1940s this was no longer so clear to him. He carried little weight with the Labour Party leadership and he must have realised this by September 1947 at the latest. Given his profound disagreement with government policies over Palestine and the Cold War, he was now never sure what to do. Loyal support of the leadership as a member of the Executive might imply agreement with the policies he hated, but resignation and public condemnation of the government could help the Conservative enemy. He therefore constantly postponed his resignation with the rationalisation that he might yet carry some influence by maintaining his position. But he was obviously deeply troubled about this.

When he finally decided to withdraw, he told his friends that he could now voice his opposition to Bevin and, to that extent, ease his conscience:

I admit that conscience is at best a pretty poor thing, but it is the only thing really one's own, and it is a deep unhappiness when, week by week, you feel you are pushing its demands into a corner out of a theory of loyalty which merely gives him and his supporters the power to go on doing evil.[13]

Once he had left, he was certain that he had taken the right decision. As the 1950 General Election approached, he told Frankfurter:

Nothing has relieved me more in years than to have left the L. P. Executive. At least this time I can speak for whom I like. How right Frida was to tell me it was simply arrogance on my part to accept responsibility without even the shadow of power. If I have little ease of mind, at least I have a bloodstream without bacteria in it . . .[14]

Laski's last years were so often dominated by moods of despair that he probably would have been far happier had he been able to bury himself in academic life. He told one of his American friends, Alfred Cohn, that his 'main joy' was a seminar at LSE:

where we have been working out just how the different strands of the intellectual revolution of the 16th–17th century came together and how they were linked together; that has been great fun.[15]

He also began to correspond with his friends about books that he had been reading – something that he had not done since the death of Holmes. And his last works again showed his relish for ideas. In 1947 he delivered an outstanding lecture on Burke at Trinity College, Dublin,[16] and his posthumous book *The Dilemma of Our Times* contained some incisive criticisms of contemporary existentialism and philosophical ethics. He also began to think seriously about writing a long-postponed book on French political thought. The three lectures that he delivered at Manchester University only a few weeks before this death, also continued to bring a vibrant approach to the study of the British political system. This work (published posthumously as *Reflections on the Constitution*) still demonstrated his ability to enliven constitutional analysis by introducing historical insights and detailed knowledge of the operation of the system in practice.

He was also presented with a further academic opportunity which might have given him some satisfaction when, in April 1947, he received a letter from Albert Einstein. This informed him that a serious effort was being made to found a new American university because of the anti-Jewish discrimination which operated elsewhere. The hope was that this would make it easier for young men and women of Jewish faith and other minorities to obtain a first-class education, while providing better career prospects for academics, who also currently faced discrimination. The university would be in

Jewish hands, but the founders were determined to develop it into an institution:

> which is enlivened by a free, modern spirit, which emphasises, above all, independent research and which does not know of discrimination for or against anybody because of sex, color, creed, national origin or political opinion.

Einstein had been given authority by the Trustees to select the first President of the University, and now wrote:

> This man would have the challenging task to help us in determining the basic foundations of the University and to select and organize the initial faculty upon whom so much depends. We all feel that among all living Jews you are the one man who, accepting the great challenge, would be most likely to succeed. Not only are you familiar with the United States and her academic institutions more intimately than many American educators, your reputation as an outstanding scholar is widespread throughout the country.[17]

The invitation could hardly have been more flattering and, to make it still more tempting, Einstein suggested that Laski should assume the leadership of the University for only two or three years so that he could then return to Britain. It seems possible that, had Laski accepted it, the task might well have given him a new lease of life. He had, for so long, criticised American universities, that the establishment of a new institution, in which he could play the leading role in determining teaching methods and research styles must have appealed to him. On the other hand, he had already told Frida that he could no longer live in the United States and perhaps this now deterred him. In any case, he turned it down, claiming that it was important for political reasons that he should remain in England.[18] It may be that this was because the Palestine situation was now at a critical juncture or, more generally, because he was still hoping to exert some influence over the Labour leadership. Brandeis University was therefore established without him.

From the point of view of his own health, happiness, and life expectation, it is a shame that he could neither accept Einstein's invitation nor bury himself in the history of political thought. Instead he tortured himself by remaining so emotionally involved with the world events that he was unable to influence. Yet however miserable he felt, he would not abandon hope or the attempt to shape political developments.

Indeed the extraordinary thing about Laski's final years was his superhuman effort to keep going and make a positive political contribution. In his inner psyche, he was gripped by moods of despair. Yet he did not reveal his feelings. Nor, despite his intentions, did he ever make public his attacks on Bevin and the Labour leadership. He wrote the introductory section of the party programme, and in the General Election of February 1950, he spoke at about forty meetings.[19] He told Frida 'I am not in the least tired, and I think my cough is better'.[20] In fact, he was now so ill with bronchitis that he could sometimes hardly stand. He did not disclose (except to Frankfurter) his fear that victory would lead the way to new 'evils', and exuded enthusiasm to Attlee.[21] Nor, when the Labour majority was decimated in the election, did he forget to write in encouraging terms to Morgan Phillips:

> This is bitter, but you must not take it too much to heart. The organisation . . . was really superb; and we'll go into the next fight with twice the ardour we went into this. But don't let anyone – and I mean anyone – discourage you.[22]

To the very end, he continued to drive himself relentlessly, trying to deny his illness and his bouts of depression and to maintain a resolute optimism. Two days before he died he thus wrote his final article in response to a very pessimistic piece by Bertrand Russell. It was on a subject which had preoccupied him increasingly since 1945: the prospect of a Third World War fought with weapons of mass destruction. Since 'Russo-American fear and suspicion had reached levels where neither could reason seriously with the other', the British government, he argued, should propose to the United Nations destruction of all weapons of mass destruction, and consideration of plans for universal disarmament. This, he maintained, might succeed if it simultaneously addressed all the fundamental problems which threatened world peace. 'Lord Russell', he proclaimed', 'builds his policy upon despair. I build my policy upon hope'.[23]

The day of his death he was due to address a new Association of Political Science at LSE. The previous day he had realised that he was too ill to do so and had sent a message, in which he expressed the hope 'that the Association will strike out boldly'.[24] This was a fitting testimony to his own values.

The death itself was painful, and traumatic for the family. On 20 March he was struck down by a new bout of bronchitis and was ordered to take six months complete rest. But within three days his lung had collapsed and an abscess burst on it. Nothing could be done as his heart was too weak for an operation, so Frida was left with him in the hospital, and he died with little medical intervention.

The cremation, which was attended by the majority of the Cabinet, was silent. Frida soon received letters from all over the world and told a friend that she wished 'Harold could have seen them, as he always heard of the rotten remarks made about him and not often the good'.[25] No doubt he would have been gratified by this. But, as Frida knew, as she wrote Heine's words on his coffin,[26] he would, above all, have wanted to be remembered as a 'soldier in the liberation war of humanity'.

Conclusion: Constructive Contradictions

When Laski died the tributes were world-wide. The Labour Party Conference passed a unanimous resolution declaring that it:

> remembers with gratitude and affection the outstanding service rendered to the Labour Movement, the cause of international solidarity and human freedom, by the late Harold Laski and instructs the National Executive Committee to establish a permanent memorial to his memory.[1]

In France, Léon Blum compared Laski to Montesquieu and de Tocqueville, claiming that no other man in Europe or America had such a profound and original knowledge of democratic thought and institutions since the seventeenth century, and that:

> In matters where I have acquired some competence – the literary and political history of France in the last two centuries – I have always found him master.[2]

Indeed the eulogies were endless. Nor were they confined to socialists. For example, when the American liberal journalist Ed Murrow heard of Laski's death, he broke into his live radio broadcast and:

> mourned the death of the friend who had taken him to task over the BBC for not reading . . . Hobbes: 'Laski was a Socialist . . . He was a man who believed . . that no body politic is healthy until it begins to itch . . . His allegiances were fierce, and neutrality was not known to him . . . More than most professors or pamphleteers, he caused people to think furiously, because it was only through the exercise of the mind that men could remain free'.[3]

Even those who opposed his theoretical work acknowledged its significance and integrity. Thus one American who wrote a deeply critical evaluation of Laski's work ended with the words:

> But few men in our day gave themselves so completely to the struggle to solve the perennial dilemma [of the problem of au-

thority versus liberty]. . . . One may also hazard the guess that few men in this century will provide so stimulating a challenge to thought upon this problem.[4]

Similarly, in Britain Max Beloff wrote that:

It would not be too much to say that just as we can call the period 1840 to 1870 . . . the 'Age of John Stuart Mill' so too the future historian may talk of the period between 1920 and 1950 as the 'Age of Laski'.[5]

And although Beloff's major point was that this age had now passed, he paid tribute to the fact that the establishment of politics as an academic subject in Britain owed more to Laski than to any other individual, and he expressed the hope that, in approaching the new problems:

the post-Laski generation of political scientists may show the same eager curiosity as Laski did, the same capacity for work, and the same disinterested devotion to the pursuit of truth.[6]

In 1950 it therefore seemed that Laski's memory would be cherished by socialists, and that his contribution to political thought would continue to be generally acknowledged. But this was not to be. The Labour Party did not establish the memorial it had pledged. Instead, two years after his death a group of his friends tried to set up a society and memorial trust which would sponsor research and issue an annual publication.[7] But this never got off the ground, and it was only in India that a Laski Institute was established and for many years succeeded in mounting a publication. When this institute opened, the General Secretary of the Labour Party was still prepared to send an effusive message:

Harold Laski will become a legend in both academic and Socialist circles which will stimulate the minds of men and women all over the world.[8]

In fact, by then it was already far too late. Socialists had not succeeded in keeping the memory alive, and Laski's reputation in non-socialist circles had plummeted. The 'age of Laski' had indeed passed. As argued in the Introduction, the Cold War was primarily responsible for his downfall. The extent of this posthumous witch-hunt may be illustrated with reference to an episode that might have been expected to be non-political.

Laski had always been a passionate antiquarian book buyer and built up a magnificent collection covering, in particular, political thought and social movements from the seventeenth to the nineteenth centuries. It was perhaps the most complete private collection on these subjects.[9] Almost as soon as he died, Frankfurter decided that Laski's American friends should buy the collection from his widow, and present it to LSE. This, he thought, would be 'the most cherished means of fructifying his significance as a scholar and teacher'.[10] The Principal of LSE, Carr-Saunders, thought this was a wonderful idea and the plan was to open up a 'Laski room' where the books could be collected.

For various reasons it took some time to launch the idea, and Frankfurter felt that as a Supreme Court Judge, he could not take the lead himself. Finally, a sponsoring committee was established and a financier, James Warburg, was entrusted with organising the appeal. He soon found it a far more difficult task than he had envisaged and, in May 1952, told Frankfurter:

> people are not too anxious these days to take the lead in this venture . . . in other words people are afraid to affiliate themselves with the project too prominently . . . After all, the Churchillian portrait of Laski is probably the best known picture of the man in this country and even those who know it to be malicious caricature know that others do not so regard it. What I am trying to say is that . . we are not only handicapped by the income bracket of our only constituency but by the fact that the project has become socially unacceptable. . . .
>
> And . . . all this is a consequence of our negative, fear-inspired foreign policy and the adoption of a devil-theory analysis of the world crisis.[11]

Frankfurter would not give up, though he admitted that the generosity of some of Laski's erstwhile friends had been 'somewhat chilled by the intimidating atmosphere of our time.'[12] But a few months later, when Warburg had managed to collect only a small proportion of the funds that were needed, Frankfurter was forced to accept defeat, confessing that 'very few things have left me so heartbroken as the failure to put through our plan'.[13] Warburg wrote to him again, painting a vivid picture of McCarthyism and its impact on the project:

> People are scared – scared to speak, write and even think – scared to be seen in certain company – scared to be seen reading the *Nation* – scared to have a book by Keynes or Laski lying on their table. Fear need not be very strong to become a powerful ally of niggardliness. Three years ago, I am sure the job could have been done. Today, I doubt very much whether anyone could do it.[14]

This was the climate in the United States which led to the sudden and dramatic decline in Laski's reputation. Attacks upon his personal qualities or political thought were acceptable and highlighted. Even the most innocuous form of association with his memory could be dangerous, as Ed Murrow was to find in April 1954 when McCarthy used his wartime friendship with Laski against him.[15] In this atmosphere it was a political act to buy some antiquarian books for presentation to a library three thousand miles away.

The situation in Britain was less dramatic but, in a more subtle way, the same process of dissociation occurred. It began at LSE, where Laski's radicalism had long troubled many of the governing body. Kingsley Martin had hoped to replace him as Professor of Government, but instead the School turned to the conservative political philosopher, Michael Oakshott. Certainly, Laski retained some support at the School. Thus the librarian and Lord Chorley played a key role in persuading the governors to put up funds to add to the amount raised by Laski's American friends so that his collection of books could be bought.[16] But the 'Laski room' was never established and the books were absorbed into the library without a list being kept.[17] Robert Mackenzie, who was at LSE from 1947, later argued that for a considerable period after his death 'the school authorities, who had been much embarrassed by Laski's political activities, half consciously set about exorcising the memory of his political role.[18] It is also particularly notable that some of the Left participated in the exorcism. Thus when Tawney, who had written a very positive appreciation of Laski immediately after his death, was approached by Kingsley Martin a year later to write about Laski's role at LSE, he declined. His excuse was that Laski's real influence had been over the staff and students in the Department of Government and that, as an economic historian, he was an inappropriate person to write the piece.[19] As Tawney and Laski had been at LSE together for thirty years and had often co-operated closely, this reveals Tawney in a less than 'saintly' light.

Naturally, there were those who tried to maintain the Laski aura. First and foremost there was Kingsley Martin himself, his first biographer. But anti-communism was at its height when the book appeared and it would probably have been impossible to counteract the negative Laski image at that stage.

If the Cold War distortions may finally be superseded, how should Laski now be evaluated? The only uncontroversial judgment about Laski is that he was a great and inspiring teacher. 'In thirty years of University work', wrote his colleague, H. L. Beales, 'I have never known anyone who inspired such devotion or had such power of instantaneous enkindlement . . . of younger minds'. Greater than all his other achievements was 'the flame he lit in people's minds'.[20] Nor did the 'flame' die. Thus twenty-seven years after his death, when Joan Abse compiled *My LSE*, she noted in the introduction:

> The longest, and clearly most deeply felt eulogies are reserved for Harold Laski who, at one time, seemed to epitomise LSE to so many people. By students he seems . . . to have been universally admired, even beloved, though perhaps few followed him uncritically.[21]

And his supreme skills as a teacher transcended any division of class, sex, or race. Krishna Menon, the Indian High Commissioner, wrote:

> His unbounded affection, generosity of mind and heart and his sense of concern, and the reality of it to the practical and the essential, are characteristics, which give him unique place among great teachers. Professor Laski's life has been the moral foundation on which many of those who really knew him and loved him have sought to build the essential structure of their thinking and social values. His great qualities of heart, mind and personality affected them more than they knew and/or can assess even now.[22]

Similar testimony could be given by Welsh miners, and women as well as men who attended LSE.[23]

Of course, part of the impact was the result of Laski's natural attributes: his personal magnetism, humour, memory, and clarity of expression. Part was also his ability to make students feel important by a vicarious association with the 'great and the good'. But there was far more to it than this, for he had a clear, and highly demanding, conception of the role and function of the university teacher.

The university, he believed, was concerned only with thought: its function was not to transform undergraduates into 'fountains of information'.[24] There were only three acceptable possibilities for a lecture:

> It must genuinely convince a student that a theme is of first-rate importance; it must . . . drive him into personal investigation of its substance. Or it must contain genuinely new knowledge or a new point of view not obtainable in the obvious books; it must, in this case, give old facts a new perspective by addition or original emphasis. Or thirdly, it must raise problems upon old material which forces the student to think out for himself the way and the nature of their solution. Lectures which do not seek to do these things have no place in a genuinely educational process.[25]

The lectures must be supplemented by 'consistent personal contact'. And education meant ten times more when built upon the foundation of friendship between student and professor. The student also needed to be driven into thinking upon a big scale:

> The essay he turns in must be read with him in detail and phrase by phrase. He must learn his faults of style, the gaps in his logic, the inadequacies of the sources he has used. The teacher must play devil's advocate against the position the student urges, insist that he give justification for his every argument, exhaust the armory of the casuist in his examination of the student's case.[26]

The teacher 'has to fill a subject with his personality', and, while 'constantly engaged in the discovery of new knowledge', must also 'be able to tread well-worn paths with a sense of vigor and freshness'. Above all, the academic must have 'a genius for friendship, with no 'cut-off' through stated office hours, for it was impossible to get to know the student's mind in this way:

> The teacher who gets the best out of his students makes his home an annex to the university. He is not prepared to divide off his life into compartments, into some of which the student cannot enter.

He entertains them, talks with them, gives them the sense that he is eager to proffer counsel.[27]

It is tempting to react to Laski's concept of the university teacher by simply saying that this ideal is no longer possible. The pressures of student numbers, teaching hours, and administration are simply too great. All this is, no doubt, true. However, it must be emphasised that, even in the first half of the twentieth century, it was impossible for the overwhelming majority of academics to aspire to Laski's conception of their function. Yet for much of his career he came very near to achieving it himself. As Robert Mackenzie recalled:

> Despite his enormous international fame, despite the outpouring of books, articles, speeches, despite his deep involvement in the politics of the Labour Party, he was more completely devoted than any university teacher I have ever known to the well-being of his students, regardless of their individual merits. . . .
> Whenever I have felt inclined to cut corners in dealing with some particularly tedious student I recall the memory of Harold Laski and it puts me to shame.[28]

Some have even argued that he was almost *too* concerned with his students – that he saw them all as 'swans' and none as 'geese'. But perhaps the supreme virtue of a teacher is to raise the aspirations of *all* students so that they try to achieve more than they would otherwise believe possible. Certainly, Laski had this effect on people.

There is one final issue about Laski as a teacher: the question of bias and objectivity. Were his fervent political opinions any obstacle to his teaching? Laski raised this question in his inaugural professorial lecture in 1926:

> My object as the occupant of this chair is not to create a body of disciples who shall go forth to preach the particular and peculiar doctrines I happen to hold. It is rather that the student shall learn the method of testing his own faith against the only solid criterion we know – the experience of mankind. That does not, of course, mean that in the exposition of political philosophy it is one's business to pretend to impartiality. In any case that is impossible; for in the merest selection of material to be considered there is already implied a judgement which reflects, however unconsciously, the inevitable bias that each of us will bring. The

teacher's function . . . is less to avoid his bias than consciously to assert its presence and to warn his hearers against it; above all, to be open-minded about the difficulties it involves and honest in his attempt to meet them. For the greatest thing he can, after all, teach is the lesson of conscious sincerity. More truth is discovered along that road than can be found on any other.[29]

Once again, to an extent which is remarkable for someone with such strong views, Laski practised what he preached. Those who differed from him politically often derived as much intellectual stimulation as those on the Left. For, ultimately, it was ideas and thought that mattered. Nehru thus recalled meeting Laski in 1948 and telling him that his ideas were now the opposite of everything that he had taught him as a student at LSE. Laski replied:

I taught you no ideas. What I taught you was to think for yourself. If your own experiences in the School of Life have caused you, through your independent thinking to come to conclusions different from my own, I am happy. For I have succeeded in my aim: I have taught you how to think.[30]

When Laski is praised as a teacher, it is sometimes implied that his academic role and beliefs about the university were somehow separable from his political views. In fact, they were an integral part of his general outlook and provide a clearer insight into the essence of his ideological position than do many of the more obviously 'political' texts.

For his conception of education in general, and the university in particular, revealed his fundamental values. At its best, he argued, higher education was to 'promote love of knowledge for its own sake, to secure that relentless curiosity of mind which insists upon truth because it cannot do otherwise'. For 'that love and that knowledge have been the parents of all that is most precious in the common life of civilization'.[31] These were, above all, 'liberal' values. To say this is not to argue that the Marxist or the conservative is indifferent to the clash of ideas or the disinterested pursuit of knowledge for its own sake. It is, rather, to suggest that the value itself is part of the liberal 'core' and, in Laski's case, his constant *emphasis* upon the ideal of free, traditional scholarship indicates that his preoccupations remained essentially 'liberal'. This, of course, becomes still more evident, when taken in conjunction with his other beliefs.

For it is impossible to read Laski's work in an open-minded way without being aware that his ideal was a humanitarian society based on creativity, tolerance, participation, the rule of law, the right of dissent, and government by discussion and debate. But if this is so, how does it relate to Laski's professed adherence first to socialism and, later, to Marxism?

The apparent incongruity in his conjunction of ideas has tended to puzzle many sympathetic critics. Some have tended to discount the Marxist terminology. As Greenleaf puts it:

> Maybe it is too harsh and cavalier a summary to say that the Marxism was mere window-dressing, but that the Marxism was in some way simply an incremental layer added to an existing palimpsest of ideas it is (I believe) unreasonable to doubt.[32]

This judgment contains an important element of truth for, as this book has stressed, the transition to 'Marxism' was indeed foreshadowed in Laski's earlier ideas, and they continued to co-exist with it. Yet it is inadequate because it implies that he did not *use* Marxist analysis, and that his interpretations and policies would have been exactly the same without it. This is untenable for, after 1934, his explanations of such phenomena as liberal-democracy, fascism, and imperialism were certainly influenced by Marxism. *The American Democracy* was not a Marxist work in any straightforward sense but, in his pre-Marxist period, Laski would not have analysed the whole of American society and institutions in terms of capitalist dynamics and their negative effects.

Another sympathetic critic put forward an alternative explanation of the co-existence of Marxism and liberalism:

> Laski had strong emotional attitudes towards politics . . . and he had immense wealth of learning in many fields. But he wrote and spoke and taught so much that he never gave himself time to find a permanent resting-place for his ideas, or to bring the vast uncoordinated mass of his knowledge under a single roof. In this respect Laski had many of the qualities of perpetual youth – always curious, always seeking, always enthusiastic over some new discovery that might provide just the key which he had been wanting to the problems of the universe.[33]

This again contains an important element of truth: there was no 'permanent resting place for his ideas' and no final work which brought them all together. However, to put it in this way is to do Laski less than justice, for it implies that he was unaware of the contradictions. I believe, that he was conscious of them and used them constructively. The judgments of two other socialist thinkers, who knew him well, make this point very effectively.

As early as 1932 H. N. Brailsford introduced Laski to an audience as follows:

> The academic student who is half of Laski is most himself . . . among the individualistic rationalists of the eighteenth century and the French Revolution; their passion for liberty burns in him. The man of experience who is the other half of him is the contemporary of the Russian revolution: he understands its imperious call to order and planning, its grasp of the significance of the machine, its passion for social equality, its sense that the whole is greater than the part. But I cannot imagine him at home in Soviet Russia, and, indeed, it is probable that either revolution would have made away with him, because of his sympathy in retrospect or anticipation with the other effort. His work is to attempt a synthesis of these two tendencies, which are shaping the world of today and tomorrow . . .
>
> Professor Laski's work would stand out by reason of its courage and its vision; but it has, I think, a still rarer distinction. He grasps both the poles of this contradiction that reads and inspires our lives, with equal integrity, and strives to reconcile them with an effort of intellectual sincerity that is itself a creative act.[34]

Brailsford's judgment was full of insight for Laski was indeed grappling with these contradictions then and for the rest of his life. It is inconceivable that he was unaware of them.

The second illuminating assessment was by John Strachey in an obituary article. Strachey had worked closely with Laski in the Left Book Club and was no stranger to contradictions, having gone through a succession of political positions himself. He wrote:

> Under the shock of his death I . . . find myself suddenly reversing one judgement I had made of his work. The very dazzling variety and copiousness of his intellectual output had always seemed to me Laski's chief weakness. It was always easy enough to point out the unresolved themes that ran through his books and articles and speeches. . . . But the pain and shock of his death makes one realise that this was certainly his main strength: that it was just

this that gave him his hold over the mind of a whole generation of the British Labour Movement. After all, the contradictions were in our minds too – in a sense they were in the objective situation itself as it had developed historically in this country. Laski performed an immense service for us by making these contradictions conscious and articulate; for he gave us thereby at least one prerequisite for solving them. No one of his time and place could have done much more. To have struggled so long and to have done this much was, we now see, something which overshadowed the contradictions.[35]

This is highly perceptive. The contradictions in Laski's writings are tantalising and sometimes frustrating. But at each stage in his life he tried to incorporate what he had learnt from his experience into his thinking, and his thought into his practice. The result was bound to be only partially coherent. Yet it was just because he could simultaneously accept more than one perspective that he also offered more insight than could be derived from any individual position. The most obvious contradiction was that between Marxism and liberalism, but this was certainly not the only one. For example, as was shown in Chapter Three, there were, by 1919, already elements of Guild Socialism, pluralism, and emergent Fabianism in his outlook. As time went on further strands were incorporated into a 'Laskian' perspective. Reality, he implied, was too complex to be encompassed within any individual theoretical framework. However, he also adopted this position because he was *never* a conventional theorist. He was always simultaneously a political actor, who was trying to effect change. Both his writing and his political activity were therefore attempts to *persuade* people to accept his conclusions. This also meant that his project was unlikely to remain anchored within neat theoretical categories. Moreover, there was one further element in Laski's outlook, which he may have wanted to deny, but which was of crucial importance: a quasi-religious conviction, stemming from his background in Judaism.

Laski's faith transcended any insights derived from evidence or logic, and always drove him to new efforts, however pessimistic he felt. Although he maintained his antipathy to all existing forms of religion, he probably knew that his own beliefs were partly nonrational. In his earliest work (*The Chosen People*), he had argued that both the 'dreamer' and the 'scientist' were necessary if a new world was to be created and, in his last major book, he even discussed 'true' religion sympathetically:

The quality that is of the essence of a religion is the inner and passionate impulse which drives those who possess it beyond and above themselves to an elevation where they can conquer the immediate desire, and the temporary caprice, in their search for a fraternal relation with all who suffer and all who are broken by the tragedy of a pain they cannot face. Religion, in this sense, can never compromise with the world; it must be willing to break it or be broken by it rather than to yield the imperative passion in which it finds its supreme expression . . . It is not even a spirit which believes that fame or knowledge or power can ever compensate for the surrender of that inner vision which persists in those who present it by the fact that its call is never denied.

This religion existed long before any of the historical religions were born, and it will live on long after many of them are dead. It has no institutions, no dogmas, no rituals, no priests; it is a spirit something of which is in the character of those who possess it; something of which also breaks into flame as that character meets experience of the world. Its possession is independent of greatness, whether of mental power or of social position, whether of wealth or of official dignity. If it is found in Socrates, it is found in Albert Schweitzer; it is unmistakable in that last supreme utterance of Vanzetti, as it is a light that gleams in the controlled, yet impressive, emotions . . . in many of the writings of Mr Justice Brandeis. I do not know how to put it better than in those magic words . . . in . . . the Book of Proverbs 'Where there is no vision, the people perish'.[36]

Laski possessed a vision of this kind and often used quasi-religious language to describe the stark alternatives facing the world. For example, in 1946 he told the Labour Party Conference:

I do not seek to under-estimate the perils of the road before us; I do not even pretend that our own generation can enter the promised land. . . . If we are still hardly out of the Valley of the Shadow of Death, we have begun to climb the Mountains of Hope. Let us remember that the more the energy with which we advance, the more hope and courage this stricken world will find in our example. Let us, therefore, with high hearts and unbreakable courage, march on to the Socialist Commonwealth.[37]

It is therefore easy to understand both the hold that he had over the rank and file of the Labour Party and the difficulties of his relationship with the leadership. A socialist theorist, with an ethical message and charismatic personality, would simultaneously inspire the members and irritate the leaders, who sought pragmatic solutions, rather than socialism, theory or high moral purpose. Many of the confrontations between Attlee and Laski were ultimately reducible to these differences: the Labour leader welcomed Laski's contribution in manifestos, when the moral high ground and an underlying rationale came in handy, but he did not want him anywhere near the levers of power.

If Laski was thus a teacher, a theorist, and a preacher,[38] there was one final quality, which accounts for his constant shifts of perspective: he was also a learner. There was an irreducible core of beliefs that remained constant throughout his life, but he was always seeking to learn from his own experience and from the history of his times. And this never stopped. In his last years he highlighted his pluralist beliefs, which he had always retained beneath the other layers, and focused on current problems. In particular, he considered two issues which are still of crucial importance in the contemporary world: de-centralisation/participation, and the relationship between the nation-state and the world community.

In *Trade Unions in the New Society* he wrote:

> the stoutest hook we can put in Leviathan is the twofold one of effective decentralization, both by area and by function on the one hand, and the evocation, on the plane of politics, of the individual citizen's interest and initiative on the other. . . .
>
> I confess to a frank fear of what I used to call the 'monistic' state . . . Its consequence is in a high degree evil.[39]

Nor was he simply criticising capitalist institutions. In the same book he stressed the danger of 'bureaucratic deformation' in nationalised industry, and elaborated eight principles to maximise decentralisation and democratisation. Moreover, in *The Dilemma of Our Times* he made clear his belief that the problems were not necessarily resolved by the overthrow of capitalism:

> the immense technological advance of the United States no more solved the problem of economic democracy than did the wholesale socialisation of the means of production in Russia. Both leave the mass of workers instruments to be manipulated for ends in the definition of which they do not in any decisive way share.

Both of them elevate the few at the price of leaving the many disciplined and insignificant because the routine they are told to follow evokes from them nothing of that initiative and spontaneity without whose evocation the quality of freedom in society in inevitably depressed.

If this be true, we need to get rid of an economic system in which ownership, by definition, becomes a method of exploiting men and women, with the power of the state mobilised to protect that exploitation. We do not achieve this objective merely by transferring ownership from private to public hands, and then seeking to plan the processes of production. The problem is the much more complicated one of planning the whole economy of the society in such a way that each worker is able, at the level of his effort, to co-operate in defining the end and the means of that part of the plan in which he is involved as producer, while as consumer and as citizen he can participate in judging the operation of the plan as he experiences its results upon himself.

That clearly involves decentralised machinery of consultation both on the side of production and on the side of consumption. It is not enough merely to change the forms of ownership in a society; it is necessary to democratise them too. Men whose nature calls for creative activity will only feel free when they are given the opportunity to go forward from the present system which makes them so largely automata, empty, without self-respect, citizens of a friendless world, to a system which, believing in man, works out in concert with him the conditions in which his full individuality has room for genuine expression.[40]

A second problem of supreme importance, which he had originally elaborated during the First World War, was the issue of national sovereignty. In 1947 he argued:

We have entered upon an epoch in which it is daily more clear that the principle of national sovereignty has exhausted its usefulness. Certain functions of government are so clearly international in character that we cannot rely upon the co-operation of so-called 'independent and equal' sovereign states to achieve the cosmopolitan law-making that has become essential. It is not only that the 'independence and equality' of states is a juristic fiction with no roots in political reality; it is a harmful fiction because it obscures the reality to which we need to pay attention. I do not pretend to foresee the stages by which we shall transcend the national state; nor do I deny that national feeling is still a deep passion to which adequate institutional respect must be paid. I can argue only that the more fully we separate the concepts of nation and state, and get clear in our own minds the area of activity over which each can legitimately range, the more fully we shall understand the issue before us.[41]

He argued that the final goal must be world government, but that, since this was not practical politics, the interim solution lay in:

the growth of a functional as distinct from a territorial federalism. If nation states could agree to pool their interests in certain areas of action, as in a single European railway system, or a single system of aviation for the American continent, if there could be joint ownership and control of electric power, say in the Danubian Valley, or an internationally governed irrigation and power authority in the Middle East, we should begin to think in supranational terms about problems. . . .

For it is only by transcending a principle the obsolescence of which hinders international cooperation at every turn that we can begin to make men realize that the little platoon which now demands their exclusive loyalty is in fact only a part of the great regiment of mankind. To get that regiment to strike its tents is the first of the duties before us. That is the condition which alone will make it possible for humanity to move forward to a higher conception of citizenship than is permitted by the narrow horizons of the nation state.[42]

He also saw the abandonment of national sovereignty as essential if international conflict were to be avoided and, from 1945, Laski was obsessed with the prospect of a Third World War, fought with weapons of mass destruction. He constantly called for international control over the development and production of atomic energy, and explicitly linked this with an argument for increasingly powerful international organisations to supersede the nation-state in other spheres.[43]

He linked the evil of national sovereignty with capitalism, but also now argued that socialism would not necessarily resolve the problem. For he asserted that the international solidarity of the working class had never been much more than a pious enunciation of hope. At present there was no *real* internationalism in either the social democratic or communist movements. Socialism provided a far better basis than capitalism for functional federalism but, to translate this into reality, socialist movements needed to step beyond the sovereign state.[44]

This final effort to understand what was happening is instructive in two ways. First, it pinpoints two fundamental and unresolved issues of the twentieth century. But secondly, this constant attempt to learn from contemporary developments provides the key to understanding Laski's thought.

In a brilliant essay on Machiavelli, Laski once wrote:

> political philosophy is, by its very nature, pragmatic. Its practitioners do not sit down to write a treatise as dispassionate and universal as an exposition of geometry. In a real sense what they attempt is autobiography, the reaction upon themselves of a special environment individually interpreted.[45]

In this sense, Laski's work was certainly 'political philosophy'. His whole life was dedicated to analysing the real world, and trying to convey his conclusions to all who would listen to him. In the attempt to understand what was happening, he made no distinction between the different branches of politics. Indeed, he was one of the last in the great tradition of political thought who tried to uncover the meaning of events without specialisation. In his inaugural lecture in 1926 he proclaimed:

> I stand here to plead for the study of politics in the terms of history. To know how our traditions and institutions have been moulded, to grasp the evolution of the forces by which their destiny has been shaped – that . . . is above all the key to their understanding.[46]

And this sense of history underpinned all his analysis so that, for example, when he discussed constitutional practice, his approach was always informed by an understanding of its development over time. Yet he also moved through such fields as law, philosophy, political sociology, comparative government, and international relations, consciously rejecting any argument that these were areas that required specific expertise. In order to interpret the world it was, he believed, vital to be a generalist rather than a specialist. Because he was constantly engaged in this effort to understand the meaning of events, his political philosophy was also 'autobiography' in the fullest meaning of the word. For instead of seeking to encapsulate the reaction upon himself 'of a special environment individually interpreted' at a particular time, Laski recorded a whole succession of such reactions in each phase of his life. We are therefore left with a set of 'readings' on history, thought, institutions, constitutions and international politics which need to be contextualised as part of a particular stage in his life.

But if he was attempting 'political philosophy', and was able to communicate a sense of importance both to his own generation and to posterity, should he be regarded as an *important* theorist? Laski's views on past thinkers are again helpful in evaluating his own contribution. He once stated:

> Every great thinker is in part the autobiography of his age. His influence springs from the fact that he expressed, in a peculiarly magistral way, some significant portion of its hopes and fears.[47]

It is a far more subjective matter than Laski implied to decide whether a thinker was simply expressing a personal autobiography or that of the age in which she or he lived. It implies that it is always possible to transcend differences in political ideology and to make an objective judgment about the merits of a particular figure, irrespective of personal sympathy or antipathy to the position expressed. One of Laski's own qualities was an extraordinary ability to understand the value of many thinkers with whom he did not agree: hence, for example, his abiding appreciation of Edmund Burke. In a similar spirit, it is surely possible – even for his opponents – to acknowledge that Laski was indeed expressing the autobiography of his age. For the real impetus behind the many stages in his life was that he was, in his deepest being, a liberal who became increasingly aware that the viability of all his values was threatened by the crisis of his era. His political development, in all its forms, was really a search for a solution for this fundamental dilemma. And his trajectory through pluralism, and Fabianism, and his simultaneous lurch towards both

Marxism and the New Deal indeed expressed the hopes of many in his age. However, in the passage quoted above, Laski also stipulated that 'great thinkers' expressed themselves in a 'peculiarly magistral way'. It is not clear that he fulfilled this requirement.

Laski wrote no single book which encapsulated his whole philosophy. The nearest was *A Grammar of Politics*, and he retained many of the beliefs that he expressed there for the rest of his life. However, he also jettisoned several of the assumptions because the whole doctrine was based on non-Marxist and gradualist conceptions of change. And in each successive phase of his writings the same problem is encountered: there are important continuities, and yet there is no overall statement which can be studied and dissected as Laski's considered contribution to political thought.

Some of his writing was repetitive and superficial, but some was superb. Nor, as has often been suggested, was the early work uniformly superior to the later writing. *The Problem of Sovereignty* was adorned with too many allusions to obscure material, and even Frankfurter chided him for making his Introduction to the *Vindiciae contra Tyrannos* somewhat pretentious.[48] However, the lecture that he delivered on Burke at Trinity College, Dublin in 1947 was regarded as outstanding by a contemporary American expert on the subject.[49] Similarly, in terms of pure literary quality and insight, passages in *The American Democracy* are magnificent. Some of his shorter essays are also particularly brilliant. W. L. Guttsman has pointed out that 'The Personnel of the British Cabinet, 1801–1924' was the first sociological study of this kind[50] so and, in my view, 'Aristocracy is Still the Ruling Class in England' foreshadowed (by almost forty years) Miliband's *The State in Capitalist Society*. Laski's short essays on political theorists and their continuing relevance were also often masterly. My own favourite is one in which he encapsulates Machiavelli's assumptions and argues that the way to avoid a situation in which 'Machiavellianism' may triumph is through social transformation.[51] Similarly, some of his general political observations, such as 'The Limitations of the Expert', contain wonderful insights into the dangers of elevating experts above politicians.[52] In fact, he had an extraordinary ability to make important political points over a vast range of subject matter in a clear and provocative manner.

However, none of this is quite equivalent to a 'magistral' work. Perhaps Laski's thoughts on Rousseau may be applied to himself:

it is important to remember that in so vast an edifice consistency cannot be looked for; that, in any case, the life of Rousseau is the glimpses of truth he caught and fearlessly recorded.[53]

Despite the inconsistency, Rousseau was, he claimed, a 'prophet to his generation'. If we consider his essential message, so was Laski.

Civilisation at its best, he was arguing, could be expressed in liberal values. It constituted a plurality of ideas, reason, compromise, and the appropriate institutional form to give expression to all these virtues. It operated internationally, above the nation-state, and through forms of federalism below it. And democracy, the highest political expression of civilisation, also required active citizens who would participate in political and economic decisions. But the whole vision was, in the final analysis, unrealisable unless it was built upon the interests of the common people. And this required substantial economic equality, for those deprived of the material and spiritual possibilities of a society could never accept it as just. Yet those who benefitted from the privileges would always seek to resist the transformation, perhaps with dire consequences. The message was that – somehow – this change must be carried out through peaceful means so that the liberal ideal could be attained in reality both within and between states. He could never bring all this together into one coherent theory, which would provide a synthesis between the various aspects. And the attempt to *persuade* all who would listen of the *need* for change was incompatible with the Marxist assumption that there was no universal reason or morality that transcended class differences.

At the end of the twentieth century, three principal weaknesses in Laski's assumptions are also discernible.

First, he remained deeply embedded in the Western rationalist tradition. Thus even though he became actively committed to anti-imperialism, particularly in India, he clearly expected an evolution towards European-style 'modernism'. Nationalism and fundamentalist religion were, he believed, irrational forces which would give way to the secular values of liberalism and socialism as industrial capitalism developed. Even those who share his prejudices must now admit that reality is more complex.

Secondly, his grasp of both capitalist and Marxist economics was rudimentary. He was perceptive in understanding the underlying value system in orthodox economics and in recognising the relationships between economics and politics. But he tended to assume – far too readily – that a socialist economy could 'work'. In his final years, he recognised some crucial *political* problems in the planned economy, but he never considered the issues of markets and consumer production under socialism. Again, with the collapse of the Soviet empire, these are fundamental problems which no socialist could now ignore.

Thirdly – and a closely related point – Laski was too optimistic about the Soviet Union. As has been argued, he was *not* an apologist for the regime, and he was not uncritical. He was, I believe, also justified in arguing that external pressure was at least partly responsible for the internal repression. And after the Second World War he became critical of the whole Leninist conception of the party and of Stalinist politics. Yet his pessimism about capitalism led him to suspend too many of his critical faculties when examining the Soviet Union. When, during the 1930s and in the wake of Stalingrad, he saw the 'exhilaration' of the Soviet Union and the principles of a new civilisation, he surely saw a mirage.

However, such judgments are based on the wisdom of hindsight. It would have been extremely difficult for Laski to have taken these points into account, particularly as he was so deeply involved in trying to change the world as well as to understand it.

One final criticism that might be made is that Laski sounded too dogmatic and certain about what would happen if his warnings were ignored. It is fitting to let him have the last word, both in defending himself on this point, and in assessing his overall contribution. At the end of his life he wrote a review of Acton's work, in which he was surely writing his own autobiography:

> whatever he said finally in print, there were frequent moods of doubt about the very foundations of his beliefs, and . . . the occasional rhetorical arrogance of his sweeping generalisations . . . was probably at least as much the protective colouration for inner doubt as it was the expression of certainties beyond the possibility of disproof. . . .
>
> [He] was a passionate constitutionalist, and he would have viewed the use of terror, red or white, to impose opinion as the indefensible sin against the dignity of man. But he knew . . . 'that a great change was needed', and to him the central principle of that change was the discovery of institutional methods which would enable liberty to bring happiness to the many . . . He sought in many directions for the secret by which that would

become possible. It may, indeed, well be that his great book was never finished simply because he sought so widely, and so profoundly, for that secret. The point is that . . . [he] . . . was honest enough, and detached enough, to see that the exercise of power by his own class . . . did injury, and not benefit, to the great principle of freedom for which he lived. A half a century almost after his death, this is even more clear to us than it was to him.[54]

Notes

The following abbreviations have been used for the location of collections of archives:

Bodleian Library Oxford = BLO
British Library of Political and Economic Science at the London School of Economics = LSE
Felix Frankfurter Papers at Library of Congress = FFP (All references are in the Frankfurter-Laski correspondence unless otherwise indicated)
Franklin D. Roosevelt Library = FDR
University of Hull, Laski correspondence, 1973 Collection = H 1973
University of Hull, Laski papers, Eastwood Collection = HE
University of Hull, Correspondence between Frida and Harold Laski = FHL
International Institute of Social History, Amsterdam = IISH
Labour Party Archives = LP
Papers (other than those of Felix Frankfurter) held at Library of Congress = LC
Public Record Office = PRO
Rockefeller Archive Center = RAC
University of Illinois = UI
Yale University Library = YUL

All letters cited are from Laski unless otherwise stated. Works by Laski are cited without the author's name.

INTRODUCTION

Notes to pp. x–xii

1. Norman Palmer, quoted in G. Eastwood, *Harold Laski* (Mowbrays, 1977) p. 94 (hereafter Eastwood, *Laski*).
2. Max Beloff, 'The Age of Laski', *The Fortnightly*, CLXVII, June 1950.
3. Kingsley Martin, *Harold Laski* (Gollancz, 1953) (hereafter Martin, *Laski*); Mark DeWolfe Howe (ed.) *Holmes-Laski Letters: The Correspondence of Mr Justice Holmes and Harold J. Laski 1916–1935*, 2 vols (Harvard University Press, 1953) (hereafter *Holmes-Laski*).
4. H. A. Deane, *The Political Ideas of Harold J. Laski* (Columbia University Press, 1955) (hereafter Deane, *Laski*).
5. *Punch*, 16 September 1953.
6. H. L. Beales, 'The Professor-Politician', *Leader*, 30 June 1945.
7. Quoted in Eastwood, *Laski*, p. 133.
8. 8 December 1921 in *Holmes-Laski*, I, pp. 386–7 (hereafter all Laski's letters to Holmes from these volumes are cited as follows: date, volume number, page. For example, 8 December 1921, I, pp. 386–7).
9. George Catlin in *American Political Science Review*, September 1953, p. 860.

10. Martin Gilbert, *Winston Churchill*, vol. IV (Heinemann, 1975), p. 675.
11. N. and J. MacKenzie (eds), *The Diary of Beatrice Webb*, vol. 4 (Virago/LSE, 1985) 22 January 1931, p. 235.
12. 22 April 1952, FFP, Container 151.
13. 15 August 1952, Kingsley Martin papers, General Correspondence, Box 12/1, University of Sussex.
14. Laski to Joe Kennedy, 12 August 1940, H 1973.
15. Kenneth O. Morgan *Labour People* (Oxford University Press, 1987) p. 98.
16. 'The Words Came too Easily', *New York Times Magazine*, 17 May 1953.
17. Deane, *Laski*, p. 333.
18. *New York Times*, 25 July 1955.
19. The 'Harold Laski Institute of Political Science' was established in Ahmedabad and published the *Laski Institute Review*. Several articles and memorial lectures on Laski have been delivered in India as well as two books, G. N. Sarma, *The Political Thought of Harold J. Laski* (Orient Longmans, 1965), and R. C. Gupta, *Harold Laski: A Critical Analysis of his Political Ideas* (Ram Prasad and Sons) 1966. Some of the work – particularly Sarma's book – is critical of Laski. But even in 1989 in India it was possible to publish a book (by A. Bhattacharjee) entitled *History of Political Thought from Plato to Laski* (Ashish).
20. The full references for the sources cited (unless already mentioned) are as follows: M. Peretz, 'Laski Redivivus', *Journal of Contemporary History*, 1 (2) 1966; B. Zylstra, *From Pluralism to Collectivism: the Development of Harold Laski's Political Thought* (van Gorcum, 1968) (hereafter Zylstra, *From Pluralism*); D. Nicholls *The Pluralist State* (Macmillan, 1975) (hereafter, Nicholls, *Pluralist State*); P. Hirst, *The Pluralist Theory of the State*, (Routledge, 1989) (hereafter, Hirst, *Pluralist Theory*); C. Palazzola, *La Liberta alla Prova – Stato e societa in Laski* (ETS, 1979) (hereafter Palazzola, *La Liberta*); W. H. Greenleaf, 'Laski and British Socialism' *History of Political Thought*, 2 (3) Winter 1981; Kingsley Martin, *Harold Laski* (Cape, 1969). (The references used here are to the 1953 edition cited in note 3). In 1974, G. Feaver also wrote a critical, but stimulating paper, 'Intellectuals and Politics: Harold Laski Revisited': delivered at the 46th Annual Meeting of the Canadian Political Science Association, University of Toronto, 3–6 June, in *Proceedings of the Annual Meetings of the CPSA* (mimeo), republished in a shorter form as 'Intellectuals and Politics: The Moral of Harold Laski,' *The Lugano Review*, 2, 1975.
21. H. N. Brailsford to Frida Laski, 26 March 1950, H 1973.
22. Joan Abse (ed.), *My LSE* (Robson, 1977) p. 151.

CHAPTER ONE

1. H. Laski, *Communism* (Williams and Northgate, 1927) [hereafter *Communism*] p 79.
2. I am grateful to Bill Williams (author of *The Making of Manchester Jewry, 1740–1875* (Manchester University Press, 1985) for this, and for much of the information on the Laski family.
3. Laski told Holmes that his father 'worshipped Gladstone'. 17 February 1925, I, 713.

4. I am grateful to Ian Bailey for this information and that concerning Harold Laski at Manchester Grammar School.
5. Sarah Laski, *Some Impressions of a Trip to India* (J. Cornish, Manchester, 1905).
6. Summary of taped interview J28, Manchester Jewish Museum.
7. Obituary of Nathan Laski, *Manchester Guardian*, 21 October 1941.
8. For Sarah Laski's obituary, see *Manchester Guardian*, 24 February 1945. (When Nathan died, Churchill wrote to Harold: 'He was a man whose heart overflowed with human feeling and whose energies were tirelessly used for other people and large causes. I feel I have lost a friend . . .'. Quoted in Martin, *Laski*, p. 12.)
9. Stella Jacobs, summary of taped interview 128, Manchester Jewish Museum.
10. Martin, *Laski*, p. 12.
11. Laski's first book, 'The Chosen People' was never published. I am very grateful to his grandson, Andrew Mathewson, for lending it to me.
12. Information supplied by Ian Bailey.
13. Reference of 17 July 1914, File 3 AJ/33 Laski Papers, Anglo-Jewish Archives, University of Southampton.
14. Letter to Frida, 2 November 1911, FHL.
15. Letter to Frida, 9 October 1911, FHL.
16. See Chapter 2.
17. This is evident from the correspondence between the two in the University of Hull archives.
18. 'The Memoirs of Frida Laski' (unpublished MS) p. 20. I am grateful to Andrew Mathewson for lending this manuscript to me. (It is worth noting that Frida Laski was ninety-two when the memoirs were written and that she talked about her life to someone else – Sheila Roberts – who transcribed the text. The style is different from Frida's.).
19. Letter to Frida, undated (between January and June 1911) FHL.
20. Letter to Frida, undated (also between January and June 1911) FHL.
21. Letter to Frida, 9 October 1911, FHL.
22. Letter to Frida, 1 August 1910, FHL.
23. Letter to Frida, undated (probably between March and June 1911), FHL.
24. Letter to Frida, undated (also between March and June 1911), FHL.
25. 'The Chosen People', p. 71.
26. Frida Laski, 'Memoirs', p. 33.
27. Letter to Frida, 15 November 1911, FHL.
28. 'The Chosen People', p. 87 (also quoted in Eastwood, *Laski*, pp. 7–8.
29. 'The Chosen People', pp. 88–9.
30. Letter to Frida, 17 August 1945, FHL.
31. Frida to Ben Huebsch (undated, 1916?), Huebsch papers, container 16, LC.
32. 'The Chosen People', pp. 69–70.
33. Ibid., p. 56.
34. Psalm 118, verse 9. (Paton, his head teacher, noted: 'He has no fear of any amount of titles and rank'. Letter to Crammer (?), 14 July 1920, H 1973.)
35. Letter to Frida, undated 1911, FHL.
36. This was Laski's favourite phrase which he attributed to Heine and quoted throughout his life.

CHAPTER TWO

1. 'Harold J. Laski' in C. Fadiman (ed.), *I Believe: The Personal Philosophies of Twenty Three Eminent Men and Women of Our Time* (Allen and Unwin, 1940) (hereafter *I Believe*) p. 163.
2. Letter to Frida, 28 March 1910, FHL.
3. Ibid.
4. Michael Freeden, 'Eugenics and Progressive Thought: A Study in Ideological Affinity', *The Historical Journal* (hereafter 'Eugenics') 22 (3) 1979.
5. Greta Jones, *Social Darwinism and English Thought* (Harvester Press, 1980) p. 99.
6. Ibid., p. 112.
7. Freeden, 'Eugenics', p. 658.
8. Frida Laski, 'Memoirs', p. 16.
9. 'The Scope of Eugenics', *Westminster Review*, July 1910 (hereafter 'Scope of Eugenics').
10. Ibid., p. 32.
11. Ibid., p. 34.
12. Ibid., p. 34.
13. Karl Pearson, *Life and Letters of Francis Galton*, vol. III, B, pp. 606–9, quoted in Martin, *Laski*, p. 16.
14. Letters to Frida, 30 October 1911, and (undated) March/April 1912, FHL.
15. Minutes of Oxford University Fabian Society, Mss. Top Oxon d. 465, BLO.
16. Ethel M. Elderton et al., *On the Correlation of Fertility with Social Value* (Cambridge University Press, 1913).
17. H. A. L. Fisher to Laski, 13 December 1910, in Laski Corr. 1, IISH.
18. Minutes of Meetings of Warden and Tutors, 6 February 1912, Modern Archive 308, New College, Oxford.
19. Letter to Frida, 18 October 1911, FHL.
20. Minutes of Meetings of Warden and Tutors, 10 July 1912.
21. Minutes of Meetings of Warden and Tutors, 9 December 1912.
22. Letter to Frida, undated (March–June) 1911, FHL.
23. 'Scope of Eugenics', p. 34.
24. *Ulula* (Manchester Grammar School Magazine), Autumn Term 1910.
25. The Beit Prize, January 1914. (The essay does not appear to have been retained, but I am grateful to the Oxford University Archivist for tracing the title.)
26. Martin, *Laski*, p. 18.
27. Ernest Barker, *Age and Youth* (Oxford University Press, 1953) (hereafter Barker, *Age and Youth*) pp. 74–6.
28. Frida Laski, 'Memoirs', pp. 22–5.
29. *Oxford Review*, 9 November 1912.
30. *Isis*, 9 November 1912.
31. *Oxford Review*, 25 October 1913.
32. *Isis*, 25 October 1913.
33. *Isis*, 6 December 1913; *Oxford Magazine*, 30 October 1913.

34. H. W. Nevinson, *More Changes, More Chances* (Nisbet and Co., 1925) p. 35.
35. *Isis*, 25 October 1913.
36. Frida Laski, 'Memoirs', p. 31.
37. He wrote to Frida: 'I am sorry indeed that you should have such a low opinion of your husband as to imagine he would have a share in so dastardly an outrage', 8 June 1913, FHL.
38. Frida Laski, 'Memoirs', pp. 31–2. (Unfortunately, Frida Laski provided no date for the incident, and no records of it exist in the Headquarters of the Surrey Constabulary.)
39. 'The Militant Temper in Politics', Fifth Suffragette Lecture, Caxton Hall, 18 November 1932. Museum of London Suffragette Collection, Z6061 (copy in Fawcett Library, City of London Polytechnic). See also Brian Harrison, *Prudent Revolutionaries* (Clarendon Press, 1987) p. 28.
40. *Oxford Review*, 26 January and 14 February 1914.
41. Minutes of Oxford University Fabian Society, Hilary Term 1914, BLO.
42. *Oxford Review*, 7 February 1914.
43. Unpublished college examination essay on Constitutional History, kindly lent by Andrew Mathewson.
44. Letter to Frida (undated), Summer Term 1914, FHL.
45. *Oxford University Gazette*; Barker, *Age and Youth*, p. 76.
46. Martin, *Laski*, p. 25.
47. 'Royalty and Rebellion', *Daily Herald*, 23 July 1914.
48. 'The Abortive Conference, *Daily Herald*, 25 July 1914. (The editorials were unsigned but Laski's style is recognisable.)
49. Review of J. A. Hobson's *Work and Wealth*, *Daily Herald*, 29 July 1914; 'The Cost of Coal', *Daily Herald*, 30 July 1914.
50. 'The Crime of the Century', *Daily Herald*, 3 August 1914.
51. 'The Die is Cast', *Daily Herald*, 5 August 1914.
52. 'Our German Brothers', *Daily Herald*, 14 August 1914.
53. 'A Moral Equivalent for War', *Daily Herald*, 13 August 1914.
54. Ibid.
55. Laski claimed to have volunteered for enlistment in Britain in 1914, in Canada in 1915 and 1916, and for the British Army under the Anglo-American Treaties of 1917 and 1918. On each occasion he was rejected and given certificates of exemption on grounds of inadequate physique. (See his application for the Chair of Political Science at the University of London, 15 December 1925, in Laski Corr. 3, IISH.) Kingsley Martin saw British, Canadian and US certificates rejecting Laski on medical grounds from all forms of military service when writing his biography (Martin, *Laski*, p. 26). When opponents claimed that Laski went to Canada to avoid fighting they were always forced to apologise.

CHAPTER THREE

1. H. MacLennan, *McGill – The Story of a University* (Allen and Unwin, 1960) pp. 79, 81.

2. Peterson to Laski, 19 April 1915, McGill University Archives.
3. *Montreal Star*, 3 September 1934.
4. Laski to Ben Huebsch, 28 February 1915, Huebsch papers, Huebsch-Laski correspondence, LC. (Copies of the Huebsch-Laski correspondence are also held at the British Library of Political and Economic Science, LSE.)
5. Ibid.
6. Laski to Frankfurter, 23 April 1916 in Laski-Lippmann correspondence, Walter Lippmann papers, YUL.
7. Laski to George Lansbury, 25 October 1914, Lansbury Collection, vol. 7, LSE Library of Political and Economic Science.
8. Frida Laski, 'Memoirs', p. 41–2.
9. Ibid., 42–3.
10. Laski to Huebsch, 9 July 1915 LC.
11. For a useful analysis of Frankfurter's character and career, see J. P. Lash's introduction to his book, *From the Diaries of Felix Frankfurter* (W. W. Norton, New York, 1975).
12. Martin, *Laski*, p. 29.
13. Transcript of Frankfurter's contribution to 'Harold Laski – A Portrait for Radio' (recorded 15 November 1961) transmitted by the BBC 13 March 1962. (FFP container 207).
14. Frida Laski, 'Memoirs', pp. 44–5.
15. *I Believe*, p. 165.
16. Samuel Rezneck to Eastwood, 1 July 1974, HE.
17. To Holmes 15 May 1920, I, p. 263.
18. S. E. Morrison (ed.), *The Development of Harvard University Since the Inauguration of President Eliot, 1869–1929* (Harvard University Press, 1930) p. 173.
19. *Crimson*, 10 May 1920, quoted in Issaac Kramnick, 'The Professor and the Police', *Harvard Magazine*, September–October 1989 (hereafter Kramnick, 'Professor and Police').
20. Laski to Holmes, 21 January 1917, I, p. 57.
21. Pound to Laski, 13 December 1917, Pound papers MS Box 175, Folder 12, Harvard Law School.
22. Zechariah Chafee, 'Harold Laski and the *Harvard Law Review*', *Harvard Law Review*, 63, June 1950.
23. Frankfurter to Laski, 10 December 1918, H 1973; Laski's application for Chair of Political Science, Laski papers, Corr. 3 IISH.
24. *I Believe*, p. 178.
25. (Undated) May 1919, Lippmann papers, YUL.
26. *New Yorker*, 16 May 1953.
27. Quoted in J. Leonard Bates, *The United States 1898–1928* (McGraw-Hill, 1976) p. 94. (Laski compiled and published Holmes's legal papers in 1920, wrote articles about him, and constantly quoted him.)
28. *I Believe*, p. 165.
29. Hirst, *Pluralist Theory*.
30. Martin, *Laski*, pp. 33–4, 72; A. W. Wright, *G. D. H. Cole and Socialist Democracy* (Clarendon Press, 1979) pp. 14–15.
31. Deane, *Laski*, Part I (e.g. pp. 29 and 43); W. J. Elliott, *The Pragmatic*

Revolt in Politics (Macmillan, New York, 1928) (hereafter, Elliott, *Pragmatic Revolt*), Ch 5. (For thorough analyses of Laski's pluralism, from contrasting viewpoints, see Zylstra, *From Pluralism* and Palazzola, *La Libertà*.)

32. He and Frida translated Léon Duguit's *Les transformations de droit public* as *Law in the Modern State* (B. Huebsch, New York, 1919).
33. For two brief discussions of such political ideas, with substantial bibliographies, see R. Pearson and G. Williams, *Political Thought and Public Policy in the Nineteenth Century* (Longman, 1984) and R. Barker, *Political Ideas in Modern Britain* (Methuen, 1978). E. Barker, *Political Thought in England* (Williams and Northgate, 1915) (hereafter, Barker, *Political Thought*) remains very useful.
34. See Nicholls, *Pluralist State.*
35. H. A. L. Fisher (ed.), *The Collected Papers of Frederic William Maitland* (Cambridge University Press, 1911).
36. Laski to Russell, 29 August 1919 in Bertrand Russell papers, McMaster University (hereafter Russell papers), also quoted in *The Autobiography of Bertrand Russell*, vol. 2 (Allen and Unwin, 1968) p. 112.
37. Ch. 2 in *Studies in the Problem of Sovereignty* (Yale University Press, 1917) (hereafter *Problem*)
38. 'The Personality of Associations', *Harvard Law Review*, XXIX (1916), and 'The Basis of Vicarious Liability', *The Yale Law Journal* December 1916, both reprinted in *The Foundations of Sovereignty* (Allen and Unwin, 1922) (hereafter *Foundations*).
39. Barker, *Political Thought*, p. 180.
40. Ibid., pp. 178, 245.
41. E. Barker, 'The Discredited State', *Political Quarterly*, 5, February 1915 (originally read on 31 May 1914).
42. Barker, *Political Thought*, p. 60.
43. Letter to Russell, 29 August 1919, Russell papers.
44. See, for example, 'The Personality of the State', *The Nation*, (New York) (hereafter 'Personality of the State') 22 July 1915.
45. Letter to Lansbury, 24 May 1915, Lansbury papers, LSE.
46. *Problem* p. 15.
47. Elliott, *Pragmatic Revolt*, p. 150.
48. To Russell, 29 August 1919, Russell papers.
49. *I Believe*, p. 165,
50. To Huebsch, 28 February 1915, LC.
51. To Huebsch, 11 June 1915, LC.
52. To Huebsch, 9 and 22 October 1915, LC.
53. 7 November 1916, I pp. 34–5.
54. To Holmes, 4 June 1917, I, p. 89.
55. 3 May 1917, FFP.
56. Information from Ian Bailey.
57. *Authority in the Modern State* (Oxford University Press, 1919) (hereafter *Authority*), Preface, written on 21 April 1918.
58. To Huebsch, 15 August 1915, LC.
59. *Problem*, pp. 273–4.
60. 'Personality of the State'

61. 'The Apotheosis of the State', *New Republic*, vii, 22 July 1916.
62. 'Personality of the State'.
63. Ibid.
64. Deane, *Laski*, pp. 15–16; Pollock to Holmes, 20 September 1919 in Mark de Wolfe Howe (ed.) *The Pollock-Holmes Letters* (Cambridge University Press, 1942) (hereafter *Pollock-Holmes Letters*) vol. 2, pp. 25–6.
65. For example, *Authority*, p. 106.
66. Elliott, *Pragmatic Revolt*, pp. 148–9.
67. 'Personality of the State'.
68. Elliott, *Pragmatic Revolt*, p. 154.
69. 13 September 1916, I, p. 19.
70. To Frankfurter, 8 May 1917, FFP.
71. 5 April 1917, I, p. 76.
72. Reprinted in *Foundations* (hereafter 'Administrative Areas', with page numbers as in *Foundations*).
73. 'Administrative Areas', p. 86.
74. Ibid., p. 77.
75. *Authority* p. 38.
76. 'Administrative Areas', p. 76.
77. Ibid., p. 70.
78. Ibid., p. 73.
79.. Ibid., p. 85.
80. Ibid., p. 84.
81. Ibid., p. 80.
82. *Authority*, pp. 88–9, 92–3.
83. Ibid.
84. 'Administrative Areas', pp. 86–8.
85. *Authority*, p. 82.
86. Ibid., p. 38.
87. 'Administrative Areas', p. 88.
88. *Authority*, p. 38.
89. Ibid., pp. 45–7.
90. Ibid., p. 121.
91. Ibid., p. 61 and 'Administrative Areas', p. 88.
92. *Authority*, p. 95.
93. 'Administrative Areas', p. 82.
94. Ibid., p. 76.
95. Ibid., p. 99.
96. *Authority*, p. 96.
97. Ibid., p. 88.
98. 20 May 1919, I, pp. 205–6.
99. *The Nation* (New York), 5 July 1919.
100. *The Nation* (London), 16 August 1919.
101. 'The Higher Learning in America' *New Republic*, xvii, 11 January 1919.
102. Holmes to Pollock, 5 April 1919 in *Pollock-Holmes Letters*, II, p. 8.
103. The following is based largely on Martin, *Laski*, pp. 35–43 and Kramnick, 'Professor and Police'.
104. To Lippmann, 10 September 1919, Lippmann papers, YUL.
105. To Lippmann, 23 September 1919, Lippmann papers, YUL.

106. Kramnick, 'Professor and Police', p. 44.
107. Letter of 9 October 1919, reprinted in *Harvard Alumni Bulletin*, xxii, 23 October 1919.
108. Martin, *Laski*, p. 38.
109. Kramnick, 'Professor and Police', p. 44.
110. 22 October 1919, I, p. 218.
111. *The American Democracy* (Allen and Unwin, 1949) p. 357.
112. Kramnick, 'Professor and Police', p. 44; Frida Laski, 'Memoirs', p. 49.
113. 5 January 1920, Russell papers.
114. To Russell, 4 December 1919, Russell papers.
115. For some examples, see Martin, *Laski*, p. 40.
116. 29 August 1919, Russell papers.
117. Martin, *Laski*, p. 43.
118. Wallas to Laski, 3 December 1919, Laski Corr. 2, IISH.
119. To Holmes, 15 February 1920, I, p. 240; to Russell, 18 February 1920.
120. 28 March 1920, I, p. 255.
121. 31 March 1921, I, p. 256.

CHAPTER FOUR

1. To Holmes, 18 July 1920, I, p. 271.
2. 14 July 1920, to Crammer (?), H 1973.
3. To Holmes, 8 September 1920, I, p. 278.
4. Frida Laski, 'Memoirs', p. 52.
5. Ibid.
6. To Holmes, 1 November 1920, I, p. 290.
7. Undated letter to Frida, mid 1920s, FHL.
8. Frida Laski, 'Memoirs', pp. 52–3.
9. To Holmes, 21 May 1927, I, p. 944.
10. 6 October 1915, in Neville Laski papers, Manchester Central Library archives.
11. Taped interview J144, Manchester Jewish Museum.
12. Frida Laski, 'Memoirs', p. 53.
13. To Holmes, 4 October 1925, I, p. 791.
14. To Holmes, 26 September 1921, I, p. 370.
15. Elliott, *Pragmatic Revolt*, p. 176.
16. Laski Corr. 3, IISH. (The other references, also at the IISH, were submitted by Ernest Barker, H. A. L. Fisher, Lord Haldane, Joseph Redlich, and Roscoe Pound.)
17. This trait was even evident in his academic work. For example, when writing about Adam Smith, he emphasised the happiness he must have felt as a result of 'cherished friendships' with the 'most illustrious' of his age. *Political Thought in England from Locke to Bentham* (Williams, 1920) (hereafter, *Political Thought*) pp. 292–3.
18. To Holmes, 2 April 1920, I, p. 257.
19. Patricia Pugh, *Educate, Agitate, Organize – 100 Years of Fabian Socialism* (Methuen, 1984) (hereafter Pugh, *Educate*) p. 152.

20. To Holmes, 20 January 1924, (I, p. 581), 12 February 1924 (I, p. 591); to Frankfurter, 22 December 1923, FFP.
21. Pugh, *Educate*, p. 52.
22. To Holmes, 12 January 1921 (I, p. 305), 11 February 1921 (I, pp. 312–13), 26 June 1921 (I, pp. 343–4), 15 May 1922 (I, pp. 427–8); to Herbert Croly, 19 March 1922 in Lippmann papers, YUL; to Frankfurter, 27 May 1922, FFP; to Frida, undated 1921, FHL.
23. To Holmes, 30 April 1921 (I, pp. 332–3), 12 May 1921 (I, pp. 336–7), 8 December 1921 (I, pp. 386–7) 24 February 1924 (I, p. 595).
24. To Holmes, 6 June 1923, I, p. 506.
25. To Holmes, 4 October 1924 (I, p. 665), 28 April 1925, I, p. 736.
26. For example, Sankey to Laski, 23 July 1924, H 1973.
27. To Laski, 12 October 1919, Laski Corr. 1, IISH.
28. Wallas to Laski, 15 April 1920, IISH Corr. 2.
29. Although he was also sometimes sceptical about whether adult education would be effective sufficiently rapidly. (See Laski to Holmes, 22 December 1919, I, p. 228.)
30. Haldane to Laski, 7 April 1920, H 1973.
31. 'Mr George and the Constitution', IV, *The Nation* (London) 20 November 1920.
32. To Lippmann, 30 September 1920, Lippmann papers, YUL.
33. To Arthur Gleason, 21 October 1921, Gleason papers, LC.
24. To Holmes, 30 April 1921, I, p. 332.
35. To Holmes, 19 April 1924, I, p. 611.
36. Ibid.
37. 'British Labor and Direct Action', *The Nation* (New York) 11 September 1920.
38. To Holmes, 1 April 1921, I, p. 324, 30 April 1921, I, p. 332.
39. To Holmes, 18 July 1920, I, p. 271.
40. To Lippmann, 3 August 1920, Lippmann papers, YUL.
41. To Lippmann, 6 August 1919, Lippmann papers, YUL.
42. To Lippmann, 3 August 1920, Lippmann papers, YUL.
43. Ibid.
44. *Karl Marx: An Essay* (Fabian Society/Allen and Unwin, 1922) (hereafter, *Karl Marx*) p. 43; 'Lenin and Mussolini' *Foreign Affairs*, II (September 1923), p. 44.
45. To Holmes, 2 April 1920, I, p. 257.
46. Review of A. Gleason, *What the Workers Want*, New Republic, XXIII, 9 June 1920.
47. R. B. H. (First Viscount) Haldane, *The Problem of Nationalization* (Allen and Unwin/Labour Publishing, 1921) (Introduction by R. H. Tawney and Laski) (hereafter *Problem of Nationalization*); see also 'Parliament and Revolution', *New Republic*, XXII, 19 May 1920.
48. For an example of anxiety, see 'The Alternative to Revolution in England', *The Nation* (New York) 9 February 1921.
49. To Holmes, 3 November 1924, I, p. 669.
50. To Lippmann, 25 November 1924, Lippmann papers, YUL.
51. To Frankfurter, 22 October 1921, FFP.
52. To Holmes, 16 June 1923, I, pp. 508–9.

53. To Holmes, 13 October 1923, I, p. 550.
54. For example, to Lippmann, 19 December 1920, Lippmann papers, YUL.
55. To Holmes, 13 October 1923, I, p. 551.
56. To Holmes, 12 February 1924, I, p. 592.
57. The book also dealt with the nation state and international institutions. This will be discussed in Chapter 8.
58. *A Grammar of Politics* (Allen and Unwin, 1925) (hereafter, *Grammar*) p. 504. (All page number references are from the edition published in 1938).
59. Ibid., p. 281.
60. Ibid., pp. 170–2.
61. Ibid., p. 246.
62. Ibid., p. 263.
63. Ibid., p. 268.
64. Ibid.
65. Ibid., pp. 272–3.
66. Ibid., p. 91.
67. Ibid., p. 106.
68. Ibid., p. 111.
69. Ibid., p. 114.
70. Ibid., p. 116.
71. Ibid., p. 130.
72. Ibid., p. 142.
73. Ibid., p. 143.
74. Ibid., pp. 154–61.
75. Ibid., p. 188.
76. Ibid., pp. 200–1.
77. Ibid., p. 436.
78. Ibid., pp. 489–504.
79. Ibid., p. 453.
80. Ibid., p. 462.
81. Ibid., pp. 534–5.
82. Ibid., pp. 209, 534–5.
83. Ibid., pp. 432, 565.
84. Ibid., p. 91.
85. Ibid., p. 217.
86. Ibid., p. 25.
87. *I Believe*, p. 168.
88. To Laski, 13 July 1925, H 1973.
89. To Holmes, 1 August 1925, I, pp. 768–9. However, the book was well regarded by many Liberals. See M. Freeden, *Liberalism Divided* (Clarendon Press, 1986) p. 311.
90. Grammar, p. 507.
91. Ibid., pp. 507–8.
92. Holmes to Laski, 1 August 1925, I, p. 769.

CHAPTER FIVE

1. Two useful sources on the General Strike, with extensive bibliographies, are Margaret Morris, *The General Strike* (Penguin, 1976) (hereafter Morris, *General Strike*) and Christopher Farman, *May 1926 – The General Strike* (Panther Books, 1974) (hereafter Farman, *General Strike*).
2. Quoted in Farman, *General Strike*, p. 43.
3. To Holmes, 30 April 1921, I, p. 332, 29 March 1923, I, p. 489), 26 September 1924, I, p. 661.
4. To Frankfurter, 24 September 1925.
5. Quoted in Farman, *General Strike*, p. 55.
6. Ibid., p. 120.
7. To Sankey, 23 October 1925, Sankey papers c505/153, BLO. See also Laski's correspondence with Ramsay MacDonald, 5, 26, and 30 November 1925, 1170/2 in MacDonald papers, PRO 30/69 2.
8. To Holmes, 21 November 1925, I, p. 802.
9. To Frankfurter, 17 December 1925, FFP.
10. 'Mr Baldwin's First Year of Office', *New Republic*, 16 December 1925.
11. To Sankey, 1 March 1926, Sankey papers c505/179 BLO.
12. Letter of 1 May 1926 published in *The Nation*, 26 May 1926.
13. Ibid.
14. To Holmes, 2 May 1926, I, pp. 838–9.
15. 'The British General Strike', *The Nation*, 16 June 1926.
16. In 'The Mining Crisis and the General Strike', Harvester microfilm, Box 9, reel 11, TUC archives.
17. T. Jones (ed. K. Middlemas), *Whitehall Diary*, vol. 2 (Oxford University Press, 1971) (hereafter Jones, *Whitehall Diary*) p. 43.
18. Ibid.
19. Morris, *General Strike*, p. 263.
20. To Holmes, 23 May 1926, II, p. 839. (For details of the concessions, see Farman, *General Strike*, p. 276).
21. Cab 23/52, 8 May 1926, quoted in Morris, *General Strike*, p. 264.
22. Ibid.
23. Jones, *Whitehall Diary*, 13 May 1926, p. 55.
24. 'The British General Strike', *The Nation*, published 16 June 1926.
25. 24 May 1926, quoted in Martin, *Laski*, p. 66. The unfavourable references to Churchill in Laski's letter to Holmes of 23 May 1926 were omitted from the published version. The original is in the Holmes papers Ms Box 4, Folder 1, Harvard Law Library (hereafter cited as unpublished version).
26. 'The Trade Unions Survey the General Strike', *New Republic*, 2 March 1927. K. Middlemas and J. Barnes endorse this interpretation in *Baldwin* (Weidenfeld, 1969) p. 420.
27. To Holmes, 23 May 1926, II, p. 840.
28. See, for example, 'The General Strike and the Constitution', *Labour Magazine*, 5 (3) July 1926.
29. To Frankfurter, 24 May 1926, FFP.
30. To Holmes, 2 May 1926, II, p. 838.

31. *Nation*, 16 June 1926.
32. *New Republic*, 2 March 1927; also 'Public Opinion and the National Strike', *Labour Magazine*, 5 (9) January 1927.
33. To Holmes, 23 May 1936, unpublished version.
34. To Frankfurter, 24 May 1926, quoted in Martin, *Laski*, p. 66.
35. Jones, *Whitehall Diary*, 13 May 1926, pp. 55–6.
36. For example, with E. J. P. Benn, *The Trade Disputes and Trade Unions Bill* (P. S. King and Son, 1927).
37. To Holmes, 23 April 1927, I, p. 935; see also Fabian Executive Committee minutes, 13 May 1926, cited in Pugh, *Educate*, pp. 154–5.
38. To Holmes 29 December 1926, II, p. 908, 7 May 1927, II, p. 940.
39. 'Present Tendencies in British Policies', *New Republic*, 13 July 1927.
40. *Karl Marx*, p. 40.
41. Ibid., p. 42.
42. Ibid.
43. Ibid.
44. To Holmes, 7 August 1921, I, p. 358.
45. To Holmes, 14 August 1921, I, p. 361.
45. To Holmes, 26 September 1921, I, p. 370.
47. *Karl Marx*, pp. 25, 44.
48. 'Lenin and Mussolini', *Foreign Affairs*, II, September 1923.
49. To Holmes, 23 May 1926, unpublished version.
50. To Frankfurter, 26 August 1926, FFP.
51. *Communism*, p. 54.
52. Ibid., p. 84.
53. Ibid., p. 240.
54. 'The Value and Defects of the Marxist Philosophy', *Current History*, October 1928, p. 23.
55. Ibid., p. 25.
56. Ibid., pp. 25–6.
57. Ibid., pp. 26–7.
58. Ibid., pp. 27–8.
59. Ibid., p. 29.
60. Ibid.
61. Ibid.
62. Ibid., p. 28.
63. Ibid.
64. Ibid., p. 29.
65. To Holmes, 24 September 1927, II, p. 981; see also Laski-MacDonald correspondence 12 and 13 September in PRO 30/69 2 1172.
66. 'The British Parties in Conference', *New Republic*, 9 November 1927.
67. Ibid.
68. Ibid.
69. To Laski, 21 November 1927, PRO 30/69 2 1172 (and Laski papers H. 1973).
70. To Laski, 23 November 1927, PRO 30/69 2 1172.
71. To Frankfurter, 18 August 1928, FFP.
72. Ibid.
73. 'England in 1929', *Yale Review*, 18 (3) March 1929.

74. Ibid.
75. To Frida, 17 April 1929, FHL; see also Laski-MacDonald correspondence, 16, 17 and 18 April 1929, PRO 30/69 2 1714/124–7.

CHAPTER SIX

1. *Grammar*, p. 598.
2. Ibid., p. 596.
3. Ibid., pp. 596, 598.
4. To Holmes, 26 September 1923, I, p. 543.
5. Ibid., 16 November 1923, I, p. 562. (W. E. Burghardt DuBois was the founder of the Pan-African Congress.)
6. Letter of 8 June 1929, PRO 30/69 2, file 1439.
7. For signs of Sankey's respect, see his letters to Laski in Sankey papers Ms Eng Hist c1070, BLO.
8. Dennis Dean, 'The Contrasting Attitudes of the Conservative and Labour Parties to Problems of Empire, 1922–1936', unpublished PhD, University of London, 1974, (hereafter Dean, 'Contrasting Attitudes') ch. 11.
9. *Grammar*, p. 598.
10. N. and J. MacKenzie (ed.) *The Diary of Beatrice Webb*, vol. 4 (Virago/ LSE, 1985) (hereafter Webb, *Diary*) 13 August 1929, p. 187.
11. Ibid., 20 October 1929, p. 198.
12. P. S. Gupta, *Imperialism and the British Labour Movement, 1914–64* (Macmillan, 1975) (hereafter Gupta, *Imperialism*) pp. 182–3.
13. Ibid.
14. To Holmes, 23 December 1929, II, p. 1210.
15. To Holmes, 18 January 1930, II, p. 1217.
16. To Frankfurter, 10 February 1930, FFP.
17. To Holmes, 12 April 1930, II, p. 1240.
18. Gupta, *Imperialism*, p. 185; Dean, 'Contrasting Attitudes', p. 328.
19. Quoted in Gupta, *Imperialism*, pp. 186–7.
20. Ibid., p. 196.
21. 'The Future of the Socialist International', undated (February 1946?) in Julius Braunthal Papers, no. 378, IISH.
22. For a detailed discussion of the complexities, see R. J. Moore, *The Crisis of Indian Unity, 1917–1940* (Clarendon Press, 1974)
23. Quoted in Denis Judd, *Lord Reading* (Weidenfeld, 1982) (hereafter Judd, *Reading*) p. 200.
24. To Huebsch, 19 September 1915, LC.
25. To Holmes, 25 May 1924, I, p. 619.
26. To Frankfurter, quoted in Martin, *Laski*, p. 64.
27. To Holmes, 1 July 1924, I, p. 628.
28. To Frankfurter, 30 June 1924, quoted in Martin, *Laski*, p. 64.
29. 'England in 1929', *Yale Review*, 18 (3) March 1929, p. 431.
30. Dean, 'Contrasting Attitudes', ch. 8.
31. To Holmes, 15 June 1930, II, p. 1261.
32. Ibid., 28 June 1930, p. 1264.

33. Ibid.
34. Judd, *Reading*, pp. 242–4,
35. Sankey to Laski, 17 January 1931, Laski papers, H 1973.
36. To Holmes, 27 December 1930, II, p. 1301, 10 January 1931, II, p. 1303.
37. To Frida, 5 March 1931, FHL. (Laski always wrote 'Gandhi' as 'Ghandi', but I have used the conventional spelling.)
38. To Holmes, 17 September 1931, II, p. 1330.
39. Paper of 19 October 1931, Sankey MSS, e 285, cited in Dean, 'Contrasting Attitudes', p. 218.
40. To Holmes, 27 September 1931, II, p. 1332.
41. To Holmes, 30 October, II, pp. 135–6, 14 November, II, pp. 1337–8, 7 December, II, pp. 1348–9; to Frankfurter, 27 September, 3 October, 22 December 1931, FFP. See also Leonard Woolf's account of a meeting between Gandhi and Labour intellectuals, in which Laski played a key role, quoted in Eastwood, *Laski*, p. 95.
42. To Holmes, 7 December 1931, II, p. 1349.
43. To Holmes, 30 October 1931, II, p. 1336.
44. To Holmes, 27 September 1931, p. 1332.
45. To Frida, 6 January 1932, FHL.
46. 'India at the Crossroads', *Yale Review*, 21 (3) March 1932, p. 502.
47. Gupta, *Imperialism*, p. 255.
48. 'The India Report', *The Nation*, 2 January 1935.
49. Quoted in Christopher Sykes, *Cross Roads to Israel: Palestine from Balfour to Bevin* (Nel Mentor, 1967) (hereafter Sykes, *Cross Roads*) p. 11. (This book has been a major source for much of the general background on the Palestine conflict summarised here.)
50. Ibid., p. 119.
51. Dennis Dean, 'The Search for a Balance: The Attitude of the Conservative and Labour Parties to the Palestine Mandate 1922–31' (unpublished article) pp. 8–10.
52. J. Gorny, *The British Labour Movement and Zionism, 1917–1948* (Frank Cass, 1983) (hereafter Gorny, *Labour and Zionism*) pp. 62–5.
53. See, for example, Sir John Chancellor to R. D. Chancellor, 21 February 1930, Chancellor Papers, Rhodes House, quoted in Dean, 'Contrasting Attitudes', p. 387.
54. Gorny, *Labour and Zionism*, pp. 56, 59–60, 75–6.
55. Webb, *Diary*, vol. 4, 2 September 1929, pp. 190–1.
56. Sykes, *Cross Roads*, pp. 122–3.
57. But Snell's views were not wholly pro-Zionist. See Gorny, *Labour and Zionism*, p. 81.
58. Letter to Frida, 28 March 1910, FHL; 'The Chosen People'. For an interesting discussion of Laski's attitudes, see also Y. Gorny, 'The Jewishness and Zionism of Harold Laski', *Midstream*, November 1977.
59. To Holmes, 27 January 1925, I, p. 703.
60. Lash, *Frankfurter*, pp. 25–6.
61. Letter to Laski, 31 May 1929; see also Frankfurter to Laski, 3 and 11 June 1929, FFP.
62. Laski to Frankfurter, 15 June 1929, FFP; to Holmes 4 June 1929, II, p. 1154; 11 June, II, p. 1156; 22 July, II, p. 1166; 2 August, II, p. 1170.

63. Frankfurter to Laski, 11 October 1929, FFP.
64. Letter to Laski, 27 May 1930, FFP.
65. Laski to Frankfurter, 7 June 1930, FFP.
66. To Frankfurter, 13 June 1930, FFP; see also Laski to Holmes, 15 June 1930, II, p. 1261. (Laski's judgment of MacDonald was probably correct. See Gorny, *Labour and Zionism*, p. 79.)
67. Quoted in Sykes, *Cross Roads*, p. 126.
68. Laski to Frankfurter, 26 October 1930, FFP.
69. Ibid.
70. Ibid.
71. Ibid.
72. Passfield to MacDonald, 3 November 1930, PRO PREM 1, 103 (Palestine).
73. Passfield to Laski, 1 November 1930, Laski Corr. 2, IISH.
74. 3 November 1930, PREM 1, 103.
75. Ibid.
76. Dean, 'Search for Balance', p. 23, quotes a letter by MacDonald to Miss L. Wald of 29 October in PRO 30/69, I.
77. Gorny, *Labour and Zionism*, pp. 99–100. The sub-committee was formed the same day: Cab 23/66 6 November 1930.
78. To Holmes, 22 November 1930, II, p. 1296.
79. To Frankfurter, 19 January 1931, FFP.
80. Committee on Palestine: Note by Henderson, 30 January 1931, CP 25 (31).
81. Text in PREM 1 103.
82. 10 February 1951 in Laski Corr. 3, IISH.
83. To Holmes, 30 November 1930, I, p. 1299.
84. To Holmes, 27 December 1930, II, p. 1301, and 10 January 1931, II, pp. 1302–3.
85. To Frankfurter, 19 January 1931, FFP.
86. To Frida, 2 June 1931, FHL.
87. To Holmes, 27 December 1930, I, p. 1302.
88. To Frankfurter, 26 October 1930, FFP.
89. To Holmes, 27 December 1930, I, p. 1302.
90. Webb, *Diary*, vol. 4, 26 October and 30 October 1930, pp. 229–31.
91. To Frankfurter, 4 January 1931, FFP.
92. To Holmes, 14 December 1924, I, pp. 686–7.
93. 'India at the Crossroads', *Yale Review*, 21 (3) March 1932, p. 500.

CHAPTER SEVEN

1. Deane, *Laski*, p. 140. (Deane acknowledged that his pessimism became more pronounced from 1930.)
2. Ibid., p. 218.
3. For a sustained analysis of Labour's economic policy, see Robert Skidelsky, *Politicians and the Slump – The Labour Government of 1929–31*, (Macmillan, 1967).

4. 'Aristocracy still Ruling in England', *Current History*, July 1930.
5. Ibid., p. 668.
6. Ibid., p. 670.
7. Ibid., p. 667.
8. Ibid., p. 673.
9. 'The Prospects of Constitutional Government', *Political Quarterly*, I, July-September 1930, pp. 323–4.
10. 'Communism as a World Force', *International Affairs*, January 1931, pp. 24–5 (hereafter 'Communism as a World Force').
11. Deane, *Laski*, pp. 134–5.
12. 'Communism as a World Force', p. 29.
13. *The Problem of a Second Chamber* (Fabian Society, 1925); *The Position of Parties and the Right of Dissolution* (Fabian Society, 1924).
14. 'The Evolution of the Parliamentary System', in H. J. Laski et al., *The Development of the Representative System in Our Times* (Librairie Payot, 1928).
15. 'Prospects of Constitutional Government', p. 314.
16. *Report of the Committee on Ministerial Powers* (Cmd 4060 HMSO, April 1932) (hereafter *Ministerial Powers*).
17. To Holmes, 3 November 1929, II, p. 1194.
18. To Holmes, 17 November 1929, II, p. 1199.
19. Laski to Holmes, 8 May 1932, II, p.1382. (The historical, theoretical and comparative analysis of the development of law-making and governmental power in the report show the influence of Laski.)
20. *Ministerial Powers*, p. 23.
21. Ibid., Annex VI, p. 137.
22. Ibid., p. 138.
23. See, for example, 'Judicial Review of Social Policy', *Harvard Law Review*, May 1926 (reproduced in *Studies in Law and Politics*).
24. *Ministerial Powers*, Annex V, p. 136.
25. Ibid., p. 112.
26. Letters to Frida: for example, 22 March and 12 April 1931, FHL.
27. To Frida, 1, 25 and 29 March 1931, FHL.
28. To Frida, 11 June 1931, FHL.
29. To Frida, 12 March and 12 April 1931 FHL.
30. To Frankfurter, 6 September 1931, FFP.
31. Ibid. (Also quoted with the wrong date in Martin, *Laski*, pp. 80–1).
32. Ibid.
33. 'Some Implications of the Crisis', *Political Quarterly*, II, October-December 1931, p. 467 (hereafter 'Some Implications').
34. Ibid.
35. For example, Neil Wood, *Communism and British Intellectuals* (Gollancz, 1959) pp. 46–7; A. J. P. Taylor, *English History, 1914–45* (Oxford University Press, 1965), p. 348.
36. 'Some Implications', p. 468.
37. Ibid.
38. *Democracy in Crisis* (Allen and Unwin, 1933) p. 157 (hereafter *Democracy*).
39. Ibid, p. 266.

40. *The Crisis and the Constitution*, pp. 51–2 (hereafter *Crisis, 1931*).
41. Ibid., p. 55.
42. Ibid., p. 54.
43. 'Account of Interview with Sir Clive Wigram', 15 November 1931 (unpublished, kindly lent by Andrew Mathewson). He made detailed proposals for controlling the monarchy in *The Labour Party and the Constitution*, (Socialist League, 1933).
44. To Frankfurter, 11 February and 17 April 1932, FFP.
45. To Frida, 19, 22 and 25 March 1931, FHL.
46. To Frida, 3 June 1931, FHL.
47. To Frida, 12 March and 30 April 1931, FHL.
48. To Holmes, 9 October 1931, II, p. 1409.
49. Quoted in Martin, *Laski* p. 85.
50. *Democracy*, pp. 32–3.
51. Ibid., pp. 84–5.
52. Ibid., p. 87.
53. Ibid., p. 263.
54. *Crisis, 1931*, p. 56.
55. To Frankfurter, 3 April 1927, FFP.
56. 'Marxism after Fifty Years', *Current History*, March 1933 (hereafter 'Marxism after Fifty Years').
57. 'The Position and Prospects of Communism', *Foreign Affairs*, October 1932 (hereafter 'Position and Prospects of Communism').
58. For a brief, but unsympathetic, analysis of the Socialist League, see Ben Pimlott, *Labour and the Left in the 1930s* (Cambridge University Press, 1977), ch. 5.
59. Ibid. See also S. Cripps et al., *Problems of a Socialist Government*, (Socialist League, 1933).
60. This reported in 1934 and Laski submitted an addendum advocating a greater willingness to learn from other countries, especially the USA, in legal education. See *Report of the Legal Education Committee* (Cmd 4663, HMSO July 1934).
61. *Democracy*, Preface.
62. Ibid., p. 266.
63. For a detailed critique, see R. Bassett, *Nineteen Thirty One: Political Crisis* (Macmillan, 1958) pp. 361–3, 393. (At the end of his life, Laski acknowledged that other authorities had not accepted his view of the monarch's role. *Reflections on the Constitution*, p. 61.)
64. For example in 'Some Implications' and 'Position and Prospects of Communism'.

CHAPTER EIGHT

1. 'The Elite in a Democratic Society', *Harpers Magazine*, September 1933, p. 464.
2. Ibid.
3. *Faith, Reason and Civilization* (Gollancz, 1944) (hereafter *Faith*), p. 133.

4. Ibid., p. 139.
5. To Holmes, 9 August 1930, II, p..1276.
6. To Holmes, 29 May 1932, II, p. 1389.
7. Information from Mrs Nancy Gilbert, a friend of Diana's.
8. To Holmes, 7 and 21 May, 13 June, 8 July, 9 September 1933 (II, pp. 1437, 1441–2, 1444, 1451–2); to Frankfurter 12 May, 13 August 1933, FFP; Alexander Sachs to Laski 7 November 1938 in Sachs papers, FDR. See also A. M. Sperber, *Murrow – His Life and Times*, (Freundlich, 1986) pp. 51, 70.
9. To Frankfurter, 13 August 1933, FFP.
10. To Frankfurter, 23 December 1933, FFP.
11. To Holmes, 10 October 1933, II, p. 1455.
12. See Chapter 12.
13. *Report of First Annual Conference of the Socialist League*, 3–5 June 1933, (Socialist League, 1933) p. 1.
14. For a full discussion and references, see Michael Newman, 'Democracy versus Dictatorship', *History Workshop Journal*, 5, Spring 1978.
15. Lord Citrine, *Men and Work* (Hutchinson, 1964) pp. 294–300.
16. *The State in Theory and Practice* (Allen and Unwin, 1935) (hereafter *State*), pp. 303–5.
17. 'A London Letter', *The Nation*, 6 June 1934.
18. *State*, p. 130.
19. Ibid., p. 143.
20. 'A London Letter'.
21. *State*, pp. 144–8.
22. Ibid., p. 158.
23. Ibid., pp. 152–3.
24. Ibid., pp. 193–5.
25. Ibid., pp. 105, 158–9.
26. In the Preface to *State* he thus described it as a sequel and philosophical elaboration of *Democracy in Crisis*, which had been completed before the advent of Nazism.
27. *State*, pp. 109, 120–1, 135, 158–9.
28. 'The Fabian Way', *Current History*, October 1934.
29. Greenleaf, 'Laski and British Socialism', p. 587.
30. *Grammar*, ch. 11, 'International Organisation'.
31. Ibid.; see also 'Law and the State', *Economica*, November 1929, reproduced in *Studies in Law and Politics* .
32. 'The Theory of an International Society' in H. Laski, A. E. Zimmern et al., *Problems of Peace* (Allen and Unwin, 1932).
33. 'Nationalism and the Future of Civilization' in *The Danger of Being a Gentleman* (Allen and Unwin, 1939) (hereafter *Danger/Gentleman*), p. 190.
34. Ibid., p. 211.
35. 'Position and Prospects of Communism', pp. 94–5.
36. 'The Economic Foundations of the Peace' in L. Woolf (ed.), *The Intelligent Man's Way to Prevent War* (Gollancz, 1933).
37. Ibid., p. 514.
38. Ibid., pp. 539–41.

39. Ibid., p. 544.
40. Ibid., p. 546.
41. *State*, pp. 254–5.
42. To Leonard Woolf, 8 March 1934, in Noel-Baker papers, 2/18 Churchill College, Cambridge, quoted in A. J. Williams, *Labour and Russia* (Manchester University Press, 1989) p. 233.
43. Laski-Emma Goldman correspondence December 1924 and January 1925 in Emma Goldman papers xix–2, IISH.
44. 'Position and Prospects of Communism', p. 95.
45. 'A Leningrad Letter', *The Nation* (hereafter 'Letter I') 18 July 1934 (written on 20 June).
46. Ibid.
47. 'A Leningrad Letter: II', *The Nation* (hereafter 'Letter II') 25 July 1934 (written on 25 June).
48. 'Letter I'.
49. 'Letter II'.
50. Webb, *Diary*, vol. 4, 13 July 1934, p. 337.
51. 'Letter I'.
52. 'On the Study of Politics', 22 October 1926, in *Danger/Gentleman*, p. 44.
53. Jose Harris, *William Beveridge: A Biography*, (Clarendon Press, 1977) p. 292 (hereafter Harris, *Beveridge*).
54. Ibid., pp. 293–4.
55. See, for example, 'Foundations, Universities and Research' in *Harpers Magazine*, August 1929, reproduced in *The Dangers of Obedience* (Harper and Bros., 1930) (hereafter *Dangers/Obedience*).
56. Ibid.; see also 'The Academic Mind', *Harpers Magazine*, April 1929 (Also in *Dangers/Obedience*).
57. Harris, *Beveridge*, ch. 12.
58. Ibid., p. 289.
59. Ibid., p. 295.
60. Ibid.
61. Ibid., p. 300, and Martin, *Laski*, p. 95.
62. Harris, *Beveridge*, p. 301.
63. Martin, *Laski*, p. 96.
64. To Laski, 20 April 1934 in Laski Corr. 2, IISH.
65. Editorial, *Daily Telegraph*, 6 July 1934.
66. Letter in *Daily Telegraph*, 10 July 1934.
67. *Daily Telegraph*, 12 July 1934.
68. Letter of 13 July in *Manchester Guardian, Times, Daily Telegraph* .
69. 'Private Wire', *Manchester Guardian*, 13 July 1934.
70. Letter from Sir E. Graham-Little, *Daily Telegraph*, 14 July 1934.
71. Quoted by Robert McKenzie in Abse, *My LSE*, p. 99.
72. Letter to Beveridge, 25 July 1934, quoted in Harris, *Beveridge*, p. 302.
73. Letter to Frank Hardie, 24 July 1934, in Frank Hardie papers, Mss Eng Lett. d458, no. 53, BLO.
74. To Frankfurter, 29 September 1934, FFP.
75. To Frankfurter, 5 August 1934, FFP.
76. To Frankfurter, 8 August 1934, FFP.
77. To Frankfurter, 5 August 1934, FFP.

78. 'Professor Laski and the Issue of Freedom', *New Statesman*, 21 July 1934 (partly quoted in Martin, *Laski*, p. 94).
79. To Frankfurter, 5 August 1934, FFP.
80. *Yale Review*, vol. 23 (3) March 1934 .
81. Ibid.
82. *New Statesman*, 21 July 1934.
83. *Manchester Guardian*, 16 July 1934.
84. See Laski to Keynes, 22 July 1934 in Keynes papers NS 2, King's College, Cambridge.
85. Editorial, *Daily Telegraph*, 6 July 1934.
86. Captain MacDonald, reported in *Daily Telegraph*, 12 July 1934.
87. Nevertheless, he told Frankfurter, who was leaving Britain after spending a year at Oxford, that it was the happiest year he could remember: 'This is a pretty poor kind of world just now. But at least I can look beyond its pains to your friendship as a lamp shining in the darkness'. Letter of 28 June 1934, FFP.
88. To Holmes, 12 November 1932, II, p. 1416. (For a useful brief source on the period, see W. E. Leuchtenburg, *Franklin D. Roosevelt and the New Deal*, Harper, 1963.)
89. 'What Will Mr Roosevelt Mean to Europe?', *Labour Magazine*, 11 (8) December 1932.
90. Ibid.
91. To Frankfurter, 29 October 1932, FFP.
92. 'President Roosevelt and Foreign Opinion', *Yale Review*, 22 (4) June 1933.
93. To Frankfurter, 13 August 1933.
94. To Holmes, 28 January 1934, II, p. 1466.
95. 'The Roosevelt Experiment', Socialist League, Forum Series No. 1 (London, 1933–4) p. 1.
96. Ibid., p. 14.
97. To Holmes, 16 December 1934, II, p. 1470.
98. 'Hitler over England', *The Nation*, 5 June 1935.
99. *I Believe*, p. 168.
100. *State*, pp. 129–30, 139–42, 144–5, 266.
101. To William O. Douglas, 10 April 1934, Douglas papers, LC.
102. He first used this phrase, which was to epitomise his aims during World War Two, in 'The Roosevelt Experiment', p. 2.

CHAPTER NINE

1. To Frida, 5 March 1931, FHL.
2. To Frankfurter, 7 March 1935, FFP.
3. Martin, *Laski*, p. 113.
4. To Frankfurter, 20 January 1936, FFP.
5. Information from Mrs N. Gilbert and Mrs T. Bristow.
6. To Frida, May 1933, FHL.
7. Information from Mr G. East.

8. To Frankfurter, 27 December 1937, FFP.
9. To Frida, 30 March, 1 and 6 April 1935, FHL.
10. To Frankfurter, 17 February 1935, FFP.
11. Frankfurter to Roosevelt's secretary, 29 March 1935, and reply in President's Personal File 140, FDR.
12. *The Rise of European Liberalism* (Allen and Unwin, 1936) pp. 249–52; to Frankfurter 28 May 1935; to Max Lerner, 13 November 1936 (Max Lerner papers, YUL). Frankfurter also sent him confidential memoranda that he was submitting to the President: to Laski 15 June 1935, FFP.
13. 'A Word to the Republicans', *Harpers Magazine*, October 1935, 'A Formula for Conservatives', *Harpers Magazine*, September 1937.
14. Martin, *Laski*, p. 121 (letter of October 1938).
15. To Roosevelt, 19 August 1939 in PSF 53, FDR.
16. *Harvard Law Review*, 54 (8) June 1941.
17. To Frankfurter 10 November 1937, 4 August 1938; to Thomas Powell, 15 January 1936, Box A 10 Powell papers, Harvard Law Library.
18. 'The Public Papers and Addresses of Franklin D. Roosevelt; *The University of Chicago Law Review*, 6 (1) December 1938, p. 34.
19. To Roosevelt, 14 May 1939, PSF 53, FDR.
20. See below.
21. Leuchtenburg, *Roosevelt and New Deal*, p. 150.
22. Some correspondence remains with such figures as Rexford Tugwell and Alexander Sachs in the Roosevelt library, and William O. Douglas and Thomas Corcoran in the Library of Congress.
23. See Harold Ickes Diaries, 24 January 1936, reel 1, LC.
24. Ben Cohen to Laski, 7 February 1937, quoted in J. Lash, *Dealers and Dreamers* (Doubleday, 1988) p. 294; Max Loewenthal repeated the request in August 1938. See Laski to Frankfurter, 21 August 1938, FFP.
25. Lash, *Frankfurter*, pp. 65–6; see also Dean Acheson, *Morning and Noon* (Hamish Hamilton, 1967) pp. 203–8.
26. To Roosevelt, 14 May 1939, PSF 53, FDR.
27. To Frankfurter, 22 June 1935, FFP.
28. To Frankfurter, 18 October 1935, FFP.
29. To Frankfurter, 29 June 1935, FFP.
30. 'The British General Election', *The Nation*, 20 November 1935.
31. Laski to Roosevelt, 5 November 1935, PPF 3014, FDR.
32. 'Problems of Labour Policy', *Labour Monthly*, March 1936.
33. See Ruth Dudley Edwards, *Victor Gollancz – A Biography* (Gollancz, 1987). Other useful sources for the Left Book Club are J. Lewis, *The Left Book Club* (Gollancz, 1970), Stuart Samuels, 'The Left Book Club', *Journal of Contemporary History*, 1 (2) 1966, and Kevin Morgan, *Against Fascism and War* (Manchester University Press, 1989).
34. See Michael Newman, *John Strachey* (Manchester University Press, 1989).
35. To Frankfurter, 18 October 1936, FFP. (Partly quoted, with the wrong date, in Martin, *Laski*, pp. 105–6.)
36. The demands were: abolition of the Means Test; TUC scales of unemployment benefit; national work of social value for distressed areas;

forty-hour week in industry and the public service; paid holidays for all workers; higher wages, and the abolition of tied cottages, for agricultural workers; co-ordinated trade union action for higher wages in industry; non-contributory pensions at sixty; immediate rehousing in 'houses that are homes'; power to get back land for the people; nationalisation of the mining industry; effective control of banks and Stock Exchanges; making the rich pay for social amelioration. Allen Hutt, *The Post-War History of the British Working Class* (Gollancz/LBC, 1937) pp. 305–6.

37. Ibid., p. 305.
38. To Frankfurter, 20 January 1937, FFP.
39. 'What is this Crime of Unity?', *Tribune*, 5 February 1937.
40. Ibid.
41. 'Unity and the Labour Party', *Labour Monthly*, March 1937.
42. Ibid.
43. To Frida, 1 April 1937, FHL.
44. *Tribune*, 30 July 1937; to Frankfurter, 3 August 1937, FFP.
45. Martin, *Laski*, p. 117.
46. NEC minutes, 23 November 1937, LP (National Museum of Labour History, Manchester).
47. To Frankfurter, 23 November 1937, FFP; NEC minutes, 14 December 1937.
48. To Frankfurter, 27 December 1937, 23 January 1938, FFP.
49. To Frankfurter, 23 November 1935, FFP.
50. To Frankfurter, 2 May 1936, FFP.
51. To Irving Dilliard (copy in Frankfurter-Laski letters, FFP), undated (early 1937?).
52. *Law and Justice in Soviet Russia* (Hogarth Press, 1935) pp. 23–4.
53. Introduction to *Liberty in the Modern State* (Pelican edition, 1937) p. 43.
54. To Frankfurter, 12 May 1937, FFP.
55. See Freda Utley, *Lost Illusion* (Allen and Unwin, 1949) pp. 220–36.
56. To Dutt, 20 October 1937, Communist Party archives. (Reference kindly supplied by Kevin Morgan.)
57. *Political Quarterly*, January-March 1938.
58. Ibid.
59. Ibid. (See also his review of W. P. and Z. K. Coates, *From Tsardom to the Stalin Constitution*, *New Statesman*, 30 July 1938).
60. 'The Labour Party Conference at Edinburgh', *Labour Monthly*, November 1936.
61. *Labour Party Conference Report* (1937), p. 158.
62. Dutt to Laski, 26 October 1937, CP archives. (Reference kindly supplied by Kevin Morgan.)
63. Gollancz to Strachey and Burns, 8 March 1937, Strachey papers. (These papers are held by the Strachey family.) Hugh Thomas is wrong in saying that this letter went to Laski, see *John Strachey* (Eyre Methuen, 1973) p. 161.
64. Both Strachey and Gollancz apologised to Dutt for Laski's review of his *World Politics, 1918–36* in *Left News*, July 1936. See Strachey to Dutt, 23 June 1936 in Strachey papers and Dudley Edwards, *Gollancz*, p. 237.

65. Dalton to Gollancz, 8 July 1937, Strachey papers.
66. Dudley Edwards, *Gollancz*, p. 263; *Left News* Editorial, August 1937.
67. F. M. Leventhal, *The Last Dissenter – H. N. Brailsford and His World* (Oxford University Press, 1985) pp. 246–8.
68. Dudley Edwards, *Gollancz*, p. 266.
69. To Brailsford, 18 January 1938. (Reference kindly supplied by F. M. Leventhal.)
70. Dudley Edwards, *Gollancz*, p. 268.
71. To Frankfurter, 25 February 1938, FFP.
72. To Frida, 22 March 1938, FHL.
73. Thomas Corcoran papers, April 1938 (Laski correspondence) LC.
74. 1 March 1938, quoted in Martin, *Laski*, pp. 119–20.
75. NEC minutes, 5 May 1938.
76. See 'Unity and the Labour Party', and his review of G. D. H. Cole's *The People's Front* (Gollancz, 1937) in *Left News*, July 1937.
77. 'Labour and the Popular Front', Laski file, Labour Party archives. (Laski's draft was altered slightly before publication but, where possible, I have quoted his original text.)
78. NEC minutes, 25 May, 27 July 1938.
79. 'Why not a Special Conference?', *Tribune*, 5 August 1938.
80. 'How will Britain Answer Roosevelt?', *Tribune*, 26 August 1938.
81. To Frankfurter, 4 August 1938, FFP.
82. 'Labour and the International Situation', Joint Labour Party/TUC statement, 7 September 1938. (Laski was involved in the early drafting, but the final version was agreed by the Shadow Cabinet and TUC General Council.)
83. To Frankfurter, 10 October 1938, FFP.
84. Richard L. Neuberger, 'Laski Says Roosevelt Hasn't Gone Far Enough' *Sunday Oregonian*, 5 March 1939.
85. Ibid.
86. Leuchtenburg, *Roosevelt and New Deal*, p. 286.
87. To Roosevelt, 5 January 1939, PSF 53, FDR. Also quoted in Martin, *Laski*, p. 120. (For Kennedy and appeasement, see W. W. Kaufmann 'Two American Ambassadors' in G. Craig and F. Gilbert, *The Diplomats* (Atheneum, 1968) vol. 2, ch. 21.)
88. To Roosevelt, 17 April 1939, PSF 53, FDR, and Martin, *Laski*, p. 122.
89. For example, 'Notes on the Way', *Time and Tide*, 15 July 1939.
90. NEC minutes, 28 June 1939.
91. 'Southport and After', *Left News*, July 1939.
92. To Rexford Tugwell, 8 September 1939 in Tugwell papers, FDR.
93. To Gollancz, 31 August 1939, Gollancz papers, cited in Morgan, *Against Fascism and War*, p. 264.
94. To Hugo Black, 31 August 1939, Hugo Black papers, LC.

CHAPTER TEN

1. T. D. Burridge, 'A Postscript to Potsdam: The Churchill-Laski Electoral

Clash, June 1945', *Journal of Contemporary History*, 12, 1977 p. 733 (hereafter 'Postscript to Potsdam').

2. Deane, *Laski*, pp. 238–9.
3. Ibid., p. 245.
4. This section is based on a wide variety of sources from Laski's general writing, political activity and correspondence in the period.
5. NEC minutes, 13 June 1941.
6. To Alfred E. Cohn, 12 April 1940, Cohn papers, RAC.
7. To Frankfurter, 17 May 1940 (in Hugo Black papers), LC.
8. *The Strategy of Freedom: An Open Letter to Students, Especially American* (Allen and Unwin, 1942) (hereafter *Strategy of Freedom*).
9. See, for example, his letters to Roosevelt, 26 August 1940 (PPF 3014) and 20 October 1940 (PSF 53), FDR.
10. Amos Pinchot in *Journal American*, 13 June 1941.
11. For a full analysis, see Kevin Jefferys, *The Churchill coalition and wartime politics, 1940–45* (Manchester University Press, 1991) (hereafter Jefferys, *Churchill Coalition*).
12. He constantly repeated this phrase, which he had first used in relation to the New Deal in 1933, to describe his theory. See *Where do we go from here?* (Penguin, 1940) ch. 3, *Reflections on the Revolution of Our Time* (Allen and Unwin, 1943) ch. 4 (hereafter *Reflections*).
13. He was highly critical between 1939 and June 1941, and most effusive in the aftermath of the victory at Stalingrad when he wrote *Faith, Reason and Civilisation* (Gollancz, 1944).
14. *Strategy of Freedom*, pp. 98–101.
15. To Cohn, 12 April 1940, RAC.
16. To Rexford Tugwell, 7 June 1940 (Tugwell Papers, FDR).
17. NEC minutes, 16 July 1940.
18. NEC minutes, 23 July 1940.
19. Policy Committee minutes, 16 August 1940.
20. Emergency Committee minutes, 23 October 1940.
21. Ibid., 5 November 1940.
22. NEC minutes 21 January 1941; Emergency Committee minutes, 12 February 1941.
23. 'The Labour Party', submitted to NEC, 4 February 1941.
24. Ibid.
25. Ibid.
26. Ibid.
27. 29 January 1941, Laski papers H 1973.
28. 20 October 1940, PSF 53, FDR.
29. To Frankfurter, 24 November 1940, FFP.
30. PREM 4, 62/5, PRO (also quoted in Burridge, *Postscript to Potsdam*).
31. Ibid.
32. Ibid.
33. Jefferys, *Churchill coalition*, pp. 53–5.
34. PREM 4 62/5.
35. Policy Committee minutes, 4 April 1941.
36. To Laski, 1 April 1941, Laski papers H 1973.
37. Morrison/Middleton correspondence in NEC minutes, 21, 22, and

26 April 1941. Laski and Morrison had mutual respect and affection, despite their political differences.

38. Policy Committee minutes, 23 May 1941.
39. NEC minutes, 30 May 1941.
40. Emergency Committee minutes, 13 and 20 June 1941.
41. NEC minutes, 25 June 1941, Policy Committee minutes, 4 July 1941.
42. Central Committee minutes, 30 July 1941.
43. 'The Labour Party and Domestic Reconstruction', Central Committee minutes, 17 September 1941.
44. Ibid.
45. To Huebsch, 17 August 1941, LC.
46. Central Committee minutes, 10 December 1941.
47. NEC minutes, 4 February 1942.
48. *The Old World and the New Society* (Labour Party, 1942) pp. 27–8; see also pp. 10, 13–14.
49. To Frankfurter, 4 August 1938, FFP; Gupta, *Imperialism*, pp. 258–9.
50. NEC minutes, 25 October 1939. (In Parliament, on 3 October Attlee had been critical of the Viceroy's declaration of war.)
51. 'Notes on Indian Policy', November 1939 in 'India file, 1935–41', LP.
52. Ibid.
53. NEC minutes, 6 February 1940.
54. Gupta, *Imperialism*, p. 267.
55. R. J. Moore, *Churchill, Cripps and India, 1939–45* (Clarendon Press, 1979) pp. 36–41 (hereafter *Churchill, Cripps*).
56. International Committee minutes, 25 November 1940.
57. To Frankfurter, 20 November 1940, FFP; to Clarence Berdahl, 7 December 1940 in Laski-Berdahl correspondence. UI. See also *Strategy of Freedom*, p. 91.
58. International Committee minutes, 20 January 1941.
59. Gupta, *Imperialism*, p. 268.
60. Minutes of joint meeting, 4 July 1941.
61. Moore, *Churchill, Cripps*, pp. 41–2.
62. International Committee minutes, 10 October 1941.
63. To Gillies, 11 December 1941 in India file, LP.
64. 'Memorandum on India', 11 December 1941, India file, LP.
65. International Committee minutes, 12 December 1941.
66. War Cabinet 19 December 1941, cited in Moore, *Churchill, Cripps*, p. 47.
67. The India League and the India Conciliation Group acted as pressure groups. See Moore, *Churchill, Cripps*.
68. To Frida, 20 January 1942, FHL.
69. Moore, *Churchill, Cripps*, p. 53.
70. Laski's draft and agreed version of 29 January 1942 in India file, LP.
71. Moore, *Churchill, Cripps*, pp. 52–3.
72. Ibid., pp. 55–6.
73. For a brief analysis, see E. Stokes, 'Cripps in India' *Historical Journal*, XIV (2) 1971.
74. See Attlee's memorandum of 2 February 1942, quoted in Moore, *Churchill, Cripps*, pp. 55–6.
75. Attlee to Gillies, 16 January 1942, India file, LP. For a different interpre-

tation of Attlee's role, see Trevor Burridge, *Clement Attlee: A Political Biography* (Cape, 1985) pp. 268–81 (hereafter *Burridge, Attlee*).

76. *Where do we go from Here?*, p. 31.
77. NEC minutes, 17 April 1940.
78. Press, Publicity and Campaign (PPC) Committee minutes, 30 July 1941.
79. 'Great Britain, Russia and the Labour Party' in Attlee papers, Mss Attlee dep 4, fols 142–8, BLO (The subsequent quotations are also from this unpublished paper.)
80. PPC Committee minutes, 21 January 1942.
81. Comments on Laski's draft, Attlee dep 4, fols 165–7, BLO.
82. Trevor Burridge, *British Labour and Hitler's War* (Deutsch, 1976) p. 84 (hereafter Burridge, *Labour and Hitler's War*).
83. To Frida (undated), late 1941, FHL.
84. Jefferys, *Churchill coalition*, p. 76.
85. NEC minutes, 8 December 1941.
86. To Frida (undated), late 1941, FHL.
87. To Frida, 1 March 1942, FHL.
88. To Frida, 2 and 3 March 1942, FHL.
89. To Frida, 4 March 1942, FHL.
90. Alan Bullock, *The Life and Times of Ernest Bevin*, vol. 2 (Heinemann, 1968) p. 187. Bevin did not respond.
91. Minutes of joint meeting, NEC minutes, 26 March 1942.
92. 25 March 1942, quoted in Martin, *Laski*, p. 153.
93. 'The Party and the Future', in NEC minutes, 9 April 1942.
94. Ibid.
95. NEC minutes, 9 April 1942.
96. Ibid.
97. To the Berdahls and Ruth Kelso, 6 April 1942, Berdahl papers, UI .
98. To Max Lerner, 12 April 1942, Lerner papers YUL.
99. Emergency Committee minutes, 16 April 1942. (The pretext for changing the decision was a government statement on controlling luxury meals.)
100. On 29 April, independent candidates gained Wallasey, with a swing of 35.7 per cent, and Rugby with a swing of 13.3 per cent against the Conservatives.
101. Emergency Committee minutes, 6 May 1942.
102. NEC minutes, 22 May 1942.
103. To Frida, 23 June 1942, FHL.
104. Frida to Huebsch, 4 June 1942 (Huebsch papers, LC).
105. *Reynolds News*, 12 and 26 July, 9 August, 6 September 1942.
106. Organisation Committee minutes, 18 August 1942.
107. NEC minutes, 12 October 1942.
108. Jefferys, *Churchill coalition*, p. 79.
109. Ibid., especially ch. 4.
110. NEC minutes, 12 October 1942.
111. NEC minutes, 28 October 1942.
112. To Frida, 11 November 1942.
113. NEC minutes, 25 November 1942.
114. Minutes of joint meeting, 17 December 1942.

115. NEC minutes, 24 February 1943.
116. NEC minutes 8 and 23 June 1943.
117. Minutes of joint meeting, 8 June 1943.
118. To Huebsch, 27 March 1943, Huebsch papers, LC.
119. Undated memorandum by Attlee, Attlee papers 2/2 1941–5, correspondence with Churchill, Churchill College, Cambridge.
120. To Frida, 19 June 1942, FHL.
121. To Frida, Undated, mid June 1942, FHL.
122. To Frida, 5 November 1942, FHL.
123. Letters to Roosevelt, 26 August 1940 (PPF 3014), 20 October 1940 (PSF 53), FDR. See also his undated memorandum (1940) for Harry Hopkins in Hopkins (24) Box 302, FDR.
124. Cohn to Laski, 30 June 1942 in Eleanor Roosevelt papers, Box 1635, FDR.
125. Ibid, Box 1650, undated 1942, FDR.
126. To Churchill, 2 July 1942, PREM 4 26/3, PRO.
127. G. E. Millard to Churchill's private secretary, 16 July 1942, PREM 4 26/3.
128. Sumner Wells to Eleanor Roosevelt, 20 July 1942, including Winant's telegram of 18 July. Eleanor Roosevelt papers, Box 853, FDR.
129. 18 July 1942, Eleanor Roosevelt papers, Box 1650, FDR.
130. Churchill's Private Office to Foreign Office, 24 July 1942, PREM 26/3.
131. Sir Ronald Campbell to Cadogan, 7 August 1942, PREM 26/3.
132. 13 August 1942, PREM 26/3.
133. FBI Files 100–148342, report of 6 October 1942; Westbrook Pegler in *New Yorker*, 26 October 1942; Amos Pinchot in *Journal American*, 13 June 1941.
134. Frankfurter diary, 26 February 1943 in Lash, *Frankfurter*, p. 199.
135. *New Statesman*, 10 April 1943.
136. Winant to Laski, 13 May 1943 in Winant papers, Box 204, FDR.
137. To Winant, 15 May 1943, Winant papers, Box 204, FDR.
138. Frankfurter diary, 26 February 1943, in Lash, *Frankfurter*, p. 199.
139. 'An Age of Transition', *Political Quarterly*, 14 (2), 1943.
140. *Marx and Today* (Fabian Society, 1943) pp. 9, 20–1.
141. *The Communist Party and the War: A Record of Hypocrisy and Treachery to the Workers of Europe* (Labour Party, 1943).
142. NEC minutes, 15 June 1943.
143. 'The Labour Party Delegation to the USSR', August 1943 in minutes of International Committee, 13 September 1943.
144. *The Economic Revolution* (Peace Aims Pamphlet no. 5, 1941) p. 22.
145. *The Germans – Are They Human?* (Left Book Club, 1941).
146. To Julius Braunthal, 18 February 1942 in Braunthal papers, no. 63, IISH.
147. There is an extensive correspondence in the Braunthal papers, IISH.
148. Burridge, *Labour and Hitler's War*, pp. 59–63.
149. See Chapter 12.
150. Attlee papers, dep 10, BLO.
151. Ibid. But Attlee's views were much less crude. See WP (43) 322, 19 July 1943, PRO.
152. Article in the *Washington Star* reported in *Daily Telegraph*, 3 August 1943.

153. NEC minutes, 25 August 1943.
154. Martin, *Laski*, p. 136.
155. To Lerner, 2 January 1944, YUL.
156. To Cohn, 3 January 1942, RAC.
157. To Winant, 22 April 1943, FDR.
158. To Huebsch, 20 August 1943, LC.
159. To Winant, 15 May 1943, FDR.
160. To Lerner, 2 January 1944, YUL.
161. To Winant, 15 February 1944.
162. NEC minutes, 27 October 1943.
163. NEC minutes, 26 April 1944. (The regulation banned any form of strike activity in essential services.)
164. NEC minutes, 16 May 1944.
165. The letter is discussed below, and is quoted in full in Martin, *Laski*, pp. 159–62.
166. Michael Foot, *Aneurin Bevan*, vol. 1 (Four Square, 1966) pp. 390–402.
167. Minutes of joint meeting, 28 June 1944.
168. Policy Committee minutes, 25 July; NEC minutes, 26 July 1944.
169. International Committee minutes, 14 December; NEC minutes, 23 December 1943.
170. International Committee minutes, 20 June 1944.
171. PREM 4 21/5, cited in Burridge, 'Postscript to Potsdam', p. 733.
172. NEC minutes, 26 July 1944.
173. 'The German Problem – Two Solutions', Laski-Vansittart Debate, 15 September 1944, Overseas News Agency.
174. To Roosevelt, 5 December 1944 (PSF 53, FDR, partly quoted in Martin, *Laski*, p. 166); to Winant, 20 August 1944.
175. Peace Aims Pamphlet, no. 28 (1944), pp. 14–15.
176. Frida Laski, 'Memoirs', pp. 51–2.
177. To Frida, 16 September 1944.
178. To Frida, 24 February 1945.
179. To Frida (undated), February 1945.
180. To Frida (undated), February 1945.
181. Deane, *Laski*, p. 239.
182. For Attlee's letter, see Martin, *Laski*, pp. 159–62.
183. (Undated) January 1945 in Attlee papers 2/2, correspondence with Churchill, 1941–5.
184. Keynes to Laski, 11 December 1939 in Keynes papers HPI.1.
185. Ibid. Unpublished writings of J. M. Keynes copyright © The Provost and Scholars of Kings' College, Cambridge, 1993.
186. Laski to Keynes, 1 and 28 January 1940, ibid.
187. Attlee papers 1/24 (Churchill College) partly quoted in Burridge, *Attlee*, p. 156.
188. Jefferys, *Churchill coalition*.
189. Ibid. The 'consensus' approach was stressed in Paul Addison, *The Road to 1945* (Cape, 1975).
190. Notes on post-war problems (1944–6) Attlee papers 1/24, Churchill College.
191. *Faith, Reason and Civilisation*, chs 8, 9, 12 and 13.
192. To Hugo Black, 17 August 1942, Black papers, LC.

CHAPTER ELEVEN

1. Henry Pelling, 'The 1945 General Election Reconsidered', *Historical Journal*, 23 (2), 1980, p. 404 (hereafter Pelling, '1945 General Election').
2. In 1944 Attlee and Dalton had agreed that it would be preferable to postpone an election until six months after a German surrender, and only then if Labour could separate from the Conservatives without too fierce a quarrel. Burridge, *Attlee*, p. 156.
3. PREM 4/65/4, quoted in Pelling, '1945 General Election', p. 399.
4. Pelling, '1945 General Election', p. 402.
5. Undated letter in Laski file, LP, quoted in full in Eastwood, *Laski*, pp. 122–3.
6. Letters of 31 May and 2 June 1945 in PREM 4 7/7, PRO.
7. Burridge, *Attlee*, p. 158.
8. Attlee papers, 1941–5, correspondence with Churchill 2/2, Churchill College.
9. To Attlee, Laski file, LP.
10. Martin, *Laski*, p. 170, quoting a memorandum by Laski to the NEC (which no longer exists in the files).
11. Ibid., pp. 169–70.
12. Ibid., p. 171.
13. Ibid., pp. 171–2.
14. To Charles Clark, 4 October 1945, Clark papers, YUL. On 5 July 1945 the *Daily Herald's* verdict on the election campaign was that the Tory party had 'recklessly exploited the name of Professor Laski because Laski is a foreign-sounding name and Professor Laski is a Jew.'
15. Pelling, '1945 General Election', p. 405.
16. Ibid., p. 406.
17. *The Times*, 4 July 1945.
18. Ibid.
19. For a full discussion, and the supporting evidence, see Burridge, 'A Postscript to Potsdam', pp. 735–7.
20. Ben Pimlott (ed.) *The Political Diary of Hugh Dalton, 1918–40, 1945–60* (Cape/LSE, 1986) (hereafter *Dalton Diary*) July 1945 p. 357.
21. Eastwood, *Laski*, pp. 341–2.
22. B. Donoughue and G. Jones, *Herbert Morrison* (Weidenfeld, 1973) pp. 341–3 (hereafter Donoughue and Jones, *Morrison*).
23. *Dalton Diary*, July 1945, p. 357.
24. *The Times*, 27 July 1945.
25. See below for a full discussion.
26. *The Times*, 13 August 1945.
27. Ibid., 12 August 1945.
28. Ibid., 18 August 1945.
29. 20 August 1945, Laski papers H 1973, also quoted in Eastwood, *Laski*, p. 132.
30. *The Times*, 25 September 1945.
31. Kenneth O. Morgan, *Labour in Power* (Oxford University Press, 1985) p. 71 (hereafter Morgan, *Labour in Power*).
32. NEC minutes, 24 October 1945.

33. To Lerner, 20 October 1945, YUL.
34. Undated manuscript, Laski papers 24/3, IISH.
35. 'Wanted: A New Constitution', *Tribune*, 28 June 1946.
36. Francis Williams, *A Prime Minister Remembers* (Heinemann, 1961) pp. 90–1.
37. NEC minutes, 24 July 1946.
38. NEC minutes, 25 February 1948. (The memorandum is in the Laski-Frankfurter correspondence, FFP.)
39. Quoted in Eastwood, *Laski*, p. 140.
40. Ibid., p. 141.
41. To Morgan Phillips, 14 December 1946, Laski papers, HE.
42. For Simon's statement and retraction, see Eastwood, *Laski*, pp. 143–4.
43. D. Hooper, *Public Scandal, Odium and Contempt* (Secker and Warburg, 1984).
44. *The Laski Libel Action – Verbatim Report* (*Daily Express*, 1947) (hereafter *Laski Libel*) pp. 227–8, 237.
45. Ibid., pp. 237, 275–82.
46. Ibid., pp. 257–82.
47. Ibid., pp. 9–10. See also Day's letter of 5 February 1976 quoted by F. Bresler, *Lord Goddard* (Harrap, 1977) (hereafter Bresler, *Goddard*) p. 155.
48. *Laski Libel*, pp. 18–40.
49. Ibid., p. 68.
50. Ibid., p. 80.
51. Bresler, *Goddard*, p. 164.
52. *Laski Libel*, pp. 72, 95, 118–19.
53. Ibid., pp. 177–8.
54. Ibid., p. 311.
55. Ibid., pp. 383, 384, 390. On Goddard's conscience, see Bresler, *Goddard*, pp. 177–8.
56. *Laski Libel*, pp. 295–301.
57. 'My Day in Court', *Atlantic Monthly*, November 1952.
58. Wentworth Day himself believed that Goddard had sympathised with him and had tried to help him in Court. Bresler, *Goddard*, p. 176.
59. To Noel-Baker, 3 December 1946 (copy in Frankfurter-Laski correspondence, FFP).
60. Quoted in Martin, *Laski*, p. 177.
61. Frida to the Cohns, 4 December 1946, RAC. The subsequent appeal launched in Britain by Morgan Phillips and in the USA by Max Lerner raised more than £2,000 over the necessary amount, which went to a Labour Party fund.
62. Ibid.
63. To Frida, 24 December 1946, FHL.
64. To Huebsch, 20 January 1947, in Huebsch papers, LC.
65. To Frankfurter, 11 May 1947, quoted in Martin, *Laski*, p. 179.
66. Letter of 10 January 1972, quoted in Bresler, *Goddard*, p. 174.
67. To Frankfurter, 11 May 1947, quoted in Martin, *Laski*, p. 179.
68. 'On Being a Plaintiff', reproduced as Appendix A in Martin, *Laski*, pp. 274–7.

69. 8 February 1946, quoted in John Chamberlain, 'Harold Laski', *Life*, 19 August 1946.
70. *New York Mirror*, 31 July 1945.
71. FBI memorandum, 26 November 1945, FBI file 100–148342.
72. *New York Times*, 4 December 1945.
73. Quoted in Eastwood, *Laski*, p. 131.
74. See Attlee papers, Dep. 22, BLO, including a letter of 14 September 1945 from the Board of Trade.
75. See, for example, *Daily Mirror*, 23 April 1946.
76. See, for example, *Los Angeles Examiner*, 13 December 1946.
77. 2 March 1948, FBI file 100–148342–7.
78. 12 July 1948, FBI file 100–148342–8. The content of the whole file remains classified.
79. *Post and Home News*, 6 April 1949.
80. Martin, *Laski*, p. 247. For further details of the tour, see ibid., pp. 247–52.
81. FBI memorandum, 12 July 1949, file 100–148342–9. (Laski's article was 'America, Good and Bad: III', *The Nation*, 9 July 1949.)
82. *Reflections on the Constitution* (Manchester University Press, 1951) p. 16.
83. *The American Democracy* (Allen and Unwin, 1949) (hereafter *American Democracy*) p. 333.
84. Ibid., p. 355.
85. Ibid., p. 363.
86. *Trade Unions in the New Society* (Allen and Unwin, 1950) (hereafter *Trade Unions*) pp. 42, 156–9; *The Dilemma of Our Times* (Allen and Unwin 1952) (hereafter *Dilemma*) pp. 88–90; 'Political Rights of Civil Servants', Laski papers, 23/4, IISH.
87. Introduction, *Liberty in the Modern State* (1948 edition, Allen and Unwin) p. 36 (hereafter *Liberty, 1948*).
88. *The Webbs and Soviet Communism* (Fabian Publications, 1947) p. 11.
89. Ibid., p. 13.
90. *Liberty, 1948*, p. 25.
91. Ibid., pp. 14–15.
92. Ibid., pp. 17–18.
93. *The Secret Battalion*, p. 21.
94. *Liberty, 1948*, pp. 27–8.
95. *Trade Unions*, pp. 87–90; *Dilemma*, pp. 104–6.
96. To Frida, 8 September 1946, FHL.
97. Ibid.
98. To Frida, 12 September 1946, FHL.
99. 'The Mote and the Beam', *New Statesman*, 6 September 1947.
100. *Dilemma*, pp. 16–17, 38, 265–6.
101. *Trade Unions*, pp. 99–100.
102. 'Towards a Universal Declaration of Human Rights' in *Human Rights: Comments and Interpretations* (UNESCO, 1948).
103. Marc Karson, 'Harold Laski and the Soviet Union', *New Politics*, Spring 1965, p. 82.
104. *Communist Manifesto – Socialist Landmark* (Allen and Unwin, 1948) (here-

after *Manifesto*) pp. 46, 80–2, 94. See also *The Secret Battalion* (Labour Party, 1946) (hereafter *Secret Battalion*) and his letter to Morgan Phillips, 27 September 1947, Laski file, LP.

105. For Blum's articles and the resolution, see *L'Oeuvre de Léon Blum*, vol. 6 (Albin Michel, 1958). The influence was reciprocal: Laski's arguments recalled those used by Blum at the Congress of Tours in 1920. See Jean Lacouture, *Léon Blum* (Seuil, 1977) pp. 163–72.
106. *Tribune*, 7 September 1945.
107. Ibid. See also *Nuova Europa*, 3 September 1945, cited in P. Sebastiani, *Laburisti Inqlesi e Socialisti Italiani* (FIAP, 1983) p. 99.
108. Healey to Dalton, 5 March 1946, Labour Party International Department 1946, Box 4, LP.
109. According to Denis Healey, Laski was then regarded in Italy 'as a figure comparable with Marx in the intellectual history of Socialism'. Martin, *Laski*, p. 183.
110. PRO FO 371 vol. 60528 ZM 1095/1/22. Pietro Nenni describes it as an important letter in *Tempo di Guerra Fredda, Diari 1943–56* (Sugarco, 1981) pp. 206–9.
111. FO 371 vol. 60529 ZM 1217/1/22, Charles to Foreign Office, 13 April 1946.
112. Ibid., minute by A. D. M. Ross.
113. *Secret Battalion*, p. 11.
114. Ibid., p. 12.
115. Ibid., p. 15.
116. To Frida, 23 April 1946, FHL; and Harry Pollitt, *Laski's Mistake* (Communist Party, 1946).
117. *Forward*, quoted in Jonathan Schneer, *Labour's Conscience – The Labour Left 1945–51*, (Unwin Hyman, 1988) (hereafter, Schneer, *Labour's Conscience*) p. 35.
118. Ibid., citing *Forward*, 16 March 1945.
119. 'The Future of the Socialist International', probably February 1946, Braunthal papers no. 378, IISH.
120. The other members were Alice Bacon, Harold Clay and Morgan Phillips.
121. To Frida, 30 July 1946, FHL.
122. Ibid.
123. Ibid.
124. To Frida, 3 August 1946, FHL.
125. This and the subsequent quotations are from 'Goodwill Mission to the USSR', submitted to the NEC 17 September 1946, discussed at the International Committee, 8 October 1946.
126. Laski to Phillips, 19 September 1946, Laski file, LP.
127. See, for example, Corliss Lamont's record of a conversation with Laski, 3 October 1946 in Laski papers, HE; *Dalton Diary*, 7 October 1946, p. 388.
128. Morgan Phillips's alleged rebuttal of Laski's claim is normally taken as decisive evidence. However, Laski's account to Frida of his prominence in the delegation and his impatience to discuss the crucial political issues is convincing. He was the only member of the delegation who was a theorist, and who had taken a long-term interest in the

Soviet Union. He would clearly have relished the opportunity for a further meeting to develop the ideas which had been touched upon in the group discussion. It is conceivable that Stalin would have believed this to be advantageous in the knowledge that Laski was the member of the delegation who would be most likely to promote the viewpoint that the USSR wanted to encourage. Since Laski was denounced as a counter-revolutionary by the Head of Propaganda of the CPSU only a few months after the visit, it might be expected that he would also have been accused of lying had there been no basis for his claim. (For the denunciation, see Martin, *Laski*, pp. 195–6.)

129. 'Britain without Empire', *The Nation*, 29 March 1947.
130. To Frankfurter, 11 May 1947, FFP.
131. To Frankfurter, 29 May 1947, FFP.
132. *Forward*, 21 June 1947, quoted in Schneer, *Labour's Conscience*, p. 36.
133. Ibid.
134. Ibid.
135. To Frankfurter, 11 July 1947, FFP, also quoted in Martin, *Laski*, p. 201.
136. To Frankfurter, 11 May 1947, FFP.
137. 'Notes on the new Belgrade Comintern', 7 October 1947 for the International Committee.
138. 'Summary of Proceedings of Antwerp Conference, 28 November–2 December 1947' in Labour Party, 'International Socialist Conference 1946, 1947', file of documents, LP.
139. *Forward*, 10 May 1947, quoted in Schneer, *Labour's Conscience*, p. 39.
140. To Frankfurter, 11 May 1947, FFP.
141. Schneer, *Labour's Conscience*, pp. 41–2, quoting *Forward*, 6 March 1948. He remained particularly bitter about Czechoslovakia until his death. See *Dilemma*. ch. 13.
142. *Chicago Daily News*, 8 April 1948.
143. *Daily Herald*, 3 July 1948.
144. To Frankfurter, 9 December 1949, FFP.
145. *Dilemma*, p. 95.
146. Ibid., pp. 267–8.
147. Ibid., chs 6, 10, and 14; also 'Is the Third World War Inevitable?' Laski papers 24/2, IISH, published posthumously in a shortened form in *The Free World*, June 1950.
148. *Dilemma*, p. 95.
149. *Liberty, 1948*, p. 22. (The passage was written in 1947.)
150. He was appalled by the expulsion of Zilliacus. *Reflections on the Constitution*, p. 80. See also Schneer, *Labour's Conscience*, pp. 123–4.
151. For a similar brief interpretation, see M. Peretz, 'Laski Redivivus', *Journal of Contemporary History*, 1 (2), 1966.
152. *Dalton Diary*, July 1945.
153. *Dilemma*, p. 116.

CHAPTER TWELVE

1. 'Patriots against Partition', *Jewish Chronicle*, 29 April 1988. (Sykes, *Cross Roads to Israel*, remains a very useful general source for the subject matter of this chapter.)
2. Gorny, *Labour and Zionism*, p. 120; to Frankfurter, 22 May 1937, FFP.
3. To Frankfurter, 20 January 1937, FFP.
4. To Frankfurter, 27 December 1937, FFP.
5. To Frankfurter, 3 August 1937, FFP.
6. *Left News*, August 1938.
7. To Frankfurter, 7 July 1937, FFP.
8. Record of a meeting of 14 October 1936 in Neville Laski papers, AJ33, Hartley Library, University of Southampton; NEC minutes, 7 January 1938.
9. To Frankfurter, 4 August 1938, FFP.
10. Martin, *Laski*, p. 212.
11. 'A Note on Anti-Semitism', *New Statesman*, 13 February 1943.
12. 1 July 1943, PREM 4 51/8, PRO.
13. O. C. Harvey to Churchill, 18 July 1943, PREM 4 51/8.
14. *New Statesman*, 9 October 1943.
15. 8 October 1943, Winant papers, FDR.
16. Obituary, *Jewish Chronicle*, 31 March 1950.
17. 'Palestine: The Economic Aspect' in J. B. Hobman (ed.), *Palestine's Economic Future: A Review of Progress and Prospects* (Percy Land Humphries and Co, 1946) (hereafter 'Palestine: The Economic Aspect') p. 37.
18. Gorny, *Labour and Zionism*, p. 181.
19. 'Palestine: The Economic Aspect', p. 39.
20. Ibid., p. 35.
21. 'Britain is the best friend the Jews have', *Forward*, 11 January 1947, quoted in Gorny, *Labour and Zionism*, p. 229.
22. 'Palestine: The Economic Aspect', p. 39.
23. Ibid., p. 39.
24. NEC minutes, 25 April 1945.
25. To Frankfurter, 4 June 1945, FFP.
26. Donoughue and Jones, *Morrison*, pp. 255–7.
27. Gorny, *Labour and Zionism*, p. 175.
28. Alan Bullock, *Ernest Bevin – Foreign Secretary, 1945–51* (Oxford University Press, 1985) (hereafter Bullock, *Bevin, 1945–51*) pp. 165–6.
29. Burridge, *Attlee*, pp. 249–53.
30. Sykes, *Cross Roads*, p. 291.
31. Cab 129 CP (45) 8 September 1945, quoted in Gorny, *Labour and Zionism*, p. 204.
32. CP (45) 156, quoted in Bullock, *Bevin, 1945–51*, pp. 170–1.
33. CM (45) 40.
34. PREM 8/89, quoted in R. Ovendale, 'The Palestine Policy of the British Labour Government, 1945–46', *International Affairs*, July 1979, p. 414.
35. NEC minutes, 26 September 1945.
36. Record of meeting of 5 October 1945 in NEC minutes, 24 October 1945.

37. 'Notes of Discussion' (22 October 1945) in NEC minutes, 24 October 1945.
38. Ibid.
39. To Berdahl, 4 October 1945, UI; to Lerner, 20 October 1945, YUL.
40. Bullock, *Bevin, 1945–51*, p. 178.
41. Ibid, pp. 176–9.
42. Gorny, *Labour and Zionism*, p. 208.
43. FO 800 vol. 484/PA/45/23, 14 November 1945.
44. 'Note on the Palestine Policy of HMG', 15 November 1945, Laski papers, 23.2 IISH.
45. International Committee minutes, 20 November 1945.
46. 'What about Palestine?', *Forward*, 24 November 1945, summarised in Gorny. *Labour and Zionism*, p. 210.
47. FO 371 vol. 52516 E3571/4/31, minute for Bevin, 18 April 1946.
48. Charles to Foreign Office, FO 371 vol. 52515 E3989/4/31, 11 April 1946.
49. Hall to Attlee, Morrison and Bevin, PREM 8 298, 15 April 1946.
50. FO 371 vol. 52515 E3989/4/31, 11 April 1946.
51. FO 800 vol. 485 PA/46/6, 11 April 1946.
52. PREM 8 298, 15 April 1946.
53. FO 371 vol. 52516 E3571/4/31, 17 April 1946.
54. Minute of 18 April 1946, FO 371 vol. 52516 E3571/4/31.
55. FO 371 vol. 52517 E3795/4/31, 26 April 1946.
56. FO 371 vol. 52517 E3766/4/31, 9 May 1946.
57. To Frida, 23 April 1946, FHL.
58. See Sykes, *Cross Roads*, for a summary.
59. DO (46) 61, cited in Bullock, *Bevin, 1945–51*, p. 256.
60. CM 39 (46) 1 May 1946, cited in Bullock, *Bevin, 1945–51*.
61. PREM 8/515, 19 February 1946, cited in Burridge, *Attlee*, p. 259.
62. 'Critical Days in Palestine', *Forward*, 11 May 1946, 'The Changing Middle East' *Forward*, 1 June 1946, both summarised in Gorny, *Labour and Zionism*, p. 228.
63. Quoted in Sykes, *Cross Roads*, p. 313.
64. Burridge, *Attlee*, p. 262.
65 C. O. S. (46) 188 (0), 10 July 1946.
66. CAB 128/6 CM (46) 67, cited in Bullock, *Bevin, 1945–51*, p. 294.
67. F. S. Northedge, 'Britain and the Middle East' in R. Ovendale, *The Foreign Policy of the British Labour Governments* (Leicester University Press, 1984) (hereafter Northedge, 'Britain and the Middle East') pp. 155–6.
68. 'Justice for the Jews', *Forward*, 20 July 1947, quoted in Gorny, *Labour and Zionism*, p. 228.
69. 'Jerusalem Bomb Outrage' *Forward*, 3 August 1946, cited in Gorny, *Labour and Zionism*, p. 228.
70. Gorny, *Labour and Zionism*, p. 200.
71. To Frida, 30 August 1946, FHL.
72. Sykes, *Cross Roads*, p. 318.
73. To Frida, 6 October 1946, FHL.
74. To Frida, 8 October 1946, FHL. Dalton mentions the conversation without details – in *Dalton Diary*, 7 October 1946, p. 388.

75. 'A Massive Failure in Palestine', *Forward*, 26 October 1946, cited in Gorny, *Labour and Zionism*, p. 228.
76. Attlee to Laski, 21 November 1946 in Laski papers, H 1973.
77. Weizmann to Laski, 13 January 1947, Laski Corr. 2, IISH.
78. 'British is the best friend the Jews have', *Forward*, 11 January 1947, summarised in Gorny, *Labour and Zionism*, p. 229.
79. Sykes, *Cross Roads*, p. 324.
80. Memo by R. Howe, 21 January 1947, FO 371 vol. 61858, and CM (47) 6 Minute 3, Confidential Annex, 15 January 1947 CAB 128/11, quoted in Bullock, *Bevin, 1945–51*, p. 364.
81. Ibid. Strachey and Shinwell also favoured partition but were not in the Cabinet.
82. CP (47) 59, 13 February 1947, in Bullock, *Bevin, 1945–51*, p. 367.
83. CP (47) 30, 14 January 1947.
84. Quoted in Gorny, *Labour and Zionism*, p. 216.
85. 'The Government must impose a Palestine Settlement' *Forward*, 15 February 1947, cited in Gorny, *Labour and Zionism*, p. 229.
86. 'Britain without Empire', *The Nation*, 29 March 1947.
87. Ibid.
88. Poale Zion representatives saw Laski in March and put forward a resolution to the Annual Conference, but were induced to withdraw it (NEC minutes, 26 March and 27 May 1947). Presumably they were given some kind of assurances, and Laski may have been referring to his role in a letter to Frankfurter, 21 June 1947.
89. To Frankfurter, 21 June 1947.
90. FO 371/61815, 12 July 1947, quoted in Bullock, *Bevin, 1945–51*, p. 448.
91. To Laski, 20 August 1947 in Laski papers, H 1973.
92. Sykes, *Cross Roads*, pp. 335–6.
93. Laski to Dalton, 19 September 1947, Peart Binns Papers, Hull. (He probably wrote to Attlee in similar terms.)
94. CP (47) 259, 18 September 1947, in Bullock, *Bevin, 1945–51*, p. 476.
95. Ibid., quoting CM 78 (47) 20 September 1947.
96. To Frankfurter, 29 September 1947, FFP.
97. Morgan, *Labour in Power*, p. 216.
98. Northedge, 'Britain and the Middle East', pp. 162–3.
99. FO 800 vol. 487 PA/47/19, Bullock, *Bevin, 1945–51*, p. 477.
100. For a convincing interpretation on these lines, see J. and D. Kimche, *Both Sides of the Hill: Britain and the Palestine War* (Secker and Warburg, 1960) (hereafter Kimche, *Both Sides*).
101. Ibid., p. 157.
102. Northedge, 'Britain and the Middle East', p. 161.
103. Sykes, *Cross Roads*, p. 345.
104. They also decided that British officers in the Transjordanian Arab League should not take part in any military action.
105. COS (48) 45 (0) 26 February 1948.
106. For an analysis, see Gorny, *Labour and Zionism*, pp. 221–33.
107. 'Note for the National Executive Committee on Certain Implications of the Palestine Problem', and NEC minutes, 23 March 1948.
108. FO 800 vol. 487/PA/48/16, Bevin to Inverchapel.

109. FO 800 vol. 487/PA/48/19, 22 April 1949.
110. Ibid.
111. FO 800 vol. 487 PA/48/33, Bevin to Amman, 13 May 1948.
112. Kimche, *Both Sides*, pp. 196–8.
113. FO 800 vol. 510/UN/48/36, 5 October 1948, quoted in Bullock, *Bevin, 1945–51*, p. 608.
114. PREM 8 1251, 11 January 1949, Bevin to Washington.
115. CAB 128/15 CM3 (49), 17 January 1949, quoted in Northedge, 'Britain and the Middle East', pp. 165–6.
116. Quoted in Bullock, *Bevin, 1945–51*, p. 652.
117. Donoughue and Jones, *Morrison* p. 435.
118. To Lerner, 16 August 1948, YUL.
119. Frida to the Berdahls, 7 March 1949, Berdahl papers, UI.
120. To Frankfurter, 9 December 1949, FFP.
121. Obituary, *Jewish Chronicle*, 31 March 1950.
122. R. Crossman and M. Foot, *A Palestine Munich?* (London, 1947).
123. Quoted in Gorny, *Labour and Zionism*, p. 174.
124. To Frida, 30 Aug 1946, FHL.
125. To Frankfurter, 11 and 29 May 1947, FFP.
126. To Frankfurter, 21 June 1947, FFP.
127. To Frankfurter, 14 February 1948, FFP.
128. Bullock, *Bevin, 1945–51*, p. 165.
129. Ibid., p. 175.
130. Quoted in Sykes, *Cross Roads*, p. 297.
131. FO 800 vol. 487 PA/48/26.
132. For further evidence of Attlee's prejudices, see Pimlott, *Dalton*, p. 596.
133. To Frankfurter, 2 December 1948, FFP.
134. Quoted in Martin, *Laski*, p. 165.
135. 9 February 1950, quoted in Eastwood, *Laski*, pp. 161–2.
136. Yaakov Morris, 'Laski's Concept of Socialism and Israel' (Harold Laski Institute of Political Science, 1970), quoted in Eastwood, *Laski*, p. 99.
137. To Frankfurter, 29 May 1947, FFP.

CHAPTER THIRTEEN

1. To Frida, 16 August 1945, FHL.
2. *The Times*, 15 November 1945.
3. Ibid., 3 May 1946; 'Britain without Empire: II', *The Nation*, 12 April 1947.
4. To Frankfurter, 21 June 1947, FFP.
5. To Braunthal, 17 February 1946, Braunthal correspondence, IISH.
6. To Frankfurter, 21 June 1947, FFP.
7. To Frankfurter, 27 September 1947, FFP.
8. *Forward*, 6 March 1948, quoted in Schneer, *Labour's Conscience*, p. 42.
9. To Cohn, 6 February 1949, RAC.
10. To Frankfurter, 9 December 1949.
11. To Cohn, 22 December 1949, RAC.

12. To Marion Frankfurter, 9 December 1949, in container 75, FFP.
13. To Cohn, 6 February 1949, RAC.
14. 9 December 1949, quoted in Martin, *Laski*, pp. 254–5.
15. To Cohn, 6 February 1949, RAC.
16. *Edmund Burke* (Falconer, 1947).
17. Einstein to Laski, 16 April 1947, Laski Corr. 1, IISH.
18. Eastwood, *Laski*, p. 84, quoting Otto Nathan.
19. Attlee to Laski, 14 February 1949, Laski papers, H 1973; PPC minutes, 14 and 21 February 1949.
20. To Frida, 9 February 1950, FHL.
21. Martin, Laski, pp. 255–6.
22. To Morgan Phillips, 25 February 1950, Laski file, LP.
23. 'Is the Third World War Inevitable?', in 24.2, Laski papers, IISH, published in a shortened version in *The Free World*, June 1950.
24. Eastwood, *Laski*, p. 163, quoting Ralph Miliband.
25. Frida to Huebsch, 20 April 1950, Huebsch papers, LC.

CONCLUSION

1. Labour Party Conference Report (1950) quoted by Morgan Phillips in a talk on Laski in 1953, Laski file, Labour Party archives.
2. *Le Populaire*, quoted in Martin, *Laski*, p. 271.
3. Sperber, *Murrow*, p. 334.
4. Carroll Hawkins, 'Harold J. Laski: A Preliminary Analysis', *Political Science Quarterly*, 3, 1950, p. 392.
5. 'The Age of Laski', *Fortnightly Review*, June 1950, p. 378.
6. Ibid., p. 384.
7. Record of Commemorative Meeting, 1 May 1952 in Kingsley Martin papers, Box 39/Rec 1, Sussex University.
8. Morgan Phillips to Purushottam Mavalankar, 17 March 1955, in Laski file, LP.
9. Carr-Saunders to Frankfurter, 15 August 1950, Box 151, FFP.
10. Frankfurter to Frida, 5 May 1950, Box 151, FFP.
11. Warburg to Frankfurter, 27 May 1952, Box 151, FFP.
12. Frankfurter to Warburg, 25 September 1952, Box 151, FFP.
13. Frankfurter to Lord Chorley, 2 February 1953, Box 151, FFP.
14. Warburg to Frankfurter, 3 February 1953, Box 151, FFP.
15. Sperber, *Murrow*, pp. 450–2.
16. G. Woledge (Librarian of LSE) to Frankfurter, 6 November 1953 in LSE archives (file on the Laski Collection).
17. Letter of 12 December 1963, in LSE archives (the Laski Collection).
18. Review of Eastwood, *Laski*, and in Abse, *My LSE*, p. 99.
19. Tawney to Martin, 1 April 1951, in Martin papers, 15/1. (Tawney's appreciation was in *Manchester Guardian*, 27 March 1950.)
20. 'Harold Laski: An Appreciation', *Fabian Journal*, May 1950.
21. Abse, *My LSE*, p. 8.
22. Quoted in G. M. Singh, 'Laski – The Teacher and the Political Scientist',

Laski Memorial Lecture at the Harold Laski Institute of Political Science, Ahmedabad, 30 June 1957, p. 7.

23. Information on the attitudes of Welsh miners was given by Michael Foot (quoting Aneurin Bevan) in a personal interview.
24. 'Teacher and Student' in *Dangers/Obedience* (originally in *Century*, 1929) (hereafter 'Teacher').
25. 'Teacher', p. 101.
26. Ibid., p. 103.
27. Ibid., p. 117.
28. *My LSE*, p. 91.
29. Reproduced in *Dangers/Gentleman*, pp. 44–5.
30. Abse, *My LSE*, p. 27.
31. 'Teacher,' p. 120.
32. 'Laski and British Socialism', *History of Political Thought*, 2 (3), Winter 1981, p. 590.
33. 'Encounter of Minds', *Times Literary Supplement*, 24 July 1953.
34. Introduction to *Nationalism and the Future of Civilization* (C. A. Watts, 1932) pp. 13–14.
35. 'Laski' in John Strachey, *The Strangled Cry* (Bodley Head, 1962), pp. 196–7 (originally in *New Statesman*, 8 April 1950).
36. *American Democracy*, p. 320.
37. Quoted in Eastwood, *Laski*, p. 134.
38. See also Kenneth O. Morgan 'Preaching and Pluralism', *Times Literary Supplement*, 2 December 1977.
39. *Trade Unions*, p. 42.
40. *Dilemma*, pp. 88–9.
41. *Liberty, 1948*, p. 31.
42. 'The Crisis in our Civilization' *Foreign Affairs*, xxvi, October 1947, p. 46,
43. See, for example, *American Democracy*, pp. 538–53; 'Is a Third World War Inevitable'?; *The Times*, 29 April 1946.
44. *Socialism as Internationalism*, Fabian International Bureau, February 1949.
45. 'Machiavelli and the Present Time' in *Dangers/Obedience*, p. 239 (originally in *Quarterly Review, 1927*).
46. *Dangers/Gentleman*, p. 35.
47. Ibid., p. 40.
48. Frankfurter to Laski, 30 March 1924, Laski correspondence in Syracuse University Library, New York.
49. Frankfurter sent Laski's lecture to an American scholar on the Burke period who said: 'It's the best thing I have ever seen on Burke ... There is no American scholar who could have come within miles of writing that address'. Frankfurter to Martin, 11 June 1952, Box 151, FFP.
50. *The British Political Elite* (1963) p. 16, cited in Peretz, 'Laski Redivivus'.
51. 'Machiavelli and the Present Time' in *Dangers/Obedience*.
52. Fabian Tract no. 235, February 1931.
53. 'A Portrait of Jean Jacques Rousseau' in *Dangers/Obedience*, p. 202 (originally in *Yale Review*, 1928).
54. Undated review of G. Himmelfarb (ed.), *Acton Redivivus: Essays on Freedom and Power*, in Laski papers, HE.

Select Bibliography

PRIVATE PAPERS

Laski Papers

There is no single collection which contains more than a small fraction of Laski's correspondence. Many of the papers were destroyed during the Second World War, and the remainder are dispersed amongst many different collections. The following are the most useful:

University of Hull (Great Britain)
This includes three separate collections:
(a) General correspondence and sundry material (cited as H 1973).
(b) Papers presented by Granville Eastwood in 1978 and 1981 (cited as HE).
(c) Correspondence between Harold and Frida Laski, presented by Professor John Saville from 1989 (cited as FHL).

The International Institute of Social History (Amsterdam, The Netherlands) (cited as IISH)
This includes:
(a) Three folders of correspondence (cited as Laski corr.).
(b) Drafts of manuscripts by Laski, some of which remain unpublished.
(c) Letters in other collections, including a particularly interesting correspondence with Julius Braunthal during the Second World War.

The National Museum of Labour History (Manchester, Great Britain) (cited as LP)
(a) File of correspondence between Laski and the Labour Party, 1938–50.
(b) File on India, 1935–41.
(c) National Executive Committee Minutes and associated papers, 1937–49.

Other Collections Containing Laski Papers, Correspondence or Other Relevant Material

In Great Britain
Archives of New College, Oxford
Attlee papers (Bodleian library, Oxford, and Churchill College, Cambridge)
The Fawcett Library, City of London Polytechnic
Frank Hardie papers (Bodleian library, Oxford)
Haldane papers (National Library of Scotland, Edinburgh)
Keynes papers (King's College, Cambridge)
George Lansbury papers (British Library of Political and Economic Science, LSE (BLPES))
Laski broadcasts (National Sound Archive, British Library)
'The Laski collection' and 'Memorial to Professor Laski' (in Library and School archives, BLPES, LSE)

Laski correspondence with Benjamin Huebsch (BLPES, LSE)
Laski family papers and sundry material in the Anglo-Jewish archive (Hartley
    Library, University of Southampton)
Laski family material (Manchester Jewish Museum)
Neville Laski papers (Manchester Central Library)
Oxford University Fabian Society Minute Books (Bodleian Library, Oxford)
Ramsay MacDonald papers (Public Record Office, Kew)
Kingsley Martin papers (University of Sussex, Great Britain)
Gilbert Murray papers (Bodleian Library, Oxford)
J. Peart-Binns papers (University of Hull)
Sankey papers (Bodleian Library, Oxford)

In the United States
Edith Abbott papers, University of Chicago
Carl Becker papers, Cornell University, Ithaca
Clarence Berdahl papers, University of Illinois at Urbana-Champaign
Hugo Black papers, Library of Congress, Washington DC
Zechariah Chafee papers, Harvard Law School Library, Cambridge
Charles Clark papers, Yale University, New Haven, Conneticut
Alfred E. Cohn papers, Rockefeller Archive Center, New York
Thomas G. Corcoran papers, Library of Congress, Washington DC
Merle Curti papers, State Historical Society of Wisconsin
William O. Douglas papers, Library of Congress, Washington DC
General Education Board papers, Rockefeller Archive Center, New York
Herbert Feis papers, Library of Congress, Washington DC
Felix Frankfurter papers, (containers 74, 75, 151, 152, 207) Library of Con-
    gress, Washington DC
Arthur Gleason papers, Library of Congress, Washington DC
Oliver Wendell Holmes Jr. papers, Harvard Law School Library, Cambridge
Harry Hopkins papers, Franklin D. Roosevelt Library, Hyde Park
Benjamin Huebsch papers, Library of Congress, Washington DC
Harold Ickes Diaries, Library of Congress, Washington DC
Robert La Follette Sr. papers, Library of Congress, Washington DC
Laski correspondence in several collections in Columbia University, New
    York City
Laski correspondence, Syracuse University, New York
Max Lerner papers, Yale University, New Haven
Walter Lippmann papers, Yale University, New Haven
Archibald Macleish papers, Library of Congress, Washington DC
Eugene Meyer papers, Library of Congress, Washington DC
Henry Morgenthau Jr. Diary, Library of Congress, Washington DC
Amos Pinchot papers, Library of Congress, Washington DC
Roscoe Pound Papers, Harvard Law School Library, Cambridge
Thomas Reed Powell papers, Harvard Law School Library, Cambridge
Eleanor Roosevelt papers, Franklin D. Roosevelt Library, Hyde Park
Franklin D. Roosevelt papers, Franklin D. Roosevelt Library, Hyde Park
Alexander Sachs papers, Franklin D. Roosevelt Library, Hyde Park
Harlan Fiske Stone papers, Library of Congress, Washington DC
Willard Straight papers, Cornell University, Ithaca

Rexford Tugwell papers, Franklin D. Roosevelt Library, Hyde Park
H. G. Wells Papers, University of Illinois at Urbana-Champaign
John Winant papers, Franklin D. Roosevelt Library, Hyde Park

In Canada
Bertrand Russell papers, McMaster University, Hamilton, Ontario
McGill University Archives, Montreal, Quebec

STATE PAPERS

Public Record Office, Kew

PREM 1, 102–3, Palestine, 1930–1
PREM 62/5, 1942
PREM 26/3, 1942
PREM 4/51/8, 1943
PREM 8 298, 1946
PREM 8/627, Palestine Policy, 1945–7
PREM 8/1251, Palestine Policy, 1948–50
FO 800 vols. 484–7, 1945–8
FO 371 vols. 52515–7, 60528–9, 60543, 1946, Italy

US Department of Justice

Federal Bureau of Investigation (Freedom of Information Release) files:
100–148342; 44–0–3893; 66–1731–458

WORKS BY LASKI

Published Correspondence

Mark DeWolfe (ed.), *Holmes-Laski Letters – The Correspondence of Mr. Justice Holmes and Harold J. Laski* (Harvard University Press, 1953) 2 volumes

Books

The American Democracy (Viking Press, 1948; Allen and Unwin, 1949)
The American Presidency (Harper and Bros., 1940; Allen and Unwin, 1940)
Authority in the Modern State (Yale University Press, 1919; Oxford University Press, 1919) Contains: 'Authority in the Modern State', 'Bonald', 'Lammenais', 'The Political Theory of Royer-Collard', 'Administrative Syndicalism in France'.
'The Chosen People' (unpublished) 1912
Communism (H. Holt and Co., 1927; Williams and Norgate, 1927)

The Danger of Being a Gentleman, and other Essays (Viking Press, 1940; Allen and Unwin, 1939). Contains: 'The Danger of Being a Gentleman' (1932), 'On the Study of Politics' (1926), 'Law and Justice in Soviet Russia' (1935), 'The Judicial Function' (1936), 'The English Constitution and French Public Opinion, 1789–1794' (1938), 'The Committee System in English Local Government' (1935), 'Nationalism and the Future of Civilization' (1932), 'Mr Justice Holmes: For his 89th Birthday' (1930)

The Dangers of Obedience, and other Essays (Harper and Bros., 1930). Contains: 'The Dangers of Obedience' (1929), 'The American Political System (1928), 'The Recovery of Citizenship' (1928), 'Teacher and Student' (1929), 'The Academic Mind' (1929), 'Foundations, Universities and Research' (1929), 'A Portrait of Jean Jacques Rousseau' (1928), 'A Plea for Equality', 'Machiavelli and the Present Time' (1927), 'Can Business be Civilized?' (1930)

Democracy in Crisis (University of North Carolina Press, 1933; Allen and Unwin, 1933)

The Dilemma of Our Times (Allen and Unwin, 1952)

Faith, Reason and Civilization (Viking Press, 1944; Gollancz, 1944)

The Foundations of Sovereignty, and other Essays (Harcourt, Brace and Co., 1921; Allen and Unwin, 1922). Contains: 'The Foundations of Sovereignty', 'The Problem of Administrative Areas (1918), 'The Responsibility of the State in England' (1919); 'The Personality of Associations' (1916), 'The Early History of the Corporation in England' (1917), 'The Theory of Popular Sovereignty' (1919), 'The Pluralistic State' (1919), 'The Basis of Vicarious Liability' (1916), 'The Political Ideas of James I (1919)

A Grammar of Politics (Yale University Press, 1925; Allen and Unwin, 1925). (The 1938 edition contained a new chapter, 'The Crisis in the Theory of the State')

An Introduction to Politics (Allen and Unwin, 1931). Published in the United States as *Politics* (J. P. Lipincott, 1934).

Liberty in the Modern State (Faber, 1930; Harper and Bros., 1930). A 1937 edition (Penguin) contained a new introduction, and the 1948 edition (Allen and Unwin) included a further substantially revised introduction.

Parliamentary Government in England (Allen and Unwin, 1938; Viking Press, 1938)

Political Thought in England from Locke to Bentham (Henry Holt and Co., 1920; Williams, 1920)

Reflections on the Constitution (Manchester University Press, 1951; Viking Press, 1951)

Reflections on the Revolution of Our Times (Allen and Unwin, 1943; Viking Press, 1943)

The Rise of European Liberalism (Allen and Unwin, 1936). American edition published as *The Rise of Liberalism* (Harper and Bros., 1936)

The State in Theory and Practice (Allen and Unwin, 1935; Viking Press, 1935)

The Strategy of Freedom (Harper and Bros., 1941; Allen and Unwin, 1942)

Studies in Law and Politics (Allen and Unwin, 1932; Yale University Press, 1932). Contains: 'The Age of Reason'; 'Diderot' (1931): 'The Socialist Tradition in the French Revolution' (1930); 'The Problem of a Second Chamber' (1925); 'The State in the New Social Order' (1922); 'The Political

Philosophy of Mr Justice Holmes'; 'The Technique of Judicial Appointment'; 'The Personnel of the British Cabinet, 1801–1924' (1928); 'Judicial Review of Social Policy', 'Procedure for Constructive Contempt'; 'Law and the State'; 'Justice and the Law' (1930)

Studies in the Problem of Sovereignty (Yale University Press, 1917; Humphrey Milford, 1917). Contains: 'The Sovereignty of the State' (1915); 'The Political Theory of the Disruption' (1916); 'The Political Theory of the Oxford Movement'; 'The Political Theory of the Catholic Revival', 'De Maistre and Bismarck', 'Sovereignty and Federalism', 'Sovereignty and Centralisation' (1916)

Trade Unions in the New Society (Viking Press, 1949; Allen and Unwin, 1950)

Where do We Go from Here? (Penguin, 1940; Viking Press, 1940)

Pamphlets, Reports, Tracts, and Published Lectures

Note: Contributions which were republished in books are not listed again.

Communist Manifesto, Socialist Landmark (Allen and Unwin, 1948)

The Crisis and the Constitution: 1931 and After, Day to Day Pamphlets No 9. (Hogarth Press, 1932)

The Decline of Liberalism, L. T. Hobhouse Memorial Trust Lectures No 10 (Oxford University Press, 1940)

The Decline of Parliamentary Government (with Josef Redlich) Foreign Policy Association Pamphlet No 74 (Foreign Policy Association, 1931)

Democracy at the Crossroads (National Council of Labour Colleges, 1934(?))

The Economic Revolution (with W. Wellock and P. W. Martin) Peace Aims Pamphlet No 5 (National Peace Council, 1941)

Edmund Burke, Address delivered to Trinity College Historical Society, University of Dublin (Falconer, 1947)

The Germans – Are They Human? A Reply to Sir Robert Vansittart (LBC/ Gollancz, 1941)

Is This an Imperialist War? (Labour Party, 1940)

Karl Marx: an Essay (Fabian Society/Allen and Unwin, 1922)

'The Militant Temper in Politics', Fifth Suffragette Lecture, 18 November 1932 (Obtainable in the Fawcett Library and the Museum of London)

The Labour Party and the Constitution Socialist Programme series No 2 (Socialist League, 1933)

The Labour Party, the War and the Future (Labour Party, 1939)

The Limitations of the Expert, Fabian Tract No 235 (Fabian Society, 1931)

London, Washington, Moscow, Partners in Peace?, Peace Aims pamphlet No 22 (National Peace Council, 1943)

Marx and Today, Fabian Society research series No 73 (Gollancz/Fabian Society, 1943)

The Old World and the New Society (Labour Party, 1942) (Drafted by Laski)

Political Offences and the Death Penalty, Sixth Roy Calvert Memorial Lecture (E. G. Dunstan and Co., 1940)

The Position of Parties and the Right of Dissolution, Fabian Tract No 210, the Fabian Society (London) 1924

Report of the Legal Education Committee, Cmd 4663 HMSO July 1934 (Minority report by Laski)
Report of the Committee on Ministerial Powers, Cmd 4060 HMSO April 1932 (Substantial drafting and dissenting note by Laski)
The Rights of Man, Macmillan War Pamphlets No 8 (Macmillan and Co., 1940)
The Roosevelt Experiment, Socialist League Forum Series No 1 (Socialist League, 1933); *The Atlantic Monthly*, 153, February 1934
The Secret Battalion: An Examination of the Communist Attitude to the Labour Party (Labour Party, 1946)
The Spirit of Co-operation, 1936 Hodgson Pratt Memorial Lecture (Manchester Co-operative Union, 1936)
Russia and the West, Policy of Britain, Peace Aims Pamphlet 43, (National Peace Council, 1947)
Socialism and Freedom, Fabian Tract No 216 (Fabian Society, 1925)
Socialism as Internationalism, Fabian Research series No 132 (Gollancz, 1949)
The Trade Disputes and Trade Unions Bill (with Ernest J. P. Benn)
Present Day Papers, No 12 (P. S. King and son, 1927)
The Webbs and Soviet Communism, Beatrice Webb Memorial Lecture No 3 (Fabian Publications, 1947)
Will Planning Restrict Freedom? (The Architectural Press, 1944)
Will the Peace Last?, Peace Aims Pamphlet, No 28 (National Peace Council, 1944)

Articles and Chapters in Books

Note: For a much fuller list of Laski's articles, see the relevant volumes of *Readers' Guide to Periodical Literature*, H. W. Wilson (New York) and *International Index to Periodicals*, H. W. Wilson (New York). The books by H. A. Deane and B. Zylstra (see pp. 424–5 below) also contain extensive lists of Laski's articles.

'An Age of Transition', *Political Quarterly*, 14, April–June, 1943
'The Alternative to Revolution in England', *The Nation*, 112, 9 February 1921
'The Apotheosis of the State', *New Republic*, 7, 22 July 1916
'Aristocracy Still the Ruling Class in England', *Current History*, 32, July 1930
'Britain without Empire', *The Nation*, 164, 29 March and 12 April 1947
'Britain's Baldwin', *Current History*, 42, August 1935
'The British Coal Strike', *The Nation*, 112, 27 April 1921
'British Communists Help Hitler', *The Nation*, 152, 15 February 1941
'British Democracy and Mr Kennedy', *Harper's Magazine*, 182, April 1941
'British Labor Reconstruction Proposals and the American Labor Attitude', *Proceedings of the Academy of Political Science*, 7 February 1919
'British Labor and Direct Action', *The Nation*, 111, 11 September 1920
'The British Parties in Conference', *New Republic*, 52, 9 November 1927
'The Challenge of Our Times', *The American Scholar*, 8, Autumn 1939
'Choosing the Planners' in G. D. H. Cole et al., *Plan for Britain* (Routledge, 1943)

'Civil Liberties in the Soviet Union,' *New Republic*, 115, 21 October 1946

'The Civil Service and Parliament' in *The Development of the Civil Service, Lectures Delivered Before the Society of Civil Servants, 1920–1921* (P. S. King and Son 1922)

'The Coal Strike and Beyond', *The Nation*, 122, 26 May 1926

'Communism as a World Force', *International Affairs*, 10, January 1931

'The Crisis in Our Civilization', *Foreign Affairs* 26, October 1947

'Data from Glasgow' in Ethel M. Elderton et al., *On the Correlation of Fertility with Social Value* (Cambridge University Press, 1913)

'Democracy at the Crossroads', *Yale Review*, 9, July 1920

'Democracy in War Time' in G. D. H. Cole et al., *Victory or Vested Interest?* (Routledge, 1942)

'Does Capitalism Cause War?' in Viscount Cecil et. al., *Does Capitalism Cause War?* (H. and E. R. Brinton, 1935)

'The Economic Foundations of Peace' in Leonard S. Woolf (ed.), *The Intelligent Man's Way to Prevent War* (Gollancz, 1933)

'Efficiency in Government' in Douglas Jay et al., *The Road to Recovery*, Fabian Society Lectures (Allan Wingate, 1948)

'The Elite in a Democratic Society', *Harpers Magazine*, 167, September 1933

'England in 1929', *Yale Review*, 18, March 1929

'English Politics Today', *New Republic*, 43, 8 July 1925

'Epitaph on a System', *New Statesman and Nation*, 24, 11 July 1942

'The Fabian Way, *Current History*, 41, October 1934

'A Formula for Conservatives', *Harpers Magazine*, 175, September 1937

'Forward from Liberalism' (review), *Left News*, January, 1937

'Freedom in Danger', *Yale Review*, 23, March 1934

'The General Strike and the Constitution', *Labour Magazine* 5 July 1926

'Getting on with Russia', *The Nation*, CL XVI, 10 January 1948

'Government in Wartime' in H. J. Laski et al., *Where Stands Democracy?* (Macmillan, 1940)

'Harold J. Laski' in Clifton Fadiman (ed.), *I Believe: The Personal Philosophies of Certain Eminent Men and Women of Our Time* (Simon and Schuster, 1939; Allen and Unwin,1940)

'The Higher Learning in America', *New Republic*, 17, 11 January 1919

'Hitler over England', *The Nation*, 140, 5 June 1935

'The India Report', *The Nation*, 140, 2 January 1935

'India at the Crossroads', *Yale Review*, 21, March 1932

'Information Please, Mr Molotov', *The Nation*, 167, 15 June 1946

'Is a Third World War Inevitable?', *The Free World*, June 1950

'A Key to Communism' (review) *New Statesman and Nation*, 10, 20 July 1935

'Knowledge as Civic Discipline' in O. Stanley (ed.), *The Way Out: Essays on the Meaning and Purpose of Adult Education* (Oxford University Press,1923)

'The Labour Party and the Left Book Club', *Left News*, August 1937

'The Labour Party Conference at Edinburgh', *Labour Monthly*, 18, November 1936

'Lenin and Mussolini', *Foreign Affairs* 2, September 1923

'A Leningrad Letter', I and II *The Nation*, 139, 18 and 25 July 1934

'Macaulay', *Ulula* (Manchester Grammar School Magazine) Autumn 1910

'The Machinery of International Relief' in L. Woolf et al., *When Hostilities*

Cease: Papers on Relief and Reconstruction Prepared for the Fabian Society (Gollancz, 1943)

'Marxism after Fifty Years', *Current History*, 37, March 1933

'The Means and the End', *New Republic*, 4, 4 September 1915

'A Mendelian View of Racial Heredity', *Biometrika*, 8, July 1911–January 1912

'Mr Baldwin attacks the Trade Unions', *New Republic*, 51, 8 June 1927

'Mr Baldwin's First Year of Office', *New Republic*, 45, 16 December 1925

'The British General Strike', *The Nation*, 122, 16 June 1926

'M. Duguit's Conception of the State' in Arthur L. Goodhart et al., *Modern Theories of Law* (Oxford University Press, 1933)

'Mr George and the Constitution' *The Nation* (London), 28, 9 and 23 October, 6 and 20 November 1920

'My Day in Court', *Atlantic Monthly* 190, November 1952

'My Impressions of Stalin' *New Republic*, 115, October 1946

'The Need for a European Revolution' in *Programme for Victory* (Fabian Society/Routledge, 1941)

'The New Test for British Labor', *Foreign Affairs*, 8, October 1929

'A Note on Anti-Semitism', *New Statesman and Nation*, 25, 13 February 1943

'A Note on Duguit', *Harvard Law Review*, 31, November 1917

'On a Jewish Soldier's Letter', *New Statesman*, 26, 9 October 1943

'Open Letter to President Roosevelt', *New Statesman and Nation*, 25, 10 April 1943

'The Outlook for Civil Liberties' in Bertrand Russell, Vernon Bartlett, G. D. H. Cole et al., *'Dare We Look Ahead?'* (Allen and Unwin, 1938)

'Palestine: The Economic Aspect' in Joseph B. Hobman (ed.) *Palestine's Economic Future* (Percy Lund Humphries, 1946)

'Parliament and Revolution', *New Republic*, 22, 19 May 1920

'People at Bay' (review) *Left News*, August 1938

'The Personality of the State', *The Nation*, 101, 22 July 1915

'The Position and Prospects of Communism', *Foreign Affairs*, 11, October 1932

'The Present Evolution of the Parliamentary System' in H. J. Laski, Ch. Borgeaud et al., *The Development of the Representative System in Our Times* (Payot et Cie, 1928)

'The Present Position of Representative Democracy' in G. B. Shaw et al., *Where Stands Socialism Today?* (Rich and Cowan, 1933)

'Present Tendencies in British Politics', *New Republic*, 51, 13 July 1927

'President Roosevelt and Foreign Opinion', *Yale Review*, 22, June 1933

'Problems of Labour Policy' *Labour Monthly*, 18, March 1936

'The Prospects of Constitutional Government', *Political Quarterly*, I, July–September 1930

'Public Opinion and the National Strike', *Labour Magazine*, 5, January 1927

'The Public Papers and Addresses of Franklin D. Roosevelt', *University of Chicago Law Review*, VI, December 1938

'Revolution by Consent', *The Nation*, 152, 22 March 1941

'The Scope of Eugenics', *Westminster Review*, 174, July 1910

'A Socialist Looks at the Cold War', *New Republic*, 117, 27 October 1947

'Some Implications of the Crisis', *Political Quarterly*, 2, October–December 1931

'Some Reflections on Government in Wartime', *Political Quarterly*, 13, January–March 1942

'Soviet Communism: A New Civilization' (review), *Political Quarterly*, 9, January–March 1938

'State, Worker and Technician' in Georges Gurvitch (ed.), *Industrialisation et technocratie* (Librairie Armand Colin, 1949)

'The Temper of the Present Time', *New Republic*, 21, 18 February 1920

'The Theory and Practice of Socialism', review, *Left Book News*, November 1936

'The Theory of an International Society' in Geneva Institute of International Relations, *Problems of Peace* (Allen and Unwin, 1932)

'Towards a Universal Declaration of Human Rights' in *Human Rights: Comments and Interpretations: A Symposium*, with an Introduction by Jacques Maritain (UNESCO, 1948)

'The Trade Unions Survey the General Strike', *New Republic*, 50, 2 March 1927

'Unity and the Labour Party', *Labour Monthly*, 19, March 1937

'The Value and Defects of the Marxist Philosophy', *Current History*, 29, October 1928

'Wanted: A New Constitution', *Tribune*, 28 June 1946

'The War', *Left News*, December 1939

'A Word to the Republicans', *Harpers Magazine*, 171, October 1935

'What Democracy Means in Russia', *New Republic*, 115, 28 October 1946

'What will Mr Roosevelt Mean to Europe?', *Labour Magazine*, 11, (8), December 1932

'Why Does Russia Act That Way?', *The Nation*, 164, 1 March 1947

Introductions and Translations

R. A. Brady, *The Spirit and Structure of German Fascism* (LBC/Gollancz, 1937) (foreword by Laski)

Edmund Burke, *Letters of Edmund Burke: A Selection*. The World's Classics, No. 237. (Humphrey Milford/Oxford University Press, 1922) (edited with an introduction by Laski)

Léon Duguit, *Law in the Modern State* (Huebsch, 1919) (translated by Frida and Harold Laski)

George P. Gooch, *English Democratic Ideas in the Seventeenth Century* (Cambridge University Press, 1927) (notes and appendices by Laski)

Richard B. H. (First Viscount) Haldane, *The Problem of Nationalization* (Allen and Unwin/Labour Publishing, 1921) (introduction by R. H. Tawney and Laski)

Oliver Wendell Holmes, *Collected Legal Papers* (Harcourt Brace, 1920) (compiled by Laski)

Hubert Languet (Junius Brutus), *A Defence of Liberty against Tyrants* (Bell and Sons, 1924) (introduction by Laski)

Louis Levy, *France Is a Democracy* (Gollancz, 1943) (introduction by Laski)

John Stuart Mill, *Autobiography*, The World's Classics, No. 262 (Humphrey Milford/Oxford University Press, 1924) (preface by Laski)

Edward Neep, *Seditious Offences*, Fabian Tract No. 220 (Fabian Society, 1926) (introductory note by Laski)

Jean Baptiste Say, *Letters to Thomas Robert Malthus on Political Economy and Stagnation of Commerce* (George Harding's Bookshop, 1936) (prefatory note by Laski)

Sir Henry Taylor, *The Statesman* (Heffer and Sons (Cambridge) 1927) (introductory essay by Laski)

BOOKS AND ARTICLES ABOUT LASKI

Max Beloff, 'The Age of Laski', *The Fortnightly*, 167, June 1950

T. D. Burridge 'A Postscript to Potsdam: The Churchill-Laski Electoral Clash, June 1945', *Journal of Contemporary History*, 12, 1977

'Harold Laski', *Clare Market Review*, 46 (1), Michaelmas 1950

T. I. Cook, 'In Memoriam', *American Political Science Review*, 44, September 1950

Herbert A. Deane, *The Political Ideas of Harold J. Laski* (Columbia University Press, 1955)

Granville Eastwood, *Harold Laski* (Mowbrays, 1977)

W. Y. Elliott, *The Pragmatic Revolt in Politics* (Macmillan, 1928)

G. Feaver, 'Intellectuals and Politics: Harold Laski Revisited', paper given at the 46th Annual Meeting of the Canadian Political Science Association, University of Toronto, 3–6 June 1974, in *Proceedings of the Annual Meetings of the CPSA* (mimeo), republished in a shorter form as 'Intellectuals and Politics: The Moral of Harold Laski', *The Lugano Review*, 2, 1975.

Y. Gorny, 'The Jewishness and Zionism of Harold Laski', *Midstream*, November 1977

W. H. Greenleaf, 'Laski and British Socialism', *History of Political Thought*, 2, (3), Winter 1981

R. C. Gupta, *Harold Laski: A Critical Analysis of his Political Ideas* (Ram Prasad and Sons, 1966)

Carroll Hawkins, 'Harold J. Laski: A Preliminary Analysis', *Political Science Quarterly*, 65, September 1950

P. Hirst, *The Pluralist Theory of the State* (Routledge, 1989)

K. C. Hsiao, *Political Pluralism: A Study in Contemporary Political Thought* (Kegan Paul, Trench, Trubner, 1927)

M. M. Kampelmann, 'Harold J. Laski: A Current Analysis', *Journal of Politics*, 10 February 1948

Marc Karson, 'Harold Laski and the Soviet Union', *New Politics*, Spring 1965

Freda Kirchwey, 'Harold Laski', *The Nation*, 170, 1 April 1950

Isaac Kramnick, 'The Professor and the Police', *Harvard Magazine*, September–October 1989

Frida Laski, 'The Memoirs of Frida Laski', (unpublished, 1976)

The Laski Libel Action (Daily Express, 1947)

R. T. McKenzie, 'Laski and the Social Bases of the Constitution', *British Journal of Sociology*, 3, 1952

H. M. Magid, *English Political Pluralism* (Columbia University Press, 1941)

Kingsley Martin, *Harold Laski* (Gollancz, 1953; Viking Press, 1953)

Kenneth O. Morgan, *Labour People* (Oxford University Press, 1987)

D. Nicholls, *The Pluralist State* (Macmillan, 1975)

C. Palazzola, *La Libertà alla Prova – Stato e società in Laski* (ETS, 1979)

M. Peretz, 'Laski Redivivus', *Journal of Contemporary History*, I (2) 1966

G. N. Sarma, *The Political Thought of Harold J. Laski* (Orient Longmans, 1965)

Roger Soltau, 'Professor Laski and Political Science', *Political Quarterly*, 21, July 1950

John Strachey, 'Laski's Struggle for Certainty' in *The Strangled Cry* (Bodley Head, 1962) (originally in *New Statesman and Nation*, 8 April 1950)

J. W. N. Watkins, 'Laski on Conscience and Counter-Revolution', *Nineteenth Century and After*, CXLV, March 1949

Lewis Zerby, 'Normative, Descriptive and Ideological Elements in the Writings of Laski', *Philosophy of Science* April 1945

B. Zylstra, *From Pluralism to Collectivism: the Development of Harold Laski's Political Thought* (Van Gorcum, 1968)

SECONDARY SOURCES

Note: Only those sources cited frequently in the text and those of particular relevance are listed.

Books

Joan Abse (ed.), *My LSE* (Robson, 1977)

Ernest Barker, *Age and Youth* (Oxford University Press, 1953)

Ernest Barker, *Political Thought in England* (Williams and Northgate, 1915)

Ernest Barker, 'The Discredited State', *Political Quarterly*, 5, February 1915

Rodney Barker, *Political Ideas in Modern Britain* (Methuen, 1978)

F. Bresler, *Lord Goddard* (Harrap, 1977)

Alan Bullock, *The Life and Times of Ernest Bevin*, vol. 2 1940–5 (Heinemann, 1968); vol. 3 1945–51 (Oxford University Press, 1985)

Trevor Burridge, *British Labour and Hitler's War* (Andre Deutsch, 1976)

Trevor Burridge, *Clement Attlee: A Political Biography* (Cape, 1985)

Dennis Dean, 'The Contrasting Attitudes of the Conservative and Labour Parties to Problems of Empire, 1922–36' unpublished PhD, University of London, 1974

Dennis Dean, 'The Search for a Balance: The Attitude of the Conservative and Labour Parties to the Palestine Mandate, 1922–31', unpublished article

B. Donoughue and G. Jones, *Herbert Morrison* (Weidenfeld and Nicolson, 1973)

Ruth Dudley Edwards, *Victor Gollancz – A Biography* (Gollancz, 1987)

Christopher Farman, *May 1926 – The General Strike* (Panther Books, 1974)

Michael Foot, *Aneurin Bevan*, vol. 1 (Four Square, 1966), vol. 2 (Paladin, 1975)

Geoffrey Foote, *The Labour Party's Political Thought – A History* (Croom Helm, 1985)

Michael Freeden, *Liberalism Divided* (Clarendon Press, 1986)

Michael Freeden, 'Eugenics and Progressive Thought: A Study in Ideological Affinity', *The Historical Journal*, 22 (3) 1979

J. Gorny, *The British Labour Movement and Zionism, 1917–1948* (Frank Cass, 1983)

J. Graham and B. A. Phythian (eds), *The Manchester Grammar School* (Manchester University Press, 1965)

P. S. Gupta, *Imperialism and the British Labour Movement, 1914–64* (Macmillan, 1975)

Jose Harris, *William Beveridge: A Biography* (Clarendon Press, 1977)

Brian Harrison, *Prudent Revolutionaries* (Clarendon Press, 1987)

B. Hooper, *Public Scandal, Odium and Contempt* (Secker and Warburg, 1974)

Allen Hutt, *The Post-War History of the British Working Class* (Gollancz/LBC, 1937)

K. Jefferys, *The Churchill Coalition and Wartime Politics, 1940–45* (Manchester University Press, 1991)

Greta Jones, *Social Darwinism and English Thought* (Harvester Press, 1980)

T. Jones (ed. K. Middlemas), *Whitehall Diary*, vol. 2 (Oxford University Press, 1971)

Denis Judd, *Lord Reading* (Weidenfeld and Nicolson, 1982)

J. and D. Kimche, *Both Sides of the Hill: Britain and the Palestine War* (Secker and Warburg, 1960)

Jean Lacouture, *Léon Blum* (Seuil, 1983)

J. P. Lash (ed.), *From the Diaries of Felix Frankfurter* (W. W. Norton, 1975)

J. P. Lash, *Dealers and Dreamers* (Doubleday, 1988)

W. E. Leuchtenburg, *Franklin D. Roosevelt and the New Deal* (Harper, 1963)

F. M. Leventhal, *The Last Dissenter – H. N. Brailsford and His World* (Oxford University Press, 1985)

J. Lewis, *The Left Book Club* (Gollancz, 1970)

N. and J. MacKenzie (eds), *The Diary of Beatrice Webb*, vol. 4 1924–43, (Virago/LSE, 1985)

H. MacLennan, *McGill – The Story of a University* (Allen and Unwin, 1960)

Kenneth O. Morgan, *Labour in Power* (Oxford University Press, 1985)

R. J. Moore, *The Crisis of Indian Unity, 1917–40* (Clarendon Press, 1974)

R. J. Moore, *Churchill, Cripps and India, 1939–45* (Clarendon Press, 1979)

Margaret Morris, *The General Strike* (Penguin, 1976)

Michael Newman, '"Democracy versus Dictatorship" – Labour's Role in the Struggle against British Fascism, 1933–36', *History Workshop Journal*, 5, Spring 1978

Michael Newman, *John Strachey* (Manchester University Press, 1989)

R. Ovendale (ed.), *The Foreign Policy of the British Labour Governments* (Leicester University Press, 1984)

R. Pearson and G. Williams, *Political Thought and Public Policy in the Nineteenth Century* (Longman, 1984)

Henry Pelling, *America and the British Left* (A. and C. Black, 1956)

Henry Pelling, 'The 1945 General Election Reconsidered', *Historical Journal*, 23, (2) 1980

Ben Pimlott, *Labour and the Left in the 1930s* (Cambridge University Press, 1977)

Ben Pimlott, *Hugh Dalton* (Cape, 1985)

Ben Pimlott (ed.), *The Political Diary of Hugh Dalton, 1918–40, 1945–60* (Cape/ LSE, 1986)

Patricia Pugh, *Educate, Agitate, Organize – 100 Years of Fabian Socialism* (Methuen, 1984)

Jonathan Schneer, *Labour's Conscience – The Labour Left 1945–51* (Unwin Hyman, 1988)

P. Sebastiani, *Laburisti Inglesi e Socialisti Italiani* (FIAP, 1983)

A. M. Sperber, *Murrow – His Life and Times* (Freundlich, 1986)

Arthur E. Sutherland, *The Law at Harvard* (Harvard University Press, 1967)

Christopher Sykes, *Cross Roads to Israel: Palestine from Balfour to Bevin* (Nel Mentor, 1967)

Betty D. Vernon, *Ellen Wilkinson* (Croom Helm, 1982)

A. J. Williams, *Labour and Russia* (Manchester University Press, 1989)

A. W. (Anthony) Wright, *G. D. H. Cole and Socialist Democracy* (Clarendon Press, 1979)

Anthony Wright, *British Socialism: Socialist Thought from the 1860s* (Longman, 1983)

Anthony Wright, *Socialisms* (Oxford University Press, 1986)

Anthony Wright, *R. H. Tawney* (Manchester University Press, 1987)

Index

Abdullah, King, 338, 342
Abrams, Case, 58
Abse, Joan, 358
Abyssinia, 185, 186
Acton, Lord, 81, 194, 373
Africa, East, 110–14
  Memorandum on Native Policy
    in, 113
Africa, Southern, 111, 112
agreements
  Anglo-German naval (1935),
    185–6
  Anglo-Soviet (1939), 201, 202
  Hoare-Laval (1935), 185
  Irwin-Gandhi, 118
  Munich (1938), 200
  Nazi-Soviet (1939), 202, 226
aid, 255
  Marshall, 303, 347
Alexander, A.V., 331
American Democracy, The, 289–91
  308, 362, 365, 371
American Presidency, The, 182
Amery, Leo, 223, 224
Anderson, Sir John, 213
Anglo-Irish settlement (1921), xii
anti-semitism, 2, 3, 58, 62, 122, 130,
  153, 157, 174, 181, 274, 311–14,
  317–18, 341, 343–5 *passim*, 350,
  404, n14
  'Note on – ' 314, 342
'appeasement', 164, 185, 190–1, 199,
  200, 203, 206, 210, 217, 307
Arabs, 122–4, 129, 130, 311, 315,
  318–21 *passim*, 327, 328, 330–9
  passim, 342, 345
  League, 320
  Legion, 338
'Aristocracy is Still Ruling in
  England', 134–6, 371
arms race, 186
associations, corporate, 39–40, 42,
  45, 46, 48, 50, 78
Asquith, Herbert, 47

Atlantic Charter, 223
Attlee, Clement, 116, 171, 196, 204,
  206, 211, 214–18, 221–6, 229–40
  passim, 244, 245, 249, 251–6,
  251–71 *passim*, 278, 279, 282,
  297, 320, 322, 323, 327, 328,
  330, 331, 333–6, 341–3 *passim*,
  346, 352, 366
Austin, John, 45
Austria, 155, 156, 158
Authority in the Modern State, 50,
  56–7
Avanti, 294

Bacon, Alice, 323
Baldwin, Stanley, 70, 76, 91–100
  passim
Balfour Declaration, 121–4 *passim*,
  129, 319
Bank of England, 142, 143
Barker, Ernest, 40
BBC, 204, 221
Beales, H.L., xi, 358
Beaverbrook, Lord, 241, 266, 274,
  308
Beloff, Max, 355
Ben Gurion, David, 320, 338
Benes, President, 304
Benn, Wedgwood, 113, 117, 222
Berlin crisis (1948), 305
Bethmann Hollweg, von, 44
Bevan, Aneurin, 187, 188, 202, 249,
  250, 279, 320, 331, 335, 339
Beveridge, William, 68, 153, 168–73,
  180, 238
  Report, 238, 239, 253, 254
Bevin, Ernest, 95, 215, 224, 230, 231,
  236, 237, 249, 259, 261, 267,
  268, 295, 297, 298, 300, 301,
  303, 320, 322–4, 326–8, 330–43
  passim, 349, 352
Binder, Pearl, 3
Blum, Léon, 294, 354
Boas, Professor, 43–4

Boothby, Robert, 281
Bosanquet, Bernard, 38–9
Boston Herald, 60–1
Boston Transcript, 61
Bradley, F.H., 37–9 *passim*
Brailsford, H.N., 69, 188, 196, 363
Brandeis, Louis, 125, 130, 365
Brandeis University, 350–1
Braunthal, Julius, 245, 347
Bulgaria, 348, 349
Bullock, Alan, 335, 336, 341
Burgin, Leslie, 206
Burke, Edmund, 370, 371, 414–49
Burns, Emile, 196, 197

Cadogan, Sir Alexander, 336, 338, 340
California, University of, 283
Callaghan, James, 271
Canada, 31–3
capitalism, 28, 49, 50, 52, 55, 57, 88, 137, 143, 150–1, 155, 156, 158, 161–4, 178, 185, 203, 209, 210, 288–9, 291, 308, 309, 366, 373
Carlton, H.C.C., 263, 271–3 *passim*
Carr-Saunders, Alexander, 172, 180, 356
Carver, Professor, 60
Catholicism, 41, 166
Chamberlain, Neville, 197, 199–201 *passim*, 206, 254
Chicago Daily News, 305
China, 131, 190
Chorley, Lord, 357
'Chosen People, The', 5, 6, 9, 10, 11, 13, 14, 344, 364
Churches in the Modern State (Figgis), 39, 41
churches, 39–40, 42, 46
 -state relations, 41–2, 45
Churchill, Winston, x, xii, 2, 4, 70, 91, 93, 94, 97, 99, 100, 191, 206, 208, 212, 215–17, 223, 225, 229–32 *passim*, 235, 238–9, 241–3, 259–66 *passim*, 298, 308, 314–15, 346
Chuter Ede, James, 321
Citrine, Walter, 155
class conflict, 48–56, 101, 147, 209

see also strikes; working class
coal, 91–100
Cohn, Alfred, 350
Cold War, xi, xiv, xv, 256, 302–9, 347, 349, 355–6
Cole, G.D.H., 26, 37, 55, 74, 150, 188, 189
Cominform, 304
Comintern, 156, 158, 159, 185, 198
Committee on Ministers' Powers, 138–40
Common Law, 36
Commonwealth, British, 338
Communism/Communists, 92–3, 103–4, 106, 136–7, 143, 145, 149–51 *passim*, 165–7, 178, 191, 206, 228, 293, 343
Communist Party, of Great Britain, 152, 154–5, 159, 160, 167, 185–7 *passim*, 192, 195–9 *passim*, 206, 228, 245, 256, 293, 295, 343
 of Soviet Union, 165, 245, 287, 296
 US, 175
Conservative Party, 69, 156, 209, 213, 214, 217, 230, 232, 254
constitutionalism, 143–4, 147, 148, 177 *see also* revolution
Cook, A.J., 95, 108
Coolidge, Calvin, 59, 61
Creech-Jones, A., 331, 332, 337, 338
Crick, Bernard, xvi
Cripps, Sir Stafford, 149, 171, 187, 190, 197, 198, 202, 221, 224, 225, 230
Crisis and the Constitution, The, 144–6
Crossman, Richard, 307, 337, 340
Crown, powers of, 140, 145–6, 150, 155, 392, n63
Curtis, Police Commissioner, 58–9, 61
Curzon, Lord, xii–xiii
Czechoslovakia, 197, 200, 304–5, 340, 347, 348

Daily Express, 263, 264, 272–4 *passim*
Daily Herald, 28–9, 169–70, 172, 212, 262, 272, 343–4

Daily Mail, 93, 94
Daily Telegraph, 170, 171, 174
Dalton, Hugh, 196, 198, 212, 215, 218, 230, 245, 250, 259, 261, 265, 320, 330–1
Danzig, 201
Dawes Plan, 91
Day, Wentworth, 273, 274
Deane, Herbert, x, xiv–xv, 37, 133, 148, 150, 205
Debs, Eugene, 57
decentralisation, 37, 51, 52, 75, 77, 78, 366–7
Defence Regulation 1AA, 249
democracy, 77, 135, 146–7, 155, 156, 158, 217, 285, 288–9, 292, 293, 372
    industrial, 51–2, 55, 75
Democracy in Crisis, 144, 146–8, 170, 275
Dilemma of Our Times, The, 307, 350, 366–7
Dimitrov, 185, 189
disarmament, 352
Donoughmore, Lord, 138
Duncan, Andrew, 215
Duff-Cooper, Anthony, 171
Dutt, Palme, 189, 193, 195
Dyer, General, 114–15

Eastwood, Granville, xv
economy, 135, 141, 149, 150, 372–3
Eden, Anthony, 241, 243, 249
education, 71, 73, 75, 149, 216, 285–6, 361, 384 n29
Edwards, Ruth Dudley, 196
Egypt, 333, 339
Einstein, Albert, 350–1
Elliott, W.J., 37
Engels, Friedrich, 159
eugenics, 17–22 *passim*
Europe, Eastern, 291, 296, 305, 311, 313, 316, 345 *see also individual countries*
Exodus 1947/President Warfield, 333
expenditure cuts, 142

Fabianism, 17, 20, 26, 48, 63, 65, 69–71, 74–6 *passim*, 159, 271, 364, 370

Fascism, 84, 150, 155–9, 181, 192, 200, 203, 205, 343
    British Union of Fascists, 150
Feisal, Prince, 125
Figgis, J. Neville, 37, 39–41
financial crisis (1929), 141–2
Finland, 226
Fisher, H.A.L., 39
Foot, Michael, 307, 337, 340
Four Freedoms, 227, 240, 247, 256
France, 28, 50, 55, 69, 104, 147, 155, 156, 160, 185, 186, 191, 200, 250, 267, 333, 338, 350
    Communist Party, 294
    Socialist Party, 294
Franco, General, 187, 267, 268
Frankfurter, Felix, xii–xiii, 32–3, 35, 36, 43, 76, 97, 103, 112, 125, 126, 129, 130, 146, 148, 153, 175, 177, 179–81 *passim*, 184, 188, 190, 197, 200, 240, 242, 244, 248, 279, 280, 283, 302, 304, 310–13 *passim*, 330, 341, 345–9 *passim*, 356, 371
'Freedom in Danger', 173
'functional federalism', 51

Galton, Sir Francis, 17, 20, 22
Gandhi, Mahatma, x, 115, 117–19, 223
Geneva Institution of International Relations, 161
Germans – Are They Human?, The, 245
Germany, 28, 29, 43–4, 46, 104, 147, 152, 153, 156, 157, 173, 190, 200, 208, 227, 244–6, 250, 305, 312, 316, 333 *see also* Nazism
Gilbert, Martin, xii
Gillespie, A.D., 43
Gillies, Williams, 245, 246
Gierke, Otto von, 39
Goddard, Lord, 273, 277, 278
Goldman, Dr Nahun, 129
Goldmann, Emma, 164
Gollancz, Victor, 187, 196
Gould, Mrs, MP, 323
Grammar of Politics, A, x, 65, 68, 77–89, 92, 109, 110, 112, 160, 371
'Great Britain, Russia and the

Labour Party', 255–6
Greece, 250, 267, 268, 302, 347
Green, T.H., 37–40 *passim*
Greenleaf, W.H., xv, 362
Greenwood, Anthony, 198, 212, 213, 215, 217, 219, 230, 320
Guild Socialists, 27, 28, 41, 55–7 *passim*, 74, 75, 87, 364
Gupta, P.S., 113
Guttsman, W.L., 371

Haganah, 324
Haldane, Lord, 69–72 *passim*, 75
Haldinstein, Frank, 43
Halifax, Lord, xiii, 241
Hall, George, 320, 322, 326–8 *passim*
Hall, Professor Edwin, 59, 60
Halls, Walter, 236
Hapgood, Norman, 33
Hardie, Keir, 16
Harrington, J., 53
Hartshorn, V., 116
Harvard Lampoon, 62
Harvard Law Review, 35
Harvard University, 32–6, 58–64
Hastings, Sir Patrick, 273, 275–6, 280
Hawkins, Carroll, 354–5
Healey, Denis, 295
health, public, 216
Heath, Arthur, 43
Hegel/Hegelianism, 29, 38 *see also* Idealism
Henderson, Arthur, 107, 125, 127–9 *passim*, 11, 142
Herron, A.R., 43
Hewart, Lord Chief Justice, 138–9
Hirst, Paul, xv
Hiss, Alger, 348
Hitler, Adolf, 152, 153, 157, 158, 163, 185–6, 191, 192, 200–3 *passim*, 205, 207, 313, 226, 227, 244, 343
Hoare, Sir Samuel, 119, 206
Hoare – Laval Pact, 185
Hobson, J.A., 17
Holdsworth, Sir William, 139
Holmes, Oliver Wendell, Jr, x, xii, 36, 42–3, 49, 56, 58, 61, 63–6 *passim*, 69, 72, 74, 76, 77, 88, 94, 97, 99, 102, 103, 106, 111, 112,

118, 124, 130, 132, 139–40, 153, 174, 177, 179
Hook, Sidney, xiv
Hoover, J. Edgar, 57, 146, 174, 282
Hope-Simpson, Sir John, 124, 126
Hopkins, Harry, 242, 348
House of Lords, 84, 100, 134, 138, 140, 145, 156
Hull, Cordell, 243
Hungary, 316, 325, 348, 349
Hutchinson, Leslie, 307
Huxley, Julian, xiii

Idealism, 37–40, 45, 46, 51, 53
ILP, 108, 149, 154, 187
imperialism, 31, 110–31, 161–2, 164, 208, 209, 309, 318, 372 *see also* capitalism
Incitement to Disaffection Act, 156
India, x, xv, 1, 3, 114–21, 131, 221–6, 244, 251, 321, 346, 355, 372
   Government of India Act (1919), 114
   League, 120–1, 131
Indians, East African, 111–12
industrial councils, 51–2, 78, 83
industrial democracy, 51–2, 55, 75
inflation, 253
Inkpin, Albert, 92
Institute of Adult Education, 71
'International Situation, The' memorandum, 198
Iran, 333
Iraq, 333
Ireland, 28, 47, 70
Irgun Zwei Leumi, 322, 329
Irwin, Lord, 116–18 *passim*
Is This an Imperialist War?, 206
Israel, 336, 338–40, 343–5 *passim*
Italy, 147, 156, 157, 185, 190, 205, 250, 294–5, 326
   PCI, 294

James, William, 37
Janowsky, O., 311–12
Japan, 162, 163, 190
Jefferys, K., 236–7, 254
Jewish Agency, 122, 124, 128, 129, 327–32 *passim*

Jewish National Fund, 328
Jews, 1–4 passim, 121–32, 153–4,
    158, 310–45 *see also* Judaism
    Board of Deputies of British – , 4,
    67, 153, 310
    Holocaust, 158, 313
Jones, Tom, 95
Joynson-Hicks, (Home Secretary),
    92–4 *passim*
Jowitt, Sir William, 238
Judaism, 2, 3, 5, 9, 11, 13–14, 158,
    364

Kantorowicz, Hermann, 153
Karl Marx, 101–2
Kennedy, Joseph, xiii, 201, 281
Kenya, 111–14
Kenyatta, Jomo, 113
Keynes, J.M., 150, 173, 253, 357
Kirov, 167, 192

Labour government, 70, 77, 90, 108,
    110–45, 266, 268–70, 288, 291,
    300, 302, 319–47
Labour movement, xv, 41, 49, 90,
    93, 159, 189, 200, 206, 208, 209,
    228, 354, 364
Labour Party, 26, 69–71, 75, 106–9,
    111–21, 134–7, 143–5, 148–9,
    154–5, 164, 186–90, 195–200,
    202–4 passim, 211–14, 216–22,
    227–40 passim, 249–50, 254,
    258–9, 263, 265–6, 276, 295–6,
    318–20, 354, 355
Labour Monthly, 189, 193
Labour Party in Perspective, The, 196
Lansbury, George, 26, 28, 31, 41
Laski, Diana (daughter), 32, 66, 67,
    153, 180, 247
Laski, Frida (née Kerry) (wife),
    7–12, 16, 18–19, 23–4, 26, 27,
    32, 33, 36, 66, 130, 141, 165,
    179–80, 200, 204, 239–40, 247,
    248, 251, 279, 280, 297–8, 340,
    344, 346, 347, 350, 353, 377n18
Laski, Harold
    and Attlee, 211–14, 217, 222–6
        passim, 229–40, 246, 249,
        252–6 *passim*, 260–2, 266–71,
        346, 366

and Churchill, x, xii, 215–17, 231,
    264, 266, 308, 314–15
and Cold War, xiv, xv, 302–9,
    347, 349
and Communism, 103–4, 136–7,
    143, 151, 155, 206, 296, 309;
    Party, 152, 155, 159, 160,
    186–7, 189, 192, 195–9, 203,
    206, 293–5 *passim*
and economics, 135, 149–51
    passim, 372–3
and Empire, 110–31
and eugenics, 7, 19–22
and fascism/Nazism, 153–5, 157,
    158, 164, 189–92, 200–3, 205,
    208, 245, 250
and Germany, 153, 244–6, 250 *see
    also* Nazism
and India, 116–21, 131, 221–6,
    346
and Judaism, 5–7, 9, 12–16, 62,
    66, 130, 132, 153–4, 276, 311,
    314–45 *passim*, 364–5
and Labour Party, x, 26, 53,
    106–9, 134–5, 145, 148–9,
    197–200, 202–4 *passim*,
    211–14, 216–23 *passim*,
    229–40, 295, 322, 334, 337,
    349, 365–6; National
    Executive, x, 190, 200, 212,
    213, 217–18, 221, 237–8,
    244–52, 258, 262, 266–71, 278,
    319, 322–3, 337, 339–40, 343,
    349–50
and Marxism, 74, 101–5, 109, 133,
    149, 159–60, 164, 178, 199,
    208, 283, 292–6, 362, 364, 371
and post-war reconstruction,
    209–10, 213–21, 235, 247, 248
and racism, 110–11, 131–2, 157
and revolution, 62, 74, 88, 99,
    101, 105, 144, 207, 263, 271–8
and Roosevelt, 174–8, 181–5, 197,
    201–2, 207, 217, 240–4, 247,
    250, 290
and Soviet Union, 60, 74, 164–7,
    178, 192–5, 209–10, 226–9,
    245, 249, 256, 287–8, 293,
    296–301, 303–4, 309, 373, 407
    n128

and United Front, 155, 164, 167,
178, 180, 185–90, 199, 203
and the US, 31–6, 57–64, 146,
174–7, 181–5, 197, 200–2, 207,
240–4, 250, 252, 281–4,
289–91, 302, 303, 305, 306,
308, 330
and war, 28–9, 31, 42–4, 160–4,
191–2, 198, 201, 203, 205–57,
352, 368, 379 n55
and working class, 28, 42, 49, 54,
72, 73, 75, 84, 91–101, 143, 209
and Zionism, xii, 124–31, 154,
310, 311, 313, 316–18, 320,
322, 325, 329, 330, 341,
344–5
as teacher, 34–5, 358–61
at Harvard, 32–6, 58–64
at LSE, xi, 63, 68–9, 153–4,
167–74, 180, 204, 350, 352–3,
357–9
character, xi–xiv, 4–5, 33, 36,
358–9, 383 n17
education, 4–7, 11, 20–30
fantasising, xi–xii, 301
health, 4–6 *passim*, 204, 246–8,
281, 347, 348, 352, 353
libel action, 271–80, 308, 346, 405
n58, 61
marriage, 8–12, 32, 67, 180, 344,
347
political philosophy, xiv–xv,
37–57, 74–89, 133–40, 144–51,
155–9, 207–11, 284–9, 350,
354–5, 362–5, 369–74;
pluralism, 37–57, 364; role of
state, 39–42, 44–50, 52–6, 74,
75, 78–9, 85, 87, 140, 160–4,
210, 217, 220, 366–9 *passim*;
sovereignty, 39, 42, 44–7
passim, 161, 164, 210, 367–9;
world outlook, 160–4 284–8
politics, xiii, 26–7, 29–30, 41, 42,
56, 63, 69–72, 76, 100, 106–9,
133, 142–4, 149, 153, 155,
159–61, 185–97, 204, 211–40,
244–6, 248–9, 258–309
relations with family, 9–14, 21–2,
27, 30, 46, 65–7, 246–7
Laski, Mabel (sister), 1, 4, 251

Laski, Naphtali and Esther
(grandparents), 1
Laski, Nathan (father), 1–4, 9–11
passim, 14, 22, 30, 65–7, 24, 246,
377 n8
Laski, Neville (brother), 1, 4, 7, 10,
42, 67, 153, 154, 251, 310, 313
Laski, Sarah (née Frankenstein)
(mother), 1–4, 9–11 *passim*, 14,
22, 30, 65–7, 246, 251
Laski Institute, 355, 376 n19
Laval, Pierre, 185
law, international, 160–1
Law and Justice in the Soviet Union,
192
League of Nations, 114, 160–3
passim, 186, 320
Left Book Club, 187, 195, 202, 206,
363
Left News, 196
Lenin/Leninism, 74, 103, 164, 193,
293
Lerner, Max, 234, 248, 339
Leys, Norman, 113
Liberal Party, 2, 28, 70–2 *passim*,
100, 134, 198
liberalism, 16, 38, 41, 56, 72, 208,
291–3 *passim*, 364, 372 *see also*
democracy
Liberty in the Modern State, 192
'Limitations of the Expert', 371
Lindsay, A.D., 68
Linlithgow, Lord, 224
Lippman, Walter, 35, 36, 40
Little Bardfield, 180, 204, 347
Lloyd George, David, 25, 70, 72, 75,
107
Locker, Berl, 129
London School of Economics, xi,
63, 68, 153, 167–74, 204, 350,
356–7
Lowell, A. Lawrence, 59, 61, 62

Macaulay, essay on, 22–3
MacDonald, Ramsay, 70, 72, 106–8,
111, 112, 116, 118, 123–9
passim, 134, 141–5 *passim*, 145,
148, 270
'Machiavelli and the Present Time',
369, 371

Mackenzie, Robert, 357, 360
Maitland, F.W., 39, 40
Manchester Grammar School, 3, 5, 376n4
Manchester Guardian, 171, 173
Manchester University, 284, 350
Manchuria, 162
Mannheim, Karl, 153
Marshall, George, 303
   Aid, 303, 347
Martin, Kingsley, x, xii, xv, 37, 63, 193, 246, 272, 283, 357, 358
Marx and Today, 244
Marx, Karl, 53, 101–5 *passim*, 193, 244, 283, 309
Marxism, xiv, 49, 52–4 *passim*, 56, 63, 74, 101–5, 109, 133, 149, 159–60, 164, 178, 189, 292–6, 307, 311, 313, 344, 361, 362, 364, 371, 372
Masaryk, Jan, 304, 305
Massingham, H. (editor, *The Nation*), 69
Mathewson, Robin (son-in-law), 180
Maxton, James, 108
May, Sir George, 142
McCarthy, Joseph, 357
McGill University, 30–3
Menon, Krishna, 120, 358
Middle East, 321, 323, 327–9, 332–3, 338, 339, 341 *see also individual countries*
Mikardo, Ian, 250
Mill, John Stuart, 73, 161, 244
miners, 70, 72–4, 90–100
Molotov, 301
Mond-Turner talks, 90, 108
'Moral Equivalent for War, A', 29
Morgan, Kenneth O., xii–xiv, xv, 268, 335
Morley, John, 72, 76
Morris, Yaakov, 344
Morrison, Herbert, 155, 198, 215, 217–19 *passim*, 230, 237, 260, 266, 271, 279, 313, 320, 327, 339
Moscow University, 165, 170
Mosley, Oswald, 150
Muggeridge, Malcolm, xi

Murrow, Ed, 243, 354, 357
Mussolini, Benito, 74, 164, 185, 186, 201, 205

Nation, The, 69–71
   US, 56–7, 93, 96, 283
National Governments, 118, 142–3, 149, 156, 184–6 *passim*, 188, 189, 191, 206, 213, 215, 216
nationalism, 131, 161–2, 372
   Arab, 122, 311, 328
   Indian, 121
   Jewish, 345
'Nationalism and the Future of Civilisation', 161
nationalisation, 54, 74–5, 83, 143, 216, 220, 230, 250, 346, 366
NATO, 305
Nazism, 17, 131, 147, 153–60, 163, 164, 201, 202, 205, 293, 307, 313
   -Soviet Pact, 202, 226
Nehru, Jawaharlal, x, 221, 361
Nenni, Pietro, 294–5, 304
Nevinson, H.W., 25
New Despotism, The (Hewart), 138
New Party, 150
New Republic, 35, 60, 106
New Statesman, 171, 173, 243, 314, 315, 342
Newark Advertiser, 264, 274, 278
Nicholls, David, xv
Noel-Baker, Philip, 163, 250, 278, 334–5
Northedge, Frederick, 335
Nottingham Guardian, 263, 271–2, 274

Oakshott, Michael, 357
O'Dwyer, Sir Michael, 115
oil, 318, 328, 329
Old World and New Society, The, 219–20, 230, 232, 233, 246
'On a Jewish Soldier's Letter', 315–16
'Open Letter to the Labour Movement', 212
Orwell, George, 287
ownership, public, 55, 230, 253, 299, 367 *see also* nationalisation

Palazzolo, Claudio, xv
Palestine, xii, 121–32, 251, 310–45,
    347, 349, 351
  Anglo-American Commission of
      Enquiry, 324, 325, 328, 329,
      332
  Morrison-Grady Plan, 329, 331
  Partition Plan, 330, 335
  Peel Report, 310, 312
  UNSCOP, 334
Palmer, A. Mitchell, 57
Pan-African Congress, 111
Pankhurst, Sylvia, 26, 30
von Papen, 147
*Parliamentary Government in
    England*, 208
'Party and the Future', 231–3
Passfield, Lord *see* Webb, Sidney
Paton, J.L. (headmaster), 5–6, 16, 66
Pearson, Sir Karl, 7, 17, 20, 21
People at Bay (Janowsky), 311–12
Peretz, Martin, xv
'Personnel of the British Cabinet
    1801–1924', 371
Peterson, Sir William, 31, 32
Pethick Lawrence, Mr and Mrs,
    23–4
Phillips, Morgan, 250, 268, 271, 297,
    301, 352
Platts-Mills, John, 307
pluralism, 37, 39, 41–57, 75, 364,
    366, 370, 372
Poale Zion, 317, 322, 325, 333, 341,
    411n88
Poland, 201, 202, 250, 311–13
    passim, 316, 325, 326, 348
police, 156
Political Ideas of Harold J. Laski see
    Deane
Political Theories of the Middle Ages,
    39
Pollitt, Harry, 92, 189, 296, 313
Popov (Secretary, CPSU), 297–8
Populaire, Le, 294
Popular Front, 187–90, 197–9
    passim, 202, 293
Portugal, 297
*Position of the Parties and the Right of
    Dissolution, The*, 70

Potsdam Conference, 261–3, 265,
    266
Pound, Roscoe, 35
prices, 83, 299
Pritt, D.N., 190, 198
Problem of Sovereignty, The, 371
'Problems of Administrative
    Areas', 50, 71
profits, 83
property, 54, 81–3 *passim*, 104, 136,
    137, 157, 253
'Public Papers and Addresses of
    Franklin D. Roosevelt, The',
    183
Pugh, Arthur, 94–6 *passim*

racism, 17, 110–11, 115, 131–2, 157,
    341 *see also* anti-semitism
Radcliffe, College, 34
rearmament, 186, 189, 192, 197, 199
Reflections on the Constitution, 350
reform, 49, 53, 56, 84–5, 136–40,
    145–6, 209–22
Reith, Lord, 213
Reuter, 267
revolution, 49, 53, 73–5, 88, 99, 101,
    144, 147, 164, 178, 207, 263,
    271–80, 308
  'by consent', 209, 217, 220, 239,
    248, 268, 272, 274
Reynolds News, 236
Ridley, George, 224
rights, 79–82, 84–6, 92, 101, 292
  Bill of, 52
  Universal of Declaration of
    Human – , 292
Rise of Euro-Liberalism, The, 208
'Road to Power, The', 211
Robbins, Lionel, 169
Rockefeller Foundation, 168
Romania, 311–13 *passim*, 316, 325
Roosevelt, Eleanor, 182, 241, 242
Roosevelt, President F.D., x, 174–7,
    181–6, 197, 200–3 *passim*, 207,
    215, 217, 227, 240, 242, 243,
    250, 286, 290, 302
Roosevelt University, Chicago, 282
Rousseau, Jean-Jacques, xvi, 45,
    371–2

Royal Institute of International
    Affairs, 136–7
Russell, Bertrand, 17, 41, 42, 57, 62,
    69, 74, 131, 352
Russia, 28, 49, 73, 74, 106 *see also*
    Soviet Union
'Hands Off' movement, 73
Revolution, 57, 74, 193

Samuel, Sir Herbert, 91, 94–8
sanctions, 186
Sankey, Lord, 69, 71, 74, 75, 111–13,
    117–18, 138, 142, 149
Saudi Arabia, 333
Schlesinger, Arthur Jr, xiv
School of Social Research, NY, 35
Secret Battalion, The, 295
Sedition Bill, 173
Shaw, Bernard, 173
Shaw Commission/Report, 123–5
    passim
Sheffer (Jewish philosopher), 62
Shinwell, Emanuel, 218, 219, 335
Shvernik (President People's
    Council), 298
Sidney Hillman Foundation, 282
Sievers, Nowell, 43
Simon, Sir John, 206
    Commission/Report, 116, 117,
    226
Smith, Herbert, 95–6
Smuts, General, 124
Snell, Henry, 124
Snowden, Philip, 106–7, 135, 142,
    143
social security, 216, 238 *see also*
    welfare state
socialism, 16, 55, 56, 74, 76, 87, 143,
    150, 162, 231, 250, 253, 259,
    289, 299, 304, 308, 312, 318–19,
    345, 347, 368–9, 372
Socialist International, 114, 227–8,
    245, 297
Socialist League, 149, 154–5, 175,
    186–9 *passim*, 195
South Africa, 114
sovereignty, 39, 42, 44–7 *passim*,
    161, 164, 210, 367–8
Soviet Communism: A New

Civilisation (Webbs), 193
Soviet Union, 58, 73, 150, 164–7,
    175, 178, 189, 191–6, 199, 200,
    209–10, 226–9, 235, 244, 245,
    249, 250, 255–6, 267, 287–8, 293,
    296–301, 303–5 *passim*, 309, 312,
    332, 337–9, 343–4, 347, 373
Labour party delegation to,
    297–301
Nazi-Soviet Pact, 202, 226
Spain, 187, 190, 191, 250, 267, 268,
    296, 347
Stalin, Josef, xii, 193, 195, 199, 227,
    256, 262, 263, 296, 298–301
    passim
Stalinism, xiv, 307, 309, 373
state, role of, 38, 40, 41, 44–50, 52–6,
    74, 75, 78–9, 85, 87, 140,
    155–64, 210, 217, 220–1, 367–9
State in Capitalist Society, The
    (Miliband), 371
State in the New Social Order, The,
    75
State in Theory and Practice, The,
    155–9, 178, 275
Steel-Maitland, Sir Arthur, 97, 98
Stern Gang, 322, 325, 328
Stocks, Mary, 173
Strachey, John, 15, 187, 188, 196,
    363–4
Strauss, George, 202
'Stresa front', 185
strikes, 26, 57, 73, 276
    Boston police, 58–63, 241
    General, 90–100, 103, 106
    La Spezia hunger, 326–8, 333
suffragism, 23–6, 41, 47
Sunday Express, 273
supranationalism, 210
syndicalism, 52, 55, 57
Syria, 333, 337

Tawney, R.H., 68, 75, 150, 169,
    357–8
taxation, 83, 236–7
Taylor, A.J.P., 23
Third International, 195, 256
Thomas, J.H., 95, 96, 107, 142
Times, The, 171

de Tocqueville, Alexis, 81
Town and Country Planning Bill, 249
Trade Disputes Act (1927), 100, 134, 141, 238
trade unions, 41, 42, 46, 48, 52, 55, 57, 69, 72–5, 90–100, 108, 135, 145, 238, 268, 291
  TUC, 90, 91, 93–9 *passim*, 108, 142, 196, 200, 214, 218, 231, 238
Trade Unions in the New Society, 366
Transjordan, 332, 337, 338
Trevelyan, Charles, 202
Tribune, 187, 188, 271, 337
Tribune Economique, La, 268
Trotsky, Leon, 193
Truman, President, 262, 263, 290, 302, 322, 328–30 *passim*, 341
  – Doctrine, 302, 332
Turkey, 302

Ulster, 28, 47
unemployment, 141, 150, 174, 216, 288
  benefit, 142, 396n36
UNESCO, 292
United Front, 154–5, 159, 164, 178, 180, 185–92, 197, 199, 203
United Nations, 292, 324, 332–4, 336–8 *passim*, 345, 352
UNSCOP, 334
United States, x, xiv, 31–6, 57–64, 111, 127, 140–2, 147, 156, 158, 168, 174–7, 181–5, 197, 200–2, 206, 207, 240–4, 250, 252, 256, 281–4, 290–1, 302, 303, 305, 307–9, 322, 324, 329, 330, 332, 338, 339, 341, 342, 351, 357, 366
  American Federation of Labour, 58, 60
  Boston police strike, 58–63, 241
  Constitution, 182
  Espionage Act (1918), 57
  FBI, 282, 309
  McCarthyism, 283–4, 357
  New Deal, x, 156, 174–8, 181, 209, 240, 371
  red scare (1918–19), 57–8

Supreme Court, 183, 184
  War Labor Policies Board, 35
Utley, Freda, 193, 195

Vansittart, Sir Robert, 250
  Vansittartism, 245, 250
Vatican, 302
Versailles peace treaty, 160, 185
Vishinsky, 192

wages, 51, 54, 74, 83, 91, 93, 237, 299, 396 n36
  cuts, 142, 150
  minimum, 19, 82
Walker, James, 245–6
Wall Street crash, 141
Wallas, Graham, 63, 68
war, 160–4
  Spanish civil, 187, 190, 191
  World (First), 28–9, 31, 42–4, 122, 160; (Second), 204–57, 278, 313–14, 341; (Third), 352, 368
Warburg, James, 356, 357
Washington, Seattle, University of, 185, 201
Webbs, 16, 26, 69, 74, 193–5 *passim*, 286
  Beatrice, xii, 16, 112–13, 167
  Sidney (Lord Passfield), 16, 18, 75, 88, 112, 123–8 *passim*, 130, 131, 168, 170, 310
Weizmann, Chaim, 122, 125, 127–9 *passim*, 311, 317, 322, 330, 331
welfare state, 211, 254, 288, 346
Wells, H.G., 17, 69
Why Capitalism Means War (Brailsford), 197
Wilkinson, Ellen, 139, 190, 198, 204, 223, 250, 260
Will The Peace Last?, 250
Wilson, Edmund, 36
Wilson, Harold, 271
Wilson, President Woodrow, 175
Winant, John, 241, 243, 244, 247, 248, 316
women's rights, 9, 24–6, 41, 47
Wood, Kingsley, 206, 215
Woolf, Leonard, 162

working class, 28, 42, 48–51 *passim*,
     53, 54, 72, 75, 90–101, 134–6,
     147, 196 *see also* class conflict;
     trade unions
working conditions, 51, 74, 80–1,
     83, 88, 396n36

Yale University, 62, 140–1

Zionism, xii, 3, 121–31, 310–45
     passim
Zylstra, B., xv

www.ingramcontent.com/pod-product-compliance
Lightning Source LLC
Chambersburg PA
CBHW072040020426
42334CB00017B/1339